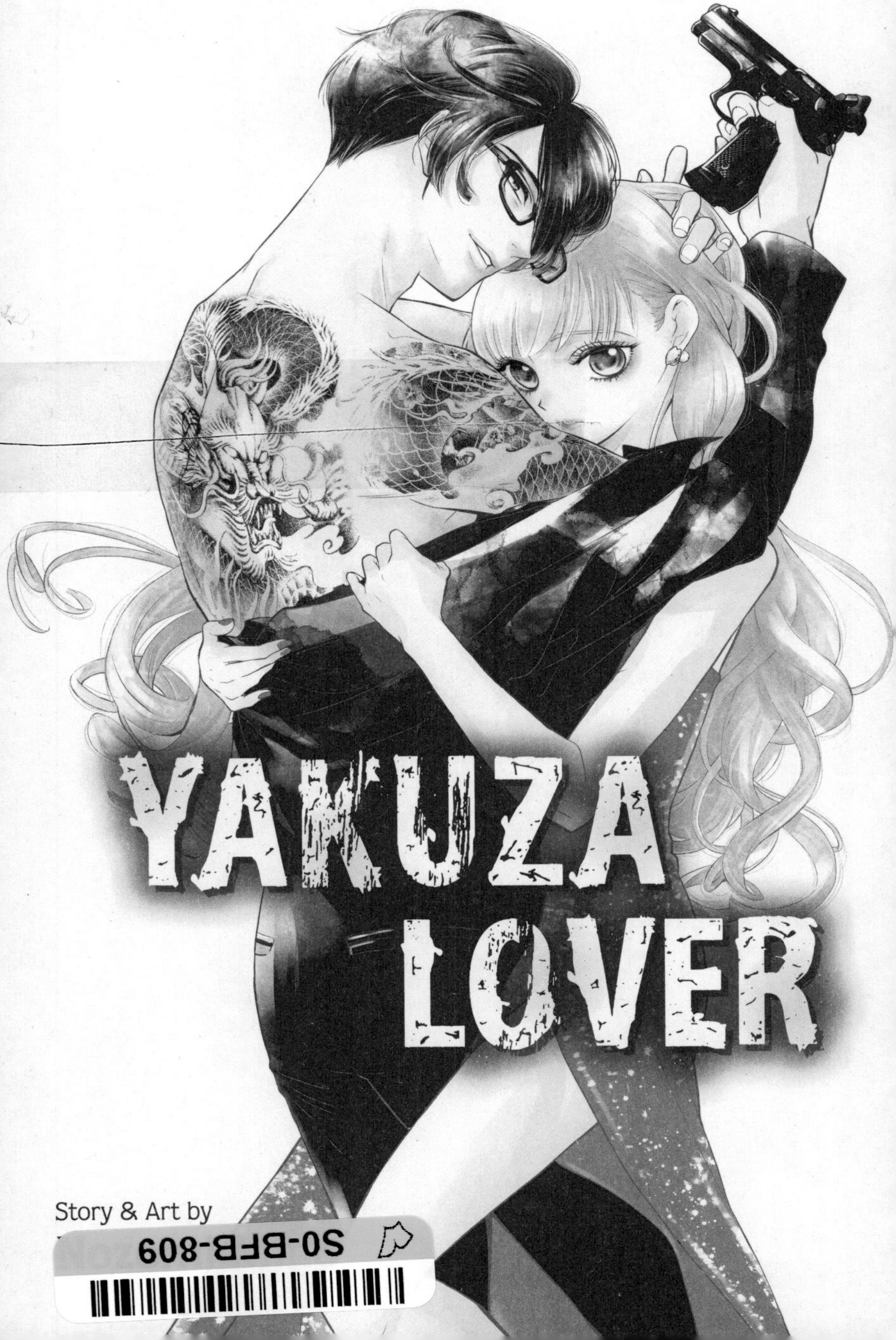

YAKUZA LOVER

Story & Art by

Contents

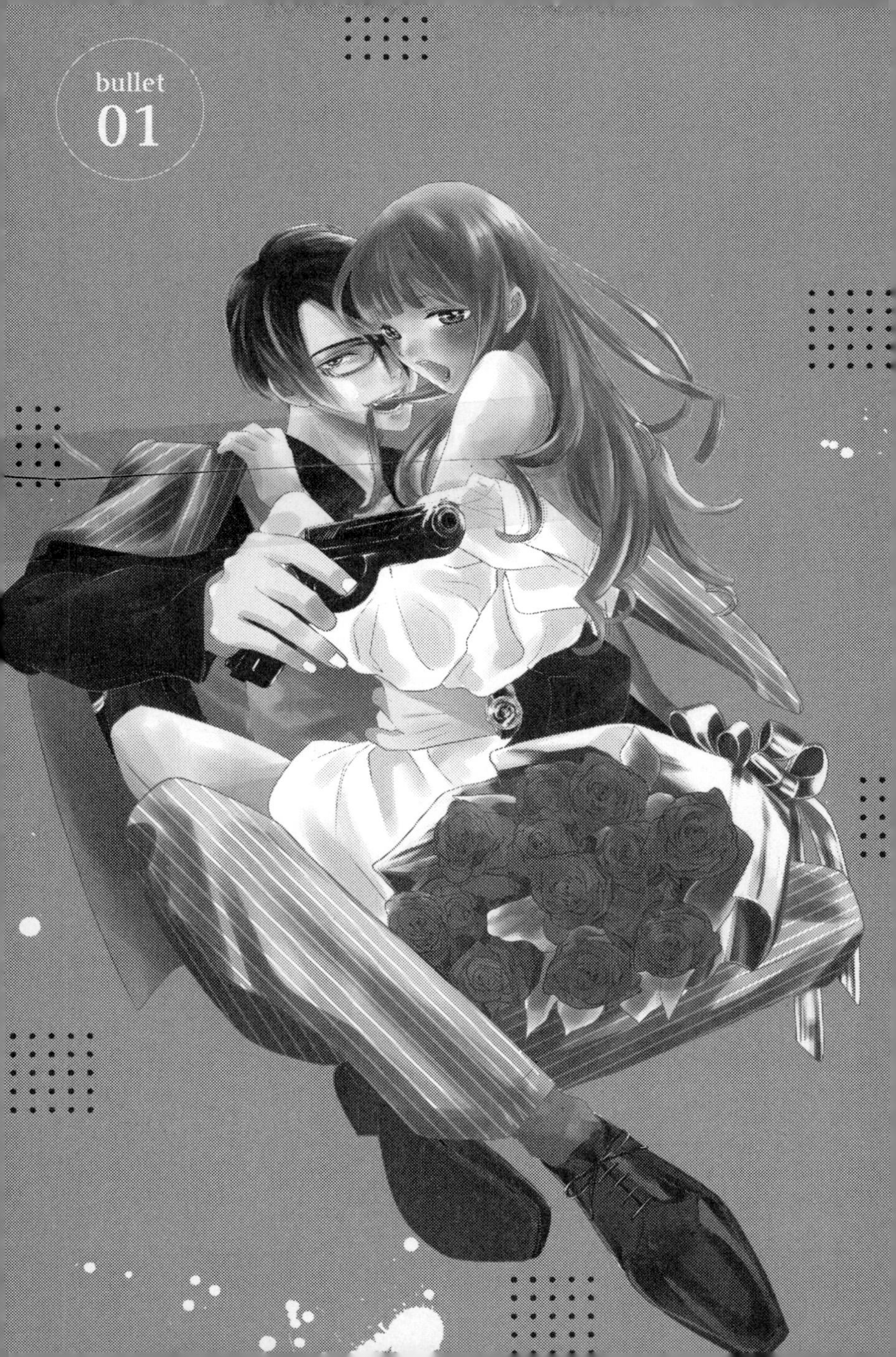
bullet
01

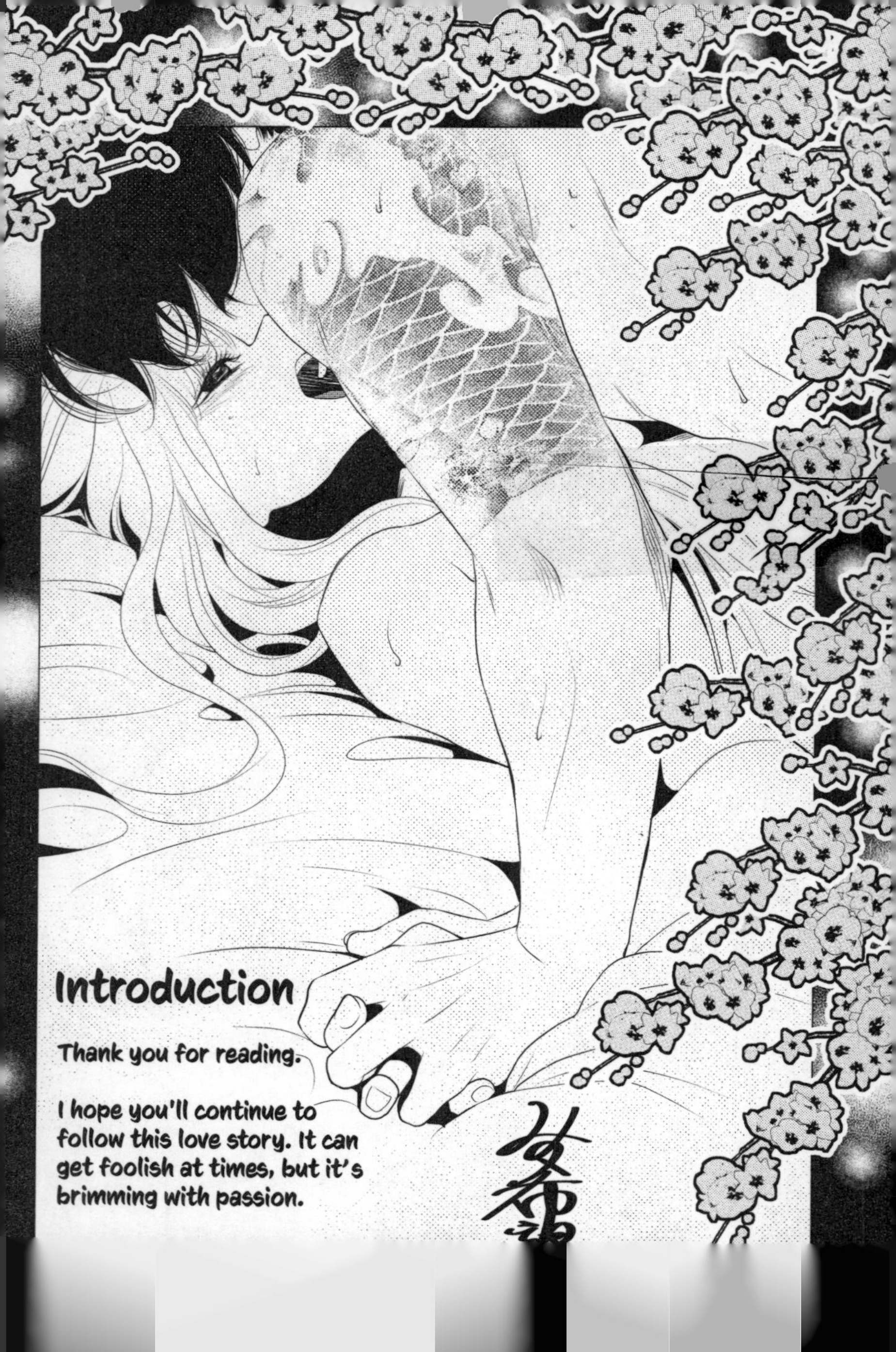

Introduction

Thank you for reading.

I hope you'll continue to follow this love story. It can get foolish at times, but it's brimming with passion.

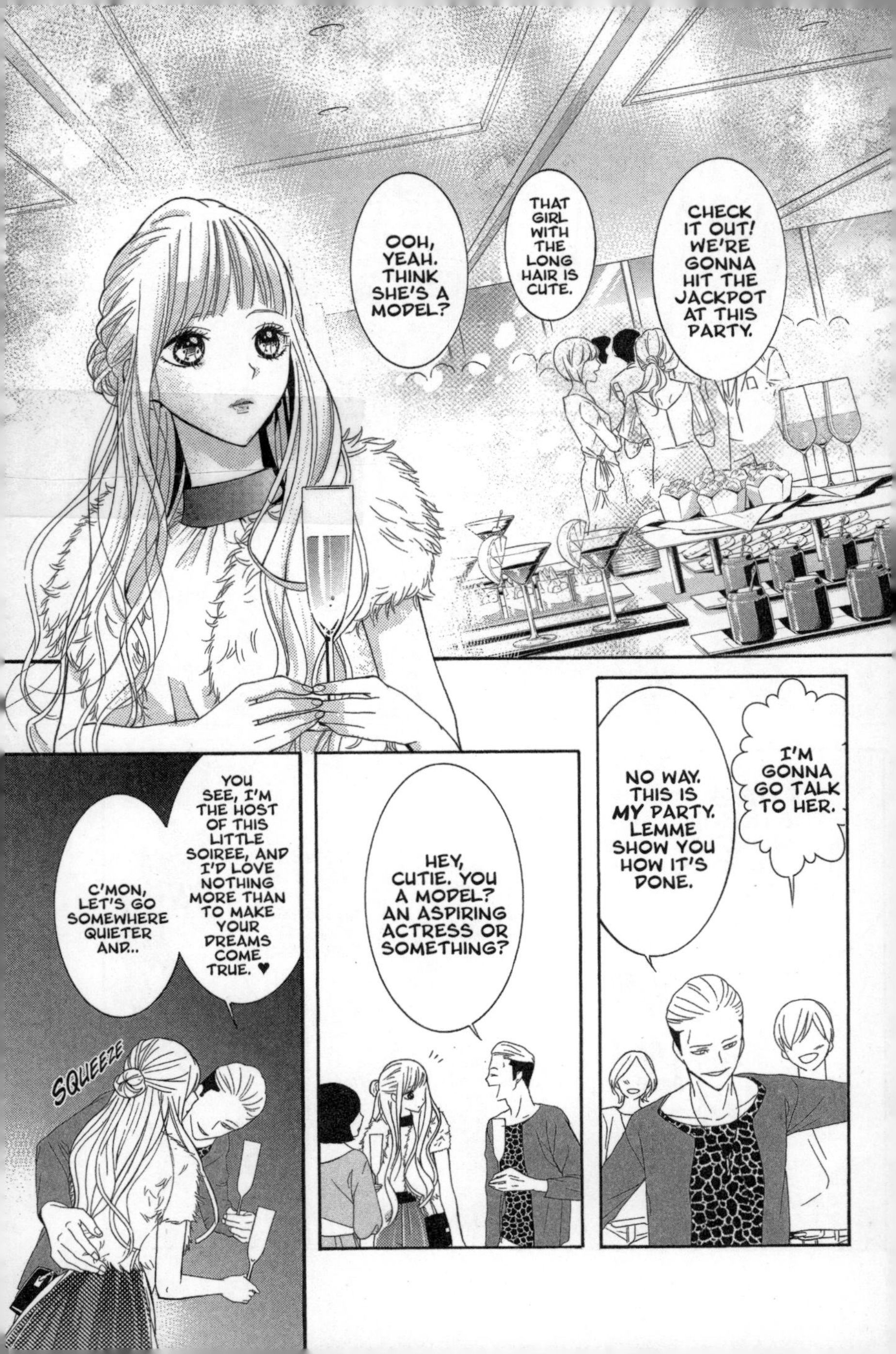
CHECK IT OUT! WE'RE GONNA HIT THE JACKPOT AT THIS PARTY.
THAT GIRL WITH THE LONG HAIR IS CUTE.
OOH, YEAH. THINK SHE'S A MODEL?
I'M GONNA GO TALK TO HER.
NO WAY. THIS IS MY PARTY. LEMME SHOW YOU HOW IT'S DONE.
HEY, CUTIE. YOU A MODEL? AN ASPIRING ACTRESS OR SOMETHING?
YOU SEE, I'M THE HOST OF THIS LITTLE SOIREE, AND I'D LOVE NOTHING MORE THAN TO MAKE YOUR DREAMS COME TRUE. ♥
C'MON, LET'S GO SOMEWHERE QUIETER AND...
SQUEEZE

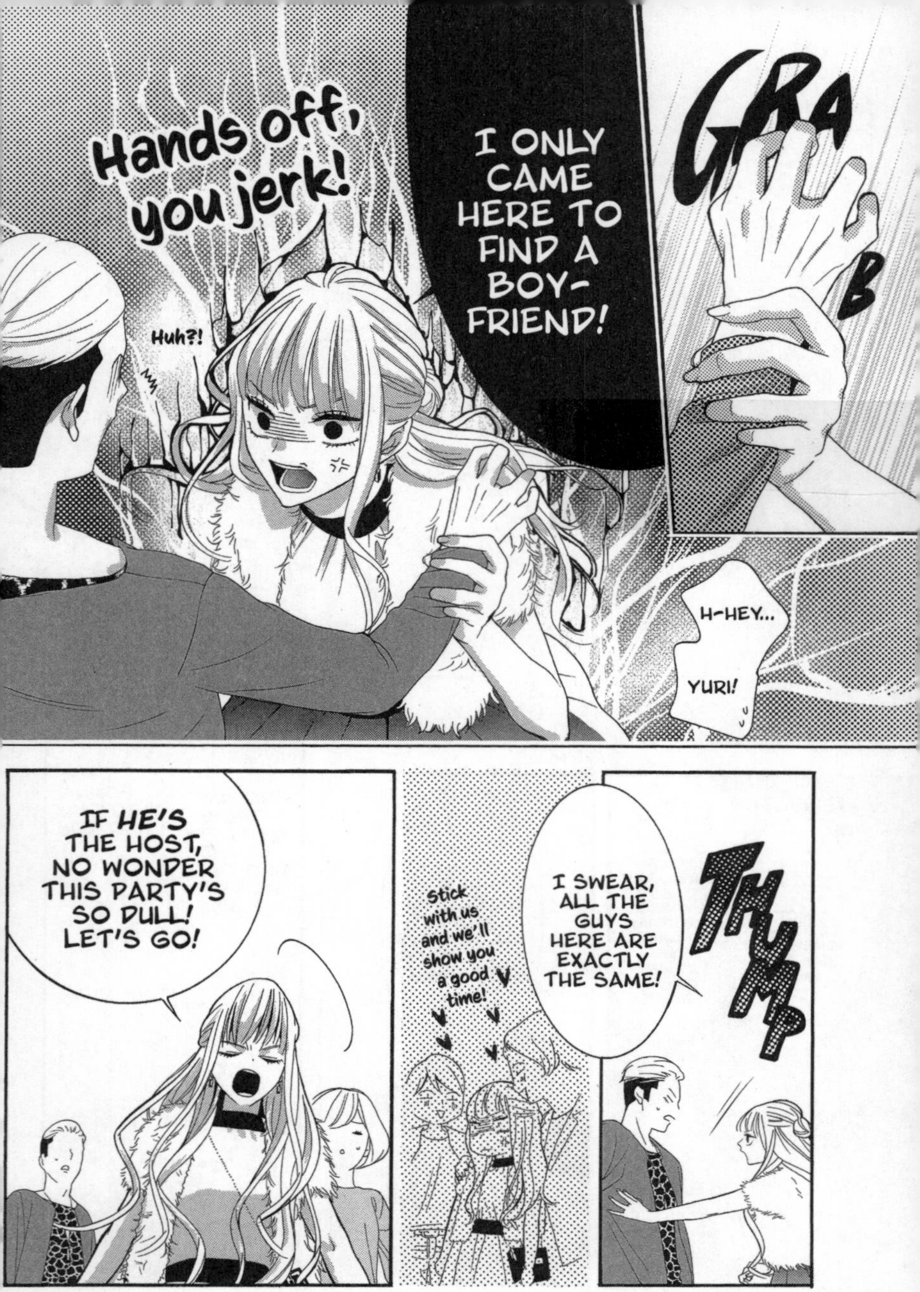
GRAB
I ONLY CAME HERE TO FIND A BOY-FRIEND!
Hands off, you jerk!
H-HEY... YURI!
Huh?!
THUMP
I SWEAR, ALL THE GUYS HERE ARE EXACTLY THE SAME!
Stick with us and we'll show you a good time!
IF HE'S THE HOST, NO WONDER THIS PARTY'S SO DULL! LET'S GO!

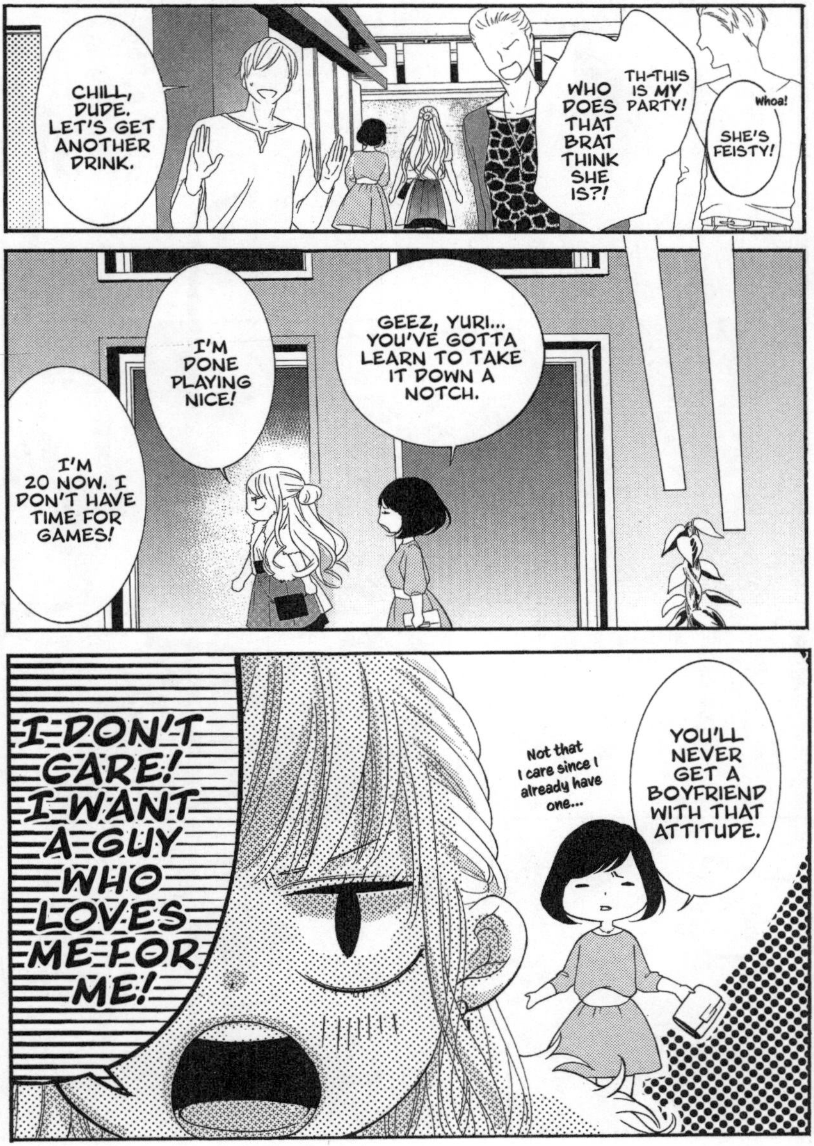
Whoa!
SHE'S FEISTY!
TH-THIS IS MY PARTY!
WHO DOES THAT BRAT THINK SHE IS?!
CHILL, DUDE. LET'S GET ANOTHER DRINK.
GEEZ, YURI... YOU'VE GOTTA LEARN TO TAKE IT DOWN A NOTCH.
I'M DONE PLAYING NICE!
I'M 20 NOW. I DON'T HAVE TIME FOR GAMES!
YOU'LL NEVER GET A BOYFRIEND WITH THAT ATTITUDE.
Not that I care since I already have one...
I DON'T CARE! I WANT A GUY WHO LOVES ME FOR ME!

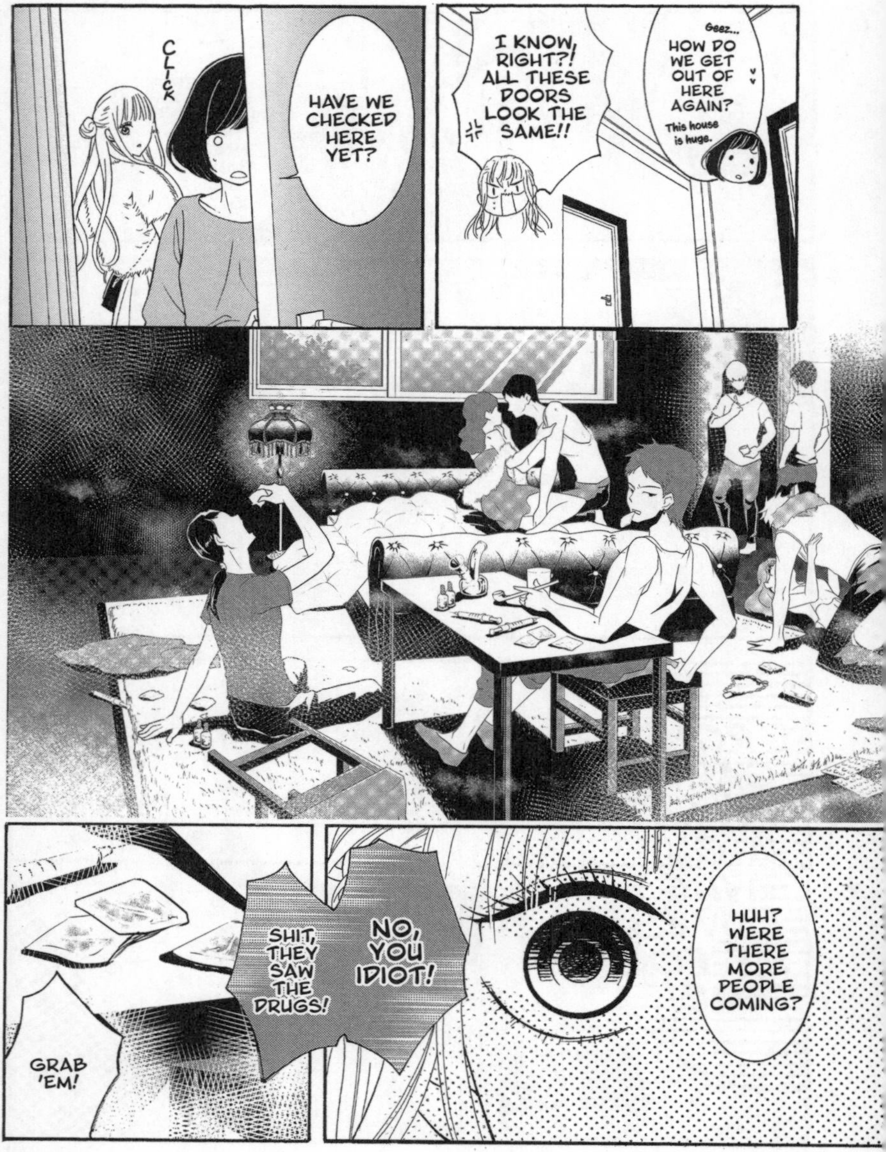
Geez...
HOW DO WE GET OUT OF HERE AGAIN?
This house is huge.
I KNOW, RIGHT?! ALL THESE DOORS LOOK THE SAME!!
HAVE WE CHECKED HERE YET?
CLICK
HUH? WERE THERE MORE PEOPLE COMING?
NO, YOU IDIOT!
SHIT, THEY SAW THE DRUGS!
GRAB 'EM!

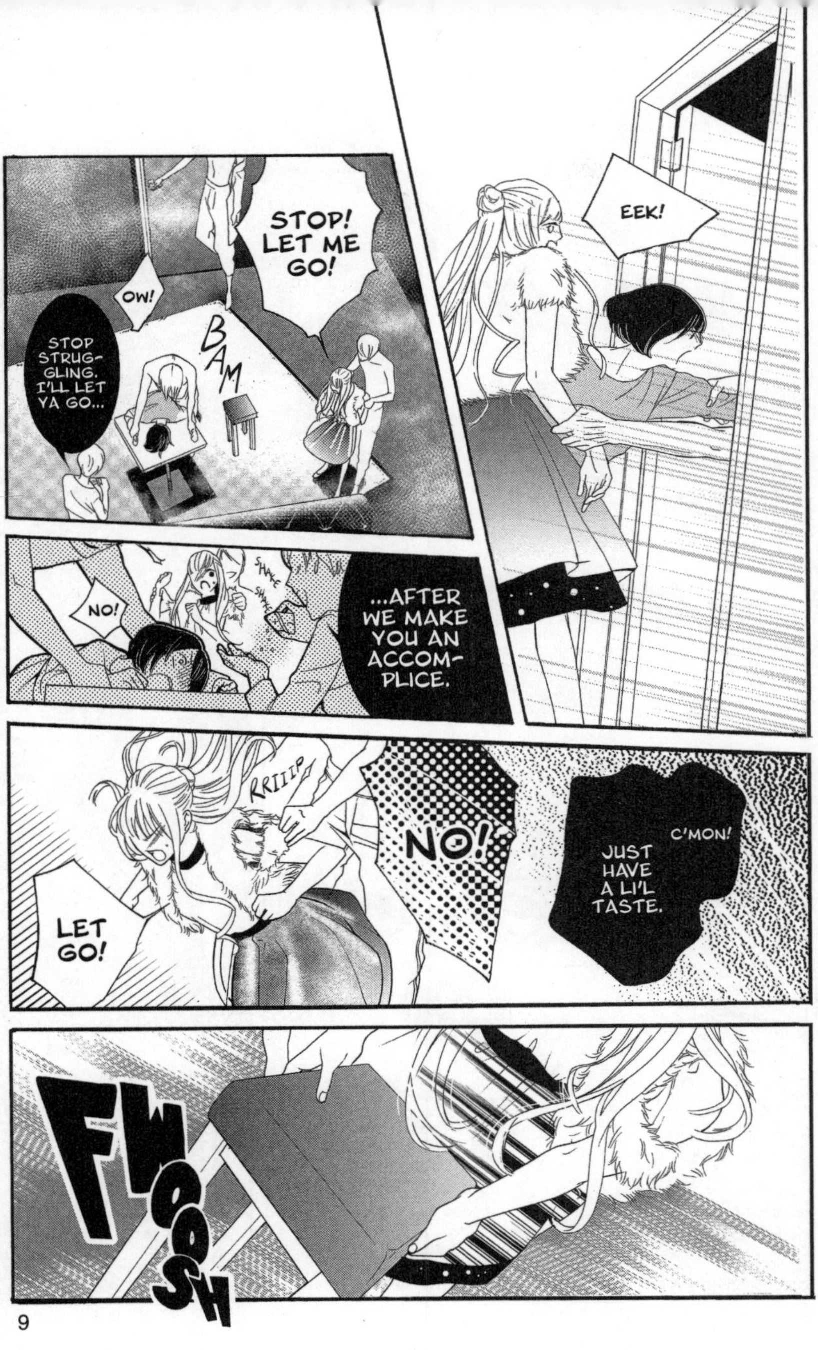
EEK!
STOP! LET ME GO!
OW!
BAM
STOP STRUG-GLING. I'LL LET YA GO...
...AFTER WE MAKE YOU AN ACCOM-PLICE.
SHAKE SHAKE
NO!
C'MON! JUST HAVE A LI'L TASTE.
NO!
RRIIIP
LET GO!
FWOOSH

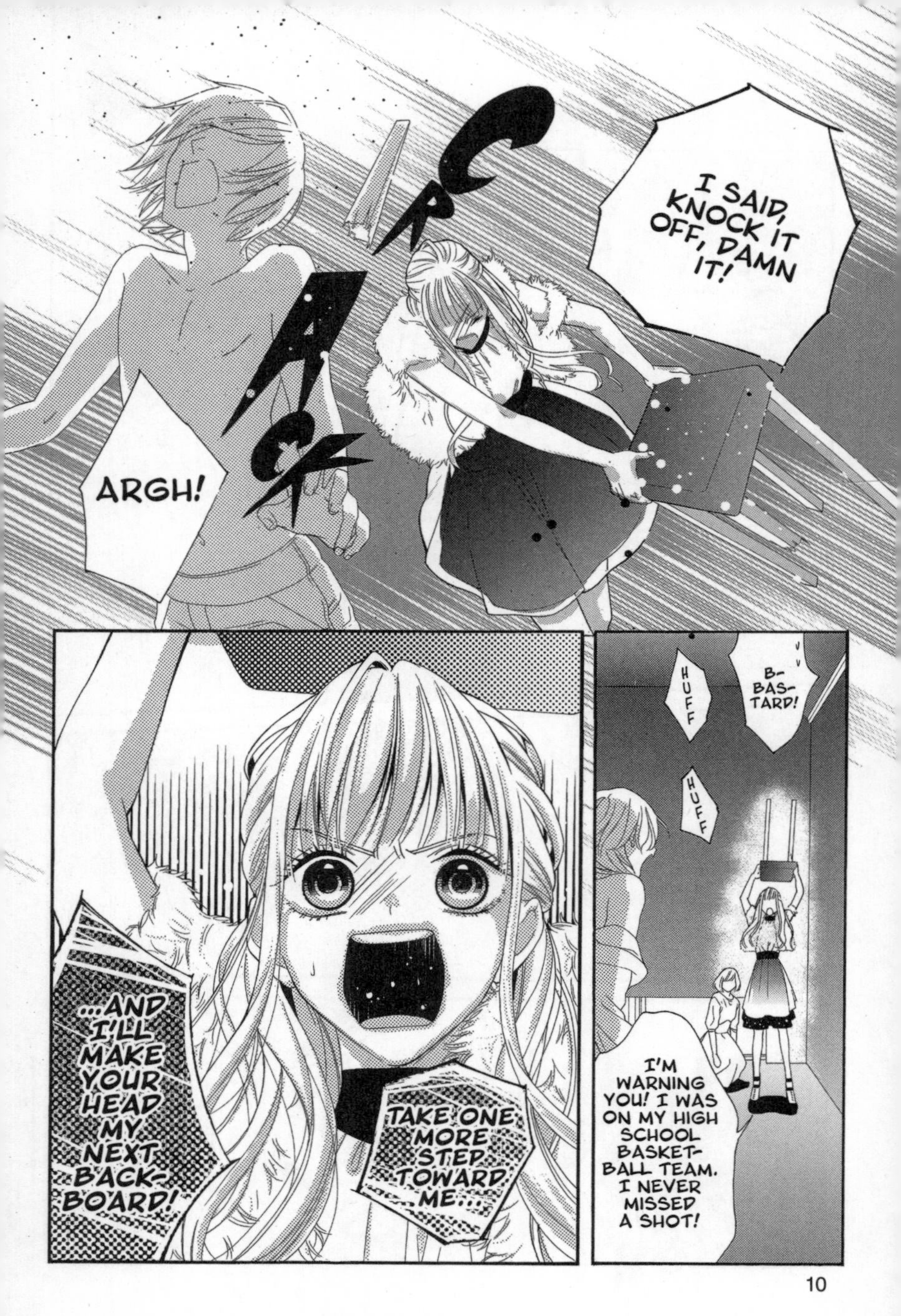
I SAID, KNOCK IT OFF, DAMN IT!
CRACK
ARGH!
B-BASTARD!
HUFF
HUFF
I'M WARNING YOU! I WAS ON MY HIGH SCHOOL BASKETBALL TEAM. I NEVER MISSED A SHOT!
TAKE ONE MORE STEP TOWARD ME...
...AND I'LL MAKE YOUR HEAD MY NEXT BACKBOARD!

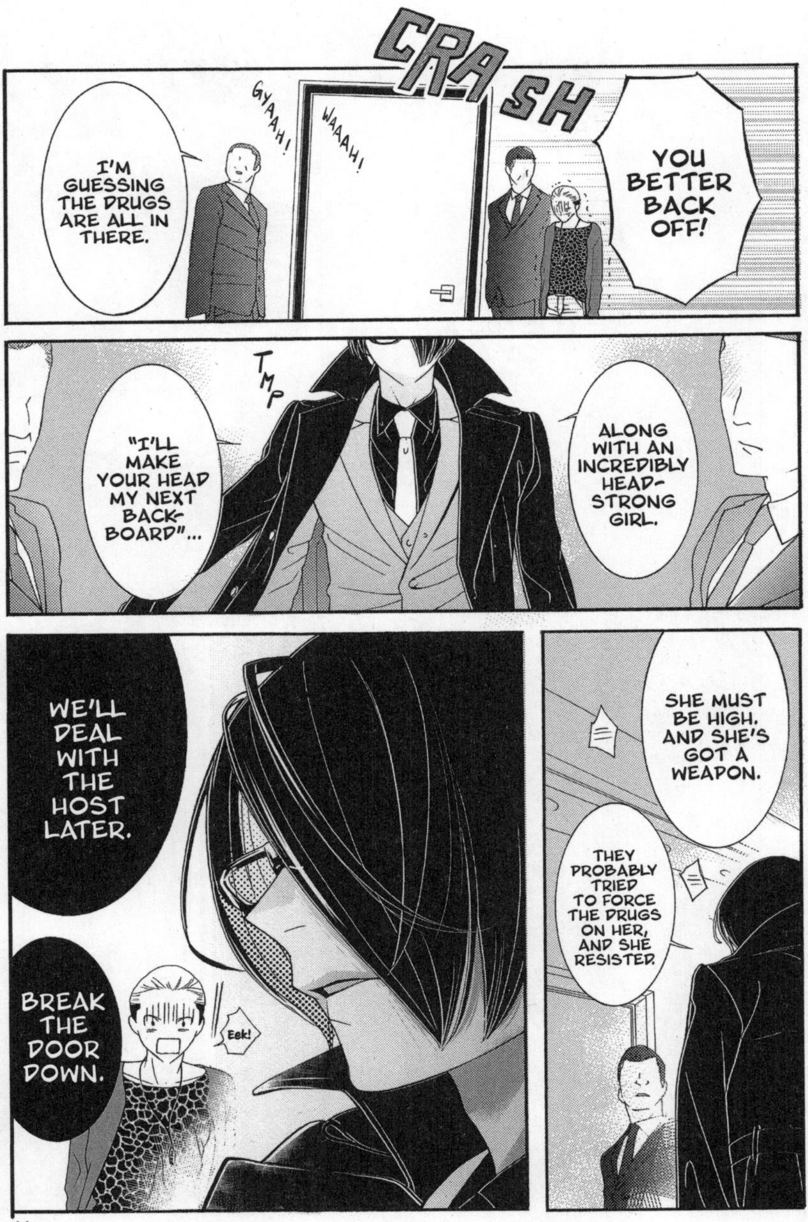
CRASH
YOU BETTER BACK OFF!
WAAAH!
GYAAAH!
I'M GUESSING THE DRUGS ARE ALL IN THERE.
ALONG WITH AN INCREDIBLY HEAD-STRONG GIRL.
TMP
"I'LL MAKE YOUR HEAD MY NEXT BACK-BOARD"...
SHE MUST BE HIGH. AND SHE'S GOT A WEAPON.
THEY PROBABLY TRIED TO FORCE THE DRUGS ON HER, AND SHE RESISTED.
WE'LL DEAL WITH THE HOST LATER.
Eek!
BREAK THE DOOR DOWN.

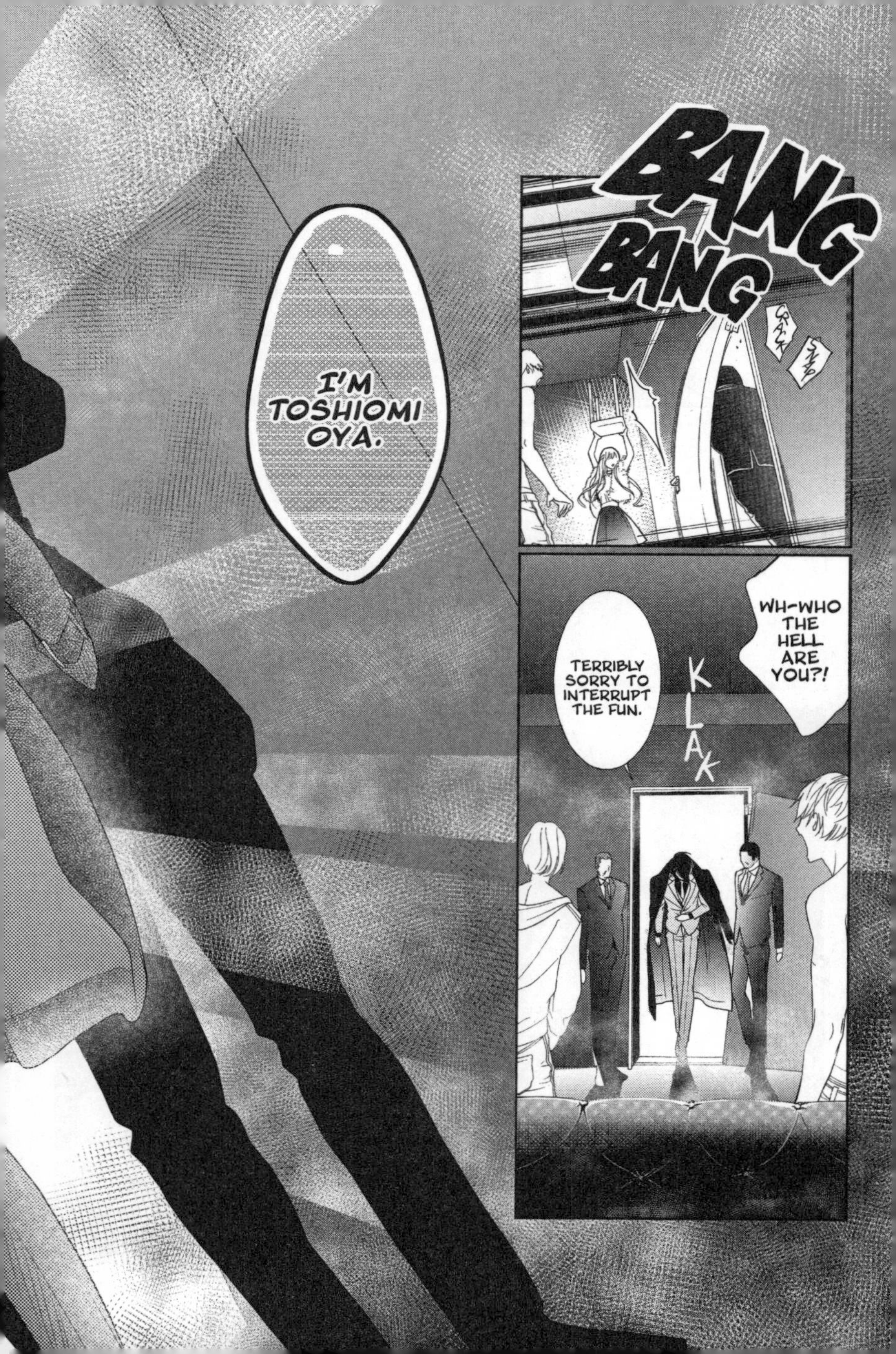
BANG
BANG
CRACK
SNAP
WH-WHO THE HELL ARE YOU?!
KLAK
TERRIBLY SORRY TO INTERRUPT THE FUN.
I'M TOSHIOMI OYA.

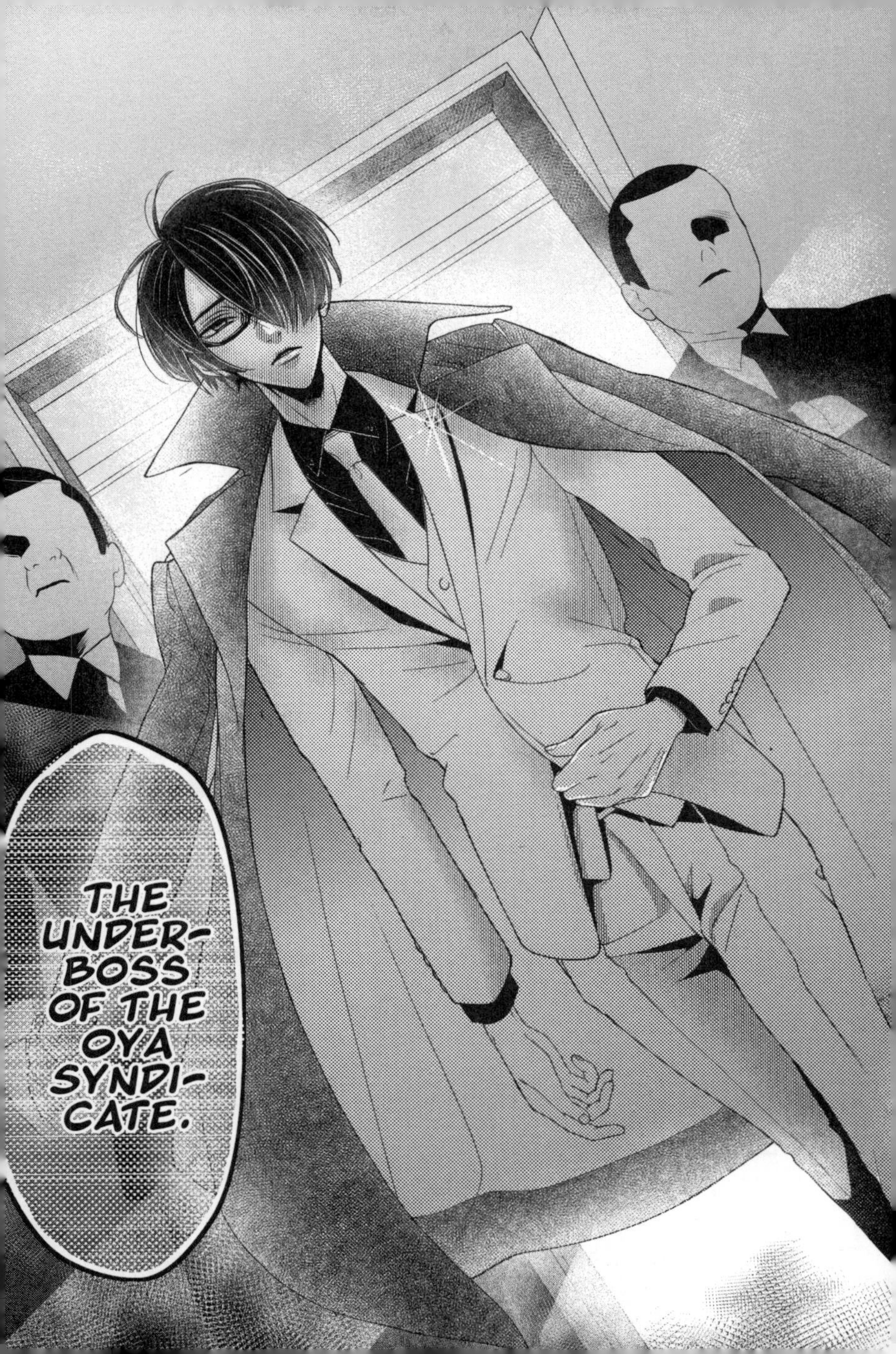
THE UNDER-BOSS OF THE OYA SYNDI-CATE.

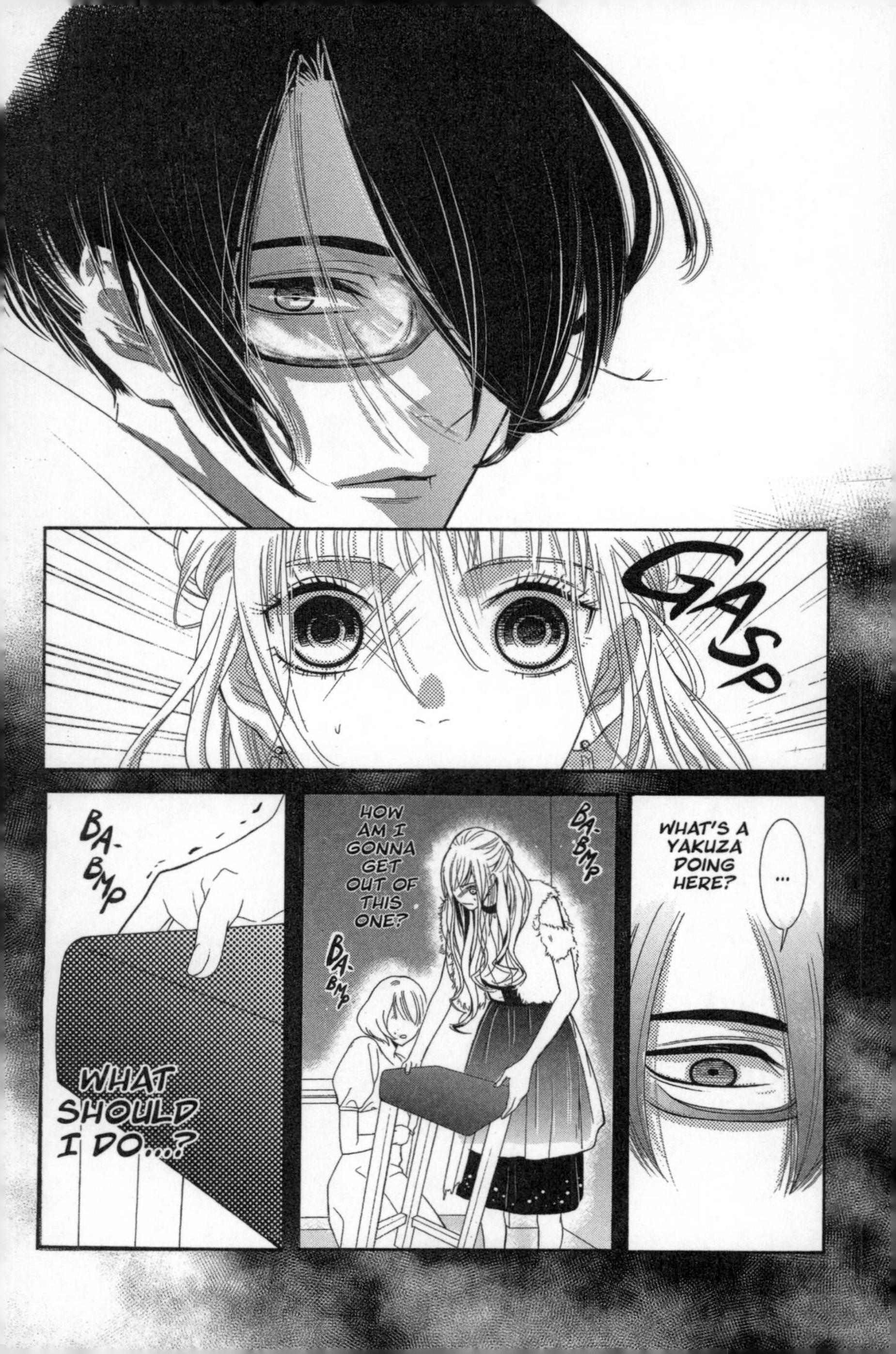
GASP
WHAT'S A YAKUZA DOING HERE?
...
BA-BMP
HOW AM I GONNA GET OUT OF THIS ONE?
BA-BMP
BA-BMP
WHAT SHOULD I DO...?

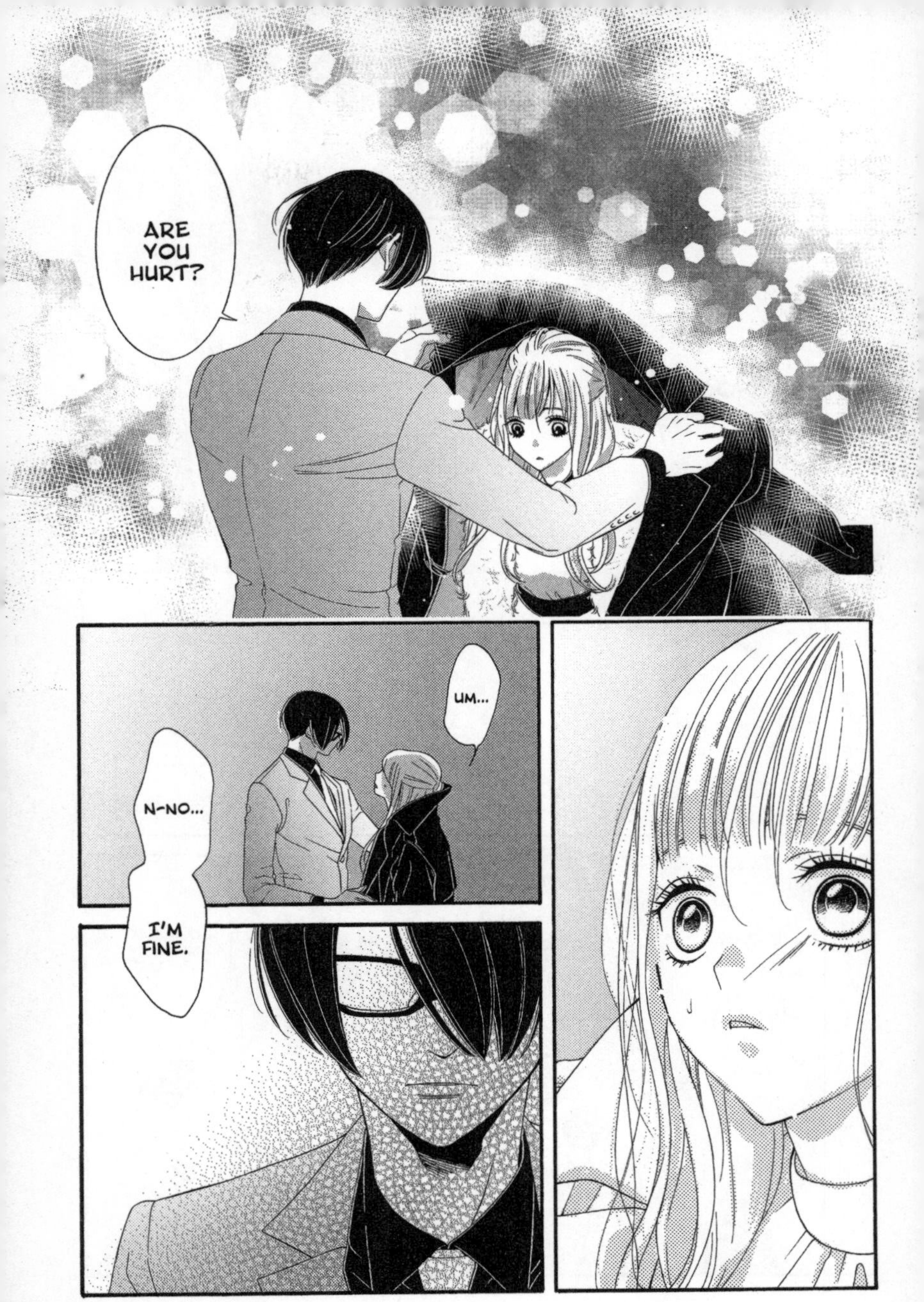
ARE YOU HURT?
UM...
N-NO... I'M FINE.

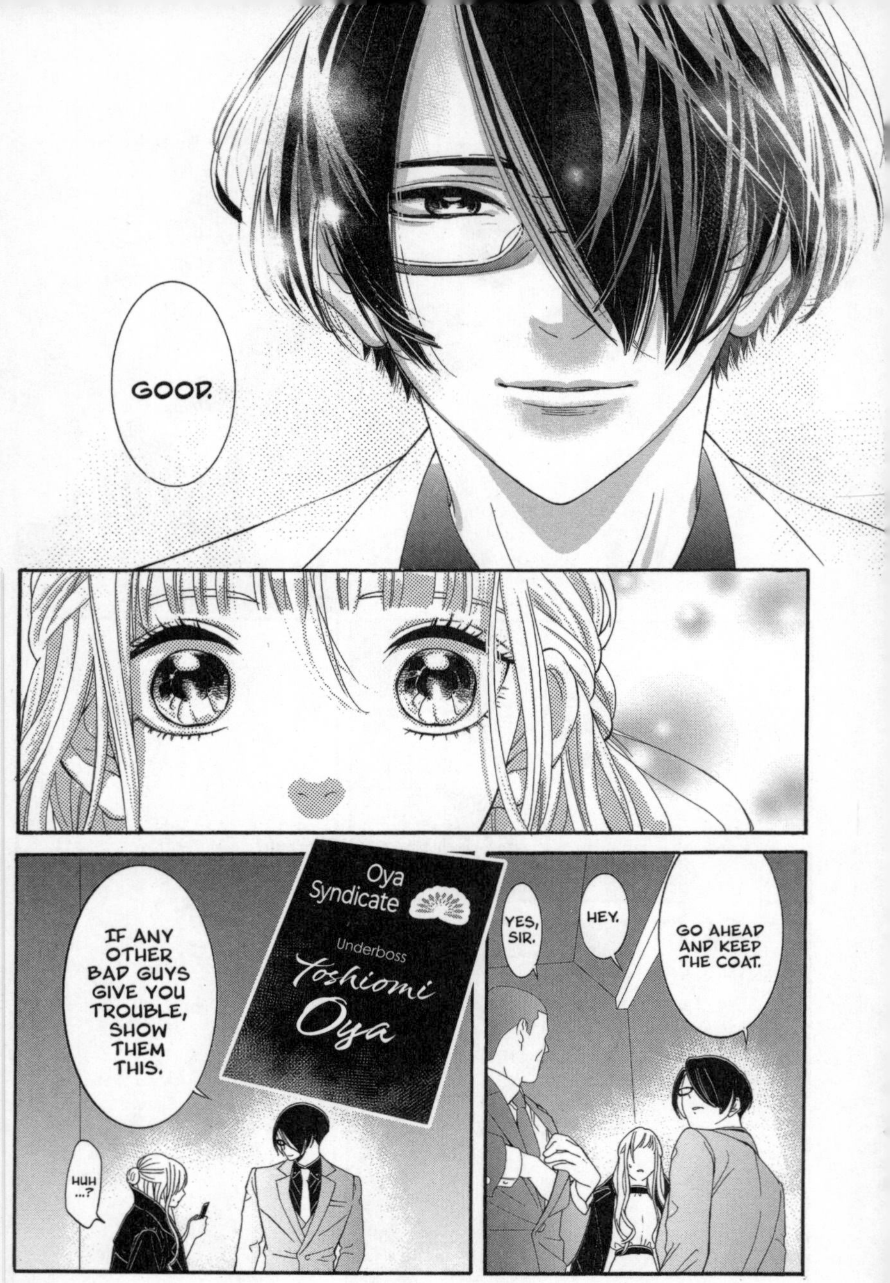
GOOD.
GO AHEAD AND KEEP THE COAT.
HEY.
YES, SIR.
Oya Syndicate
Underboss
Toshiomi Oya
IF ANY OTHER BAD GUYS GIVE YOU TROUBLE, SHOW THEM THIS.
HUH ...?

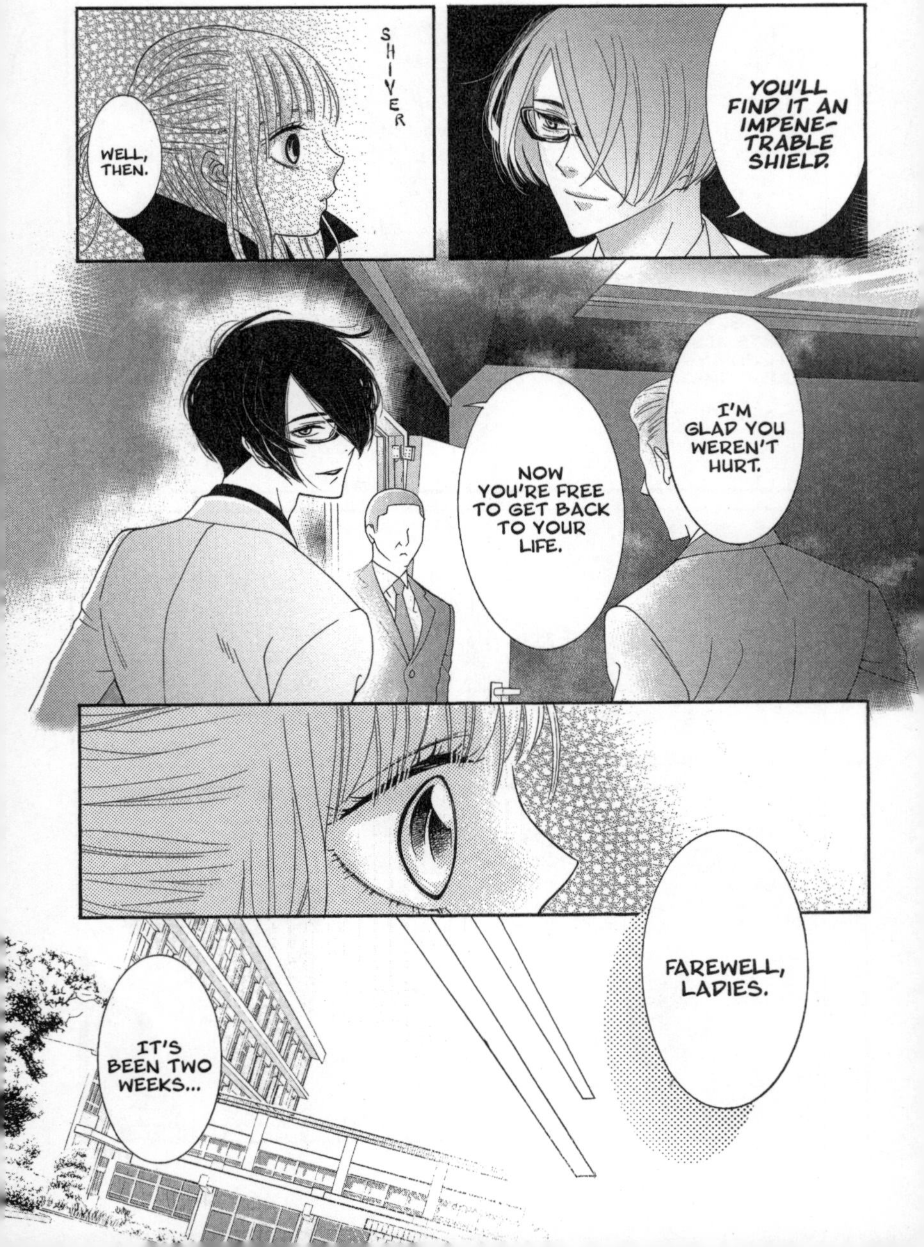
YOU'LL FIND IT AN IMPENE-TRABLE SHIELD.
SHIVER
WELL, THEN.
I'M GLAD YOU WEREN'T HURT.
NOW YOU'RE FREE TO GET BACK TO YOUR LIFE.
FAREWELL, LADIES.
IT'S BEEN TWO WEEKS...

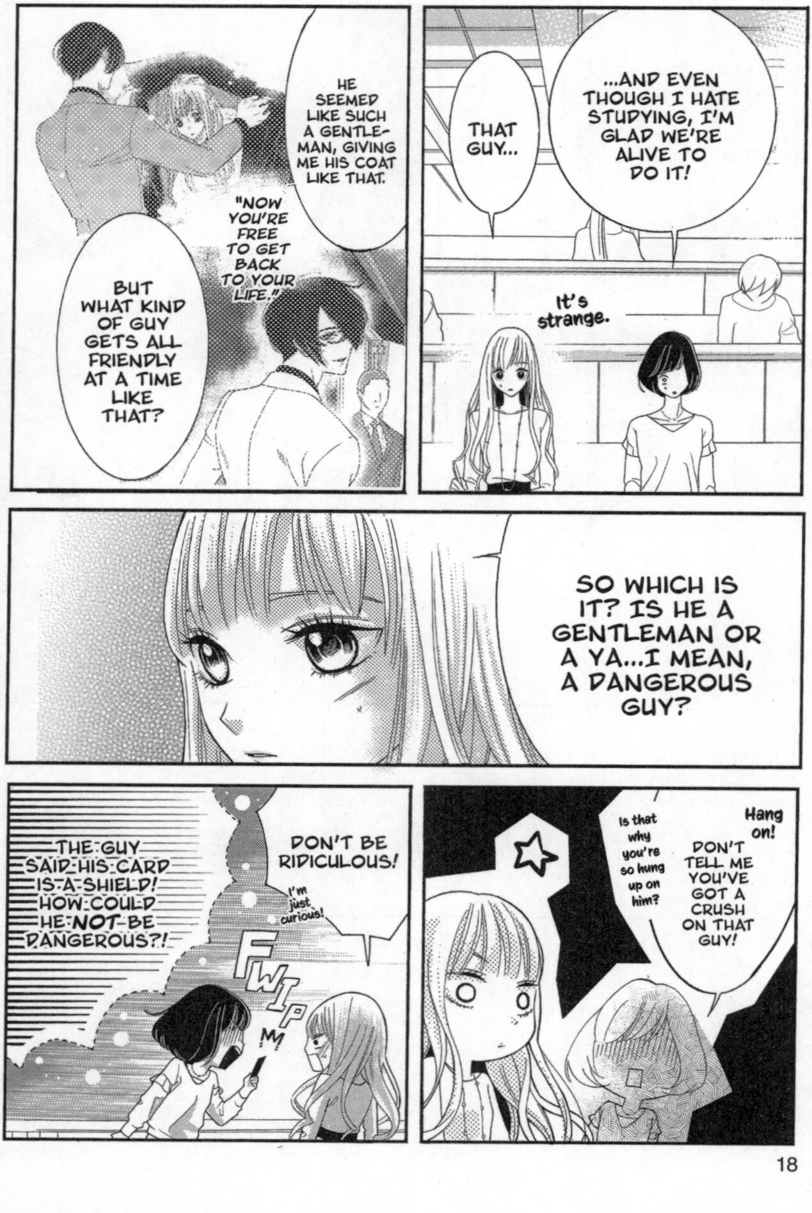
...AND EVEN THOUGH I HATE STUDYING, I'M GLAD WE'RE ALIVE TO DO IT!
THAT GUY...
It's strange.
HE SEEMED LIKE SUCH A GENTLE-MAN, GIVING ME HIS COAT LIKE THAT.
"NOW YOU'RE FREE TO GET BACK TO YOUR LIFE."
BUT WHAT KIND OF GUY GETS ALL FRIENDLY AT A TIME LIKE THAT?
SO WHICH IS IT? IS HE A GENTLEMAN OR A YA...I MEAN, A DANGEROUS GUY?
Hang on!
DON'T TELL ME YOU'VE GOT A CRUSH ON THAT GUY!
Is that why you're so hung up on him?
DON'T BE RIDICULOUS!
I'm just curious!
THE GUY SAID HIS CARD IS A SHIELD! HOW COULD HE NOT BE DANGEROUS?!
FWIP
M!

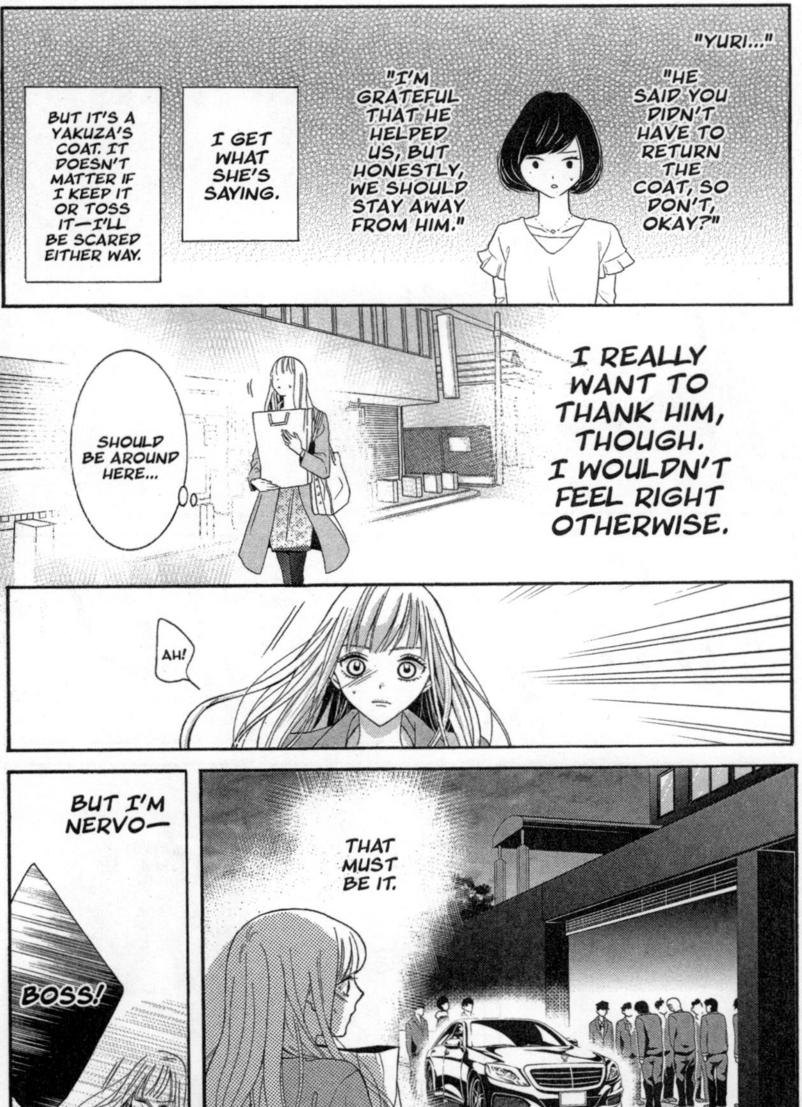
"YURI..."
"HE SAID YOU DIDN'T HAVE TO RETURN THE COAT, SO DON'T, OKAY?"
"I'M GRATEFUL THAT HE HELPED US, BUT HONESTLY, WE SHOULD STAY AWAY FROM HIM."
I GET WHAT SHE'S SAYING.
BUT IT'S A YAKUZA'S COAT. IT DOESN'T MATTER IF I KEEP IT OR TOSS IT—I'LL BE SCARED EITHER WAY.
I REALLY WANT TO THANK HIM, THOUGH. I WOULDN'T FEEL RIGHT OTHERWISE.
SHOULD BE AROUND HERE...
AH!
THAT MUST BE IT.
BUT I'M NERVO—
BOSS!

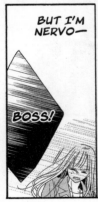

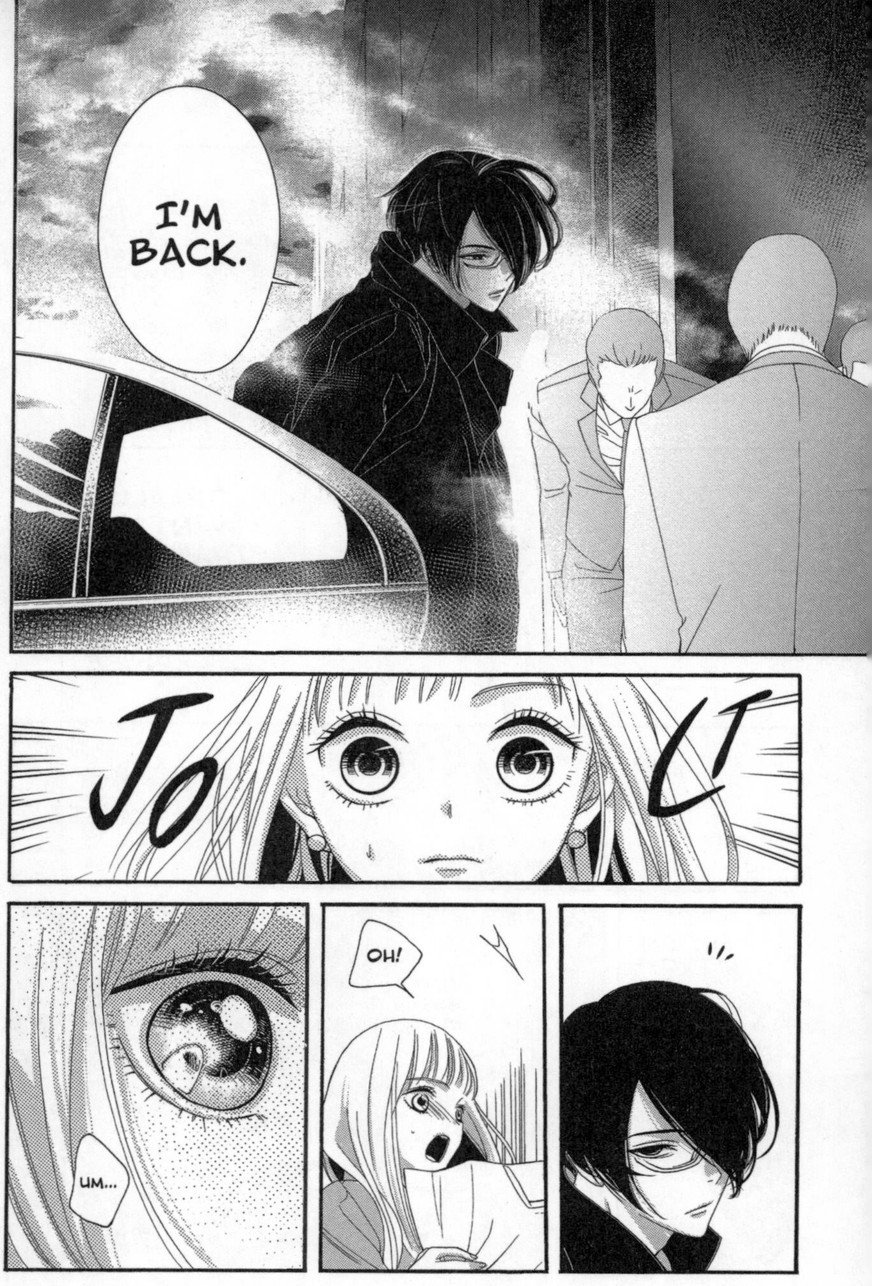
I'M BACK.
JOLT
OH!
UM...

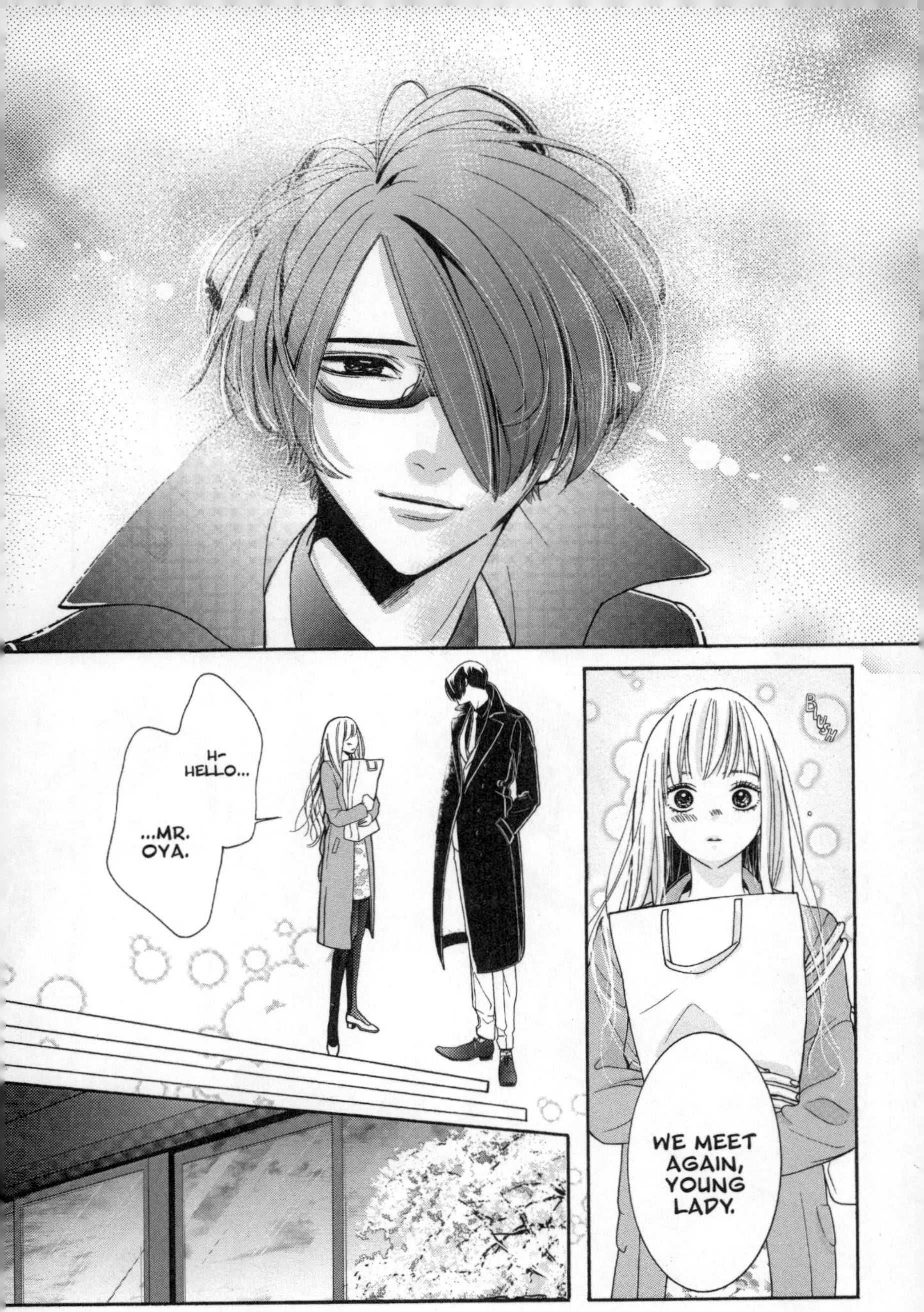
BLUSH
WE MEET AGAIN, YOUNG LADY.
H-HELLO...
...MR. OYA.

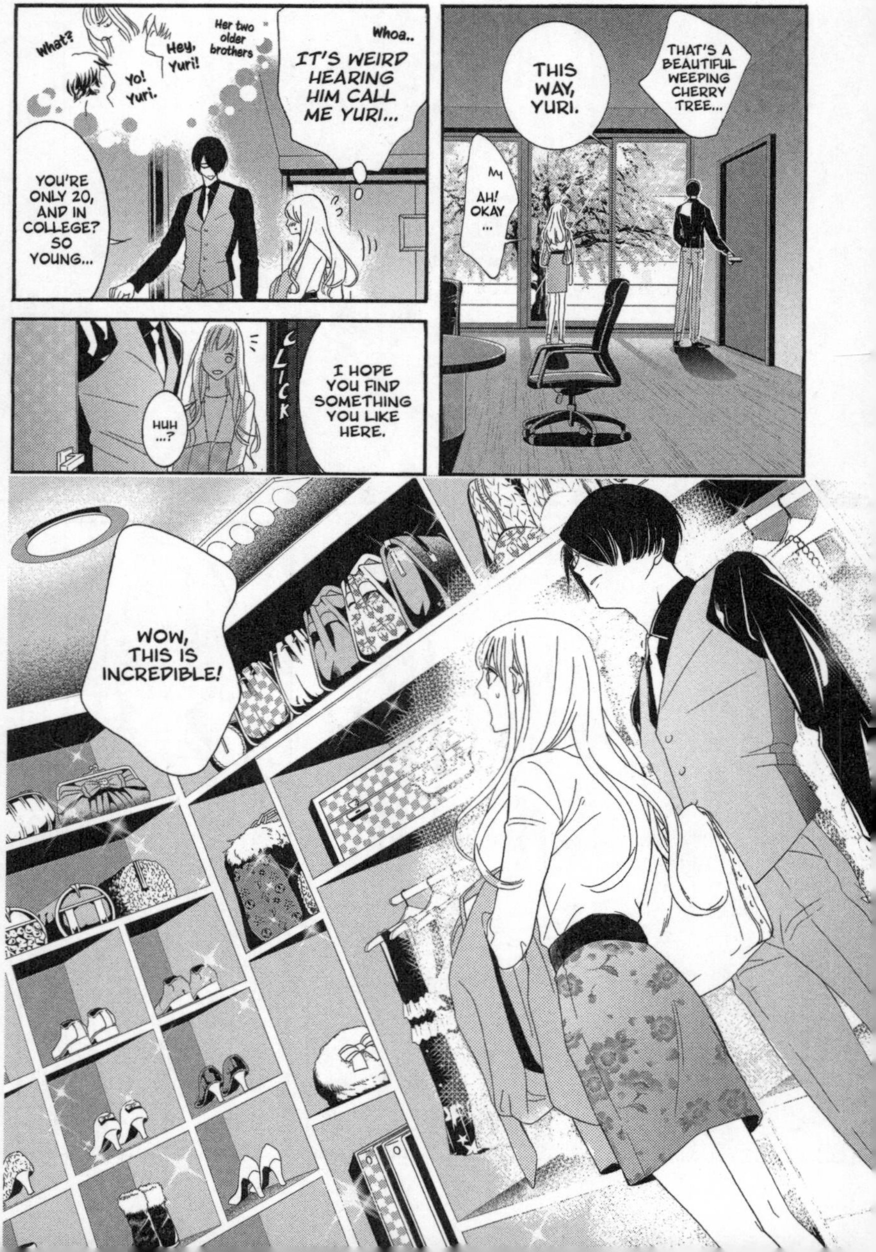
THAT'S A BEAUTIFUL WEEPING CHERRY TREE...
THIS WAY, YURI.
AH! OKAY ...
Whoa.. IT'S WEIRD HEARING HIM CALL ME YURI...
Her two older brothers
Hey, Yuri!
What?
Yo! Yuri.
YOU'RE ONLY 20, AND IN COLLEGE? SO YOUNG...
I HOPE YOU FIND SOMETHING YOU LIKE HERE.
CLICK
HUH ...?
WOW, THIS IS INCREDIBLE!

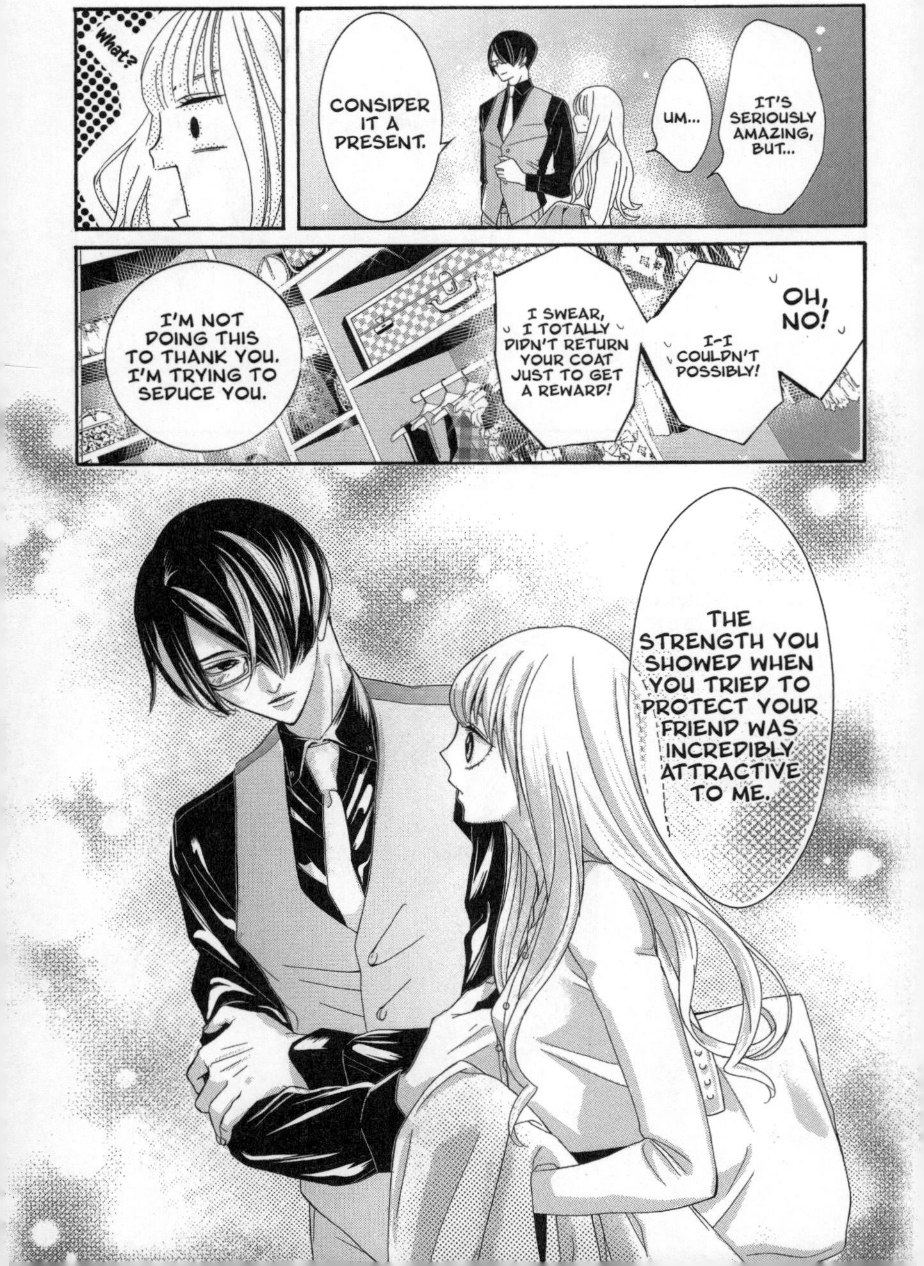
IT'S SERIOUSLY AMAZING, BUT...
UM...
CONSIDER IT A PRESENT.
What?
OH, NO!
I-I COULDN'T POSSIBLY!
I SWEAR, I TOTALLY DIDN'T RETURN YOUR COAT JUST TO GET A REWARD!
I'M NOT DOING THIS TO THANK YOU. I'M TRYING TO SEDUCE YOU.
THE STRENGTH YOU SHOWED WHEN YOU TRIED TO PROTECT YOUR FRIEND WAS INCREDIBLY ATTRACTIVE TO ME.

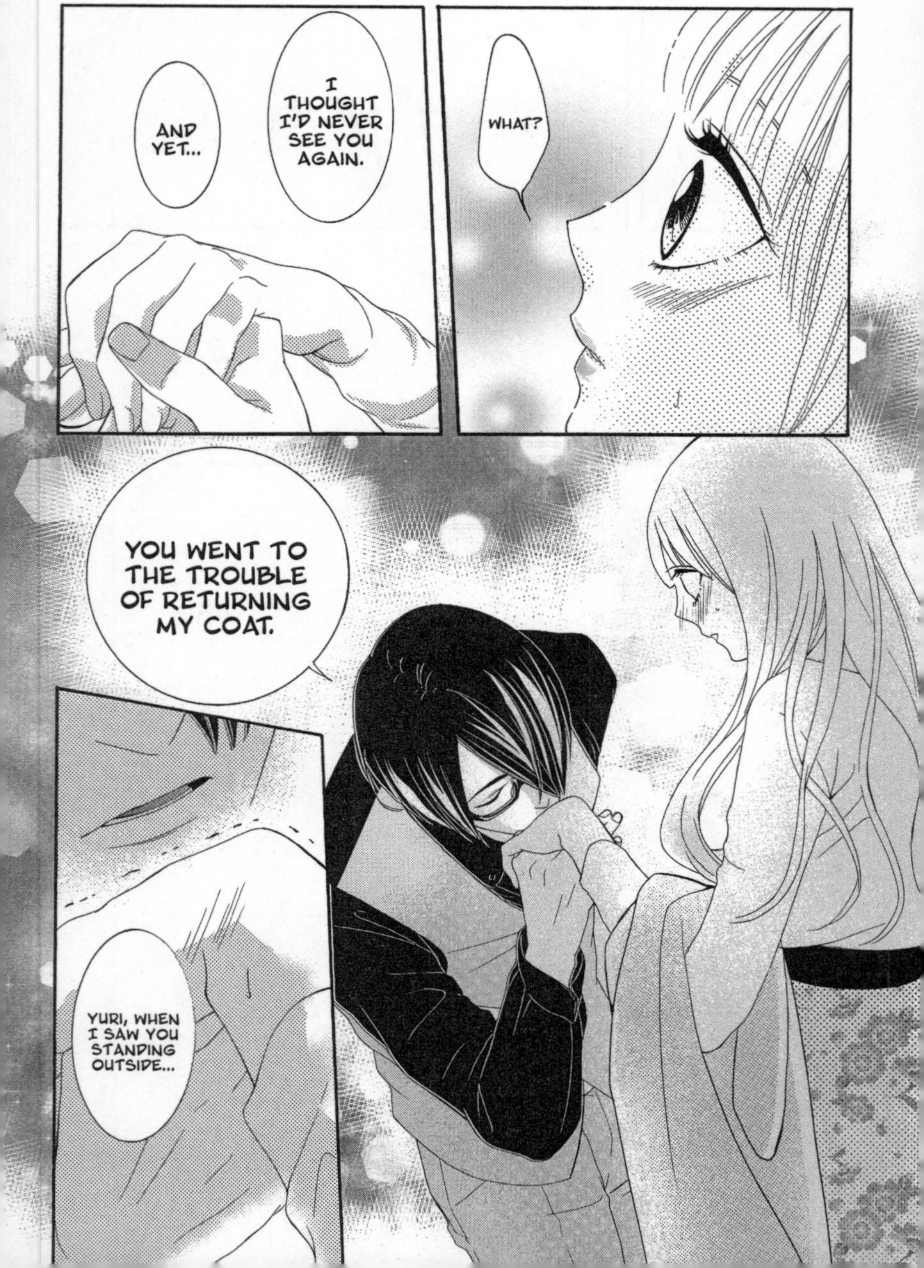
WHAT?
I THOUGHT I'D NEVER SEE YOU AGAIN.
AND YET...
YOU WENT TO THE TROUBLE OF RETURNING MY COAT.
YURI, WHEN I SAW YOU STANDING OUTSIDE...

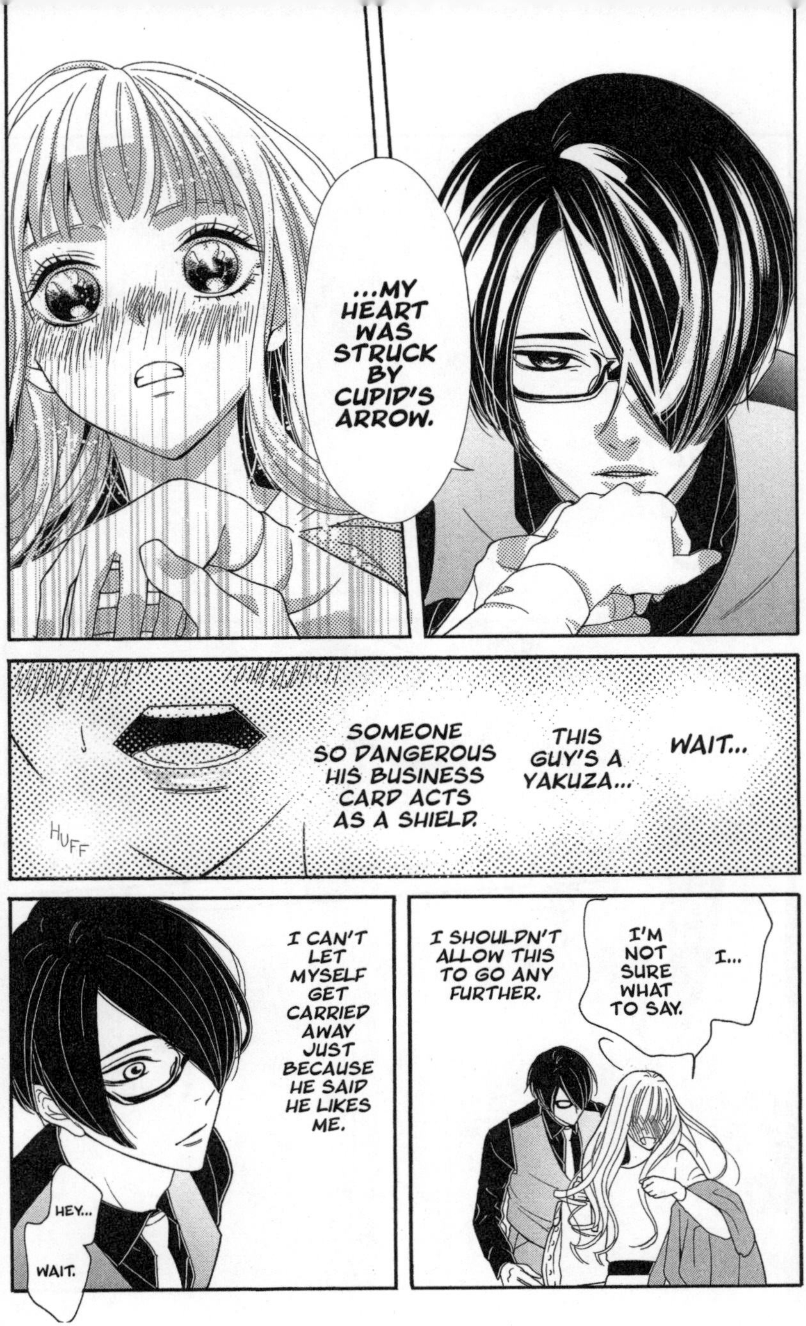
...MY HEART WAS STRUCK BY CUPID'S ARROW.
WAIT...
THIS GUY'S A YAKUZA...
SOMEONE SO DANGEROUS HIS BUSINESS CARD ACTS AS A SHIELD.
HUFF
I...
I'M NOT SURE WHAT TO SAY.
I SHOULDN'T ALLOW THIS TO GO ANY FURTHER.
I CAN'T LET MYSELF GET CARRIED AWAY JUST BECAUSE HE SAID HE LIKES ME.
HEY...
WAIT.

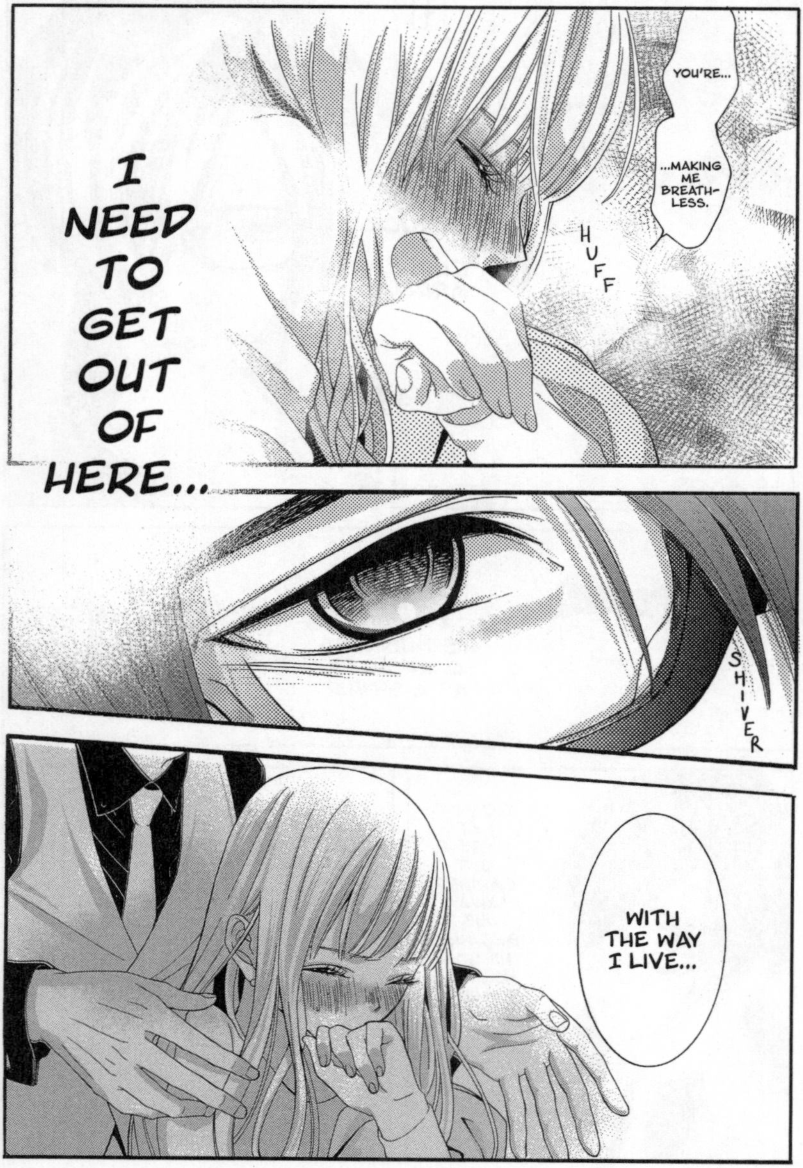
YOU'RE...
...MAKING ME BREATHLESS.
HUFF
I NEED TO GET OUT OF HERE...
SHIVER
WITH THE WAY I LIVE...

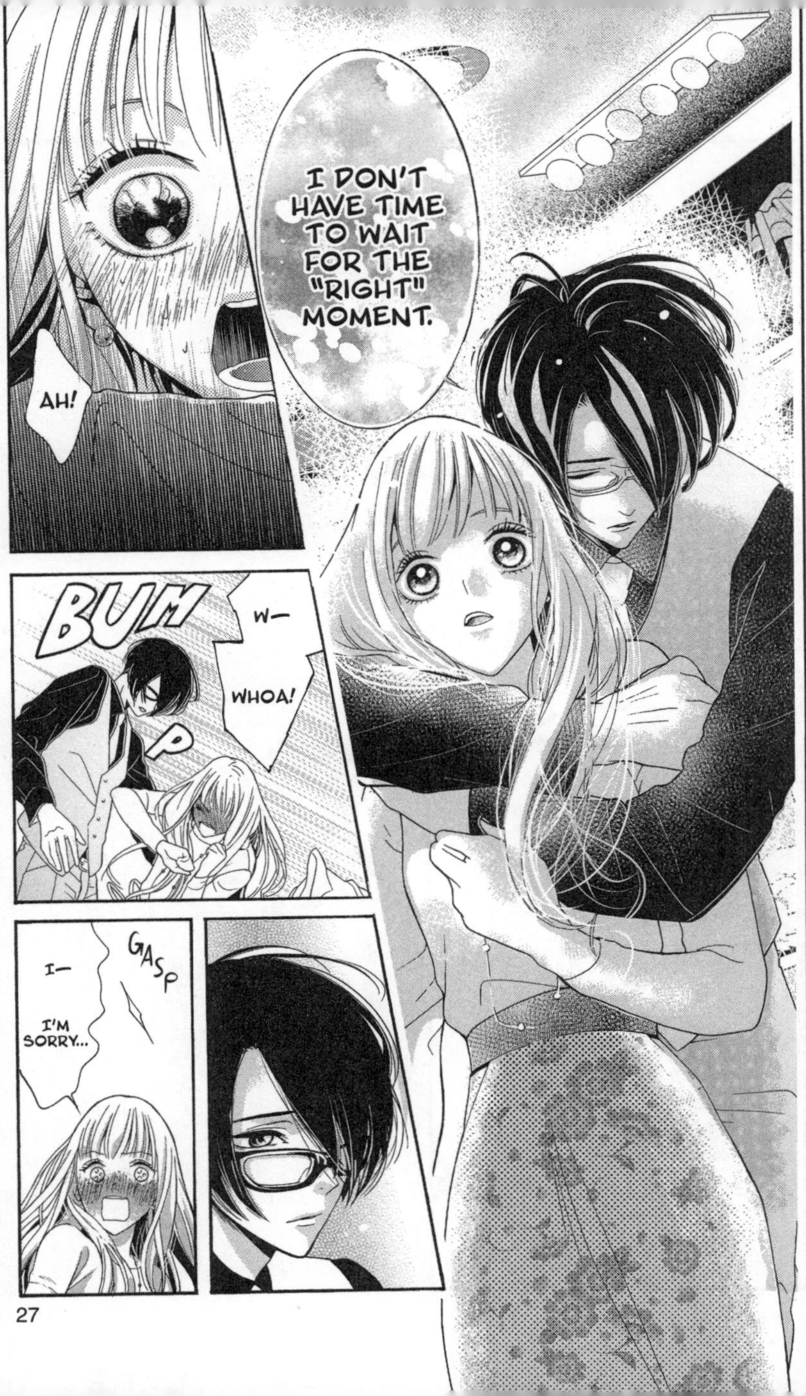
I DON'T HAVE TIME TO WAIT FOR THE "RIGHT" MOMENT.
AH!
BUMP
W—
WHOA!
GASP
I—
I'M SORRY...

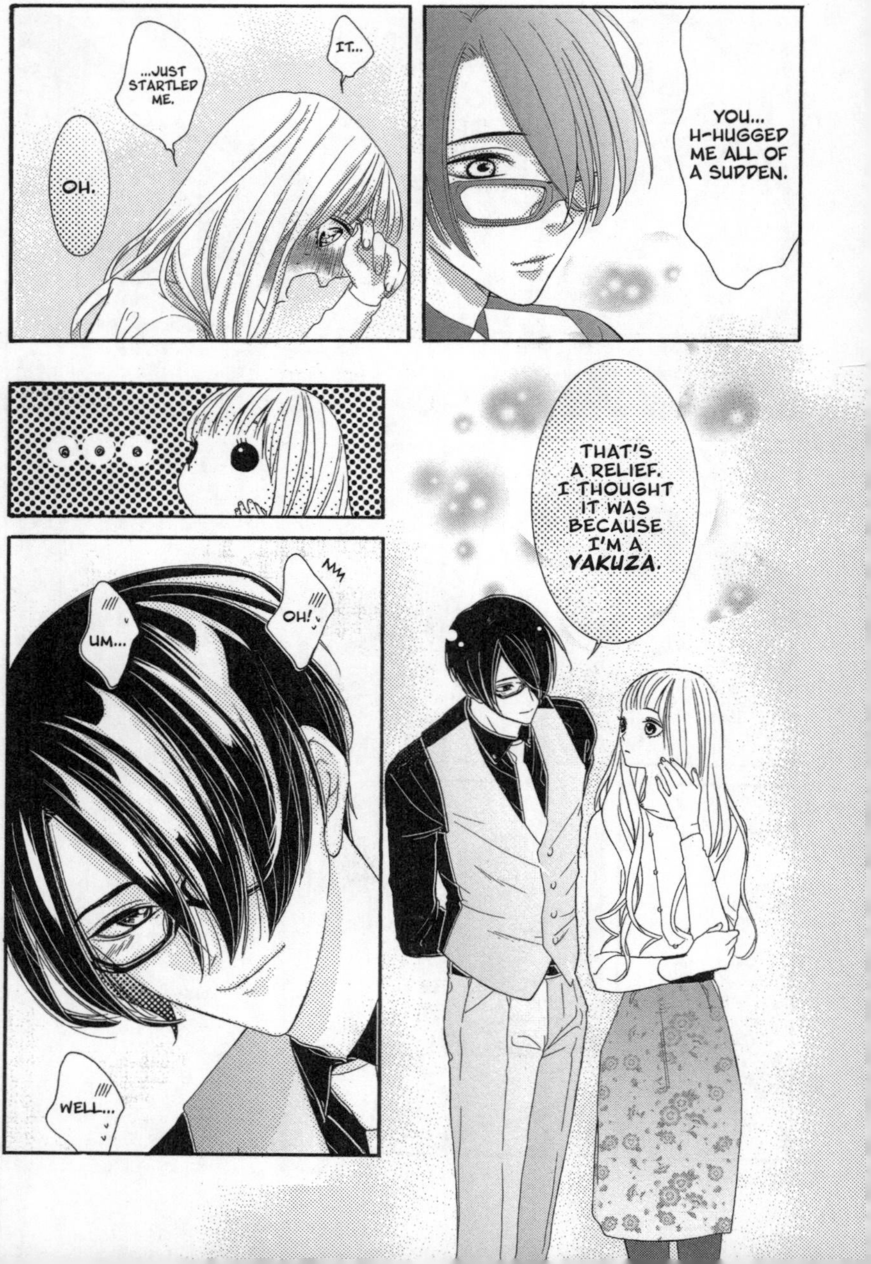
YOU... H-HUGGED ME ALL OF A SUDDEN.
IT...
...JUST STARTLED ME.
OH.
THAT'S A RELIEF. I THOUGHT IT WAS BECAUSE I'M A YAKUZA.
OH!
UM...
WELL...

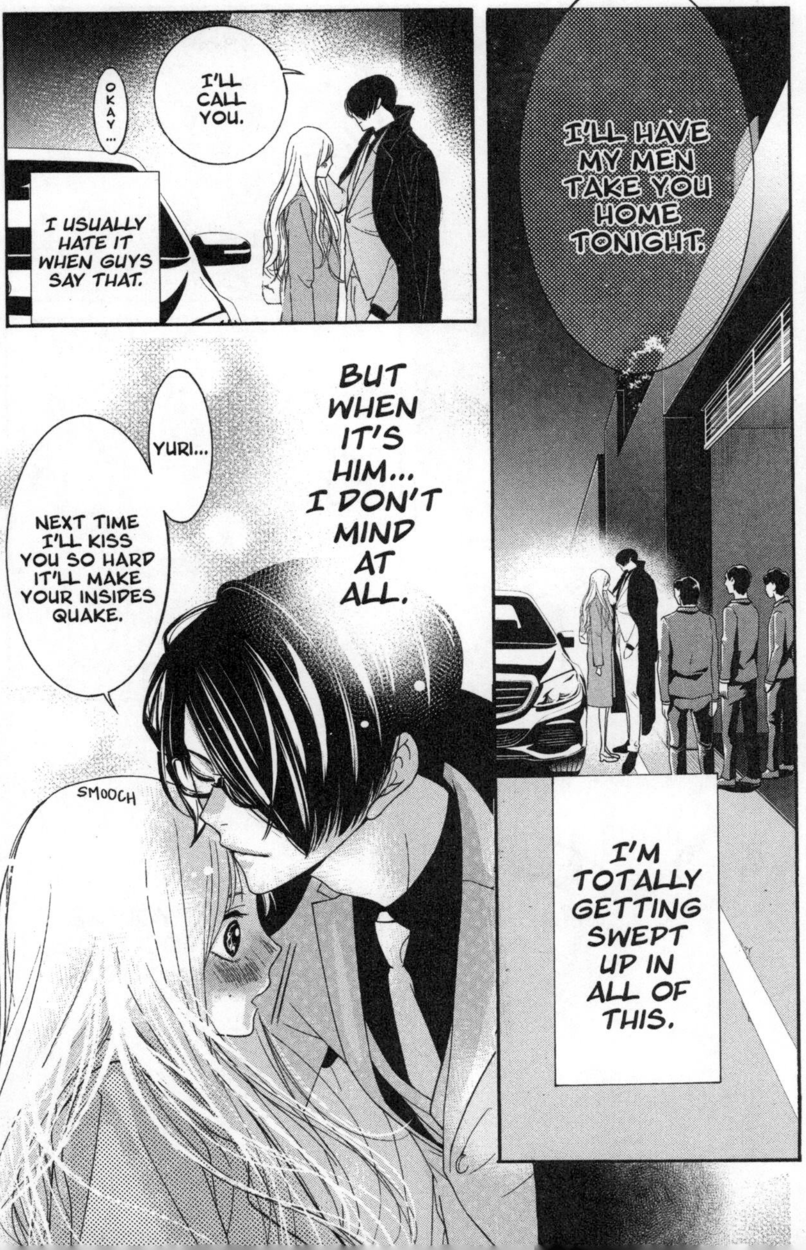
I'LL HAVE MY MEN TAKE YOU HOME TONIGHT.
I'M TOTALLY GETTING SWEPT UP IN ALL OF THIS.
I'LL CALL YOU.
OKAY...
I USUALLY HATE IT WHEN GUYS SAY THAT.
BUT WHEN IT'S HIM... I DON'T MIND AT ALL.
YURI...
NEXT TIME I'LL KISS YOU SO HARD IT'LL MAKE YOUR INSIDES QUAKE.
SMOOCH

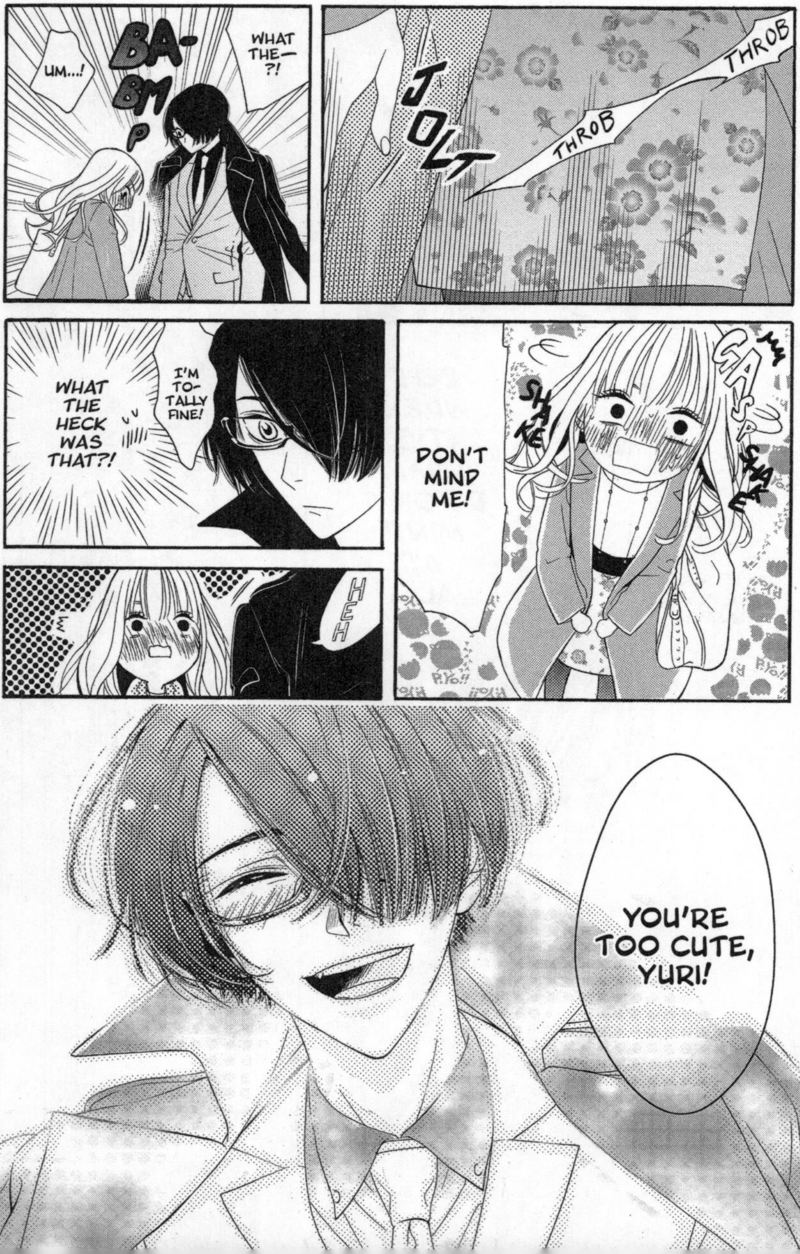
THROB
THROB
JOLT
WHAT THE—?!
BA-BMP
UM...!
GASP
SHAKE
SHAKE
DON'T MIND ME!
I'M TOTALLY FINE!
WHAT THE HECK WAS THAT?!
HEH
YOU'RE TOO CUTE, YURI!

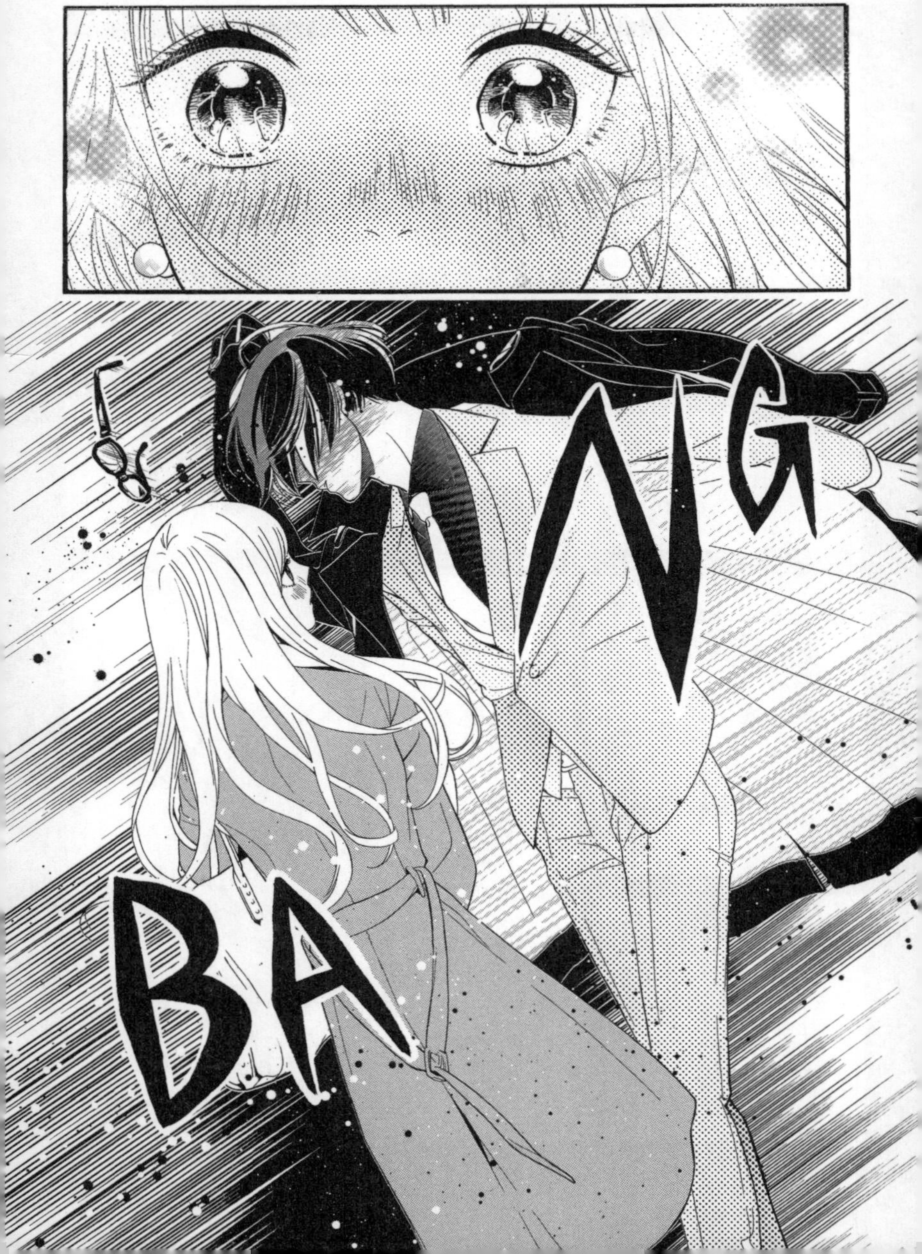
BANG

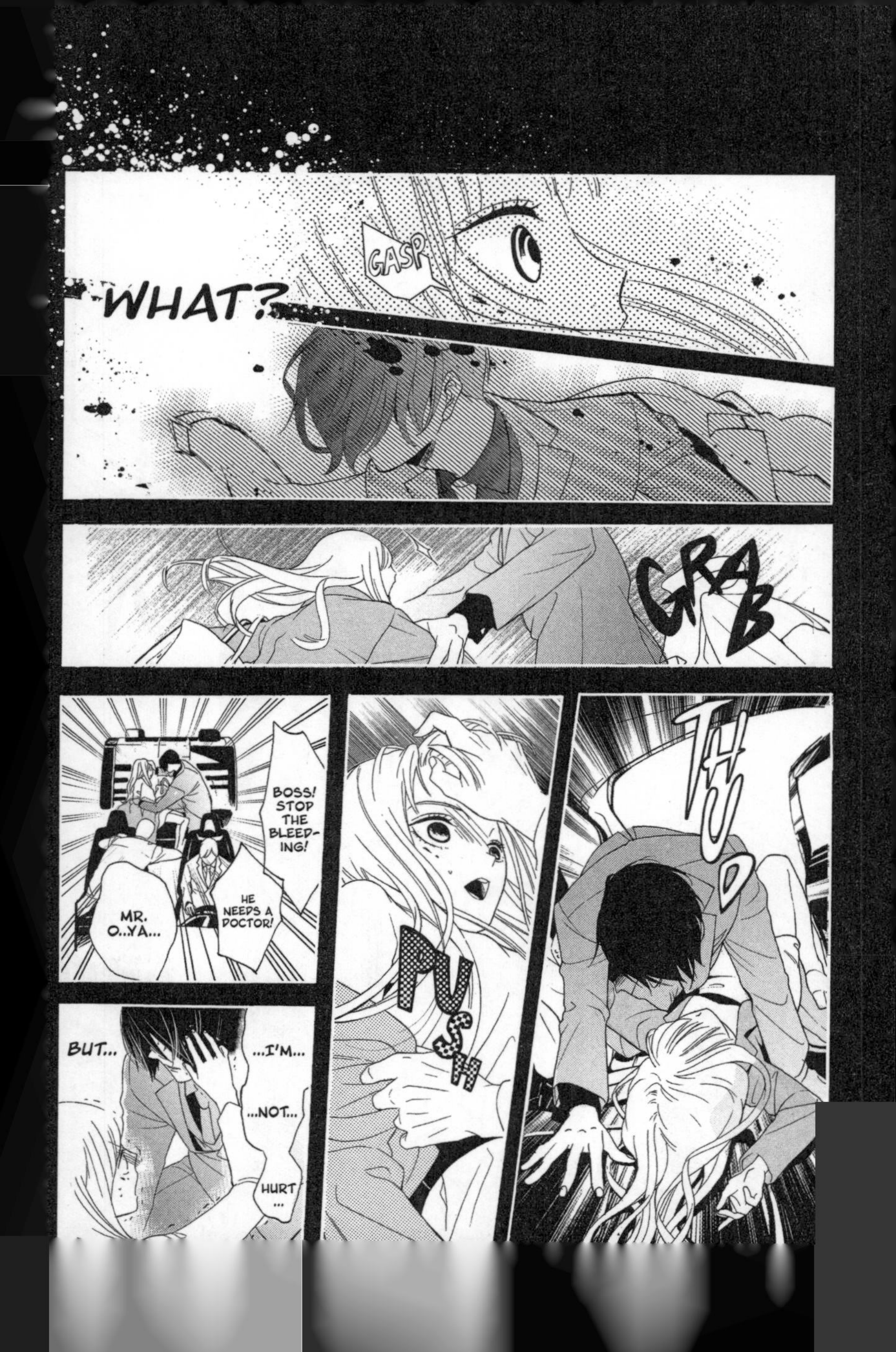
GASP
WHAT?
GRAB
THUD
PUSH
BOSS! STOP THE BLEED-ING!
HE NEEDS A DOCTOR!
MR. O..YA...
BUT...
...I'M...
...NOT...
HURT...

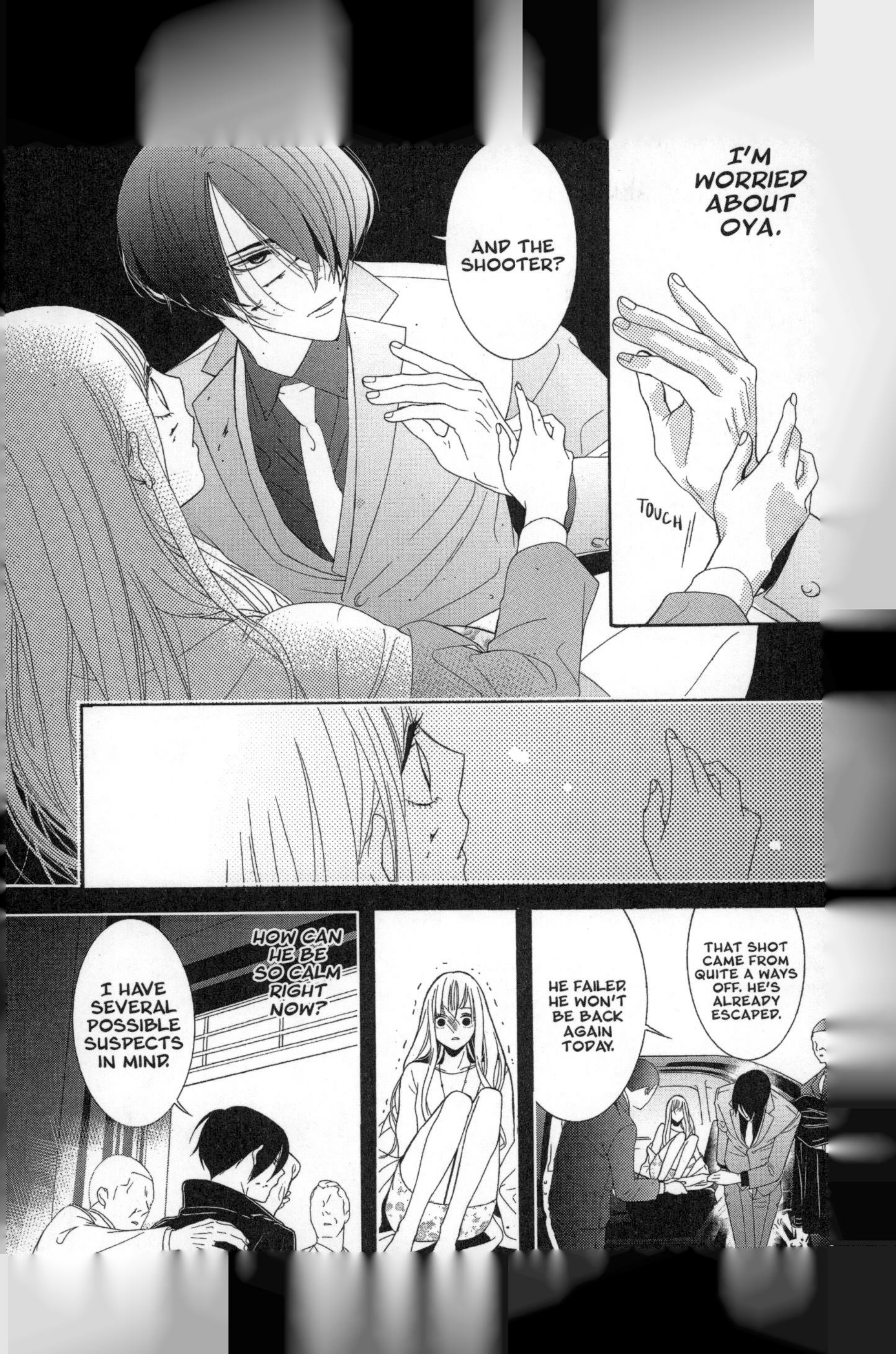
I'M WORRIED ABOUT OYA.
TOUCH
AND THE SHOOTER?
THAT SHOT CAME FROM QUITE A WAYS OFF. HE'S ALREADY ESCAPED.
HE FAILED. HE WON'T BE BACK AGAIN TODAY.
HOW CAN HE BE SO CALM RIGHT NOW?
I HAVE SEVERAL POSSIBLE SUSPECTS IN MIND.

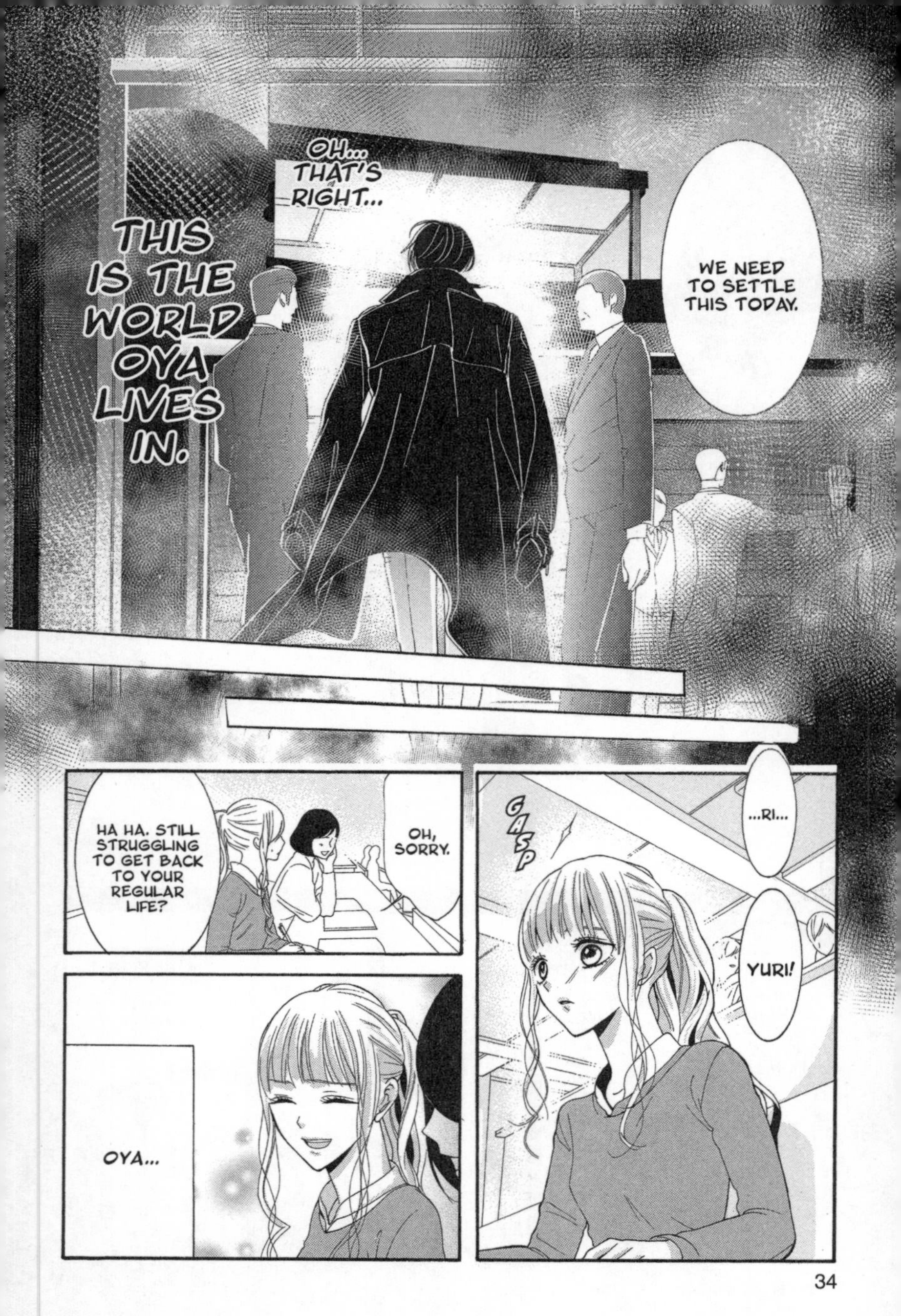
WE NEED TO SETTLE THIS TODAY.
OH... THAT'S RIGHT...
THIS IS THE WORLD OYA LIVES IN.
...RI...
GASP
YURI!
OH, SORRY.
HA HA. STILL STRUGGLING TO GET BACK TO YOUR REGULAR LIFE?
OYA...

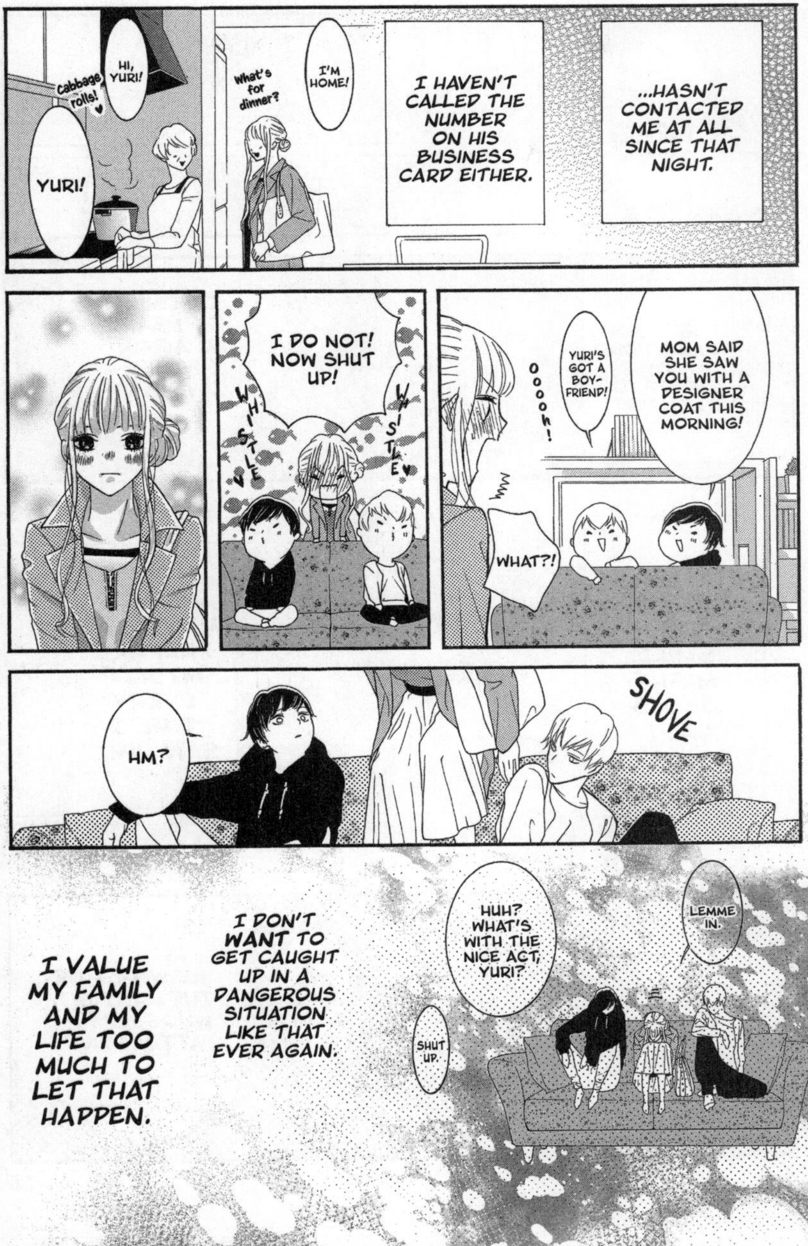
...HASN'T CONTACTED ME AT ALL SINCE THAT NIGHT.
I HAVEN'T CALLED THE NUMBER ON HIS BUSINESS CARD EITHER.
I'M HOME!
What's for dinner?
HI, YURI!
Cabbage rolls! ♥
YURI!
MOM SAID SHE SAW YOU WITH A DESIGNER COAT THIS MORNING!
YURI'S GOT A BOY-FRIEND!
Ooooh!
WHAT?!
I DO NOT! NOW SHUT UP!
WHISTLE ♥
WHISTLE ♥
SHOVE
HM?
LEMME IN.
HUH? WHAT'S WITH THE NICE ACT, YURI?
SHUT UP.
I DON'T WANT TO GET CAUGHT UP IN A DANGEROUS SITUATION LIKE THAT EVER AGAIN.
I VALUE MY FAMILY AND MY LIFE TOO MUCH TO LET THAT HAPPEN.

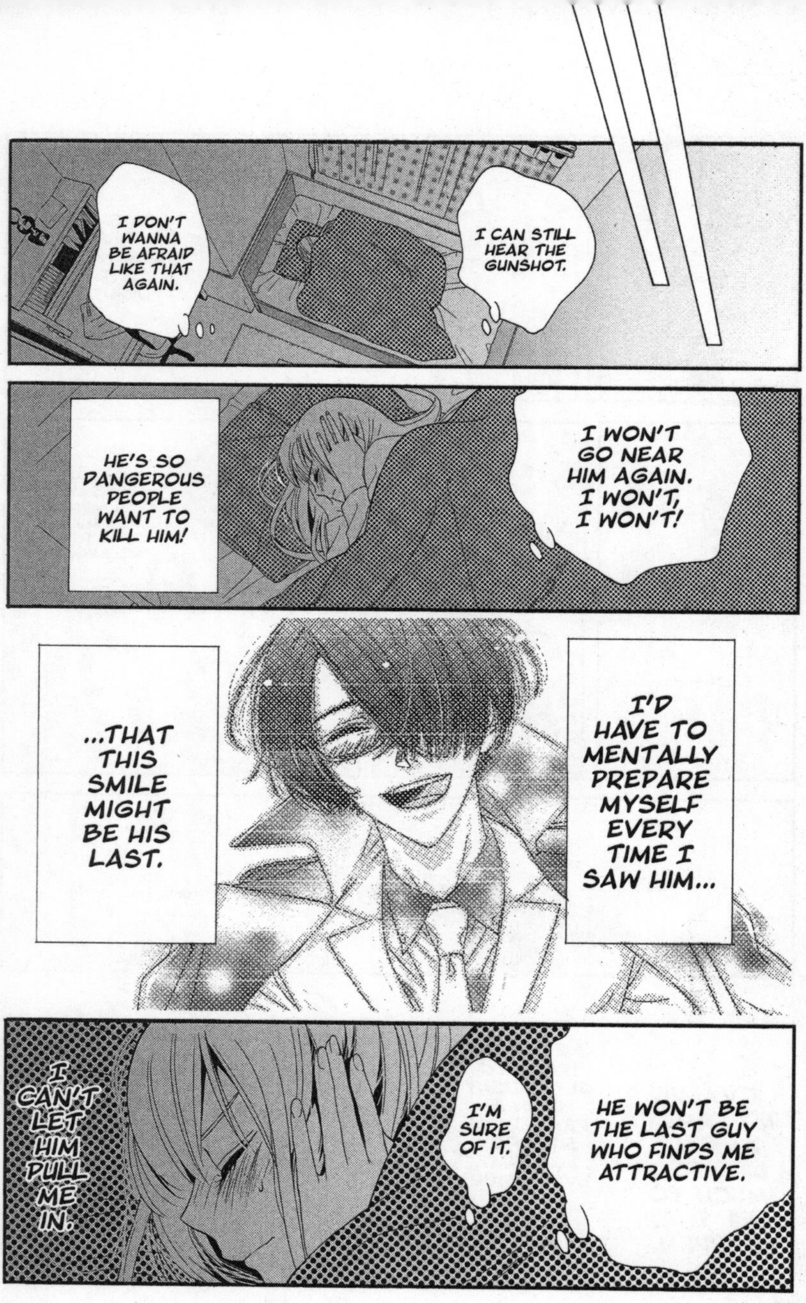
I CAN STILL HEAR THE GUNSHOT.
I DON'T WANNA BE AFRAID LIKE THAT AGAIN.
I WON'T GO NEAR HIM AGAIN. I WON'T, I WON'T!
HE'S SO DANGEROUS PEOPLE WANT TO KILL HIM!
I'D HAVE TO MENTALLY PREPARE MYSELF EVERY TIME I SAW HIM...
...THAT THIS SMILE MIGHT BE HIS LAST.
HE WON'T BE THE LAST GUY WHO FINDS ME ATTRACTIVE.
I'M SURE OF IT.
I CAN'T LET HIM PULL ME IN.

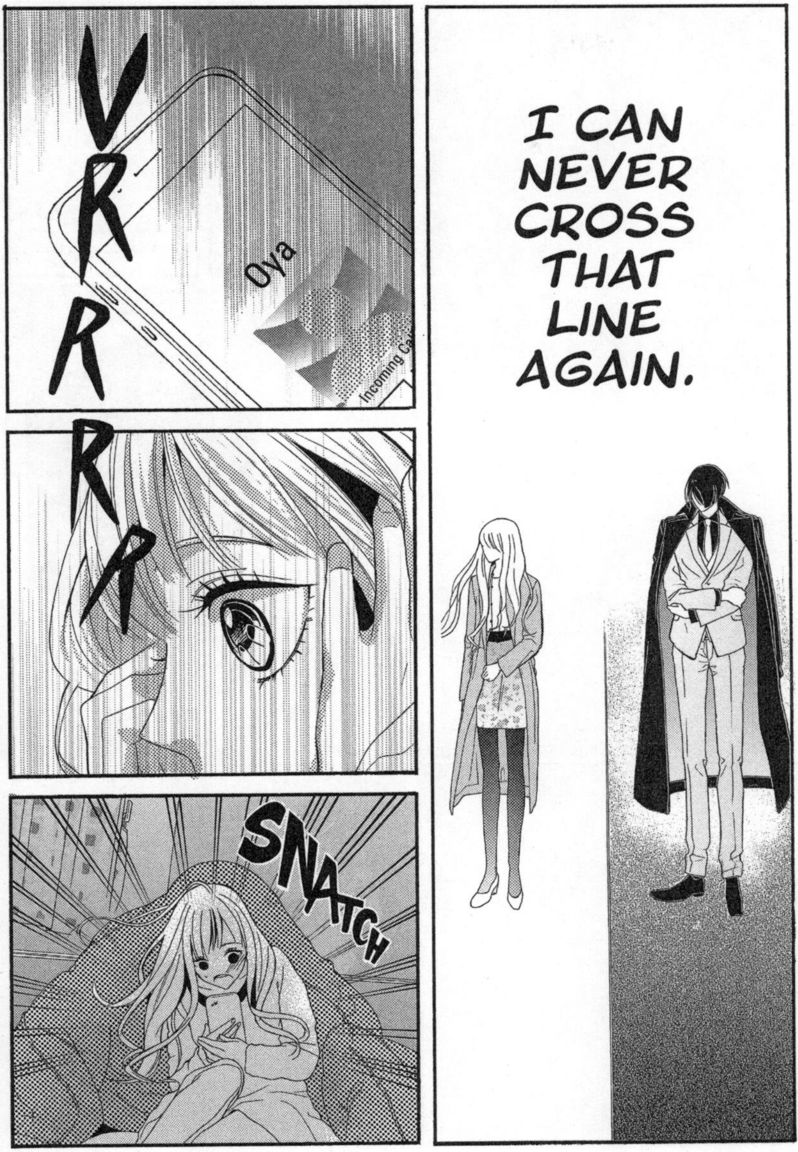
I CAN NEVER CROSS THAT LINE AGAIN.
VRRRR
Oya
SNATCH

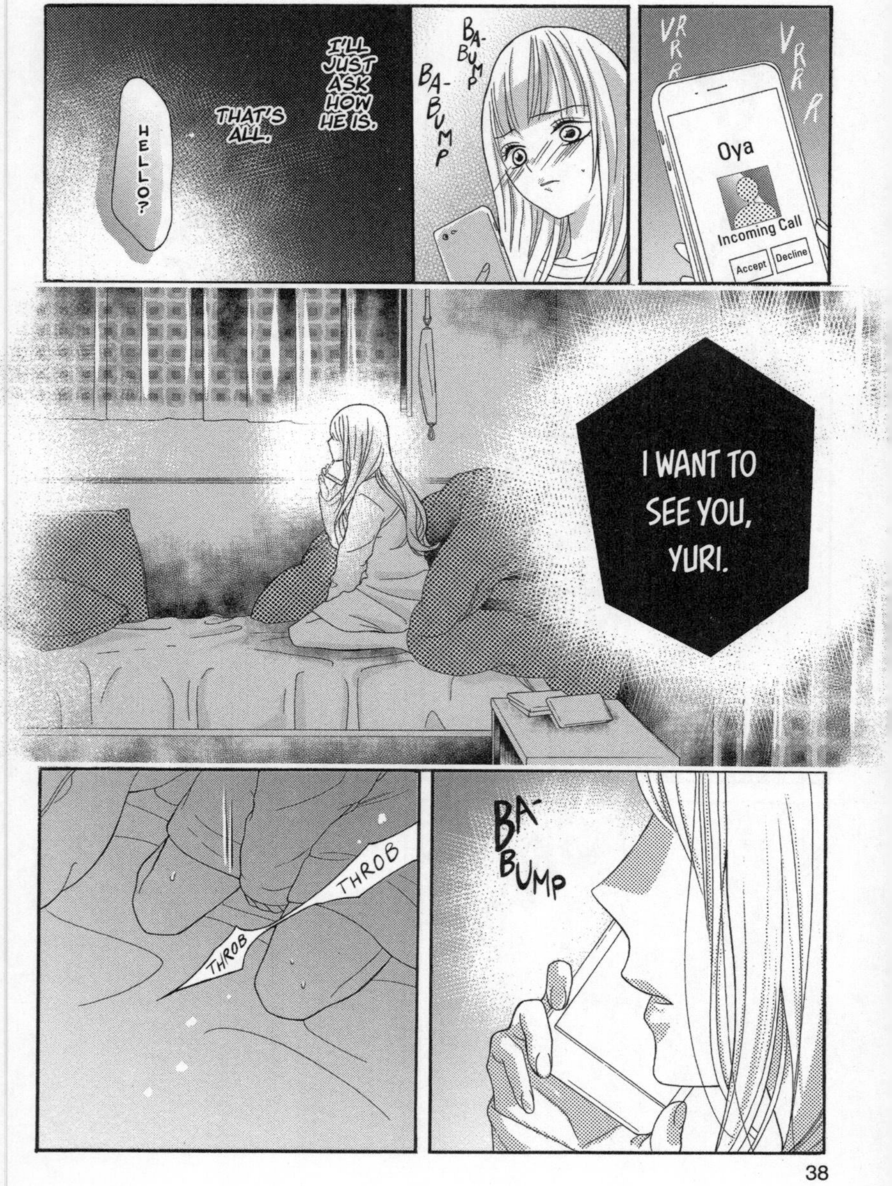
VRRR
VRRR
Oya
Incoming Call
Accept
Decline
BA-BUMP
BA-BUMP
I'LL JUST ASK HOW HE IS.
THAT'S ALL.
HELLO?
I WANT TO SEE YOU, YURI.
BA-BUMP
THROB
THROB

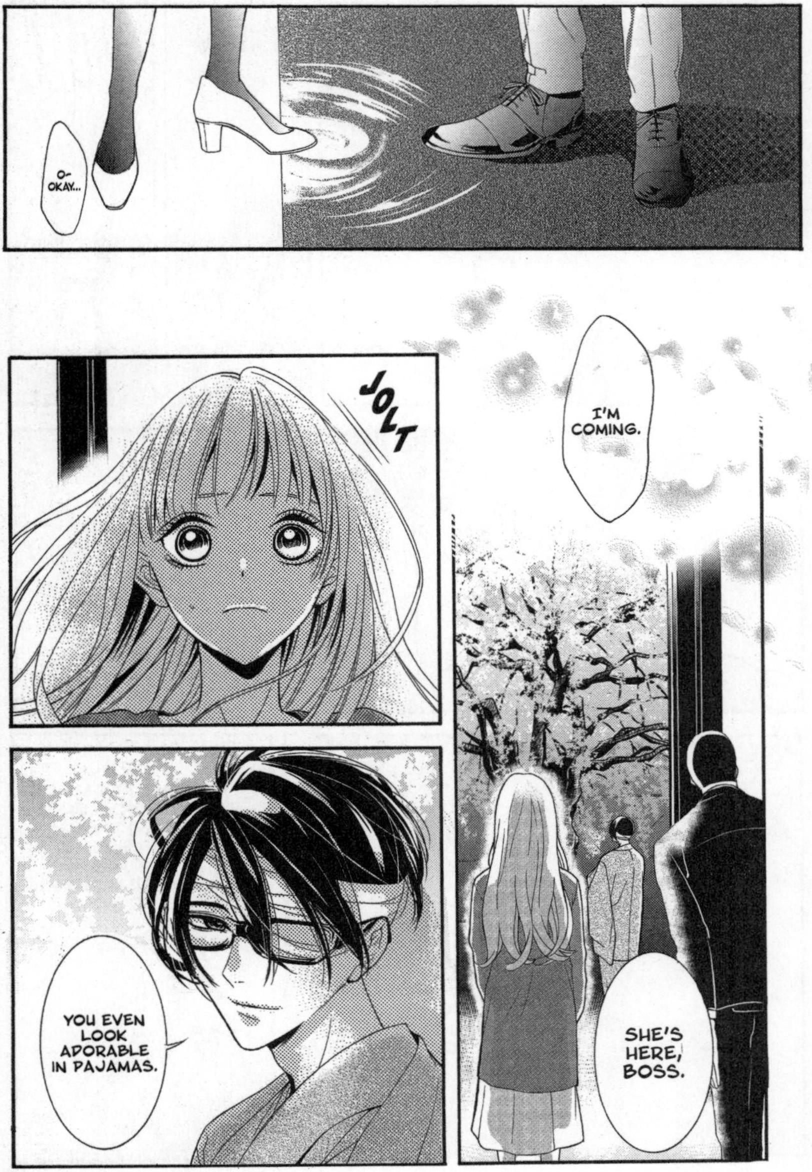
O-OKAY...
I'M COMING.
SHE'S HERE, BOSS.
JOLT
YOU EVEN LOOK ADORABLE IN PAJAMAS.

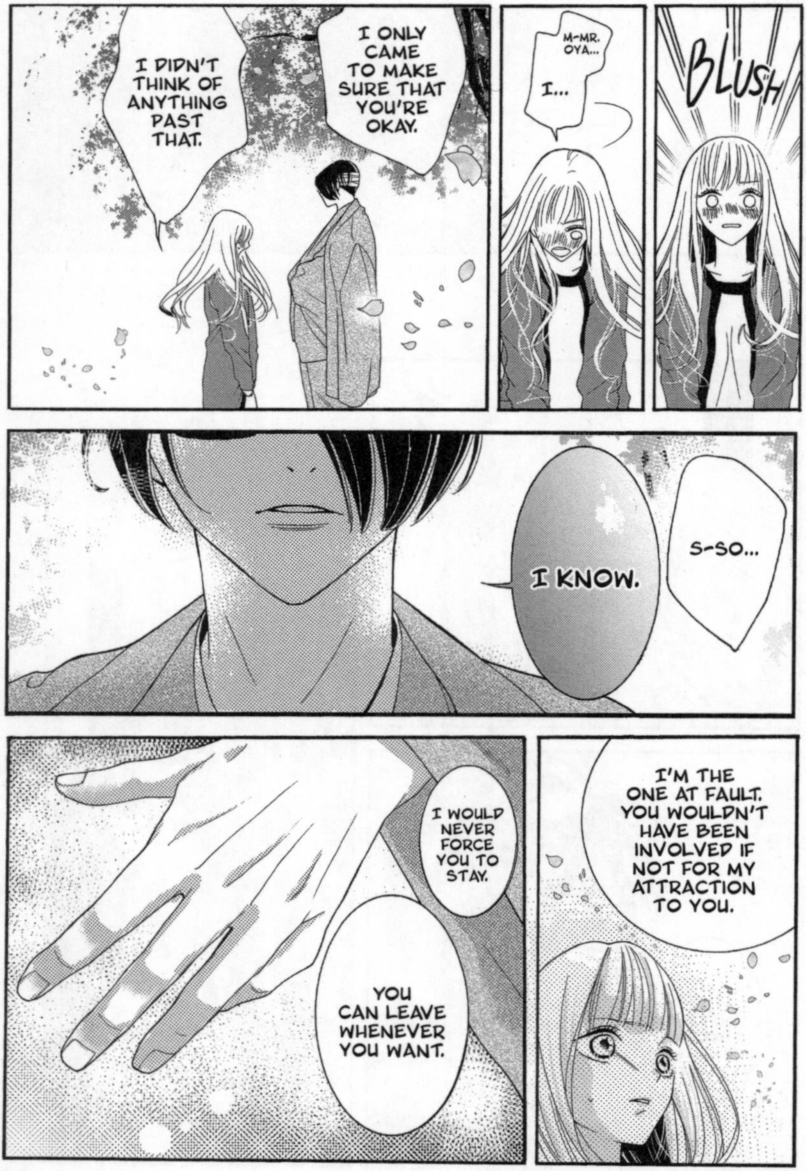
BLUSH
M-MR. OYA...
I...
I ONLY CAME TO MAKE SURE THAT YOU'RE OKAY.
I DIDN'T THINK OF ANYTHING PAST THAT.
S-SO...
I KNOW.
I'M THE ONE AT FAULT. YOU WOULDN'T HAVE BEEN INVOLVED IF NOT FOR MY ATTRACTION TO YOU.
I WOULD NEVER FORCE YOU TO STAY.
YOU CAN LEAVE WHENEVER YOU WANT.

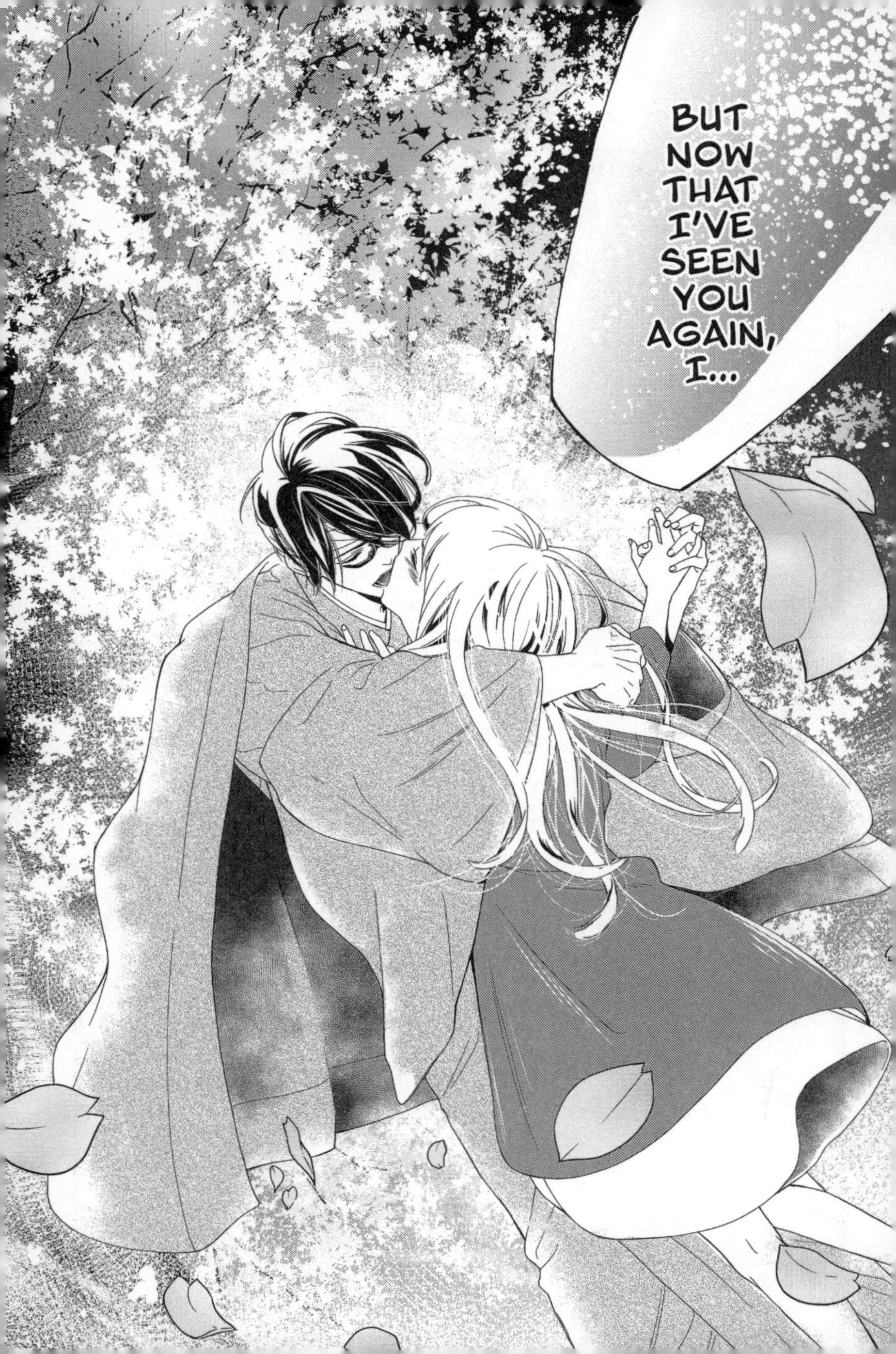
BUT NOW THAT I'VE SEEN YOU AGAIN, I...

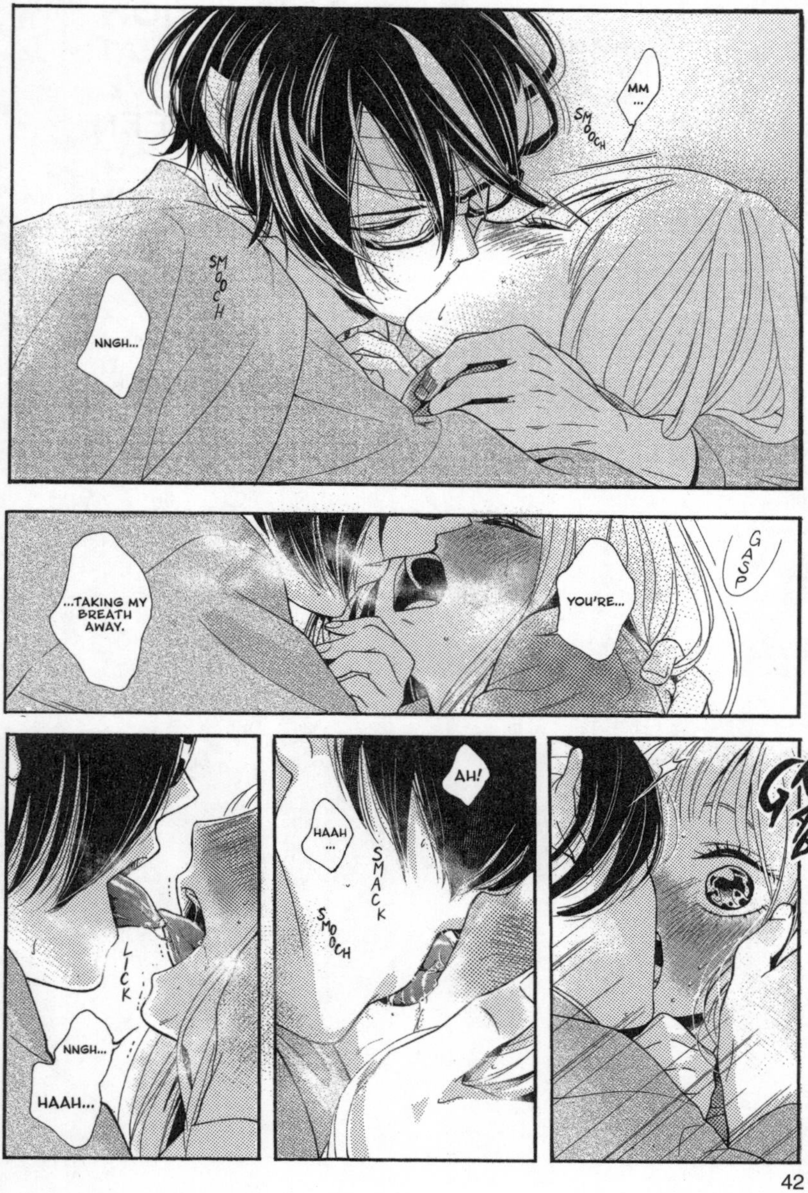
MM...
SMOOCH
SMOOCH
NNGH...
GASP
YOU'RE...
...TAKING MY BREATH AWAY.
GRAB
AH!
SMACK
HAAH...
SMOOCH
LICK
NNGH...
HAAH...

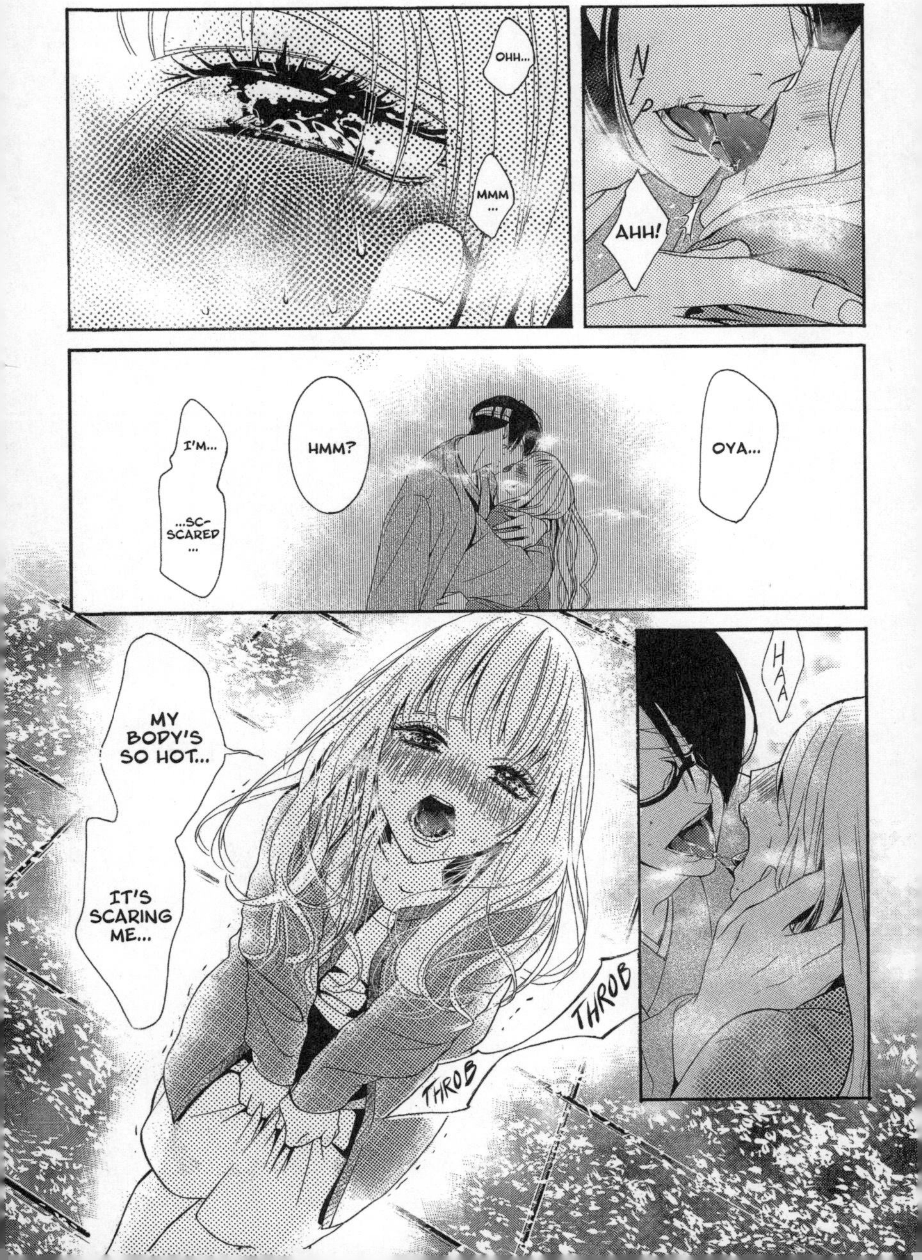
NIP
AHH!
OHH...
MMM...
OYA...
HMM?
I'M...
...SC-SCARED...
HAA
MY BODY'S SO HOT...
IT'S SCARING ME...
THROB
THROB

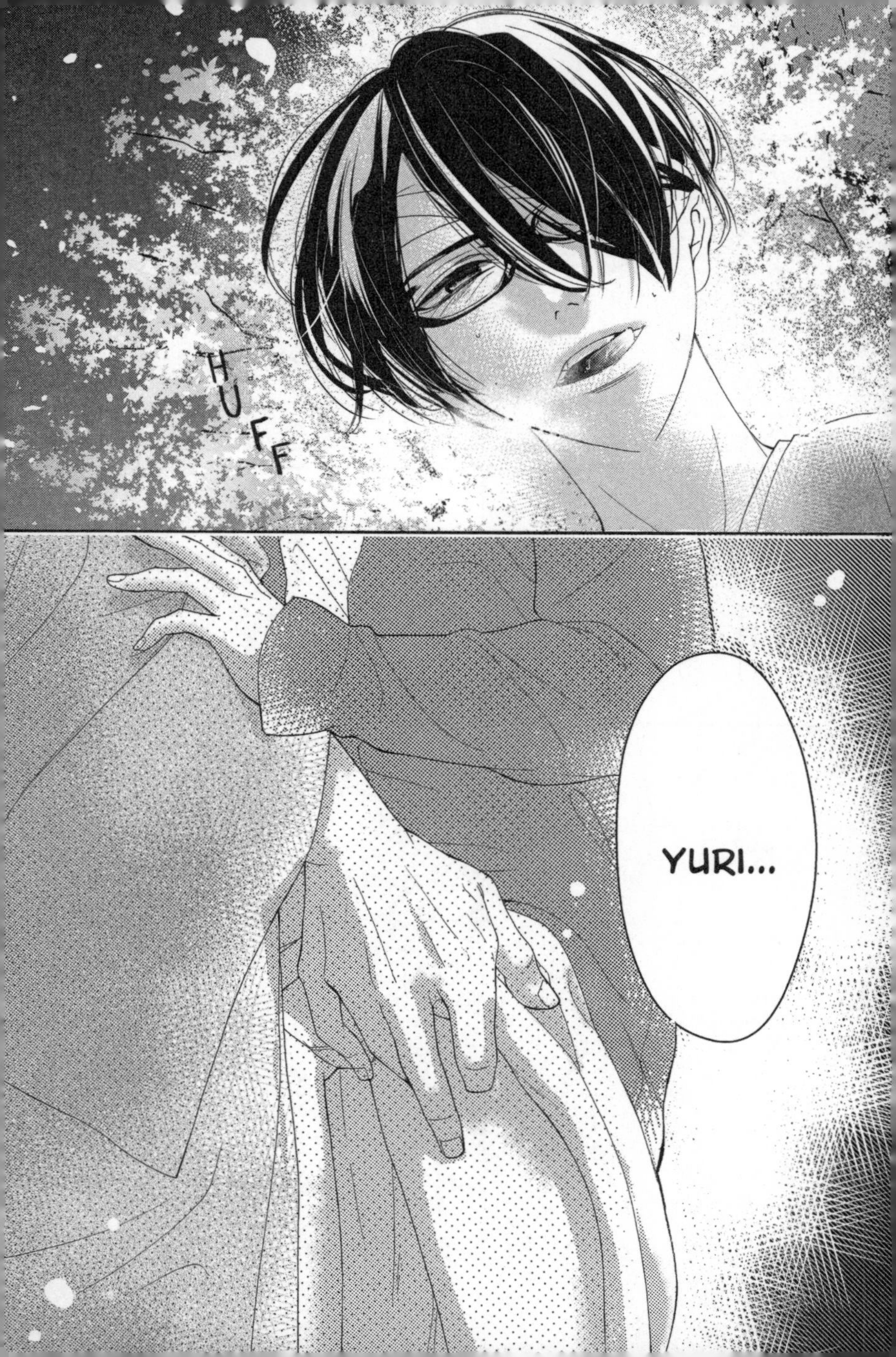
HUFF
YURI...

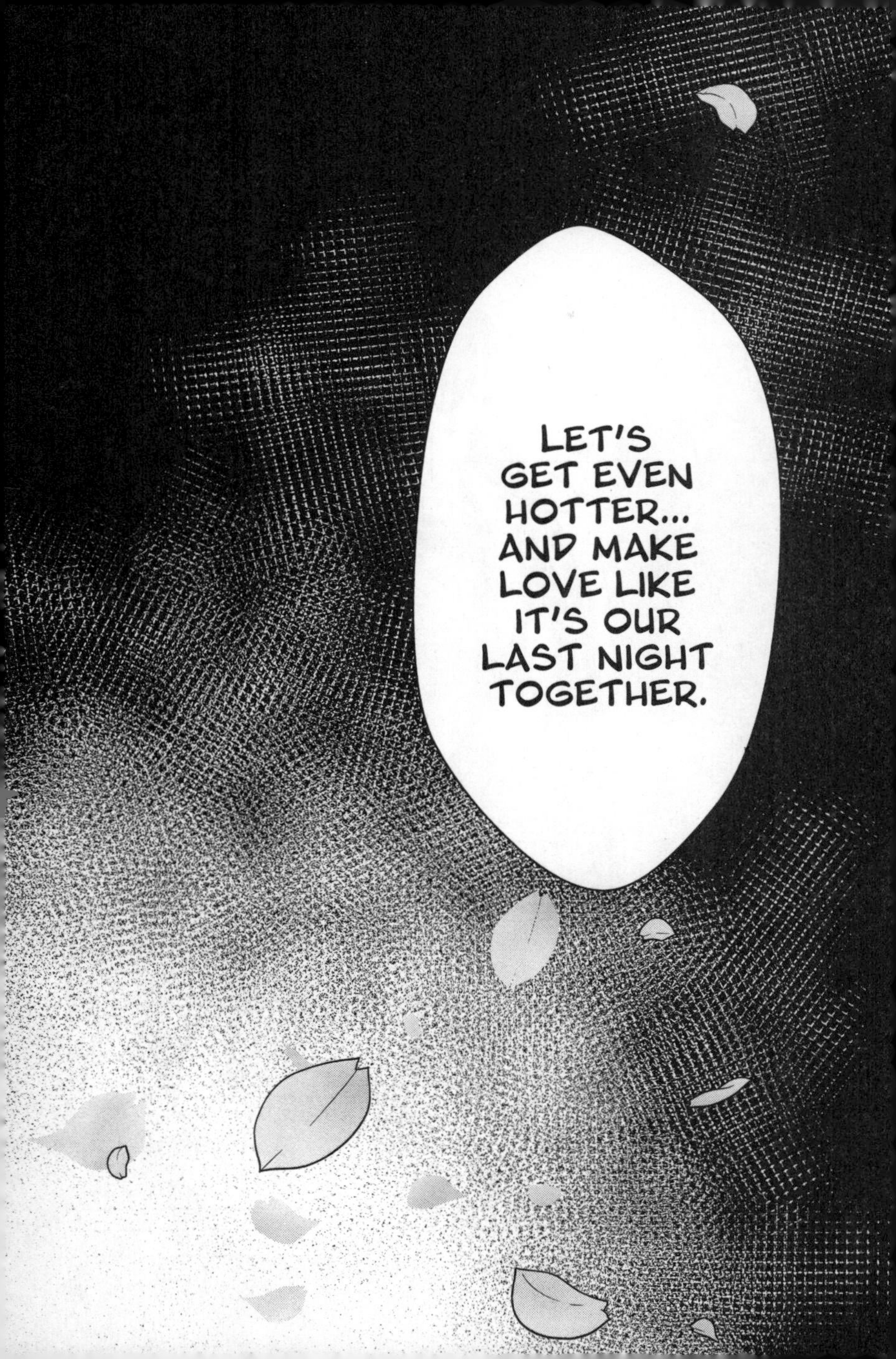
LET'S GET EVEN HOTTER... AND MAKE LOVE LIKE IT'S OUR LAST NIGHT TOGETHER.

bonus bullet 01 secret scene

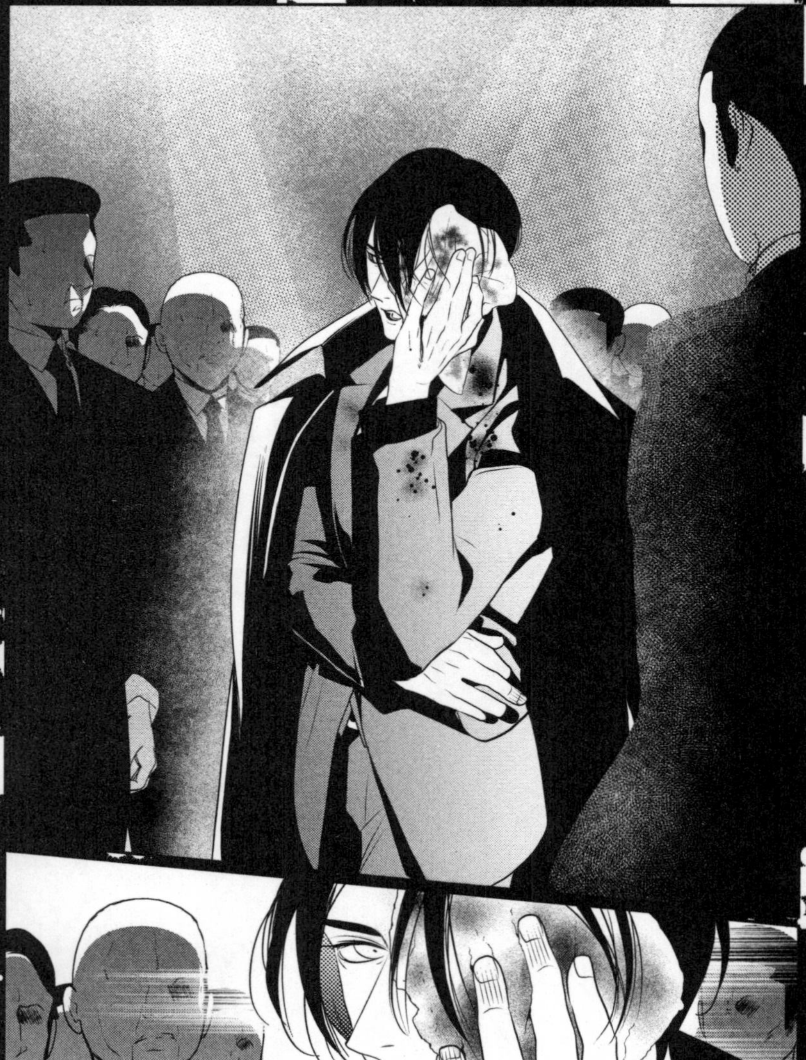

bullet 02

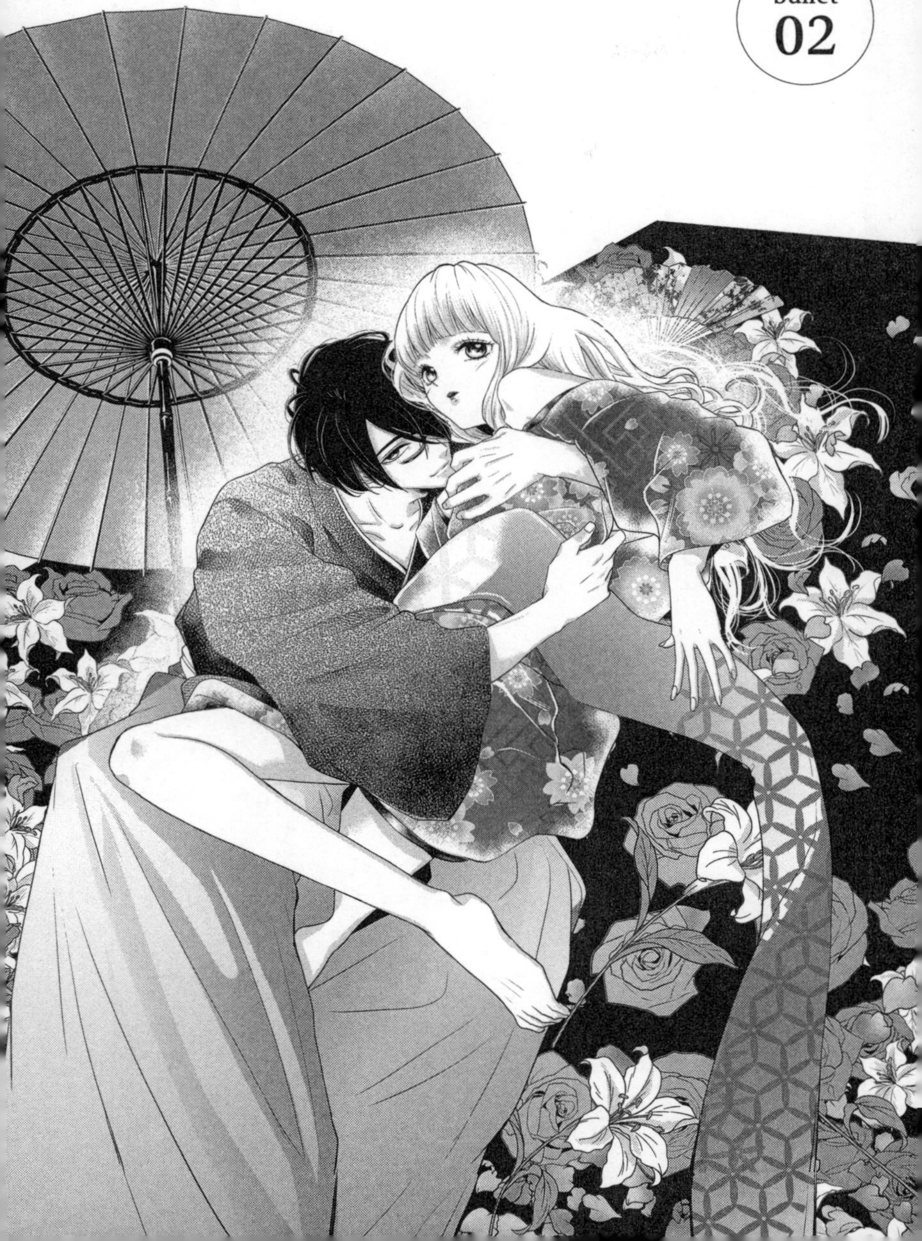

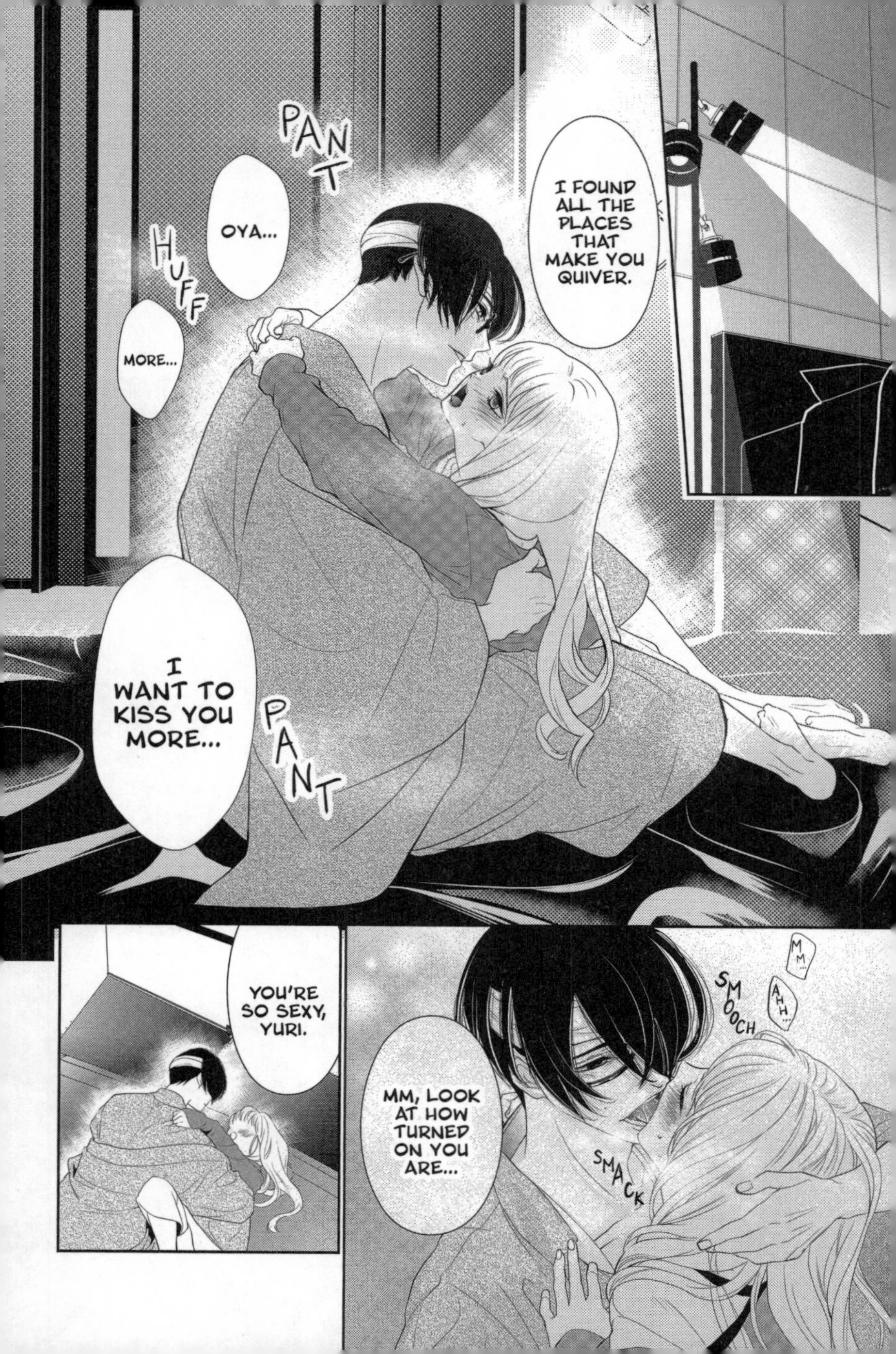
I FOUND ALL THE PLACES THAT MAKE YOU QUIVER.
PANT
OYA...
HUFF
MORE...
I WANT TO KISS YOU MORE...
PANT
MM...
AHH...
SMOOCH
MM, LOOK AT HOW TURNED ON YOU ARE...
SMACK
YOU'RE SO SEXY, YURI.

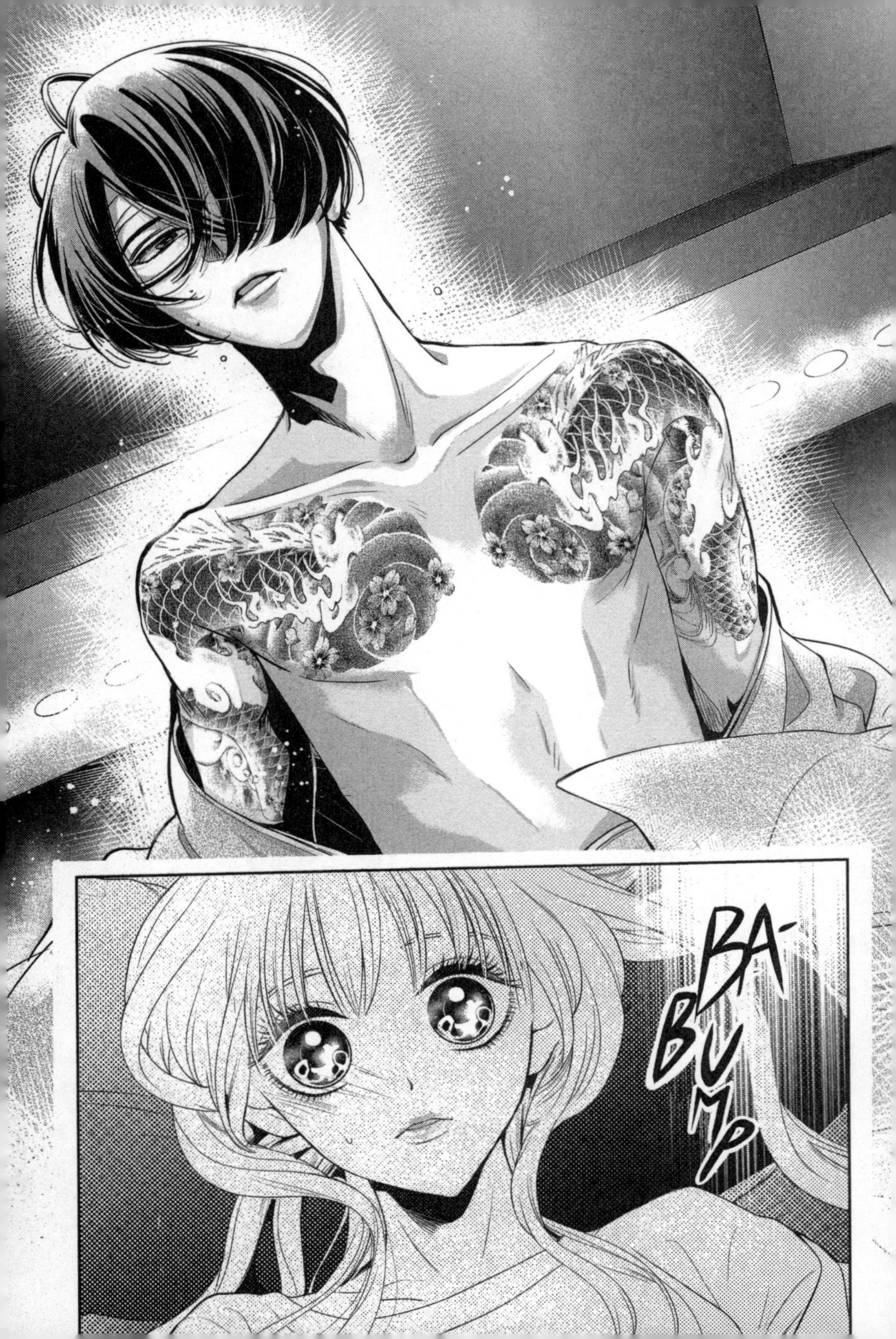
BA-BUMP

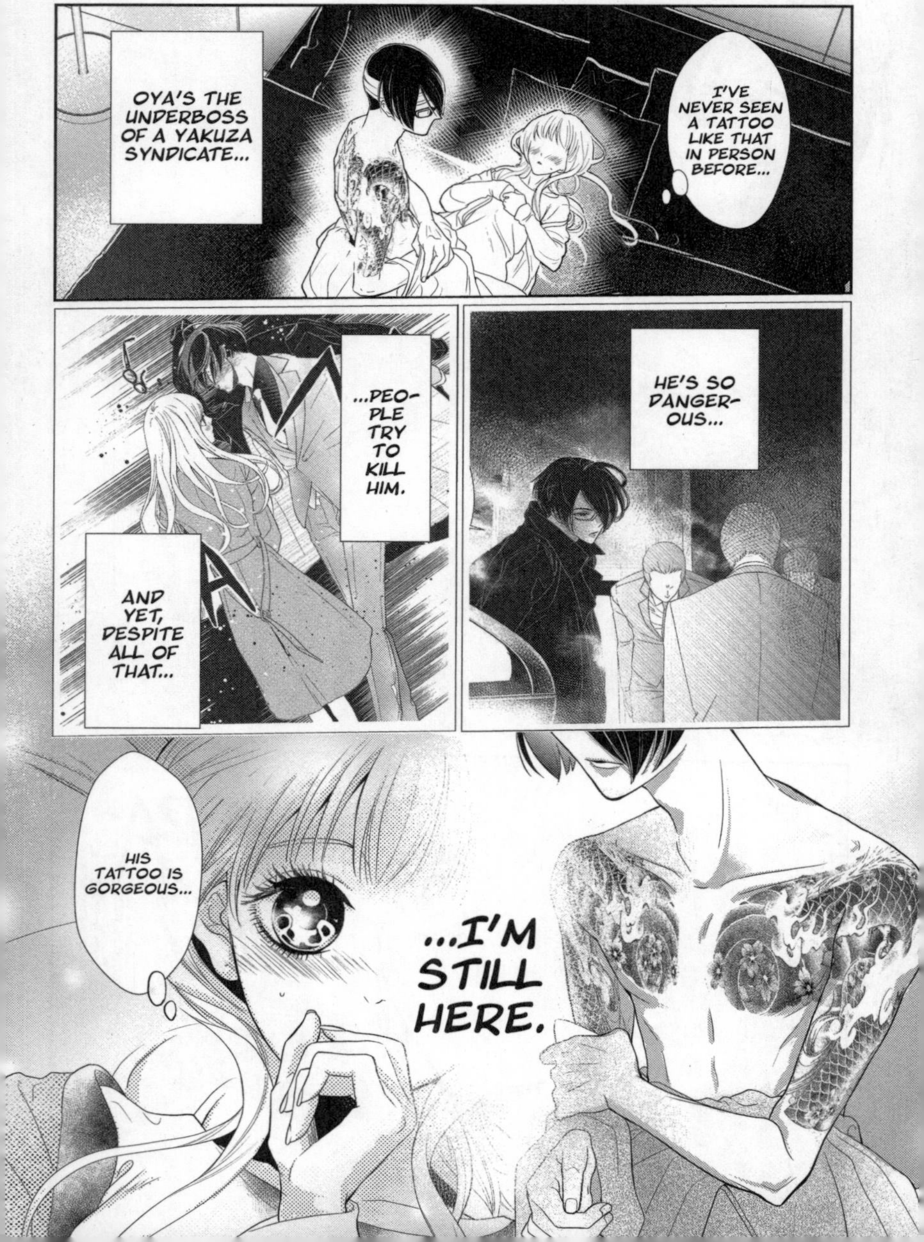
I'VE NEVER SEEN A TATTOO LIKE THAT IN PERSON BEFORE...
OYA'S THE UNDERBOSS OF A YAKUZA SYNDICATE...
HE'S SO DANGER-OUS...
...PEO-PLE TRY TO KILL HIM.
AND YET, DESPITE ALL OF THAT...
HIS TATTOO IS GORGEOUS...
...I'M STILL HERE.

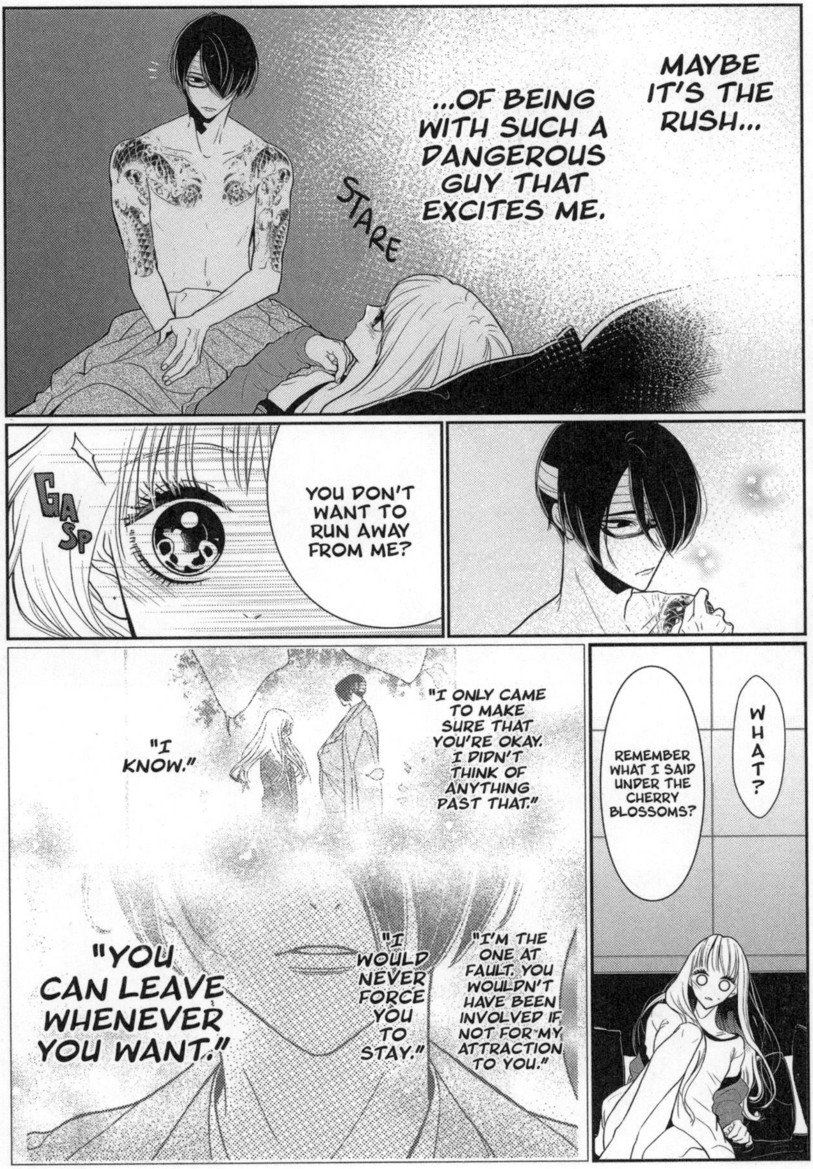
MAYBE IT'S THE RUSH...
...OF BEING WITH SUCH A DANGEROUS GUY THAT EXCITES ME.
STARE
YOU DON'T WANT TO RUN AWAY FROM ME?
GASP
WHAT?
REMEMBER WHAT I SAID UNDER THE CHERRY BLOSSOMS?
"I ONLY CAME TO MAKE SURE THAT YOU'RE OKAY. I DIDN'T THINK OF ANYTHING PAST THAT."
"I KNOW."
"I'M THE ONE AT FAULT. YOU WOULDN'T HAVE BEEN INVOLVED IF NOT FOR MY ATTRACTION TO YOU."
"I WOULD NEVER FORCE YOU TO STAY."
"YOU CAN LEAVE WHENEVER YOU WANT."

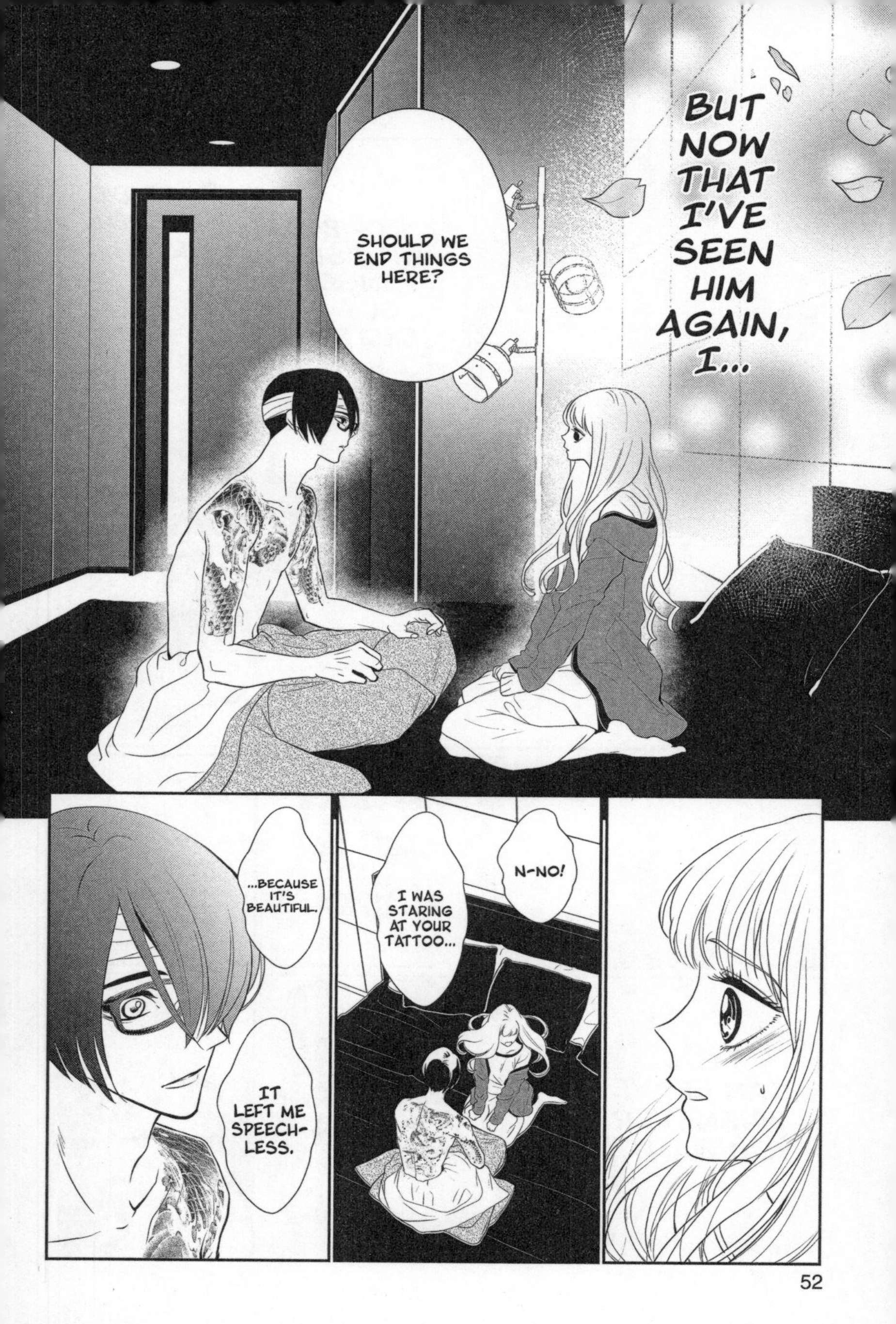
BUT NOW THAT I'VE SEEN HIM AGAIN, I...
SHOULD WE END THINGS HERE?
N-NO!
I WAS STARING AT YOUR TATTOO...
...BECAUSE IT'S BEAUTIFUL.
IT LEFT ME SPEECH-LESS.

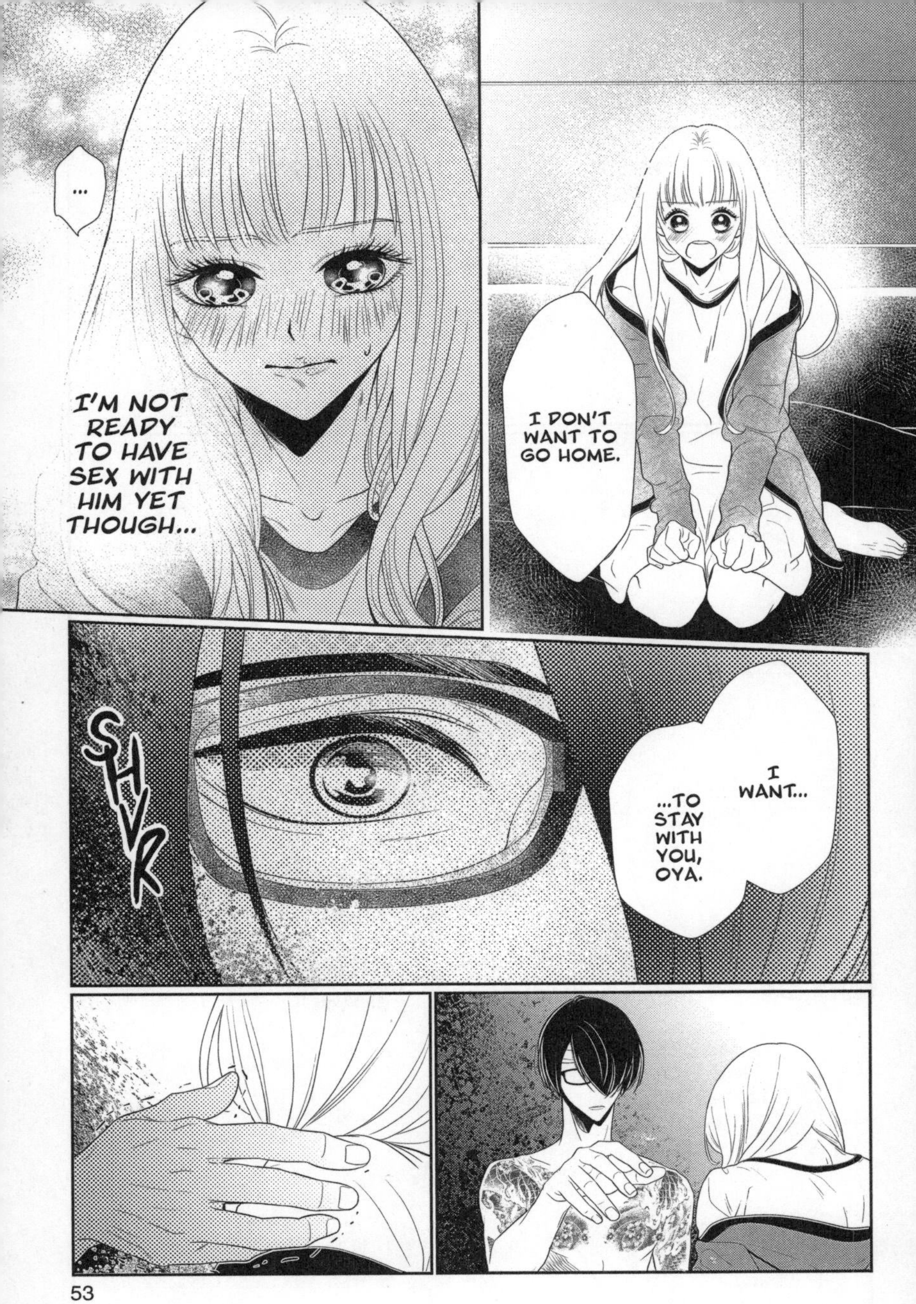
I DON'T WANT TO GO HOME.
...
I'M NOT READY TO HAVE SEX WITH HIM YET THOUGH...
I WANT...
...TO STAY WITH YOU, OYA.
SHVR

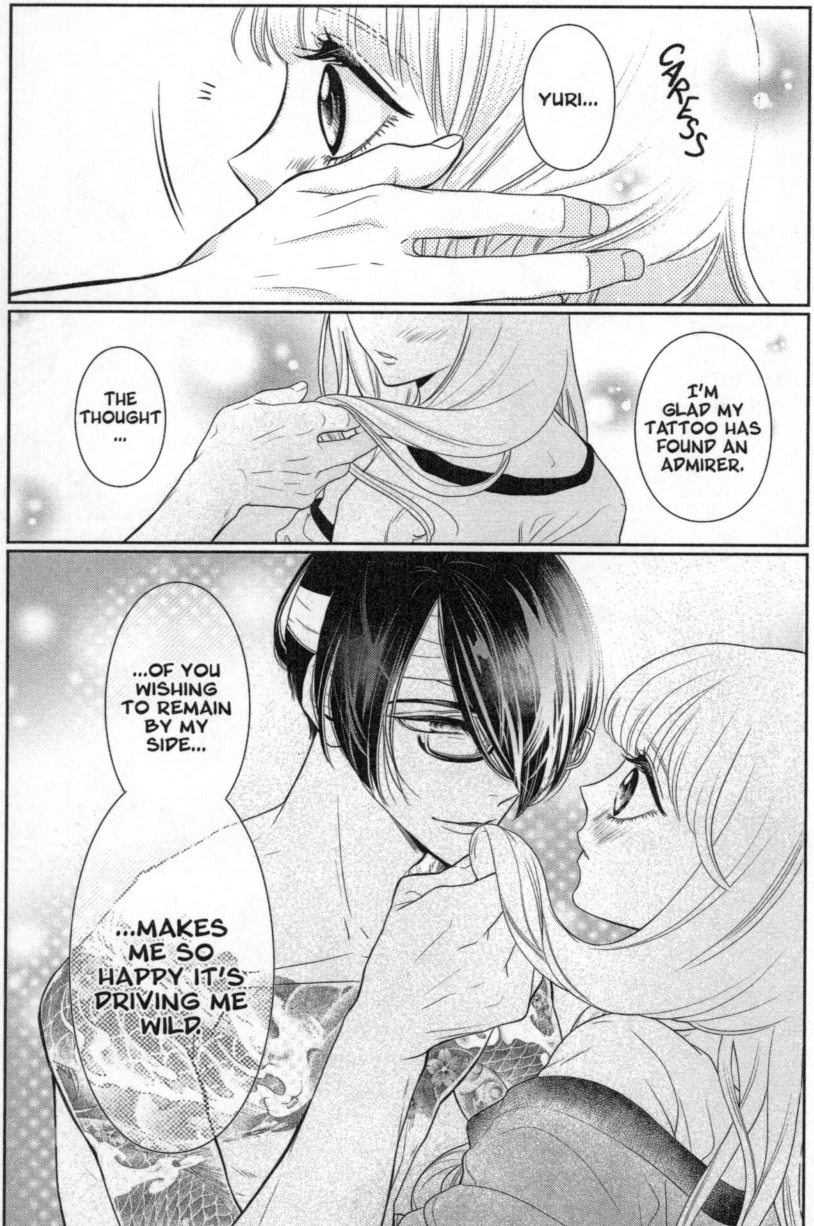
CARESS
YURI...
I'M GLAD MY TATTOO HAS FOUND AN ADMIRER.
THE THOUGHT ...
...OF YOU WISHING TO REMAIN BY MY SIDE...
...MAKES ME SO HAPPY IT'S DRIVING ME WILD.

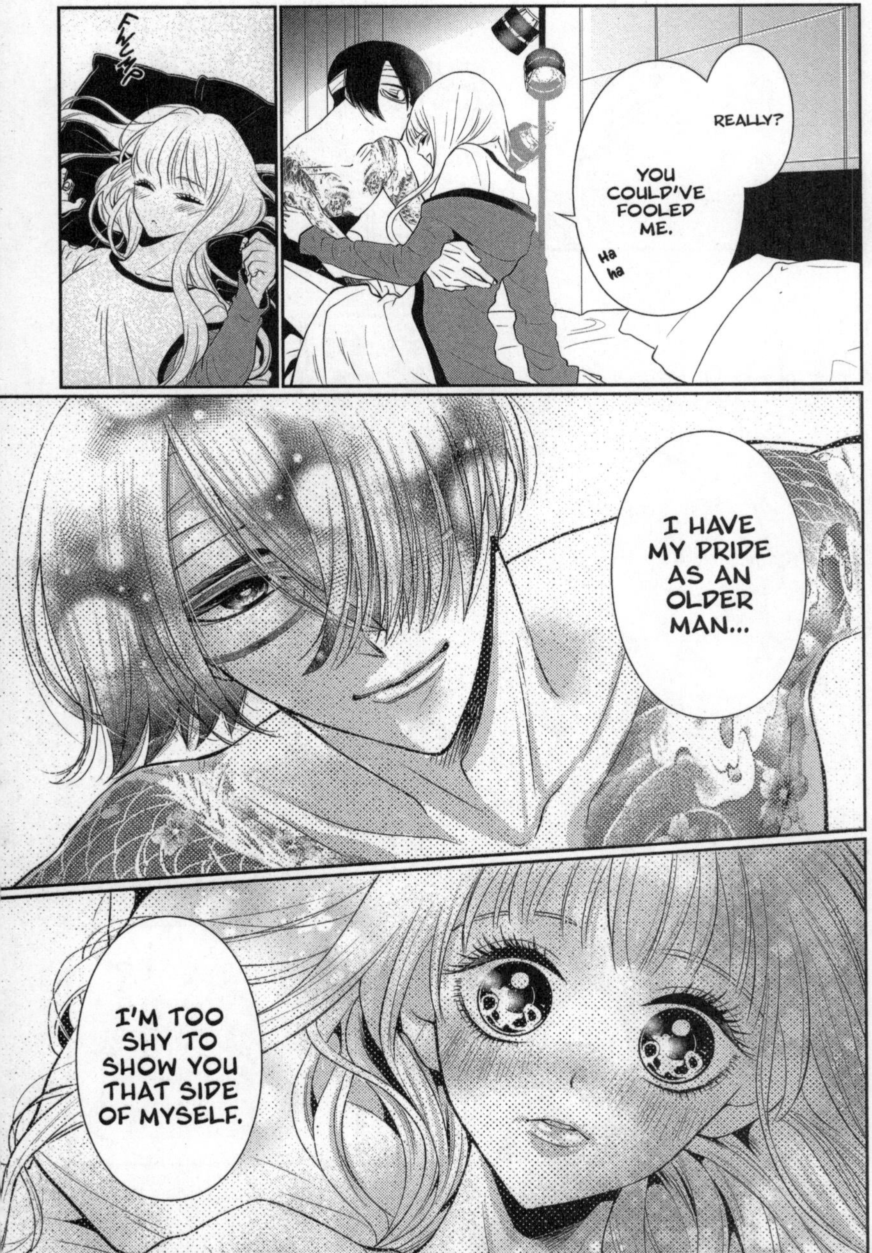
REALLY?
YOU COULD'VE FOOLED ME.
Ha ha
FWUMP
I HAVE MY PRIDE AS AN OLDER MAN...
I'M TOO SHY TO SHOW YOU THAT SIDE OF MYSELF.

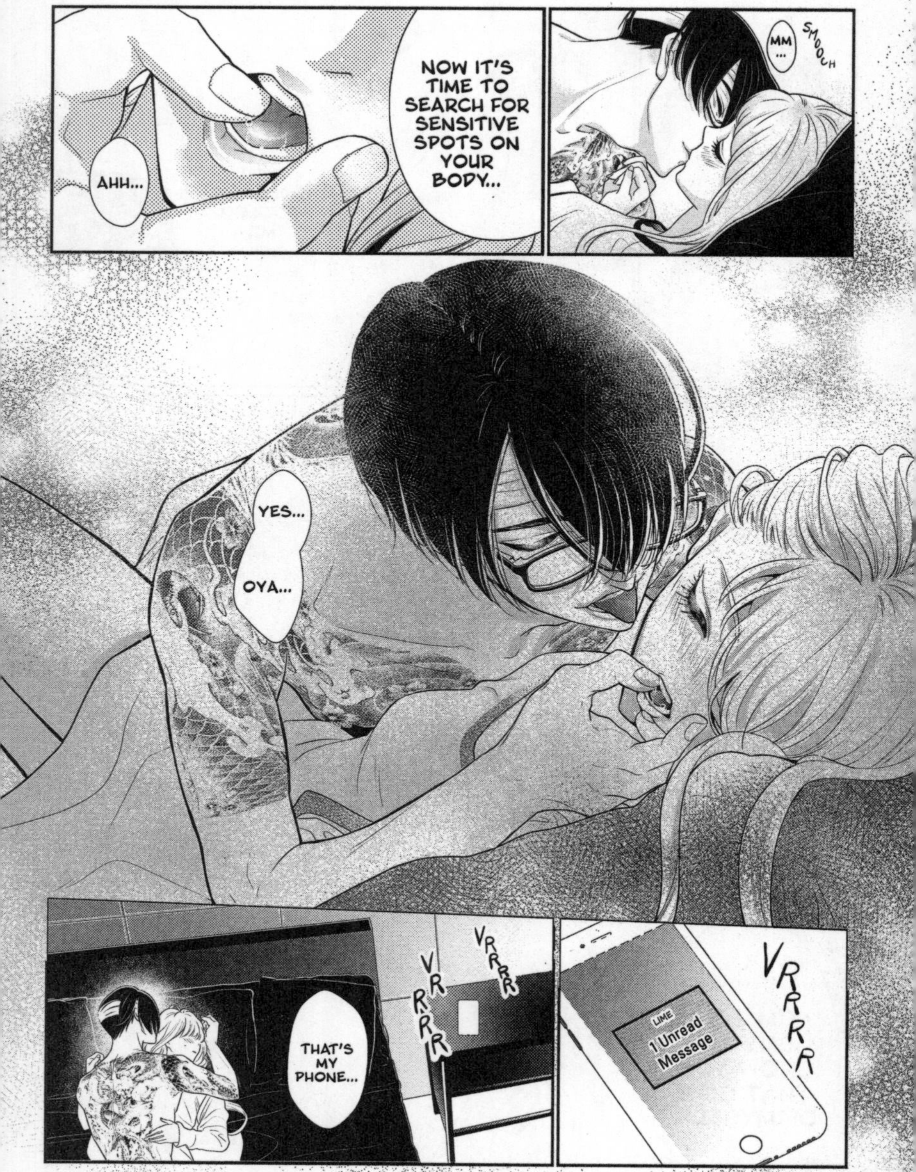
MM...
SMOOCH
NOW IT'S TIME TO SEARCH FOR SENSITIVE SPOTS ON YOUR BODY...
AHH...
YES...
OYA...
VRRRR
LIME
1 Unread Message
VRRRR
VRRRR
THAT'S MY PHONE...

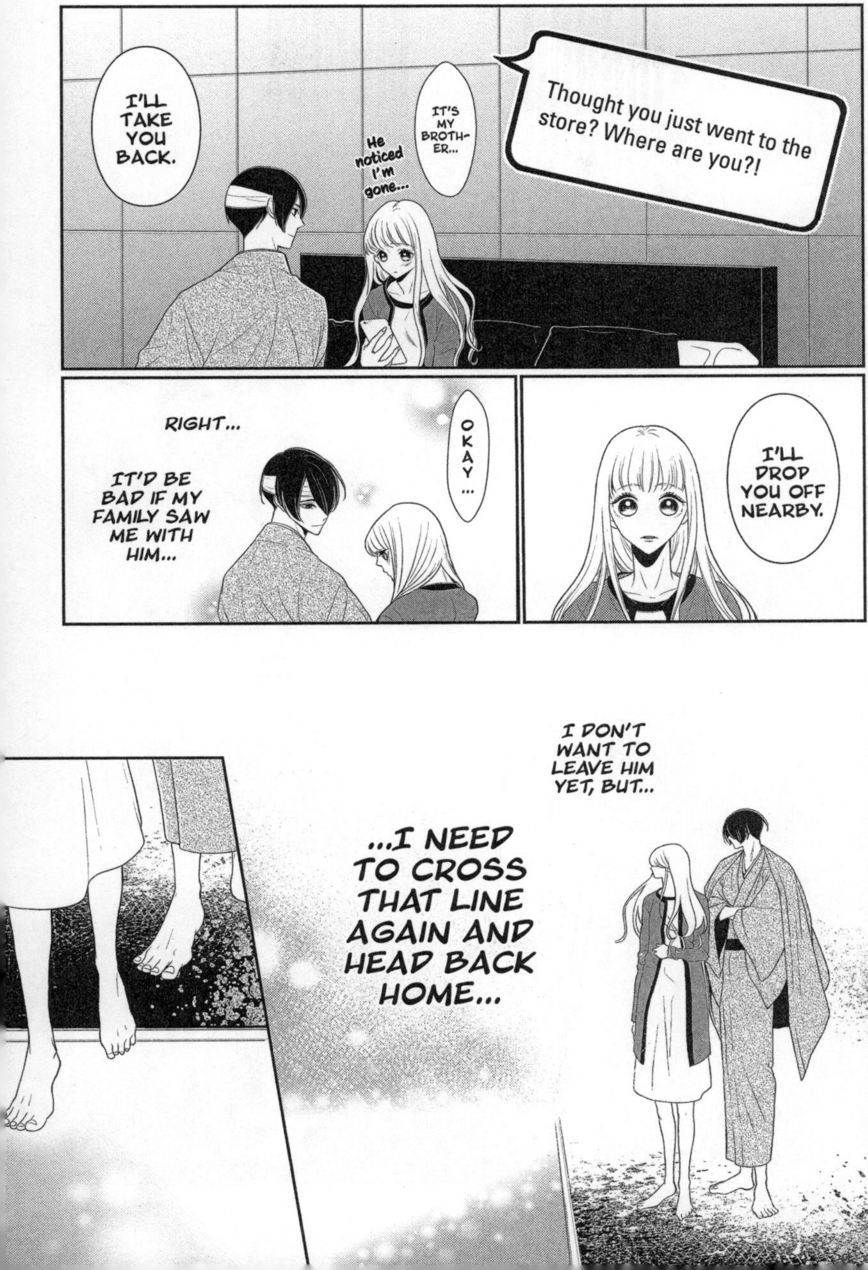
Thought you just went to the store? Where are you?!
IT'S MY BROTHER...
He noticed I'm gone...
I'LL TAKE YOU BACK.
I'LL DROP YOU OFF NEARBY.
OKAY...
RIGHT...
IT'D BE BAD IF MY FAMILY SAW ME WITH HIM...
I DON'T WANT TO LEAVE HIM YET, BUT...
...I NEED TO CROSS THAT LINE AGAIN AND HEAD BACK HOME...

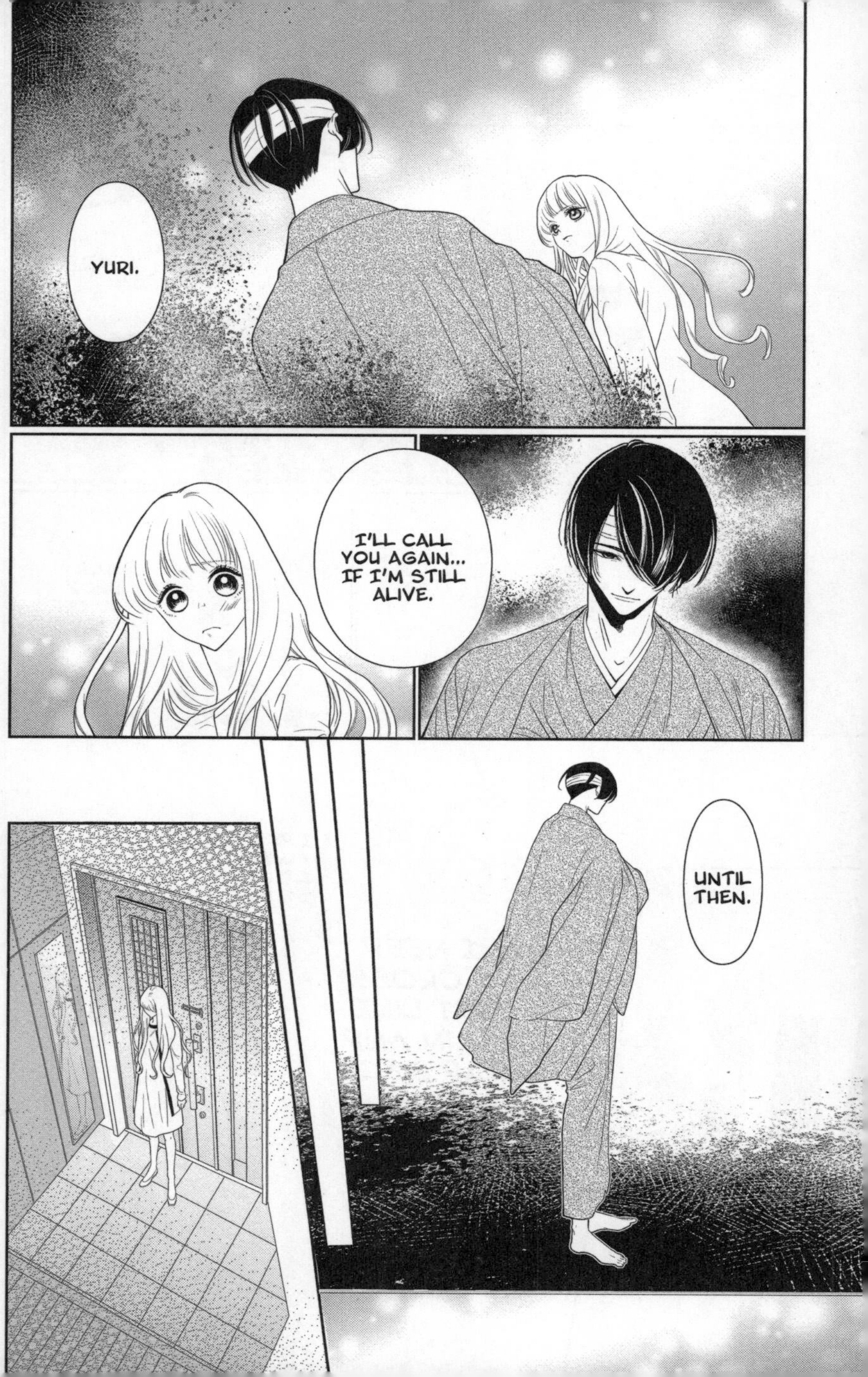
YURI.
I'LL CALL YOU AGAIN... IF I'M STILL ALIVE.
UNTIL THEN.

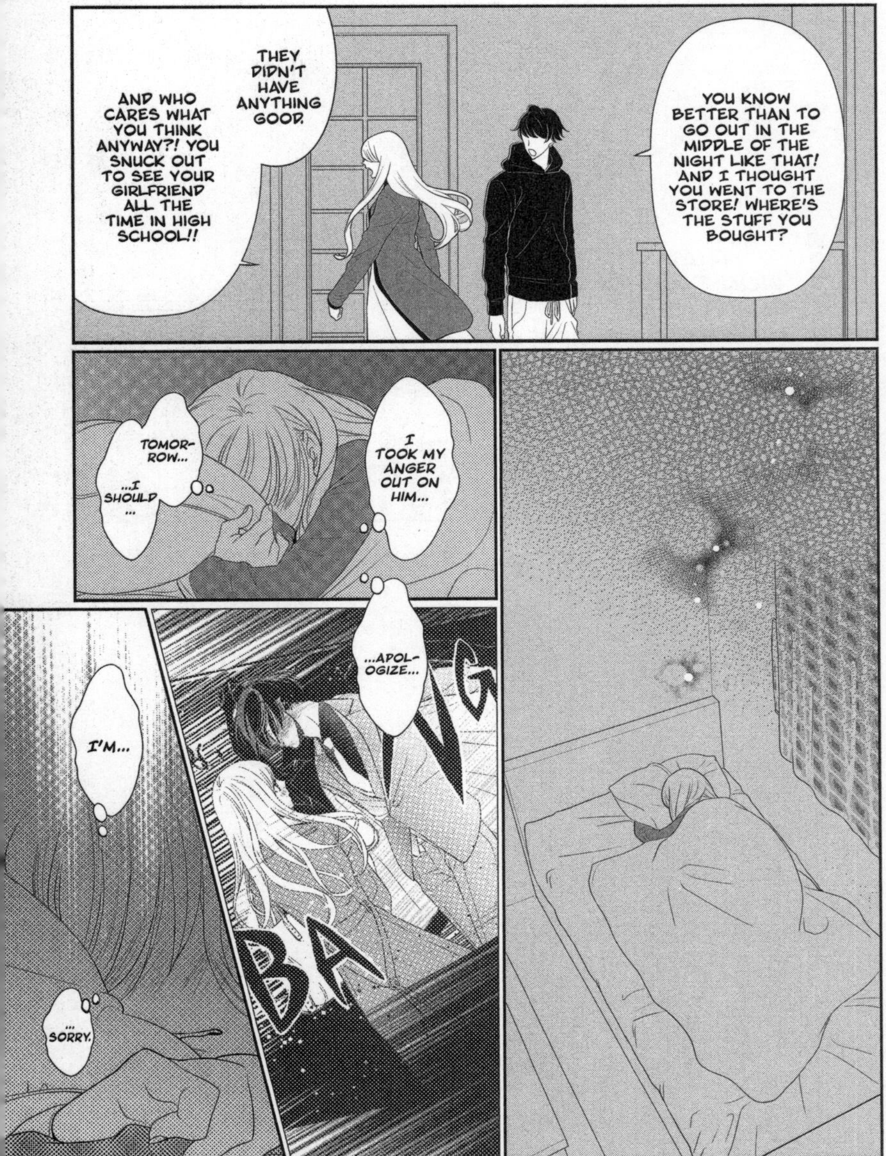
YOU KNOW BETTER THAN TO GO OUT IN THE MIDDLE OF THE NIGHT LIKE THAT! AND I THOUGHT YOU WENT TO THE STORE! WHERE'S THE STUFF YOU BOUGHT?
THEY DIDN'T HAVE ANYTHING GOOD.
AND WHO CARES WHAT YOU THINK ANYWAY?! YOU SNUCK OUT TO SEE YOUR GIRLFRIEND ALL THE TIME IN HIGH SCHOOL!!
I TOOK MY ANGER OUT ON HIM...
TOMORROW...
...I SHOULD...
...APOLOGIZE...
BANG
I'M...
...SORRY.

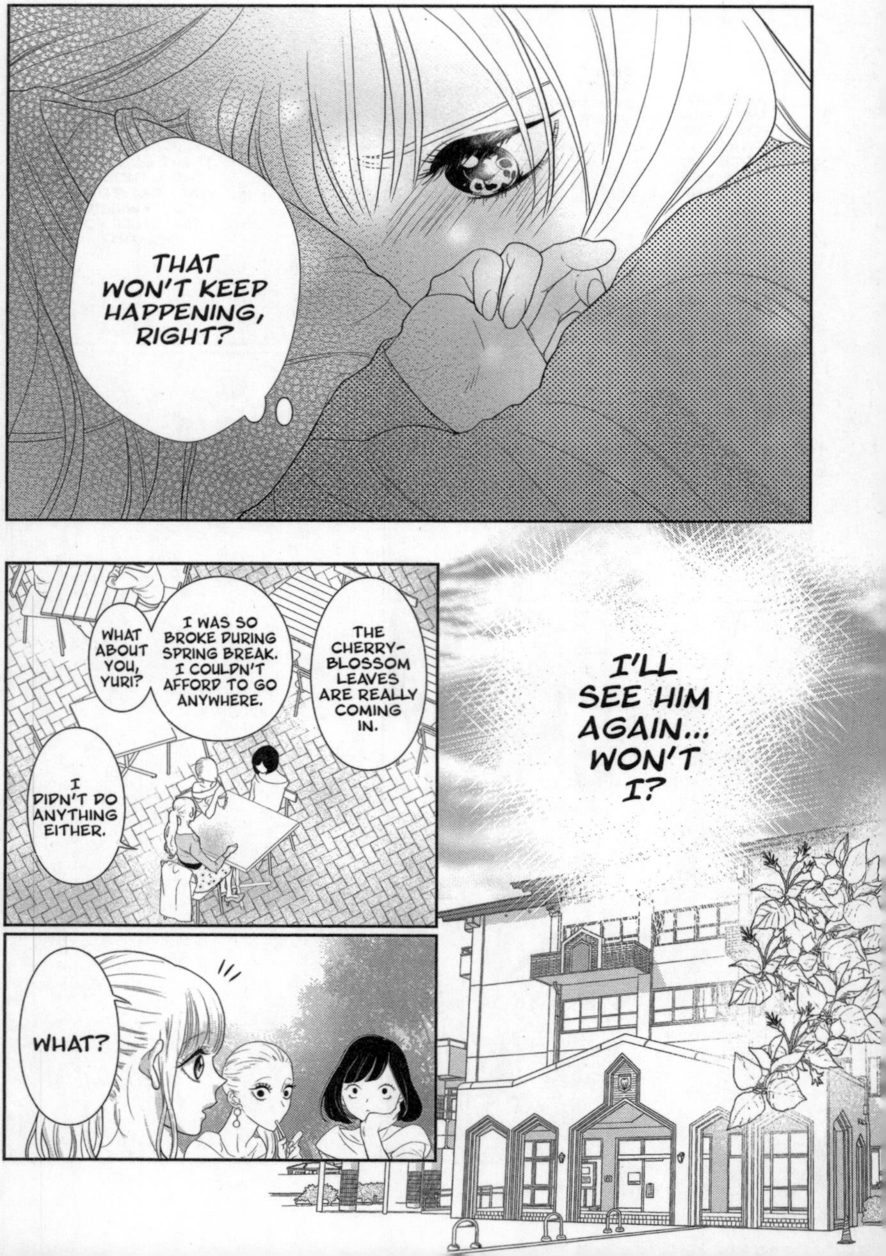
THAT WON'T KEEP HAPPENING, RIGHT?
I'LL SEE HIM AGAIN... WON'T I?
THE CHERRY-BLOSSOM LEAVES ARE REALLY COMING IN.
I WAS SO BROKE DURING SPRING BREAK. I COULDN'T AFFORD TO GO ANYWHERE.
WHAT ABOUT YOU, YURI?
I DIDN'T DO ANYTHING EITHER.
WHAT?

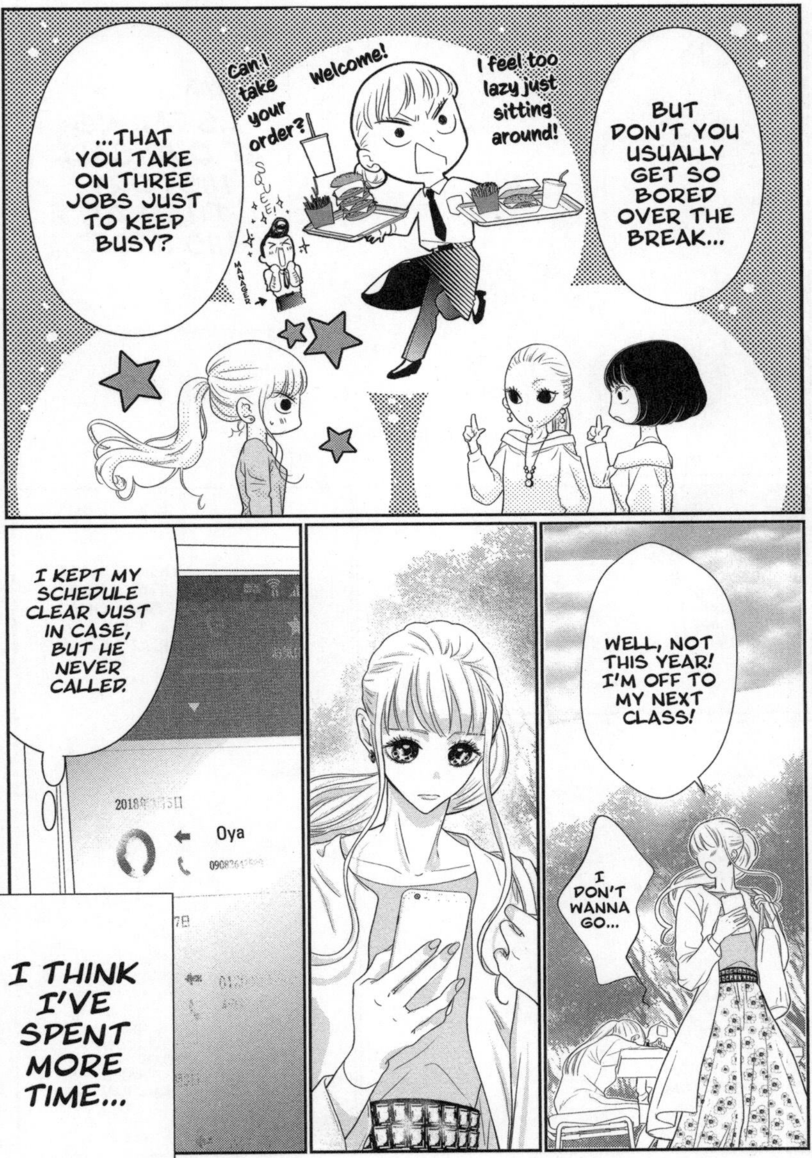
BUT DON'T YOU USUALLY GET SO BORED OVER THE BREAK...
I feel too lazy just sitting around!
Welcome!
Can I take your order?
SQUEE!
MANAGER
...THAT YOU TAKE ON THREE JOBS JUST TO KEEP BUSY?
WELL, NOT THIS YEAR! I'M OFF TO MY NEXT CLASS!
I DON'T WANNA GO...
I KEPT MY SCHEDULE CLEAR JUST IN CASE, BUT HE NEVER CALLED.
Oya
I THINK I'VE SPENT MORE TIME...

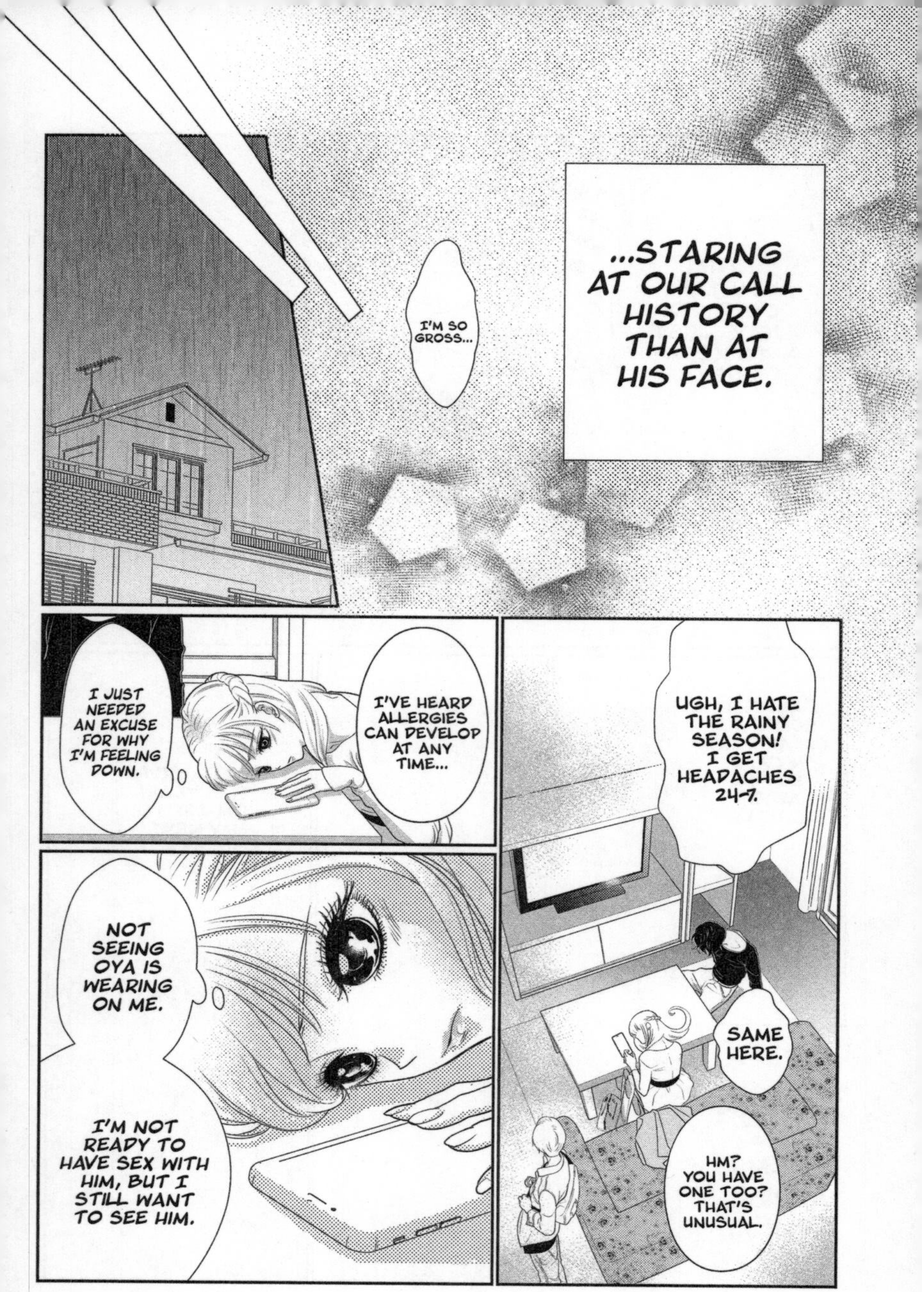
...STARING AT OUR CALL HISTORY THAN AT HIS FACE.
I'M SO GROSS...
UGH, I HATE THE RAINY SEASON! I GET HEADACHES 24-7.
SAME HERE.
HM? YOU HAVE ONE TOO? THAT'S UNUSUAL.
I'VE HEARD ALLERGIES CAN DEVELOP AT ANY TIME...
I JUST NEEDED AN EXCUSE FOR WHY I'M FEELING DOWN.
NOT SEEING OYA IS WEARING ON ME.
I'M NOT READY TO HAVE SEX WITH HIM, BUT I STILL WANT TO SEE HIM.

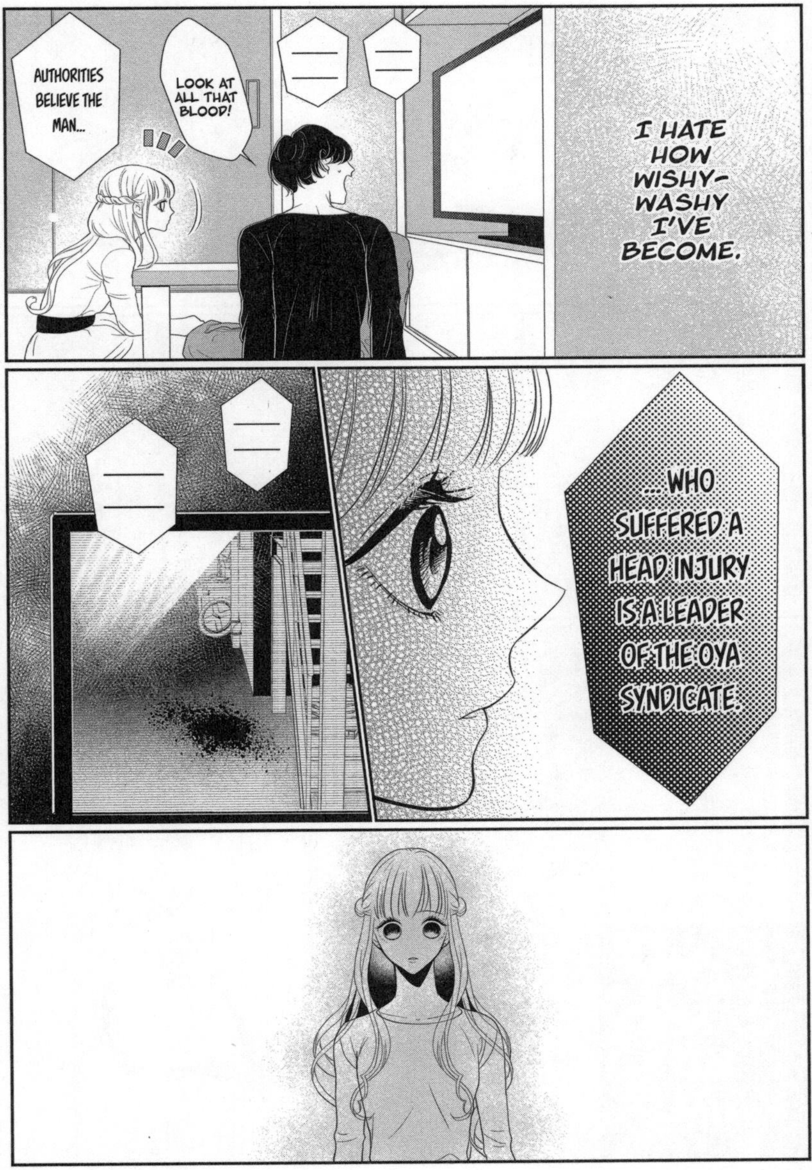
I HATE HOW WISHY-WASHY I'VE BECOME.
LOOK AT ALL THAT BLOOD!
AUTHORITIES BELIEVE THE MAN...
...WHO SUFFERED A HEAD INJURY IS A LEADER OF THE OYA SYNDICATE.

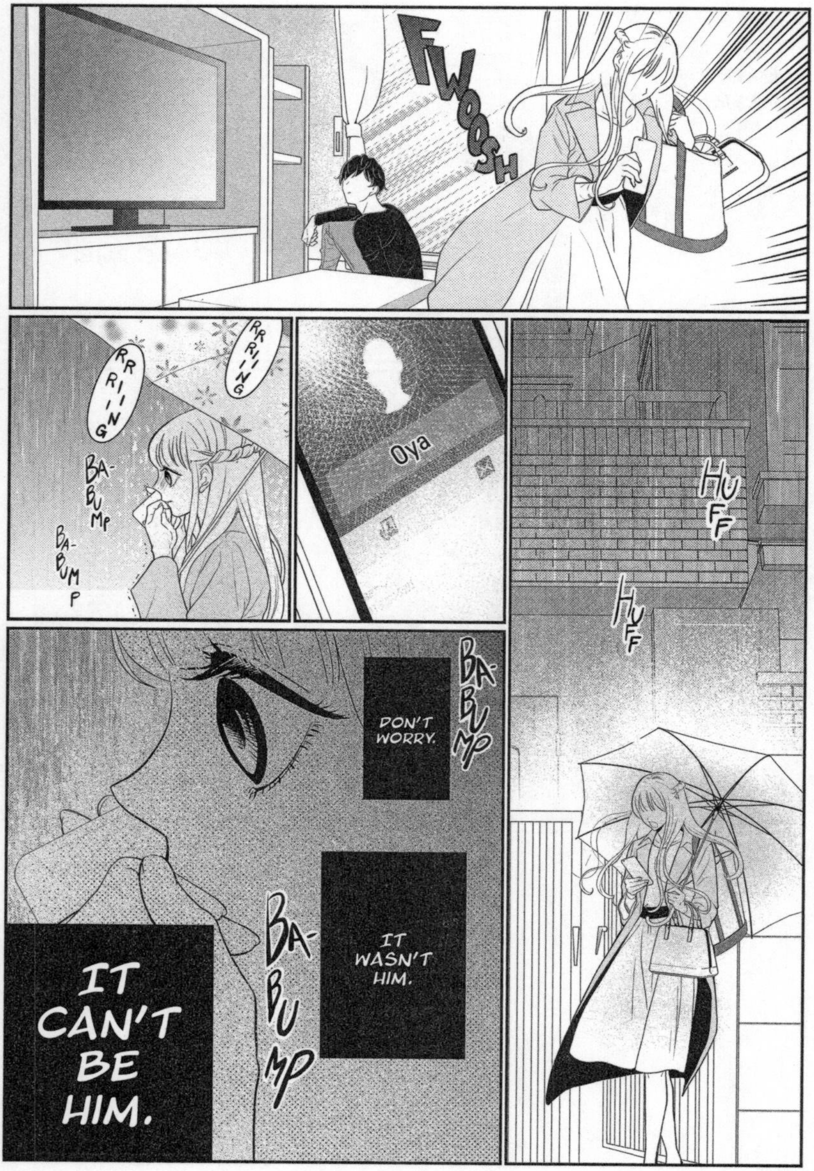
FWOOSH
HUFF
HUFF
Oya
RRRIIING
RRRIIING
BA-BUMP
BA-BUMP
DON'T WORRY.
BA-BUMP
IT WASN'T HIM.
BA-BUMP
IT CAN'T BE HIM.

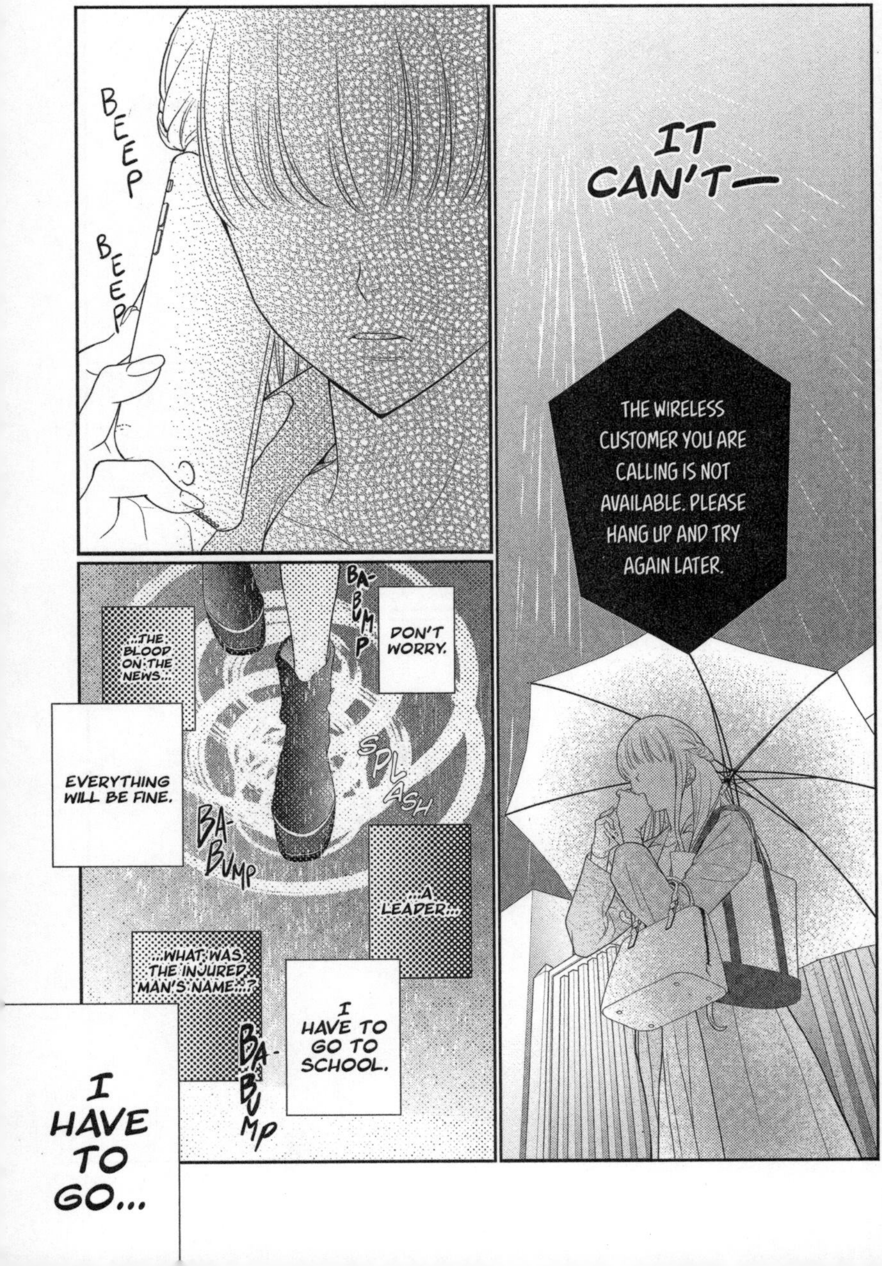
IT CAN'T—
THE WIRELESS CUSTOMER YOU ARE CALLING IS NOT AVAILABLE. PLEASE HANG UP AND TRY AGAIN LATER.
BEEP
BEEP
BA-BUMP
DON'T WORRY.
...THE BLOOD ON THE NEWS...
EVERYTHING WILL BE FINE.
SPLASH
BA-BUMP
...A LEADER...
...WHAT WAS THE INJURED MAN'S NAME...?
I HAVE TO GO TO SCHOOL.
BA-BUMP
I HAVE TO GO...

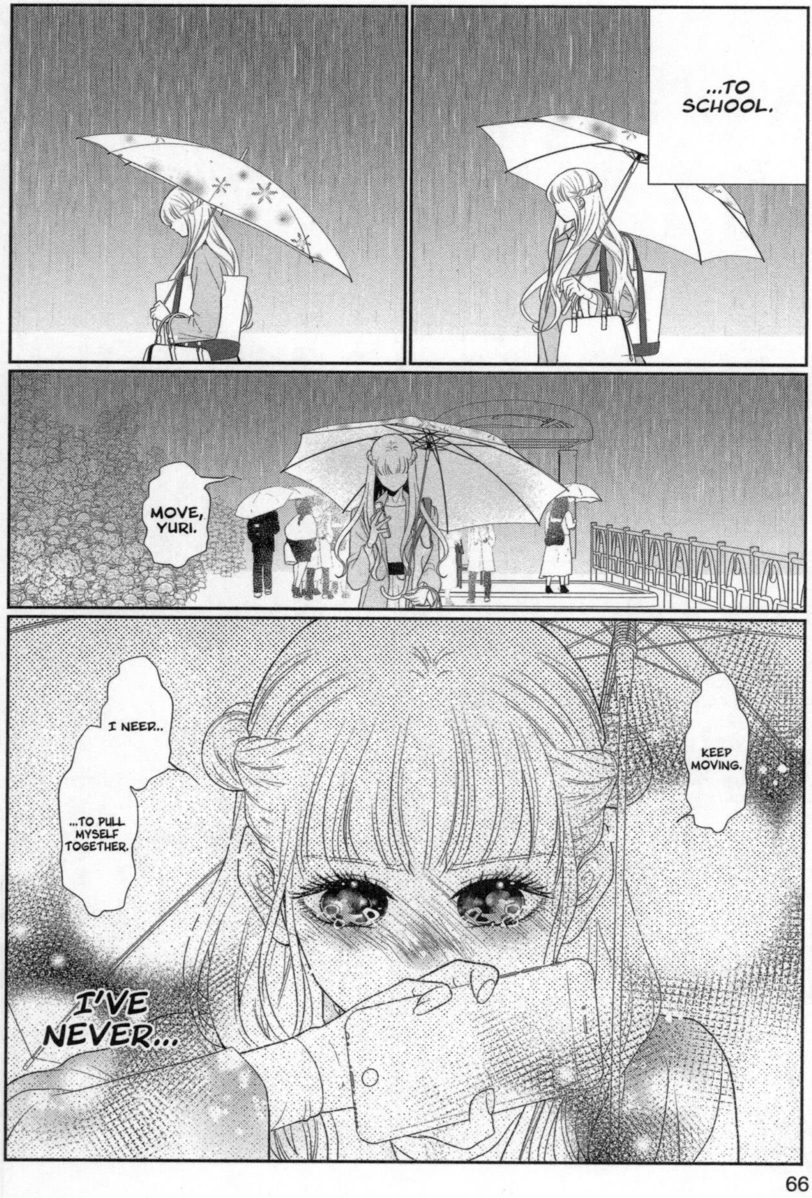
...TO SCHOOL.
MOVE, YURI.
KEEP MOVING.
I NEED...
...TO PULL MYSELF TOGETHER.
I'VE NEVER...

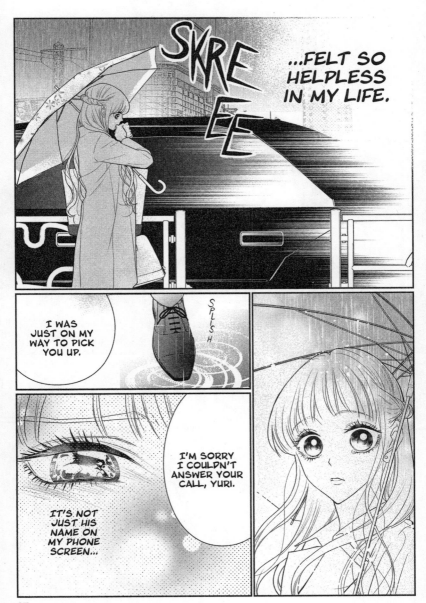

SKREEEE

...FELT SO HELPLESS IN MY LIFE.

SPLISH

I WAS JUST ON MY WAY TO PICK YOU UP.

I'M SORRY I COULDN'T ANSWER YOUR CALL, YURI.

IT'S NOT JUST HIS NAME ON MY PHONE SCREEN...

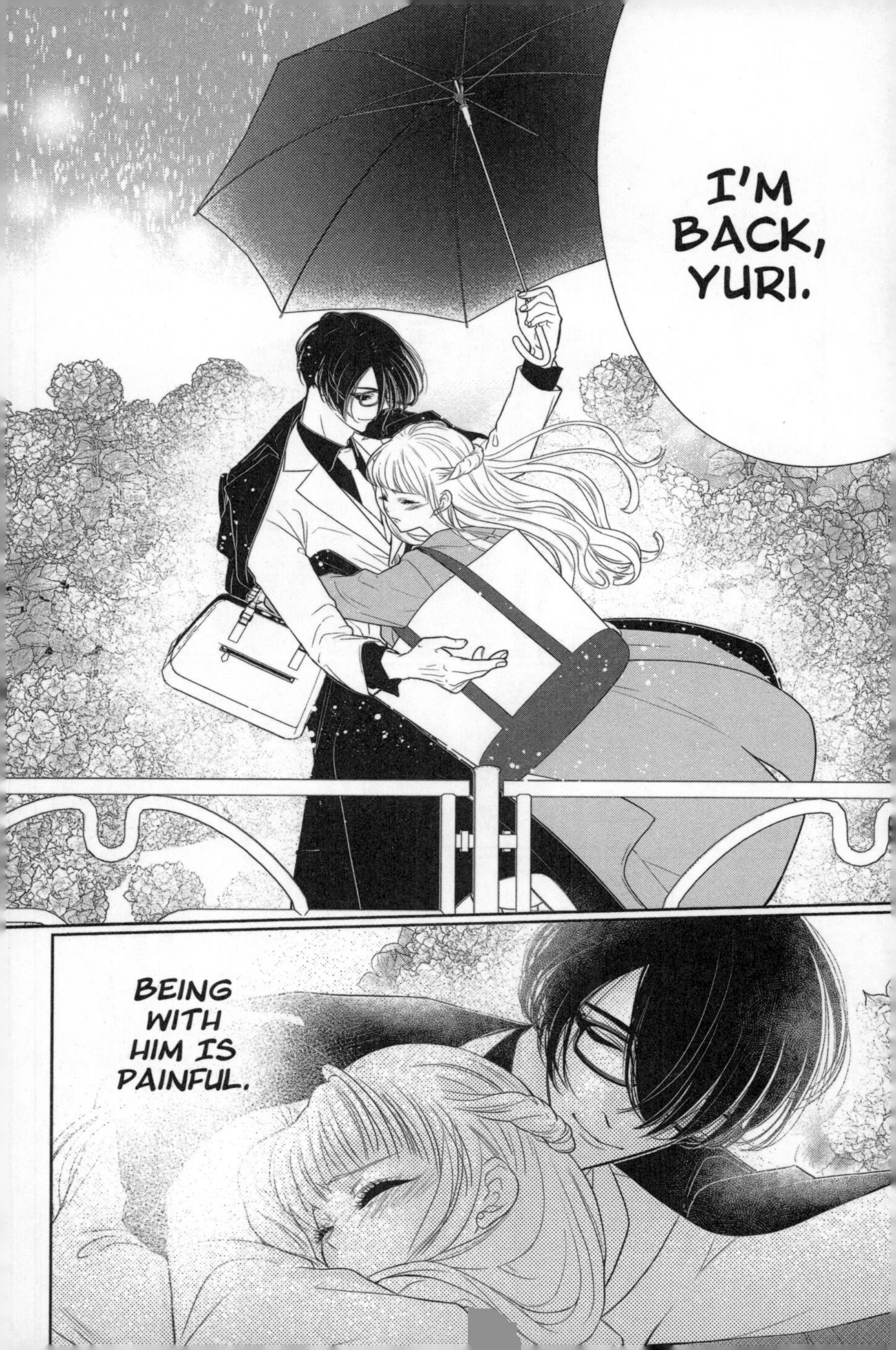
I'M BACK, YURI.
BEING WITH HIM IS PAINFUL.

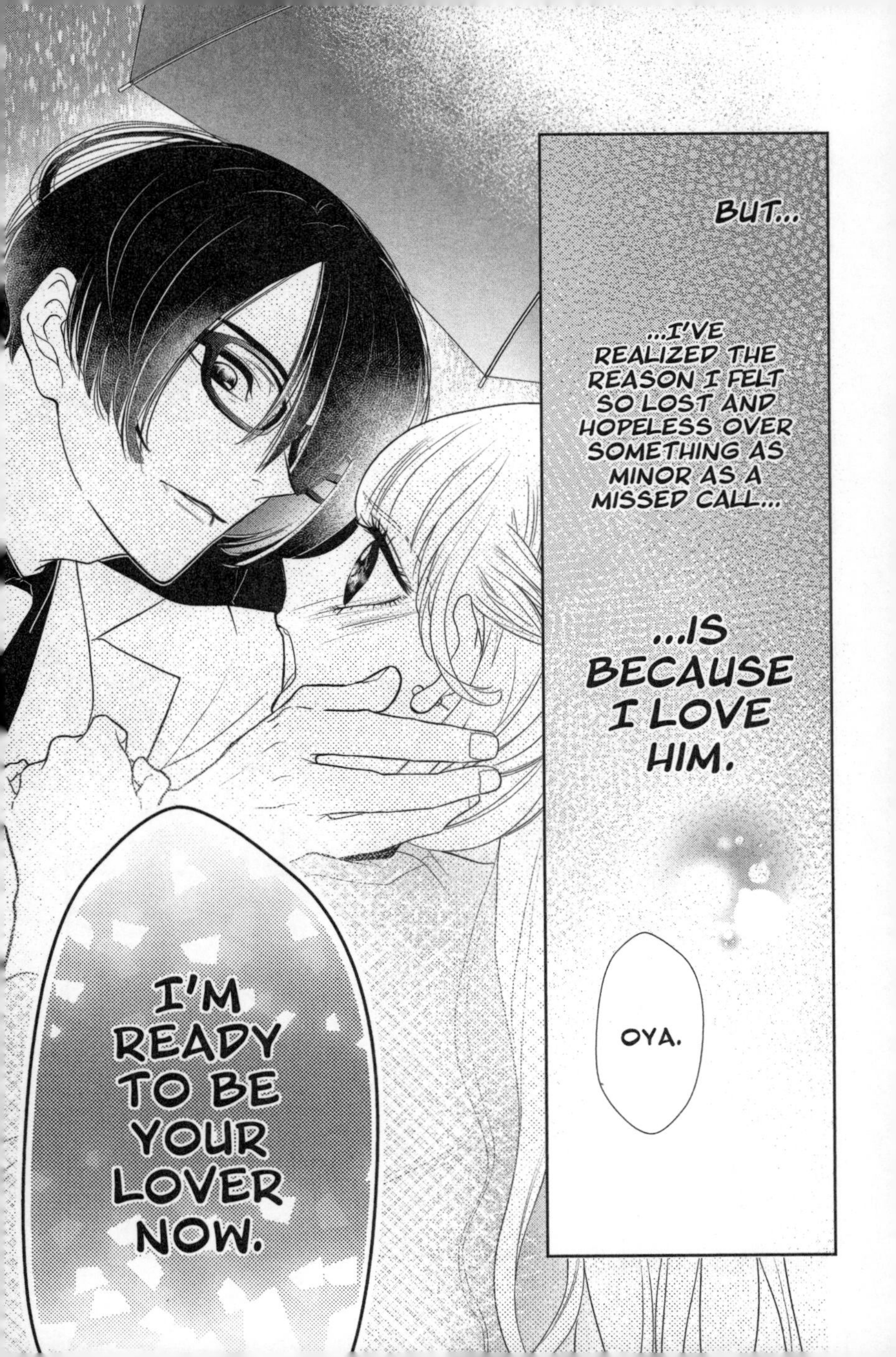
BUT...
...I'VE REALIZED THE REASON I FELT SO LOST AND HOPELESS OVER SOMETHING AS MINOR AS A MISSED CALL...
...IS BECAUSE I LOVE HIM.
OYA.
I'M READY TO BE YOUR LOVER NOW.

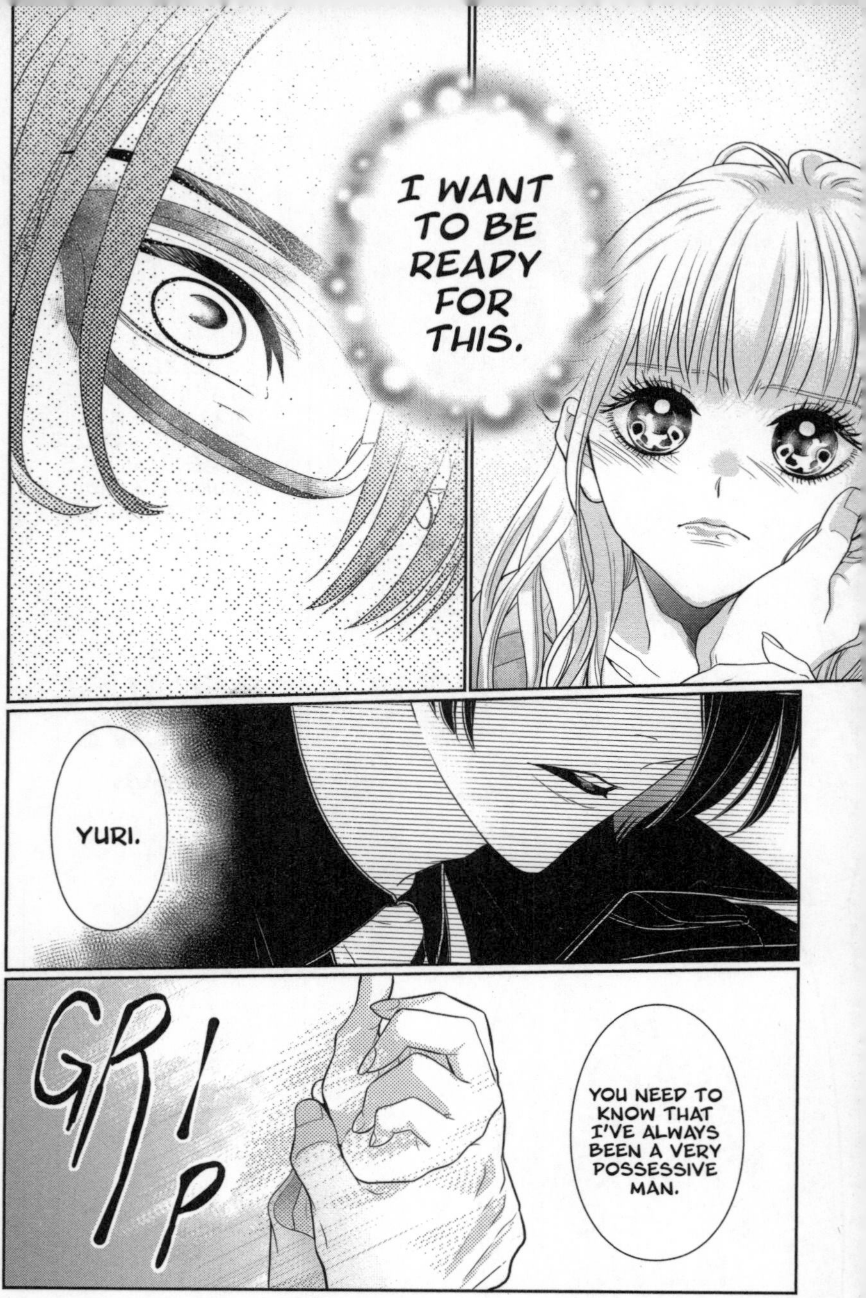
I WANT TO BE READY FOR THIS.
YURI.
YOU NEED TO KNOW THAT I'VE ALWAYS BEEN A VERY POSSESSIVE MAN.
GRIP

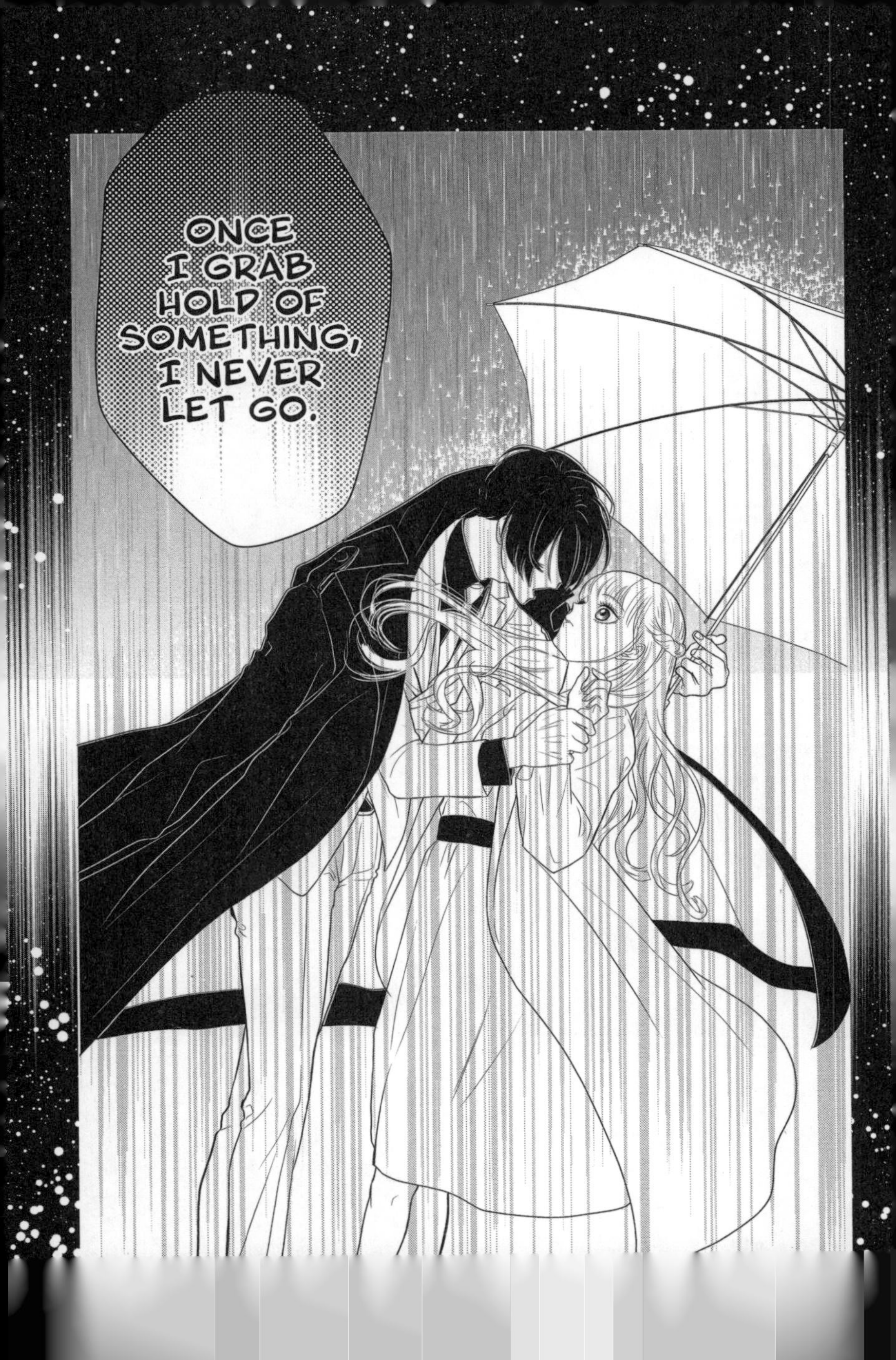
ONCE I GRAB HOLD OF SOMETHING, I NEVER LET GO.

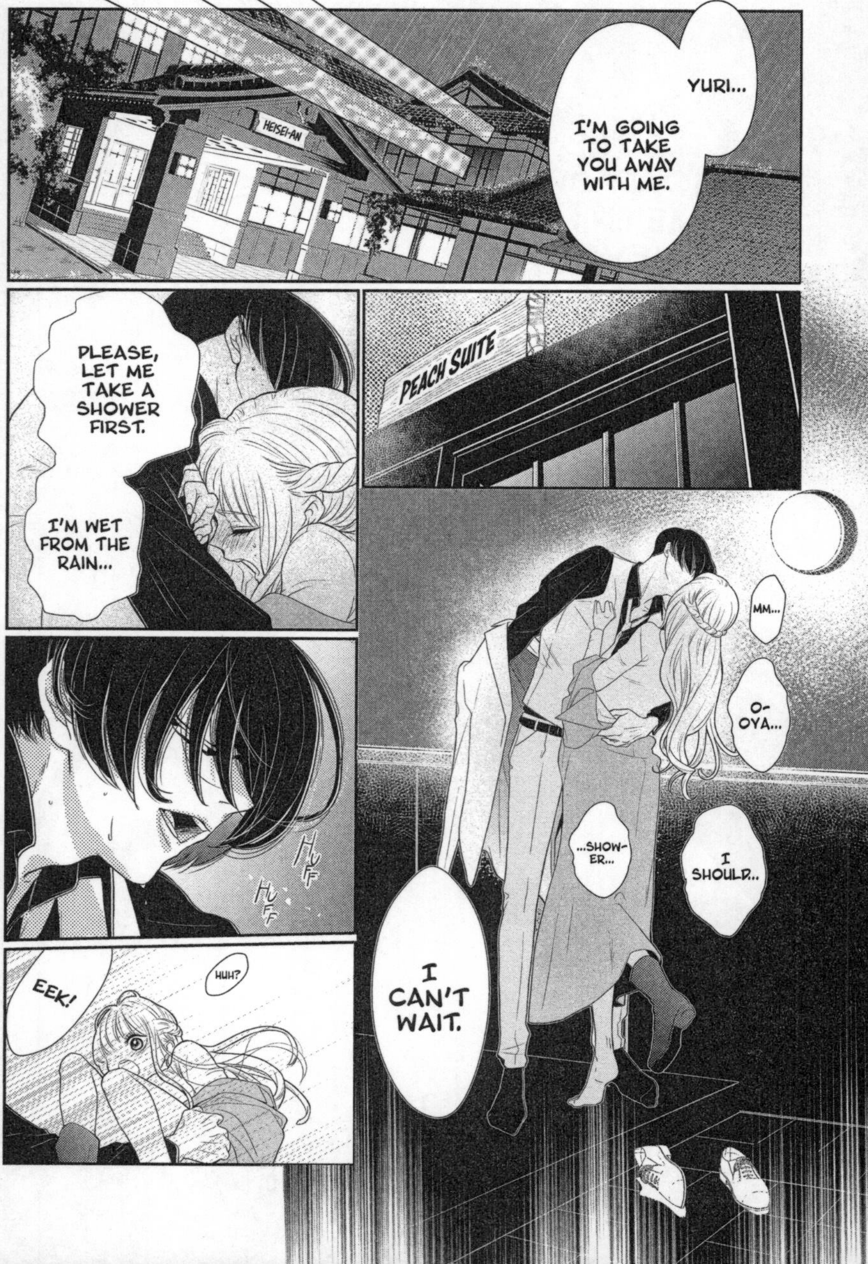
HEISEI-AN
YURI...
I'M GOING TO TAKE YOU AWAY WITH ME.
PEACH SUITE
PLEASE, LET ME TAKE A SHOWER FIRST.
I'M WET FROM THE RAIN...
MM...
O-OYA...
I SHOULD...
...SHOWER...
I CAN'T WAIT.
HUFF
HUFF
HUH?
EEK!

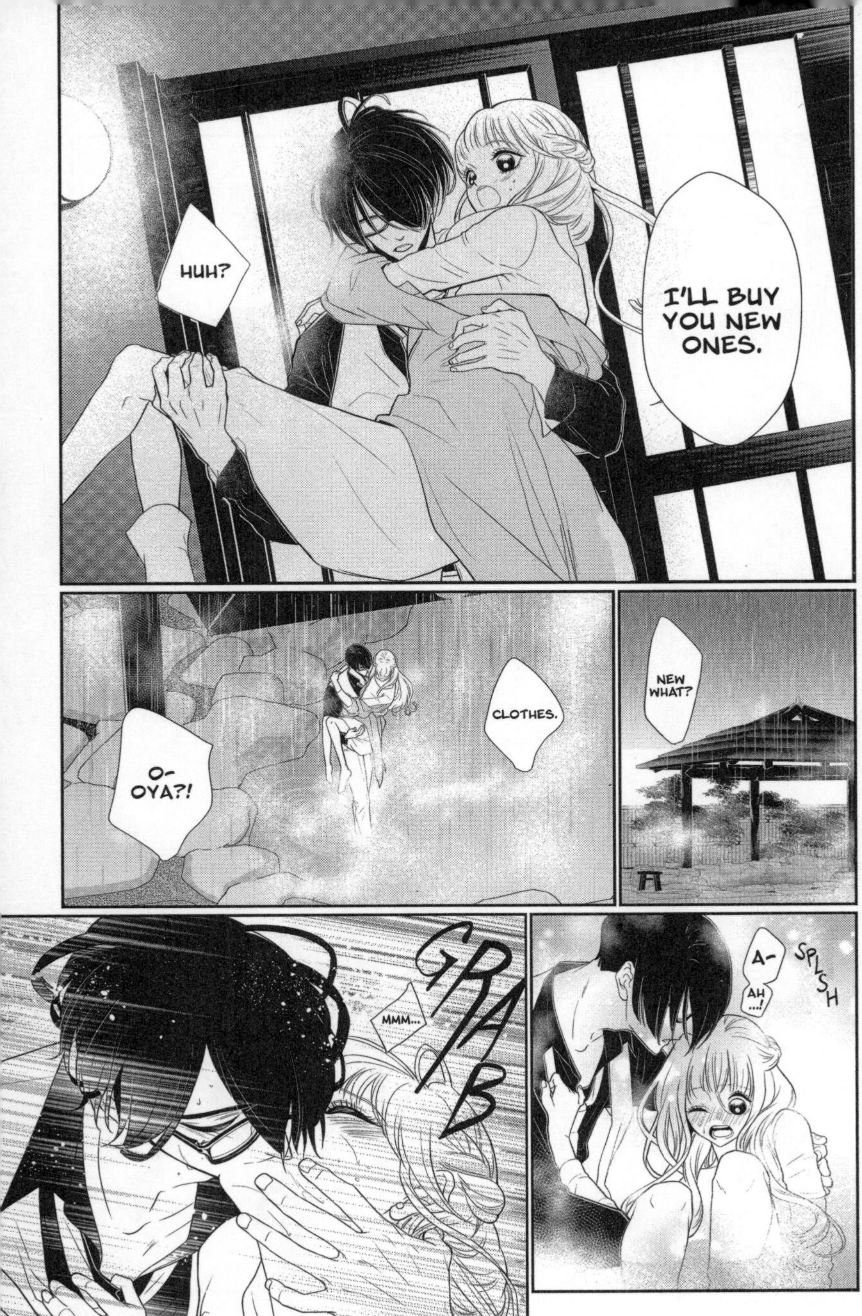
I'LL BUY YOU NEW ONES.
HUH?
NEW WHAT?
CLOTHES.
O-OYA?!
A-
AH ...!
SPLSH
GRAB
MMM...

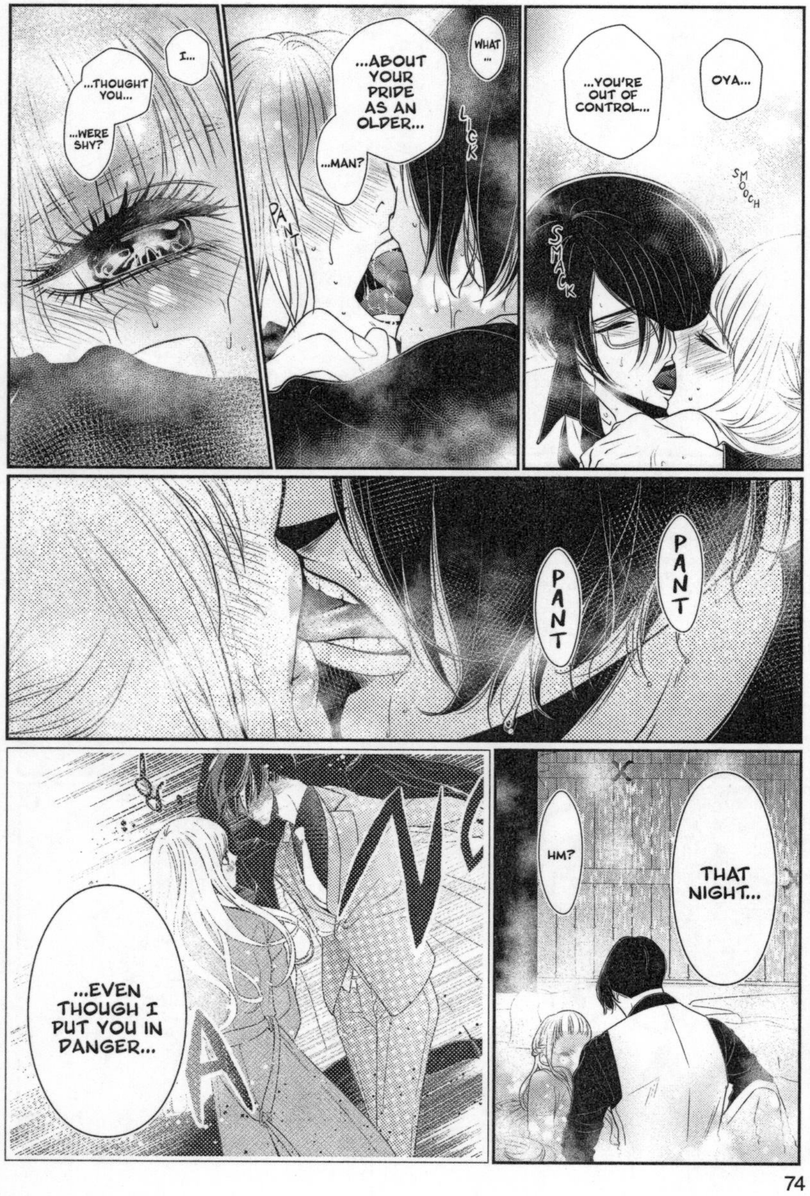
OYA...
...YOU'RE OUT OF CONTROL...
SMOOCH
SMACK
WHAT...
...ABOUT YOUR PRIDE AS AN OLDER...
...MAN?
LICK
PANT
I...
...THOUGHT YOU...
...WERE SHY?
PANT
PANT
THAT NIGHT...
HM?
...EVEN THOUGH I PUT YOU IN DANGER...

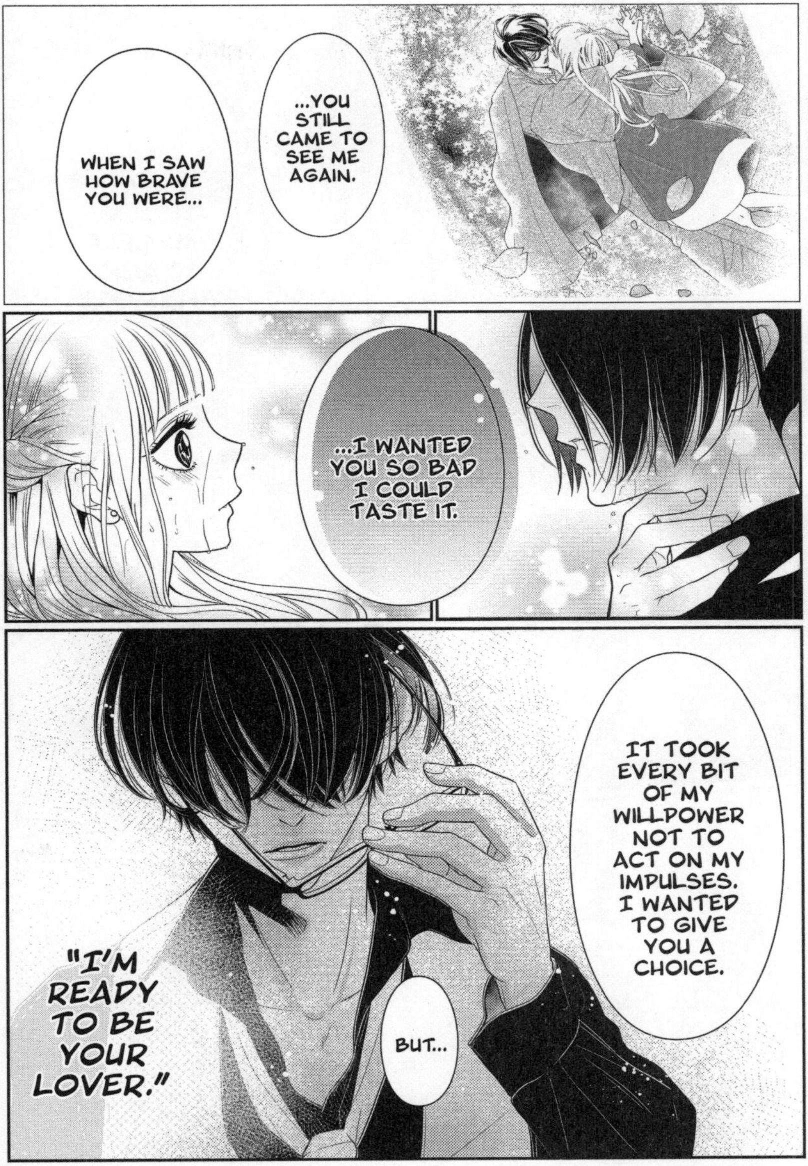
...YOU STILL CAME TO SEE ME AGAIN.
WHEN I SAW HOW BRAVE YOU WERE...
...I WANTED YOU SO BAD I COULD TASTE IT.
IT TOOK EVERY BIT OF MY WILLPOWER NOT TO ACT ON MY IMPULSES. I WANTED TO GIVE YOU A CHOICE.
BUT...
"I'M READY TO BE YOUR LOVER."

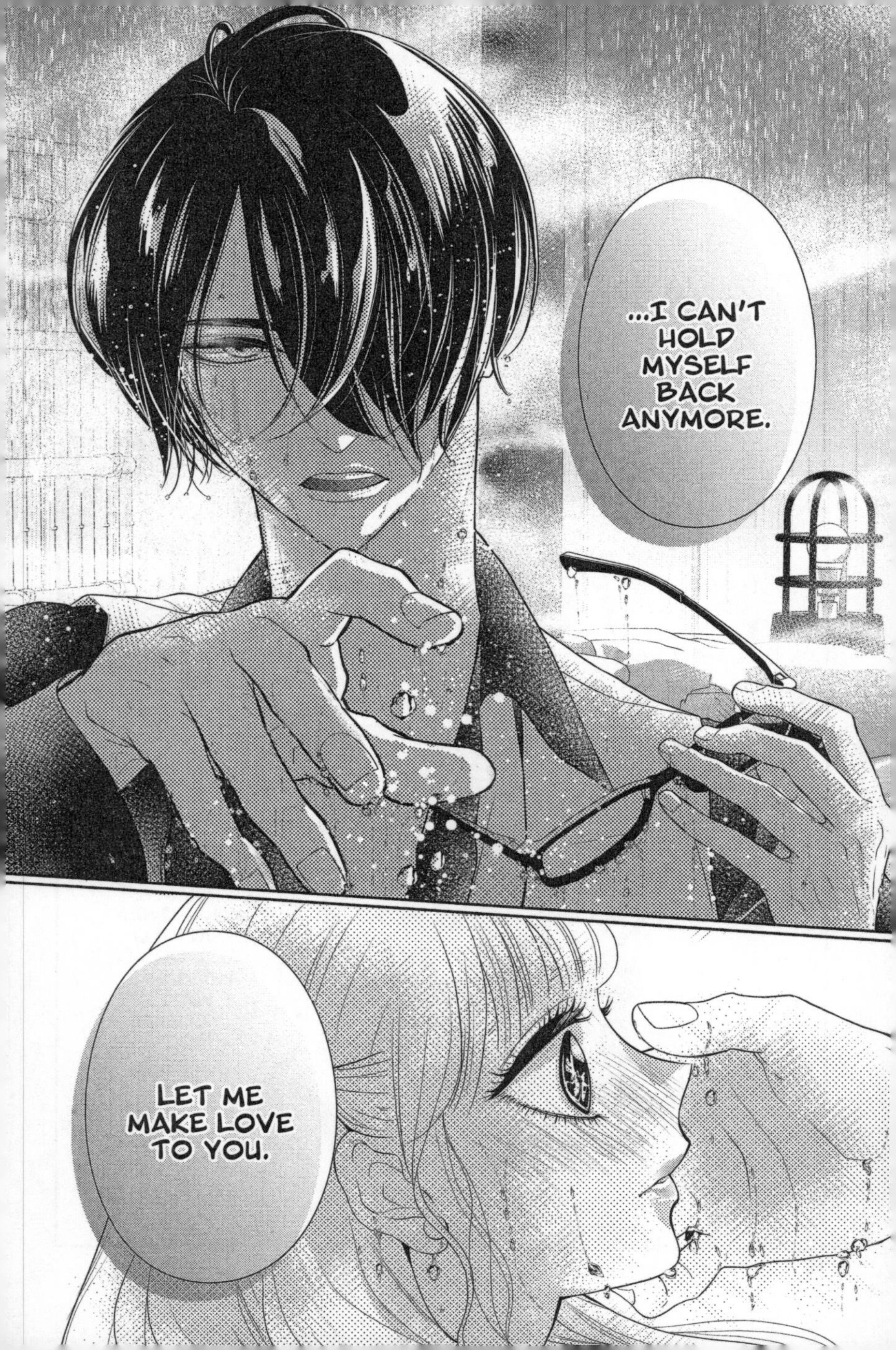
...I CAN'T HOLD MYSELF BACK ANYMORE.
LET ME MAKE LOVE TO YOU.

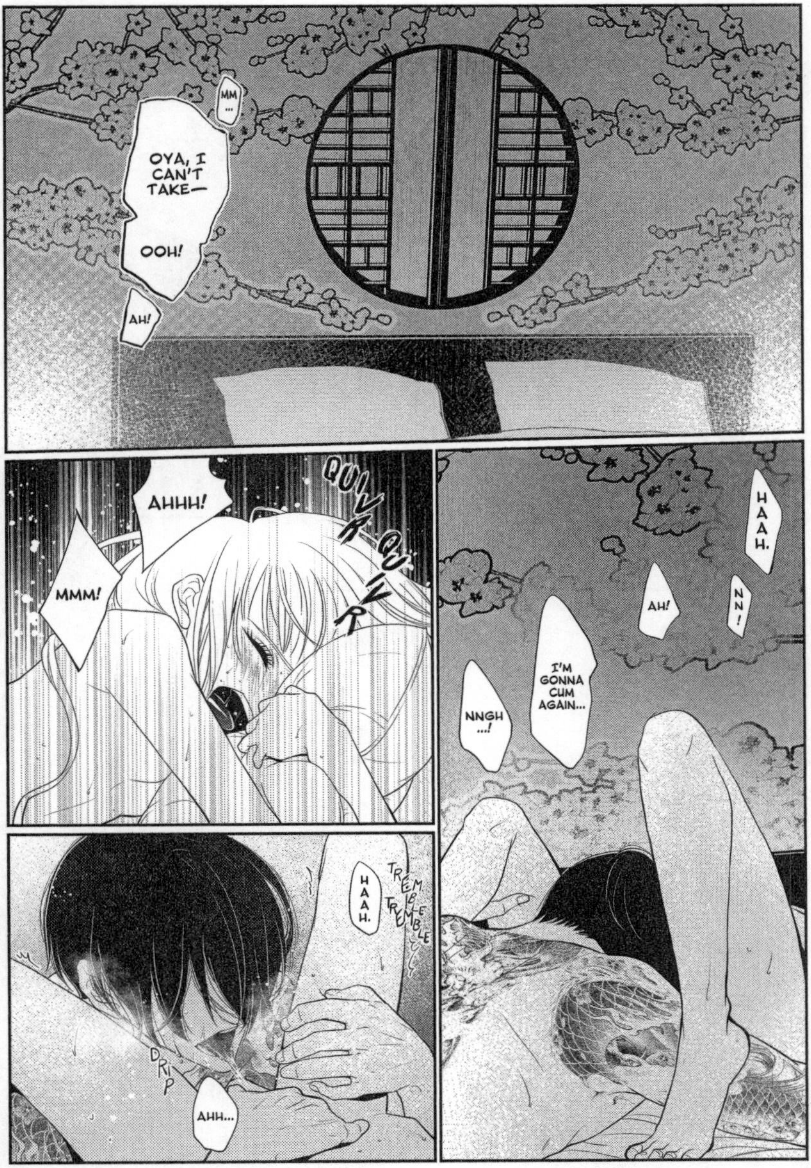
MM...
OYA, I CAN'T TAKE—
OOH!
AH!
HAAH.
NN!
AH!
I'M GONNA CUM AGAIN...
NNGH...!
QUIVR QUIVR
AHHH!
MMM!
TREMBLE TREMBLE
HAAH.
DRIP
AHH...

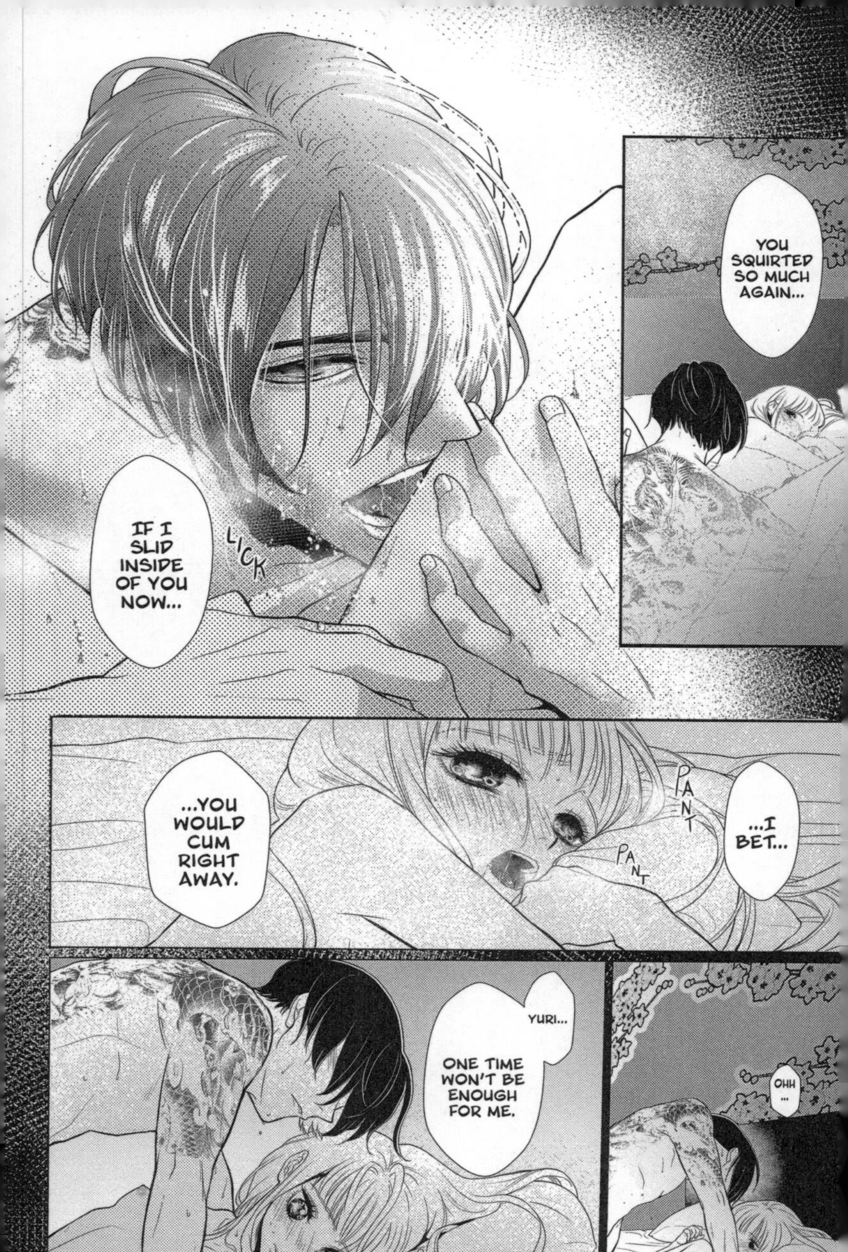
YOU SQUIRTED SO MUCH AGAIN...
IF I SLID INSIDE OF YOU NOW...
LICK
...I BET...
PANT
PANT
...YOU WOULD CUM RIGHT AWAY.
OHH ...
YURI...
ONE TIME WON'T BE ENOUGH FOR ME.

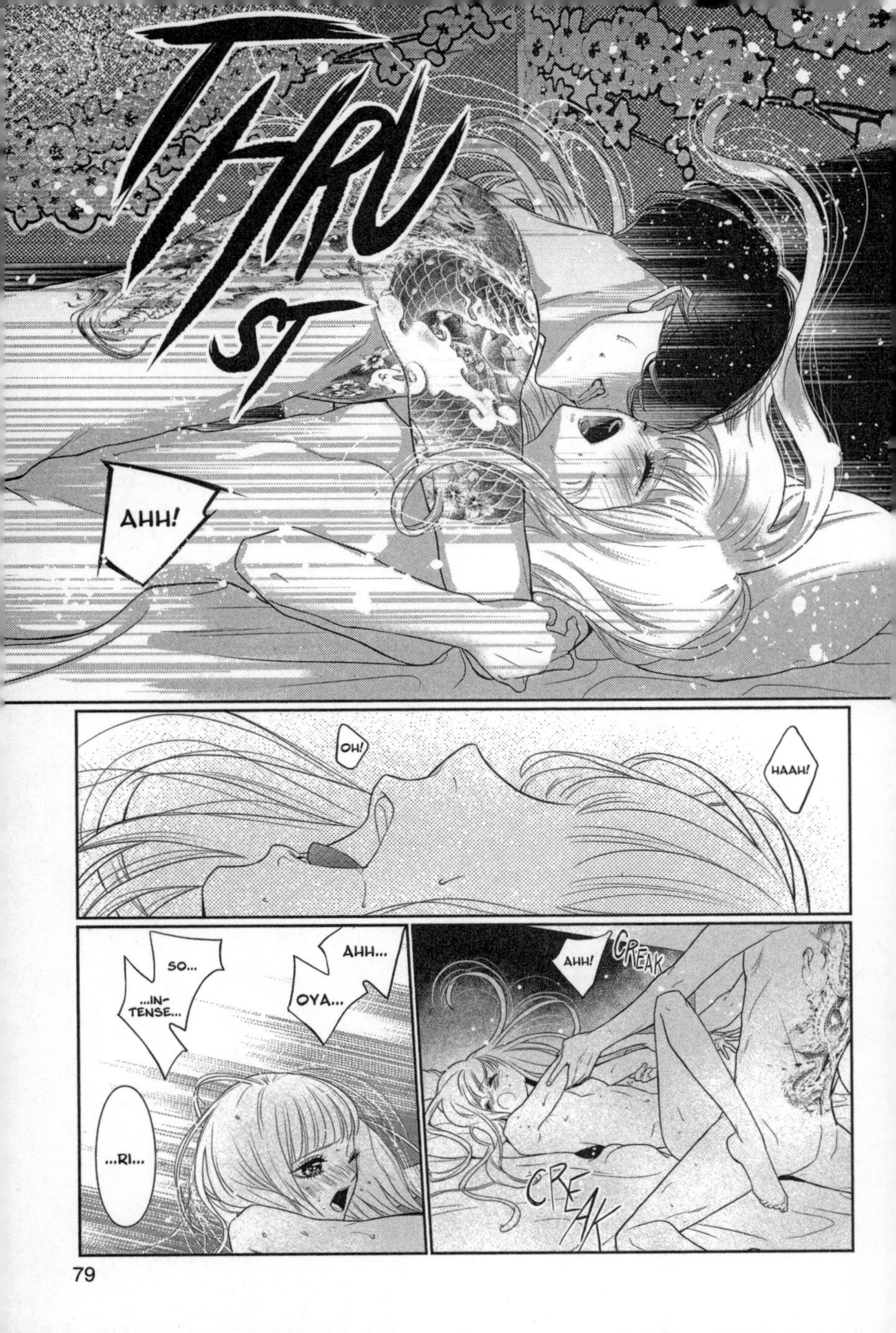
THRUST
AHH!
HAAH!
OH!
AHH!
CREAK
CREAK
AHH...
OYA...
SO...
...IN-
TENSE...
...RI...

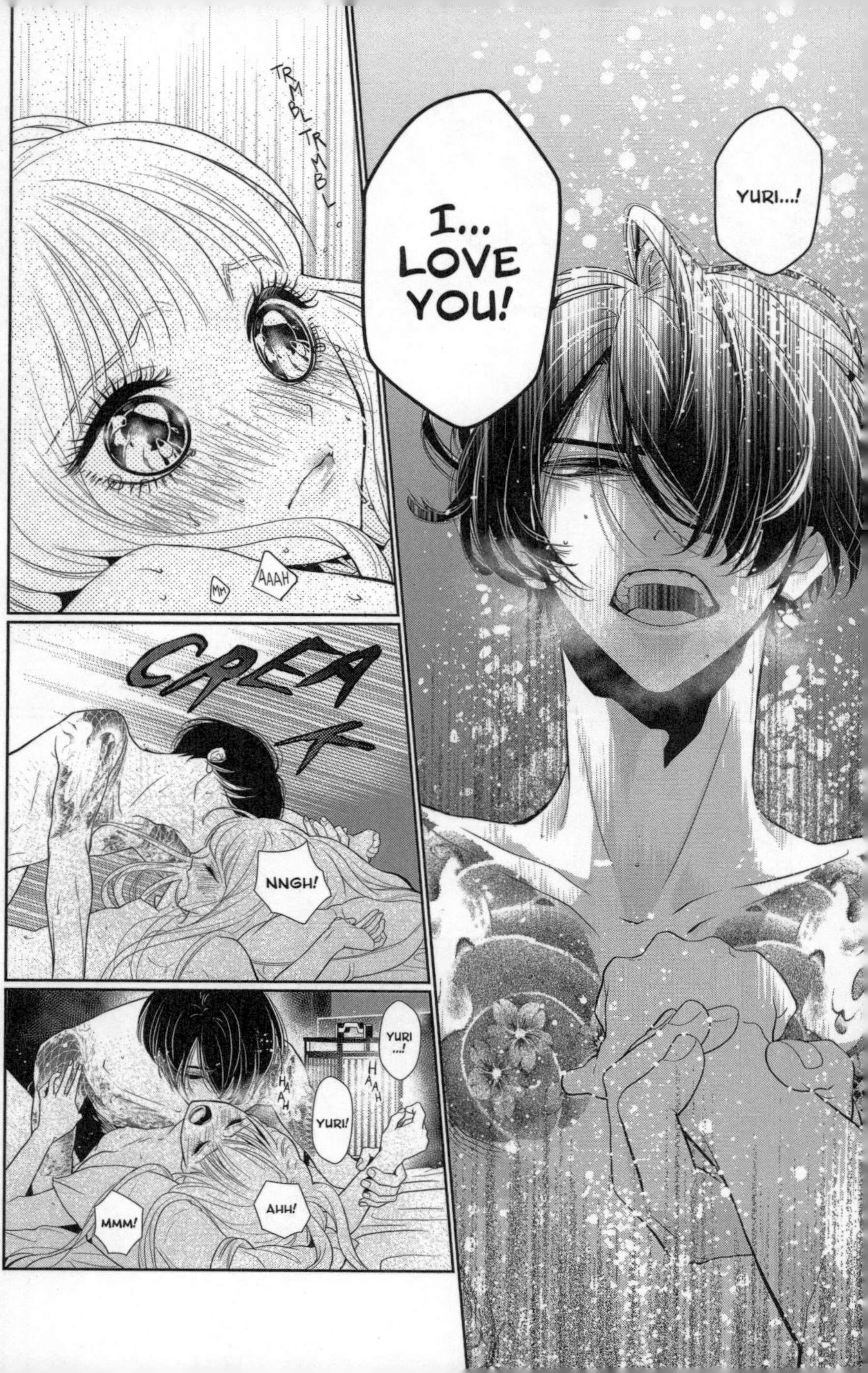
YURI...!
I... LOVE YOU!
TRMBL TRMBL
AAAH
MM
CREAK
NNGH!
YURI...!
HAAH
HAAH
YURI!
AHH!
MMM!

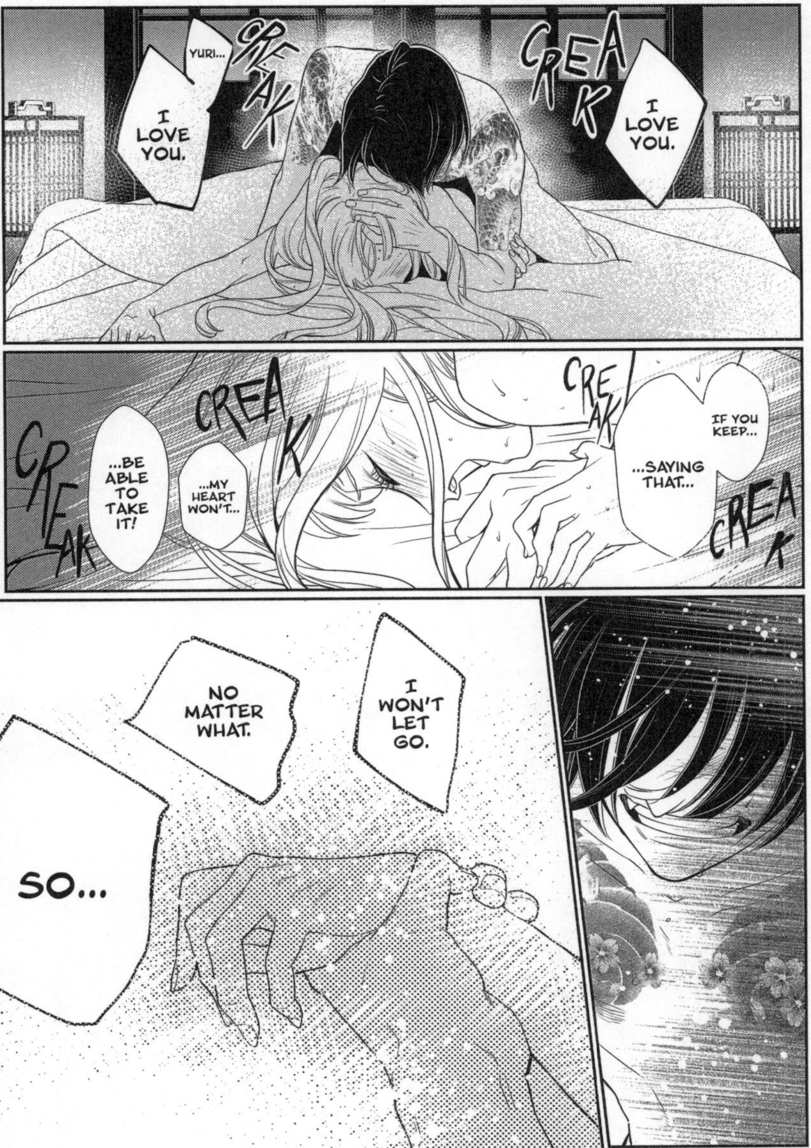
CREAK
I LOVE YOU.
CREAK
YURI...
I LOVE YOU.
CREAK
IF YOU KEEP...
...SAYING THAT...
CREAK
CREAK
...MY HEART WON'T...
...BE ABLE TO TAKE IT!
CREAK
I WON'T LET GO.
NO MATTER WHAT.
SO...

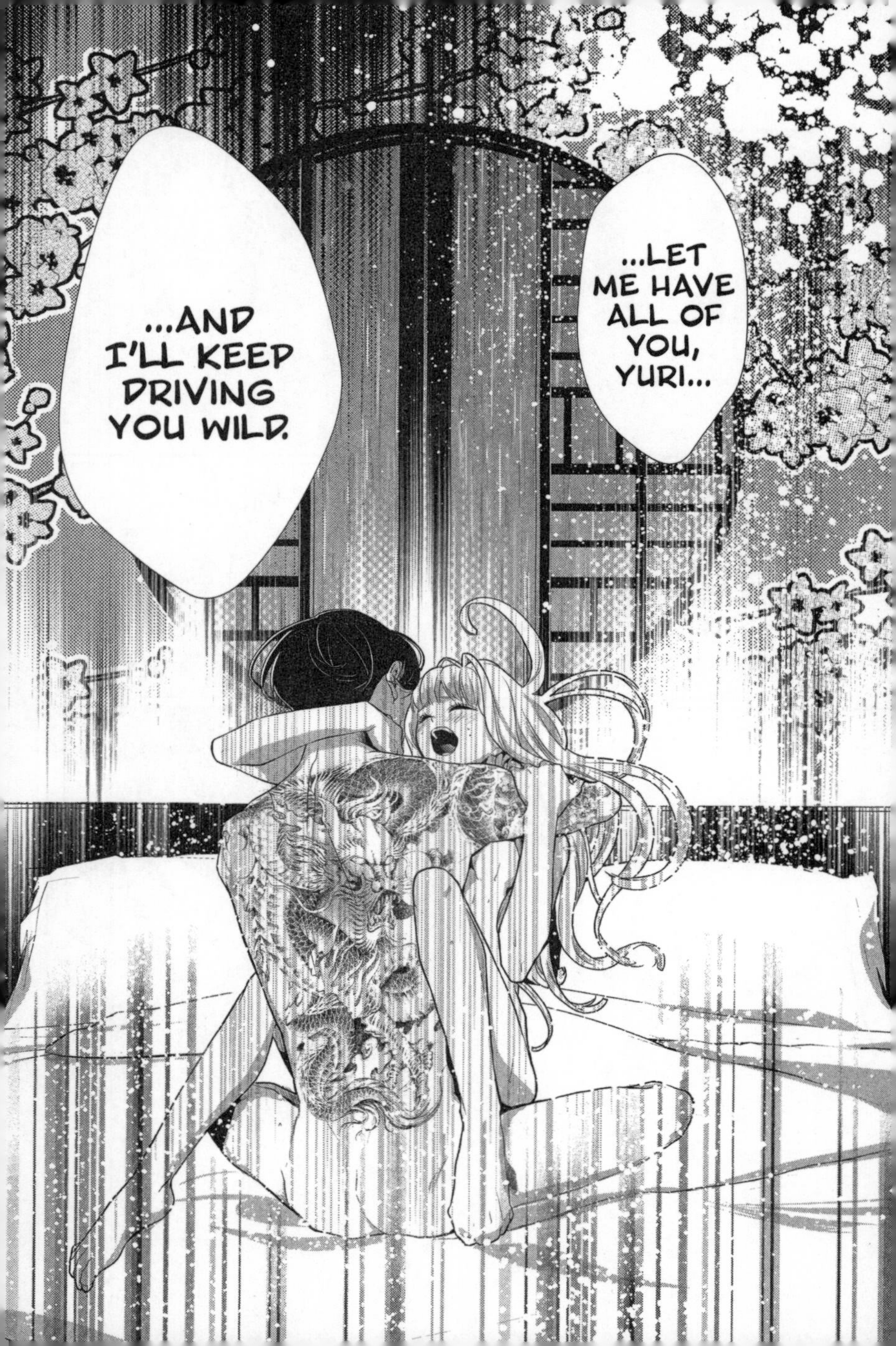
...LET ME HAVE ALL OF YOU, YURI...
...AND I'LL KEEP DRIVING YOU WILD.

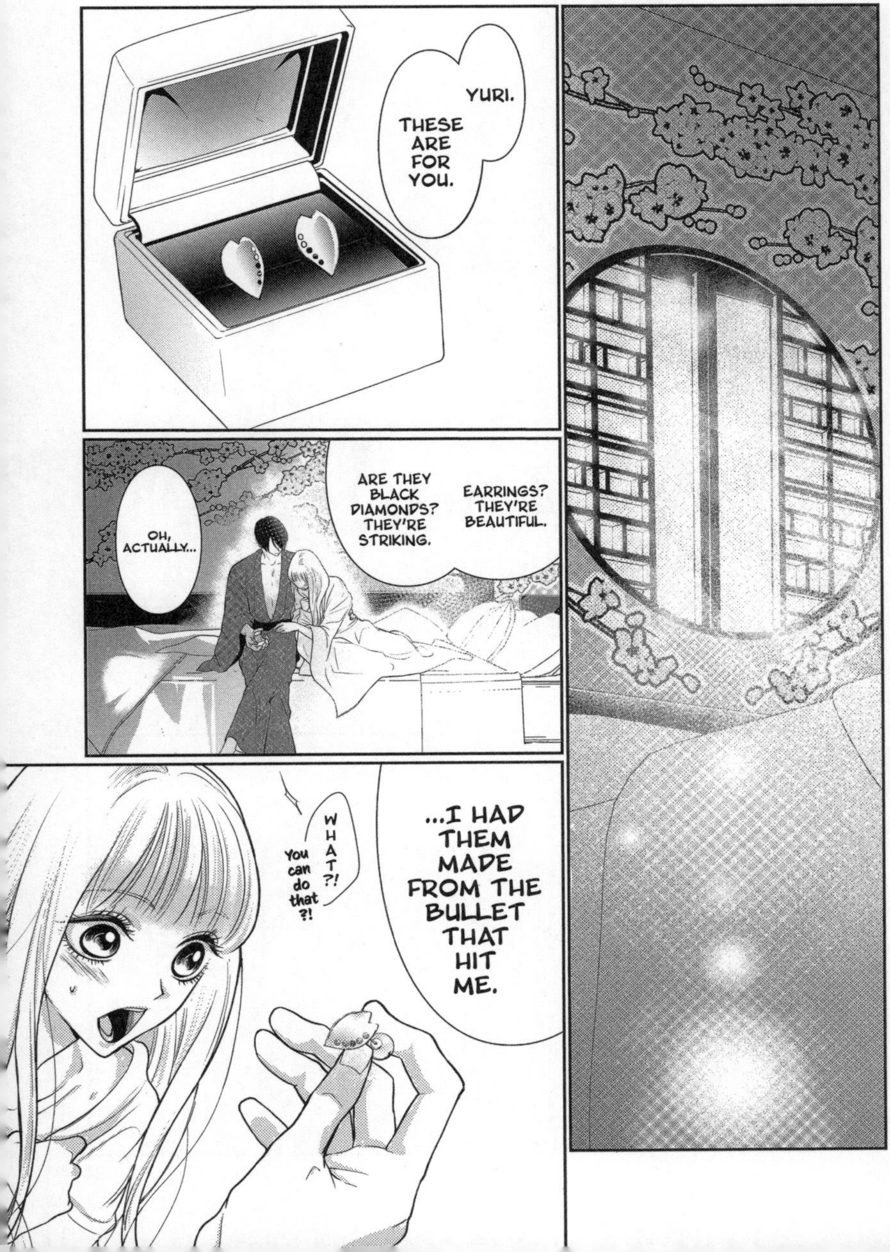
YURI.
THESE ARE FOR YOU.
EARRINGS? THEY'RE BEAUTIFUL.
ARE THEY BLACK DIAMONDS? THEY'RE STRIKING.
OH, ACTUALLY...
...I HAD THEM MADE FROM THE BULLET THAT HIT ME.
WHAT?!
You can do that?!

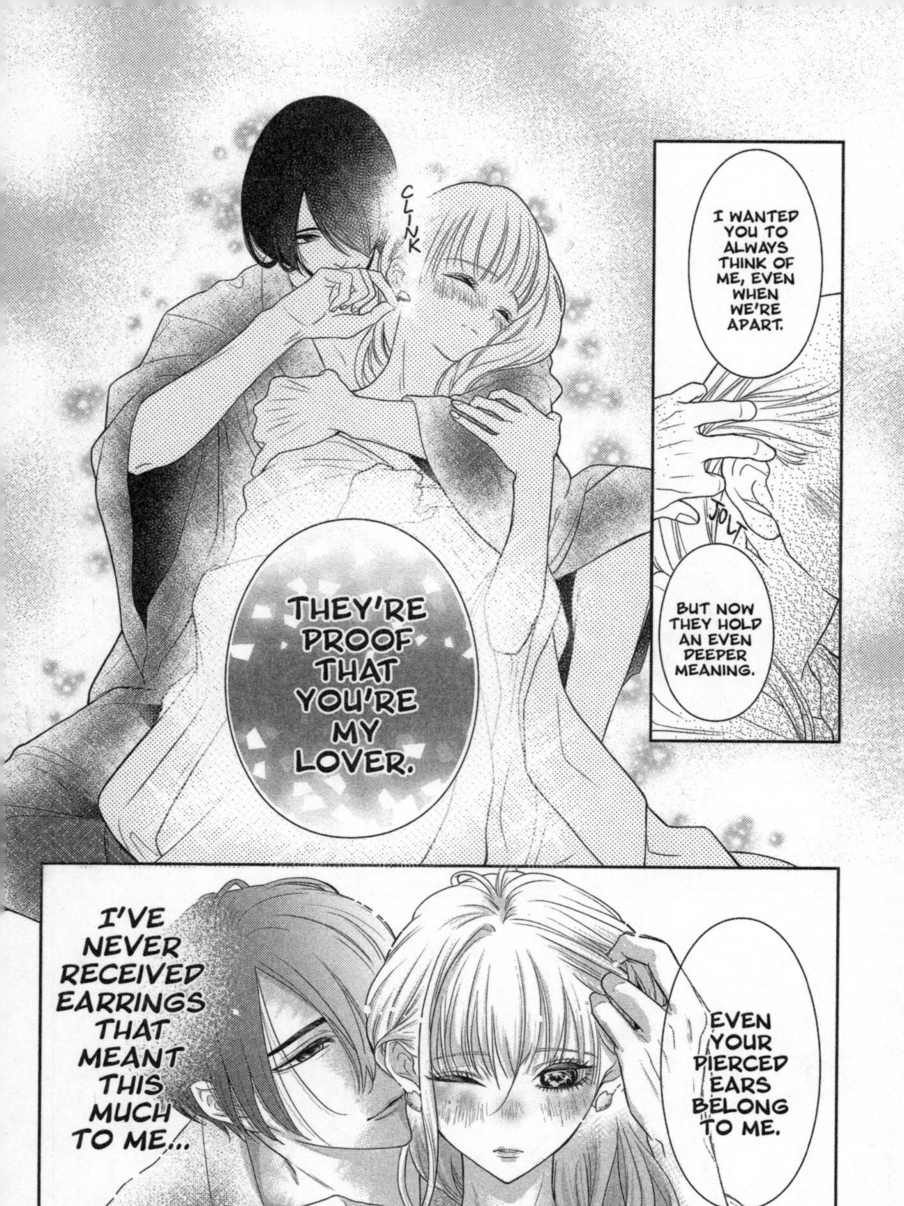
I WANTED YOU TO ALWAYS THINK OF ME, EVEN WHEN WE'RE APART.
JOLT
BUT NOW THEY HOLD AN EVEN DEEPER MEANING.
CLINK
THEY'RE PROOF THAT YOU'RE MY LOVER.
EVEN YOUR PIERCED EARS BELONG TO ME.
I'VE NEVER RECEIVED EARRINGS THAT MEANT THIS MUCH TO ME...

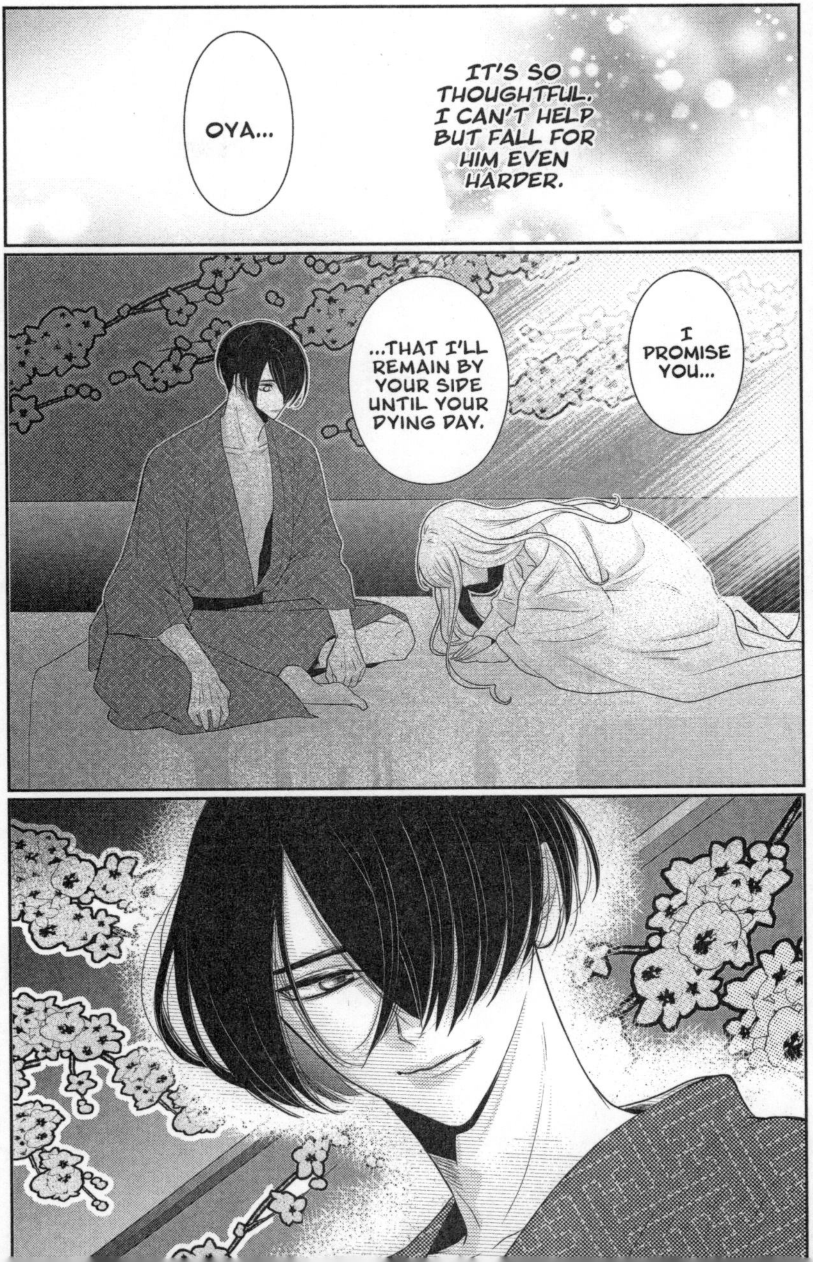
IT'S SO THOUGHTFUL. I CAN'T HELP BUT FALL FOR HIM EVEN HARDER.
OYA...
I PROMISE YOU...
...THAT I'LL REMAIN BY YOUR SIDE UNTIL YOUR DYING DAY.

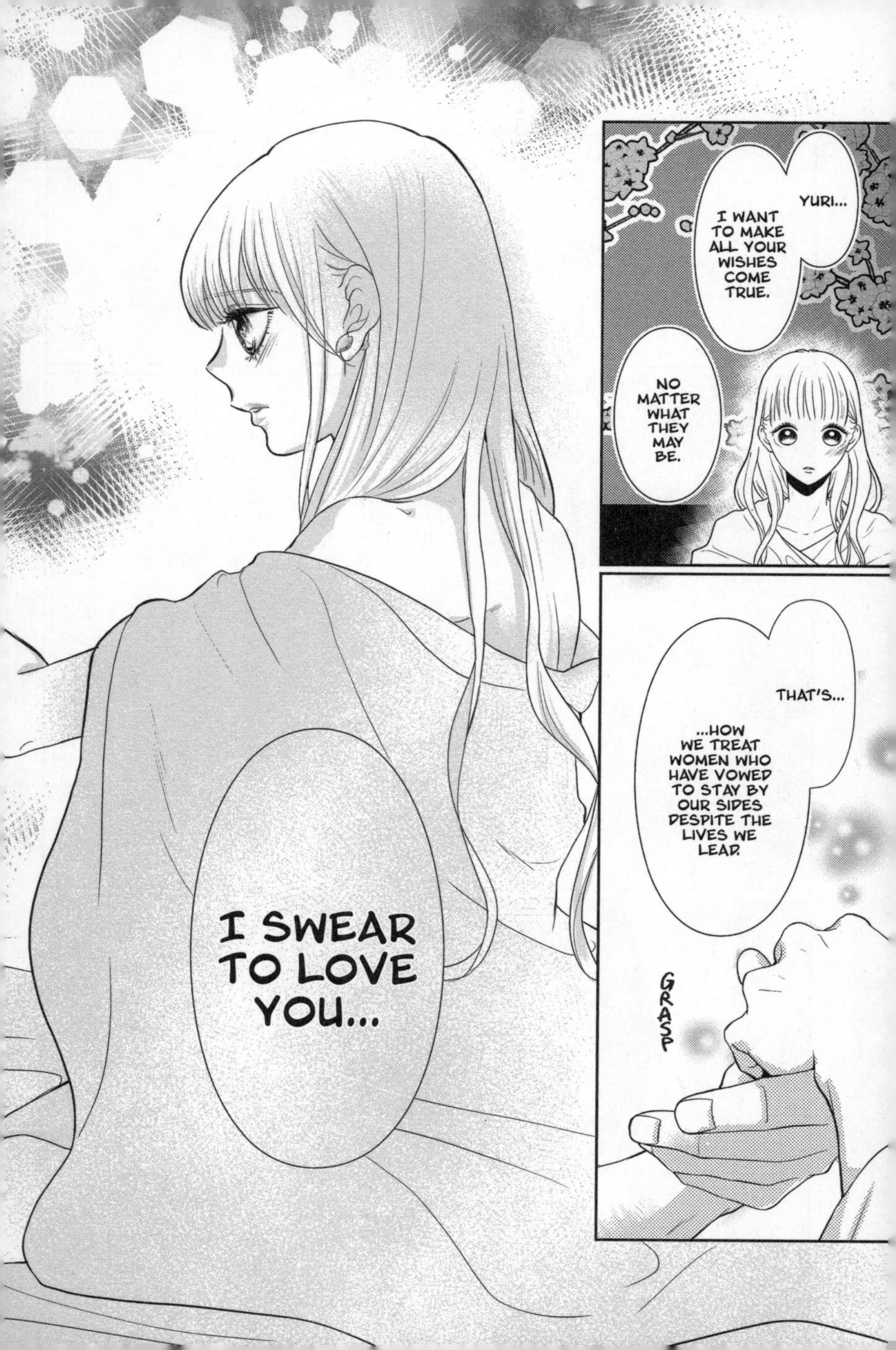
YURI... I WANT TO MAKE ALL YOUR WISHES COME TRUE.
NO MATTER WHAT THEY MAY BE.
THAT'S...
...HOW WE TREAT WOMEN WHO HAVE VOWED TO STAY BY OUR SIDES DESPITE THE LIVES WE LEAD.
GRASP
I SWEAR TO LOVE YOU...

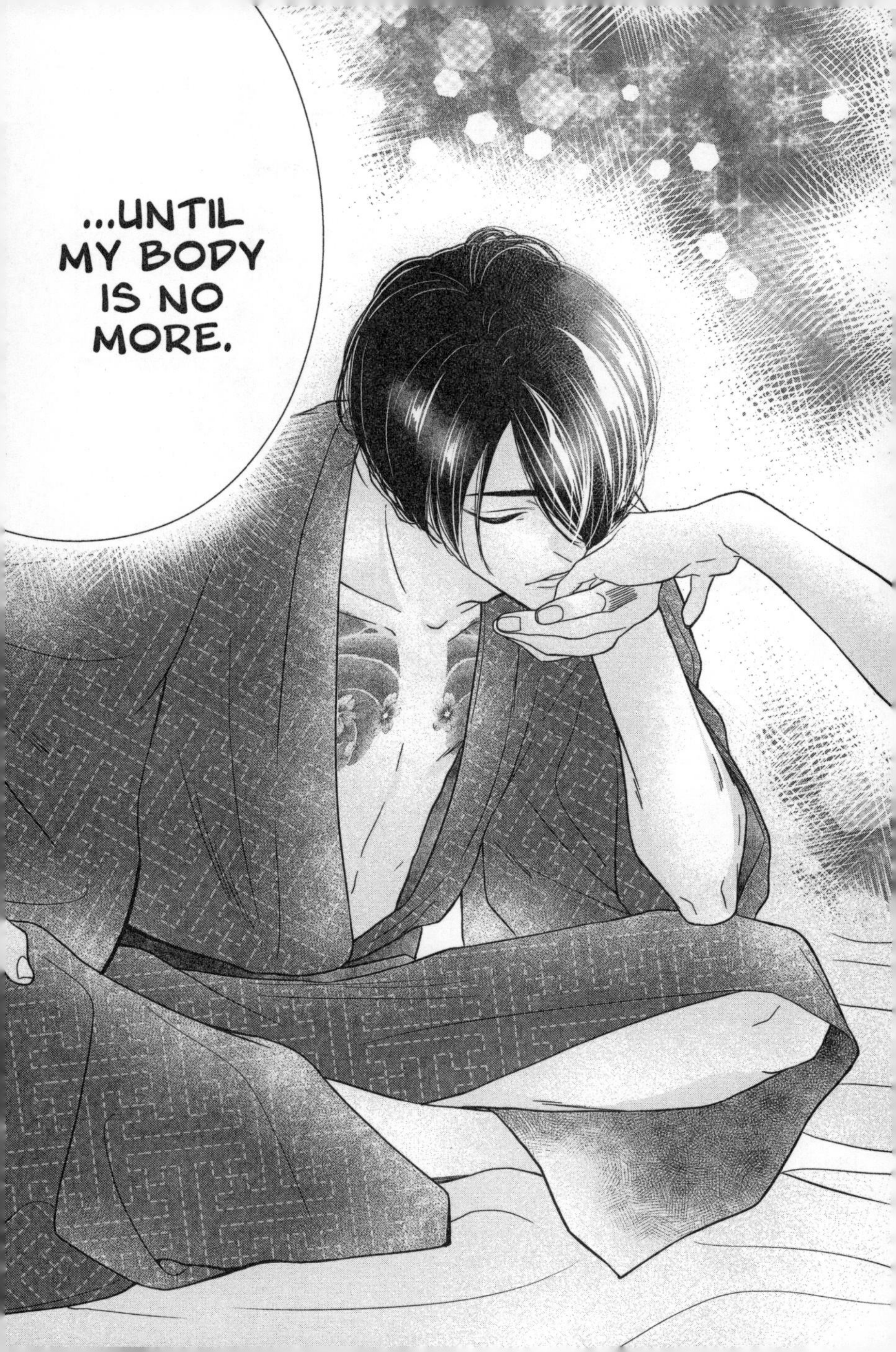
...UNTIL MY BODY IS NO MORE.

bonus bullet 02 secret scene

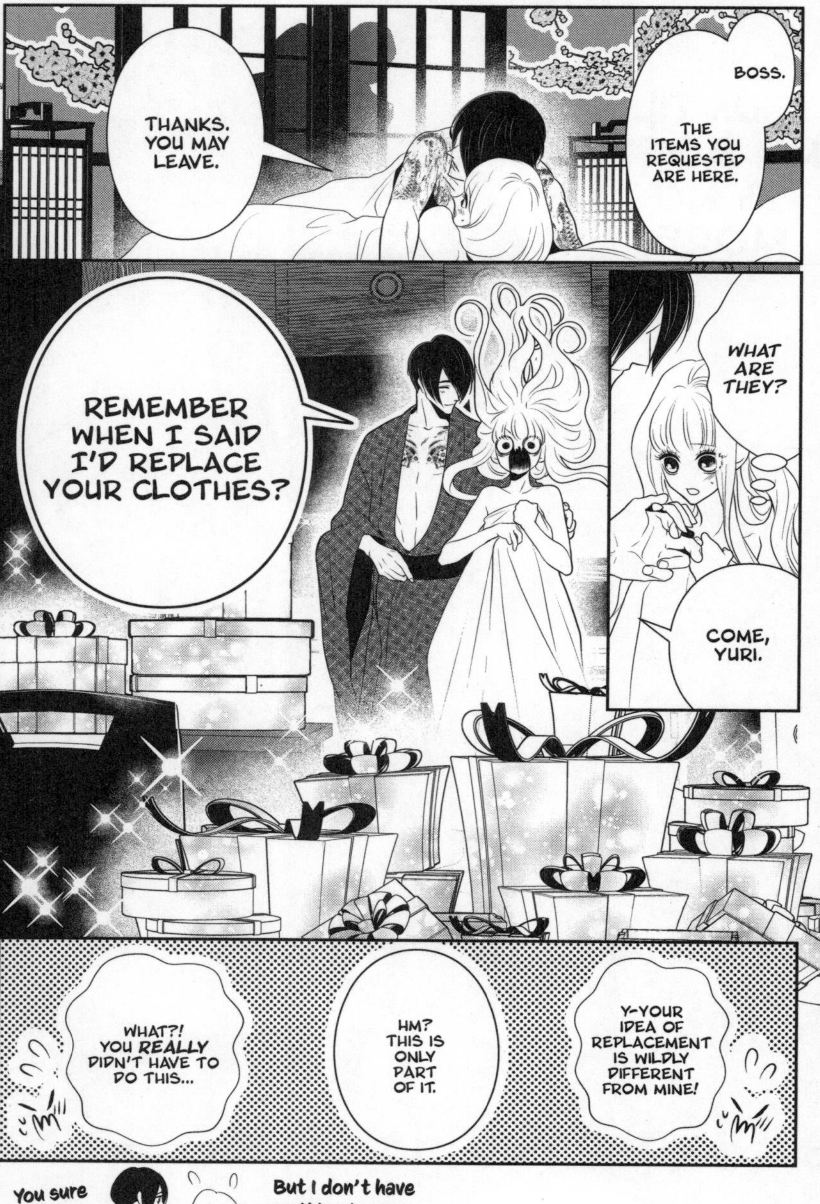
BOSS.
THE ITEMS YOU REQUESTED ARE HERE.
THANKS. YOU MAY LEAVE.
WHAT ARE THEY?
COME, YURI.
REMEMBER WHEN I SAID I'D REPLACE YOUR CLOTHES?
WHAT?! YOU **REALLY** DIDN'T HAVE TO DO THIS...
HM? THIS IS ONLY PART OF IT.
Y-YOUR IDEA OF REPLACEMENT IS WILDLY DIFFERENT FROM MINE!
But I don't have anything to wear, so I'll take one...
You sure that's enough?

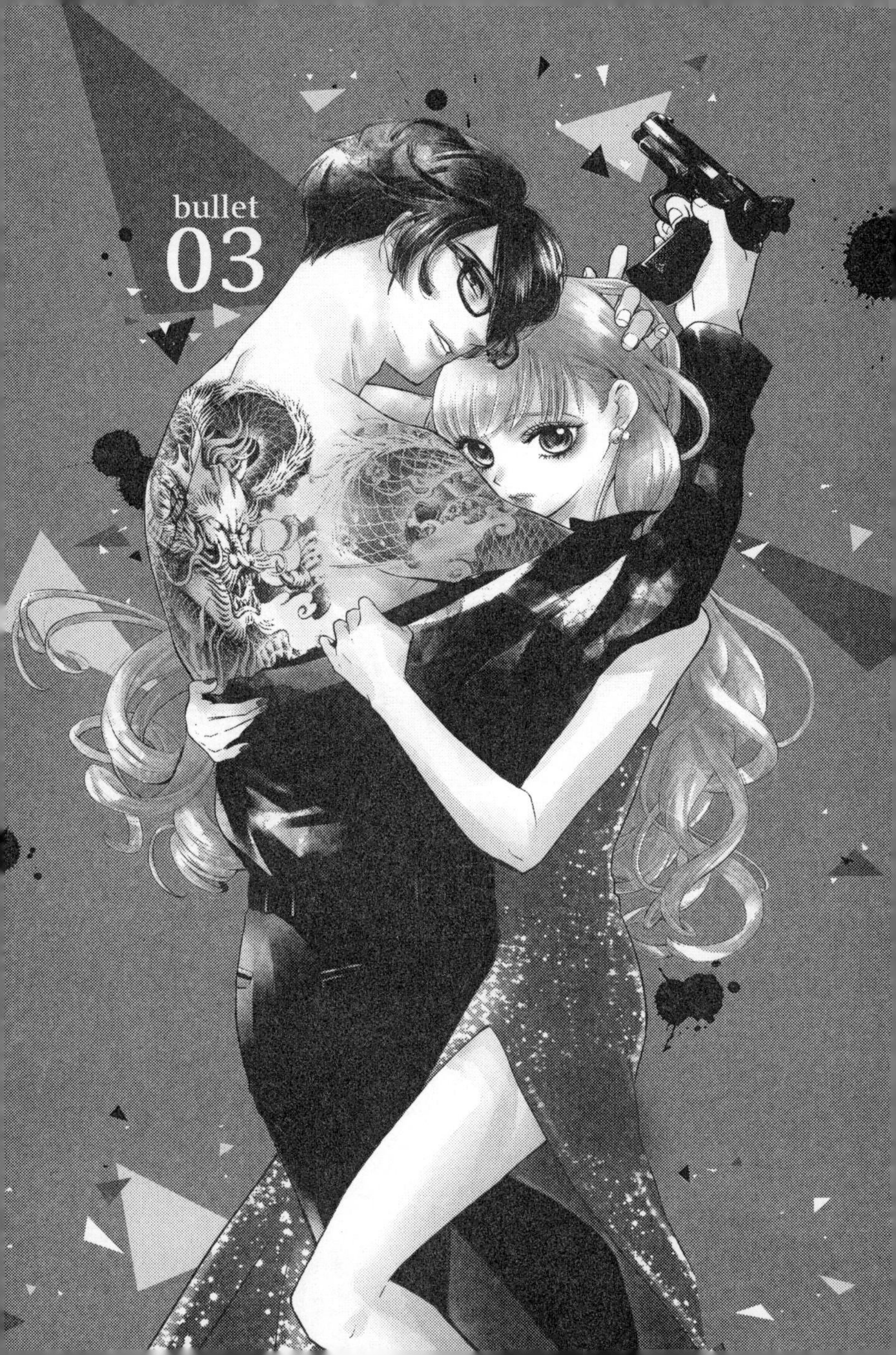
bullet
03

Special Thanks

🌸 MY READERS

🌸 CHEESE! EDITORIAL DEPARTMENT

🌸 EDITOR: MORIHARA

🌸 DESIGNER: ITOU (BAYBRIDGE STUDIO)

🌸 EVERYONE AT THE PRINT SHOP

🌸 ASSISTANTS:
ISHIDA, ISHIKURA,
TOYONAGA, SAITO

🌸 EVERYONE INVOLVED IN
PUBLISHING THIS MANGA

🌸 MY FAMILY, FRIENDS AND CAT

🌸 ROCK MUSIC, CIGARETTES,
COFFEE, VANILLA MOCHI ICE CREAM
AND HOJICHA

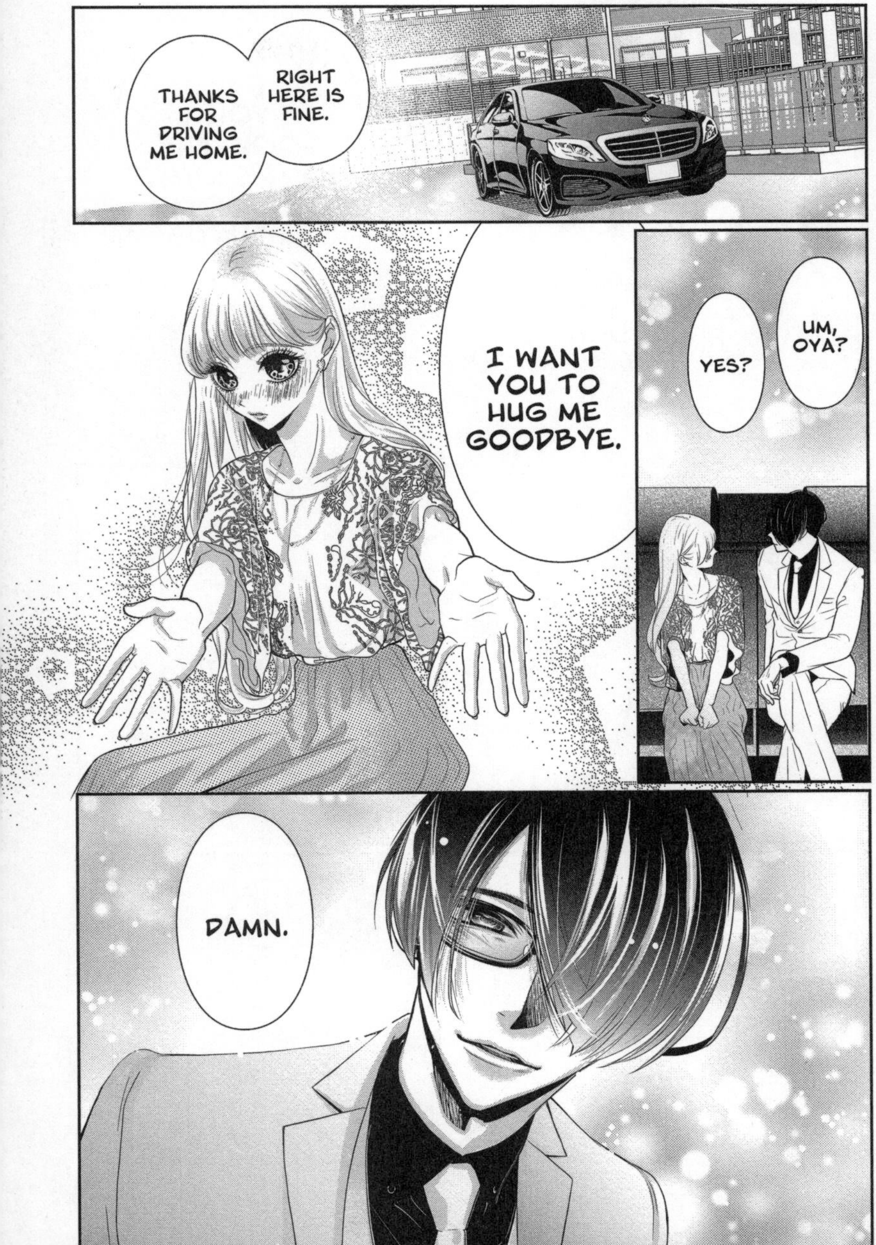
RIGHT HERE IS FINE.
THANKS FOR DRIVING ME HOME.
UM, OYA?
YES?
I WANT YOU TO HUG ME GOODBYE.
DAMN.

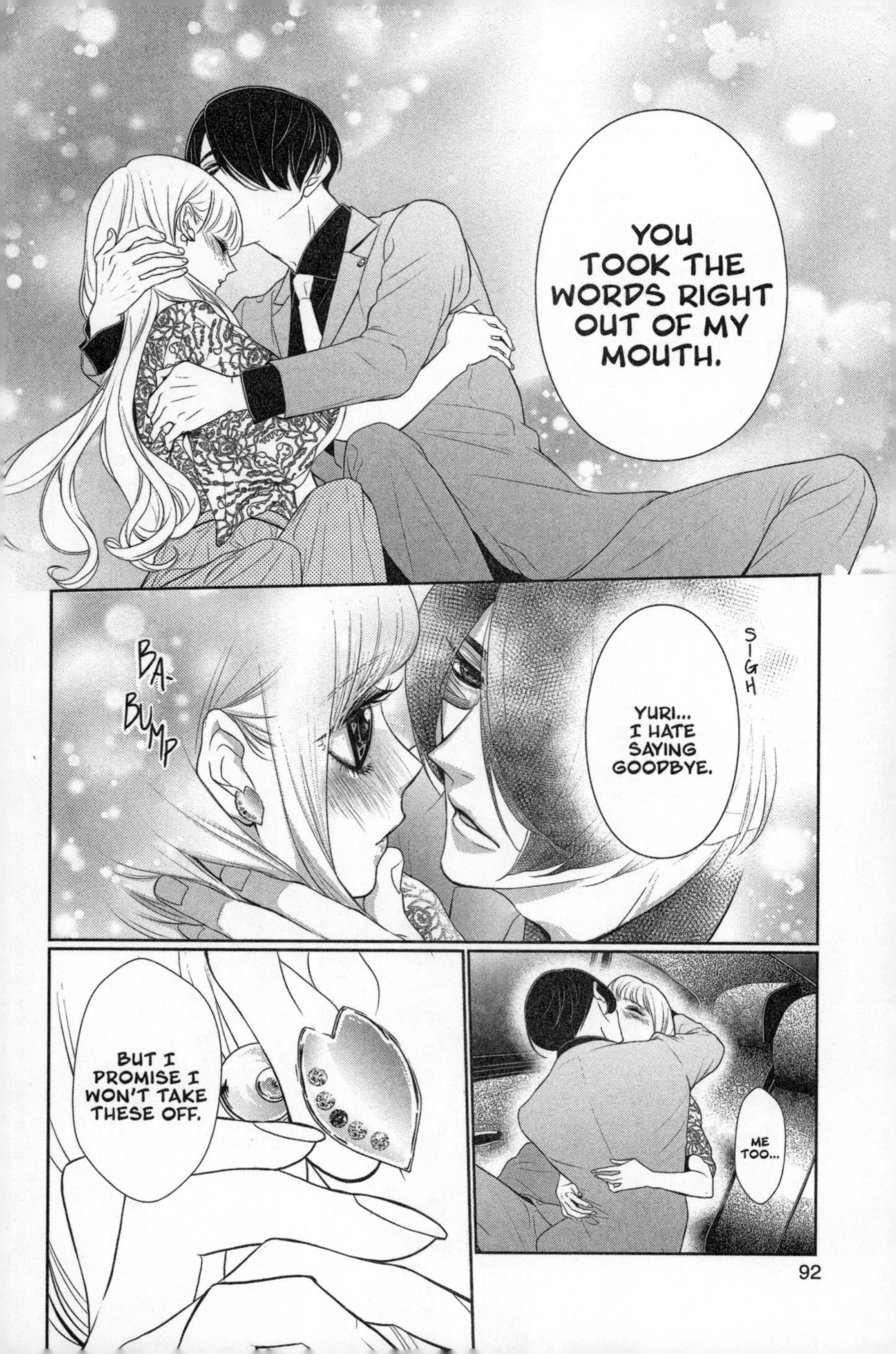
YOU TOOK THE WORDS RIGHT OUT OF MY MOUTH.
SIGH
YURI... I HATE SAYING GOODBYE.
BA-BUMP
ME TOO...
BUT I PROMISE I WON'T TAKE THESE OFF.

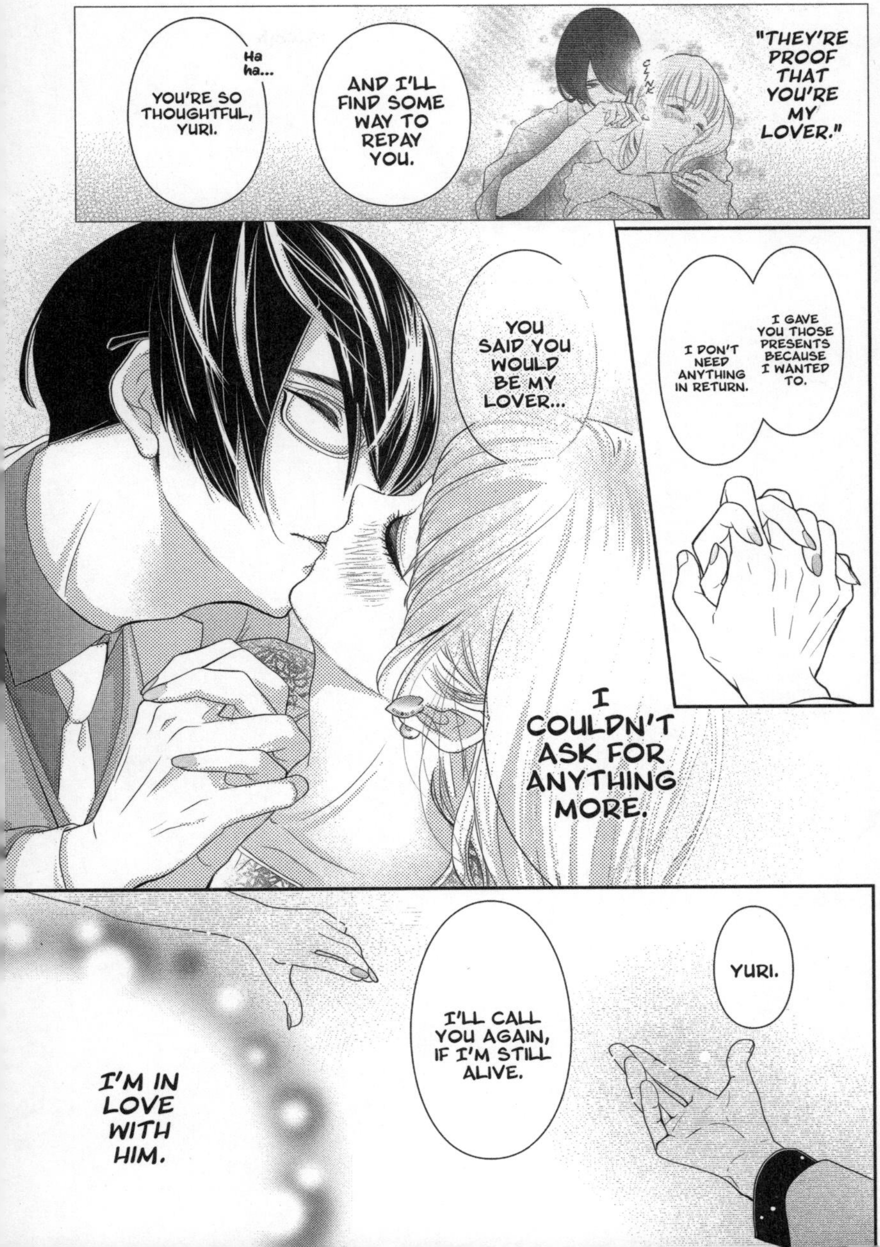
"THEY'RE PROOF THAT YOU'RE MY LOVER."
CLINK
AND I'LL FIND SOME WAY TO REPAY YOU.
Ha ha...
YOU'RE SO THOUGHTFUL, YURI.
I GAVE YOU THOSE PRESENTS BECAUSE I WANTED TO.
I DON'T NEED ANYTHING IN RETURN.
YOU SAID YOU WOULD BE MY LOVER...
I COULDN'T ASK FOR ANYTHING MORE.
YURI.
I'LL CALL YOU AGAIN, IF I'M STILL ALIVE.
I'M IN LOVE WITH HIM.

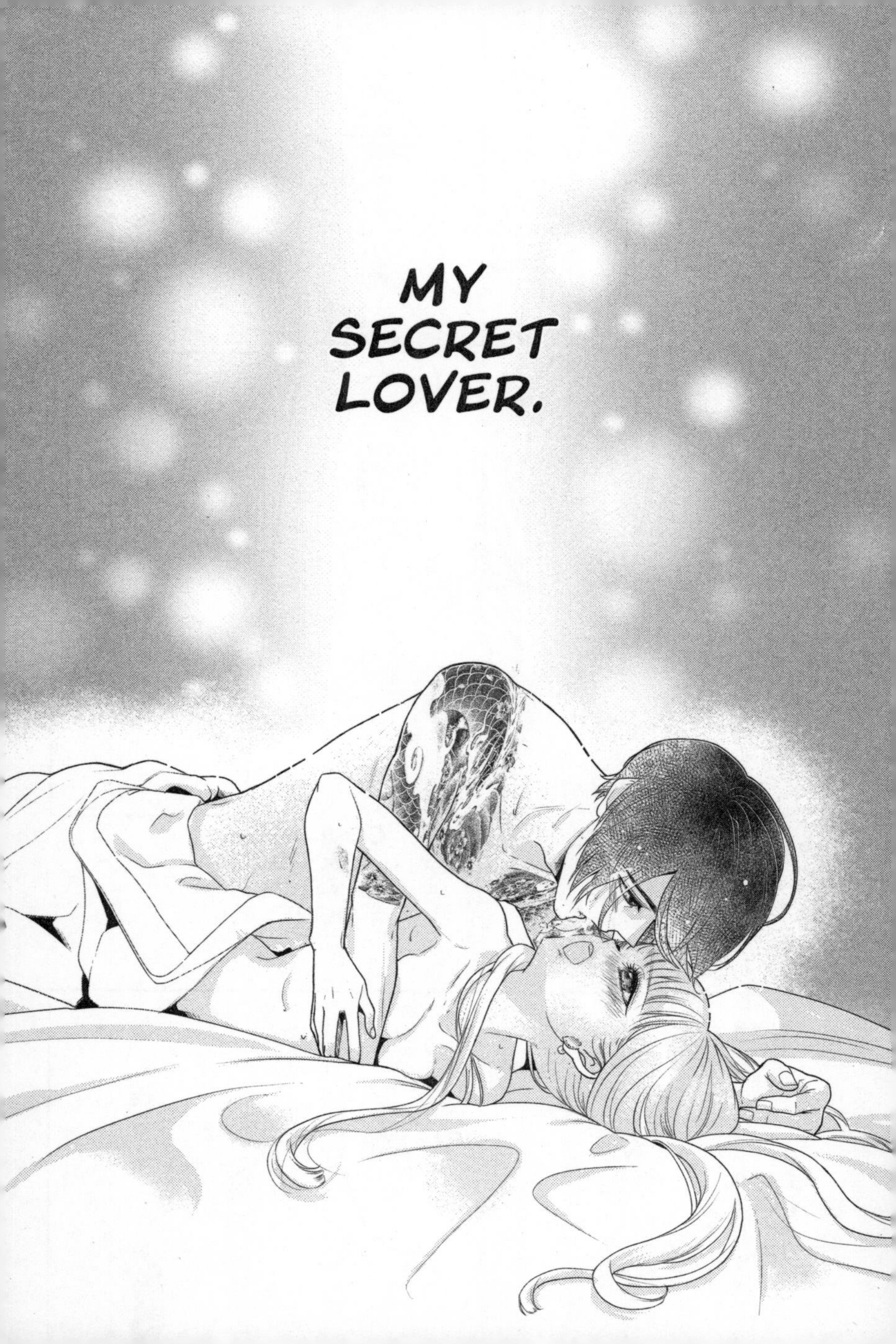
MY SECRET LOVER.

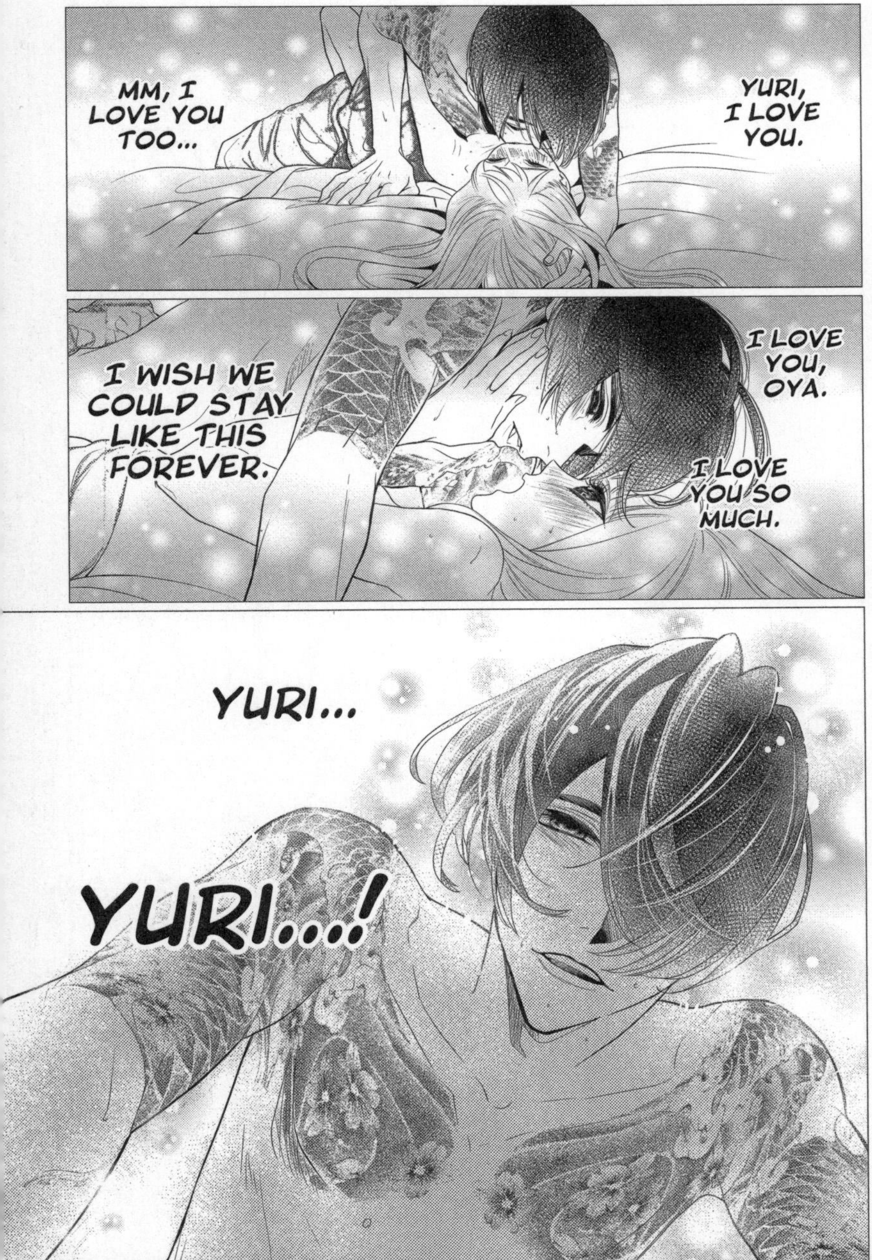
YURI, I LOVE YOU.
MM, I LOVE YOU TOO...
I LOVE YOU, OYA.
I LOVE YOU SO MUCH.
I WISH WE COULD STAY LIKE THIS FOREVER.
YURI...
YURI...!

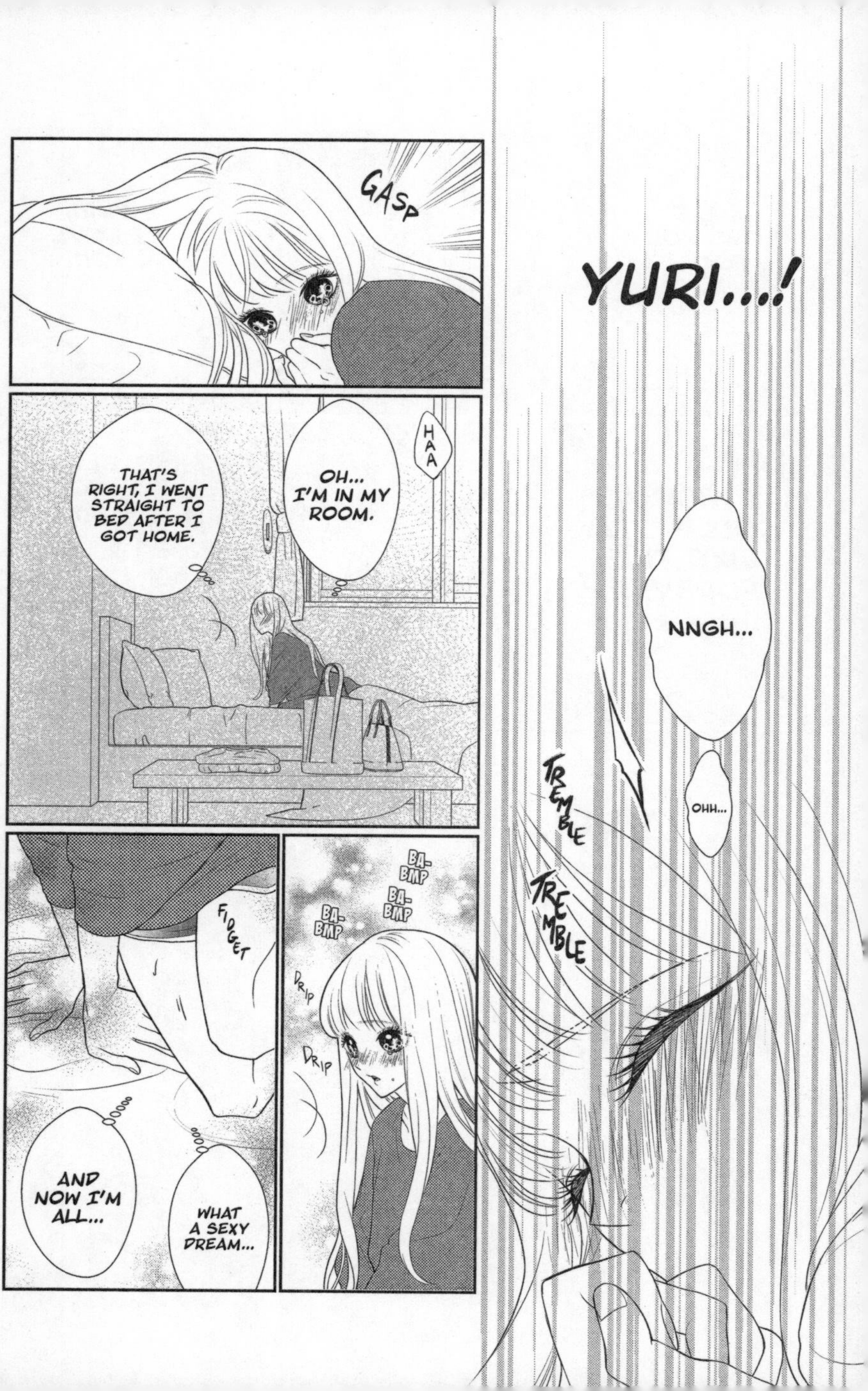
YURI...!
NNGH...
OHH...
TREMBLE
TREMBLE
GASP
HAA
OH... I'M IN MY ROOM.
THAT'S RIGHT, I WENT STRAIGHT TO BED AFTER I GOT HOME.
BA-BMP
BA-BMP
BA-BMP
DRIP
DRIP
FIDGET
WHAT A SEXY DREAM...
AND NOW I'M ALL...

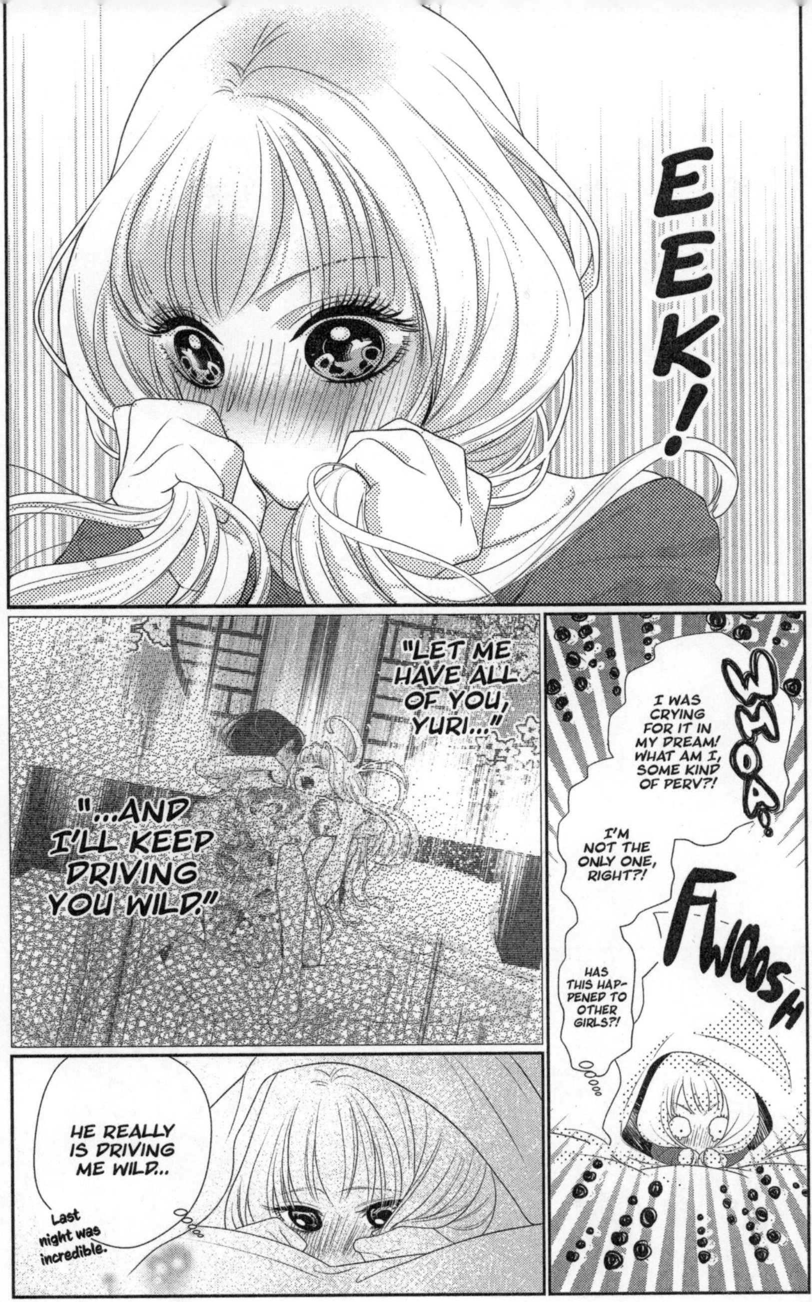
EEEK!
WHOA
I WAS CRYING FOR IT IN MY DREAM! WHAT AM I, SOME KIND OF PERV?!
I'M NOT THE ONLY ONE, RIGHT?!
FWOOSH
HAS THIS HAPPENED TO OTHER GIRLS?!
"LET ME HAVE ALL OF YOU, YURI..."
"...AND I'LL KEEP DRIVING YOU WILD."
HE REALLY IS DRIVING ME WILD...
Last night was incredible.

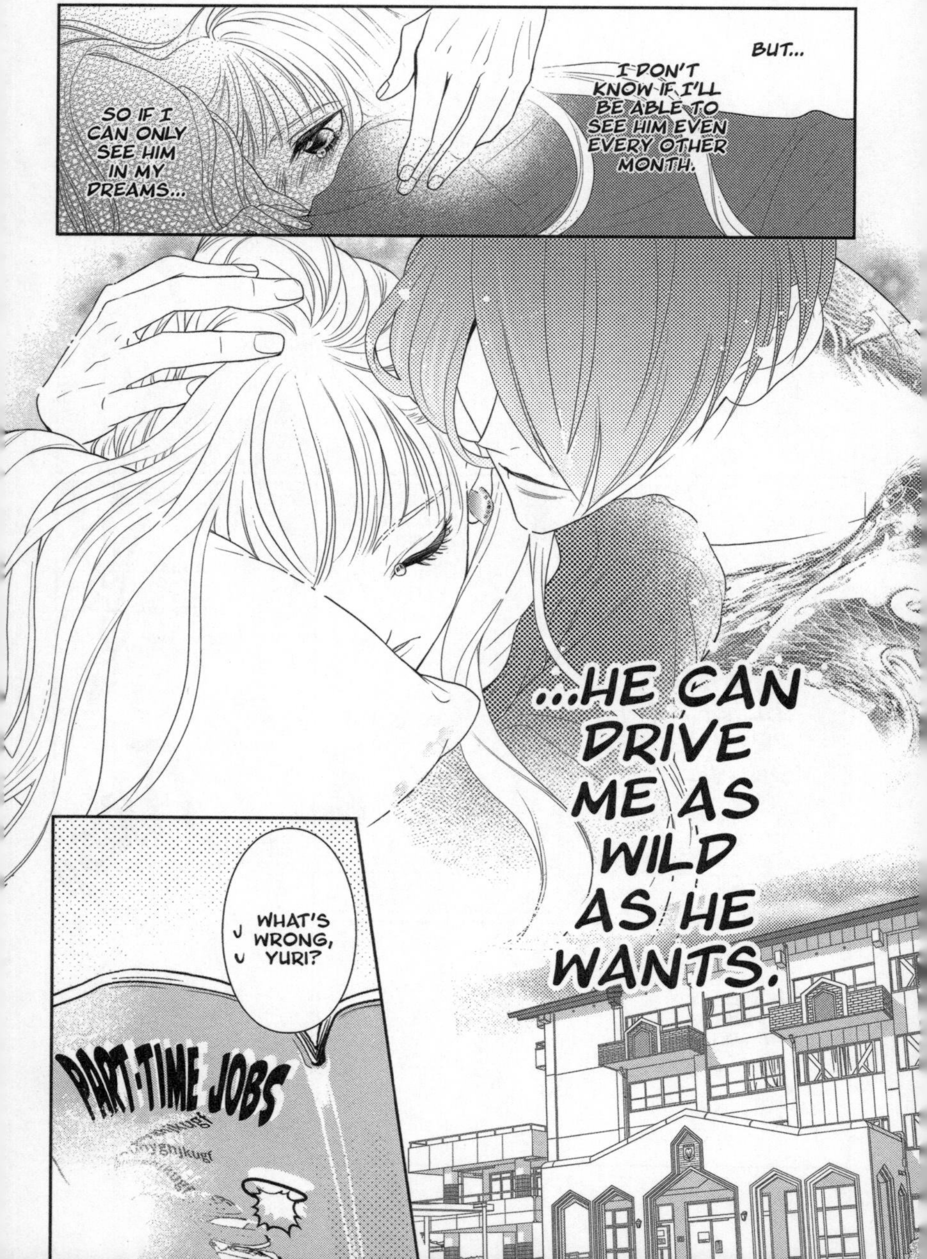
BUT...
I DON'T KNOW IF I'LL BE ABLE TO SEE HIM EVEN EVERY OTHER MONTH.
SO IF I CAN ONLY SEE HIM IN MY DREAMS...
...HE CAN DRIVE ME AS WILD AS HE WANTS.
WHAT'S WRONG, YURI?
PART-TIME JOBS

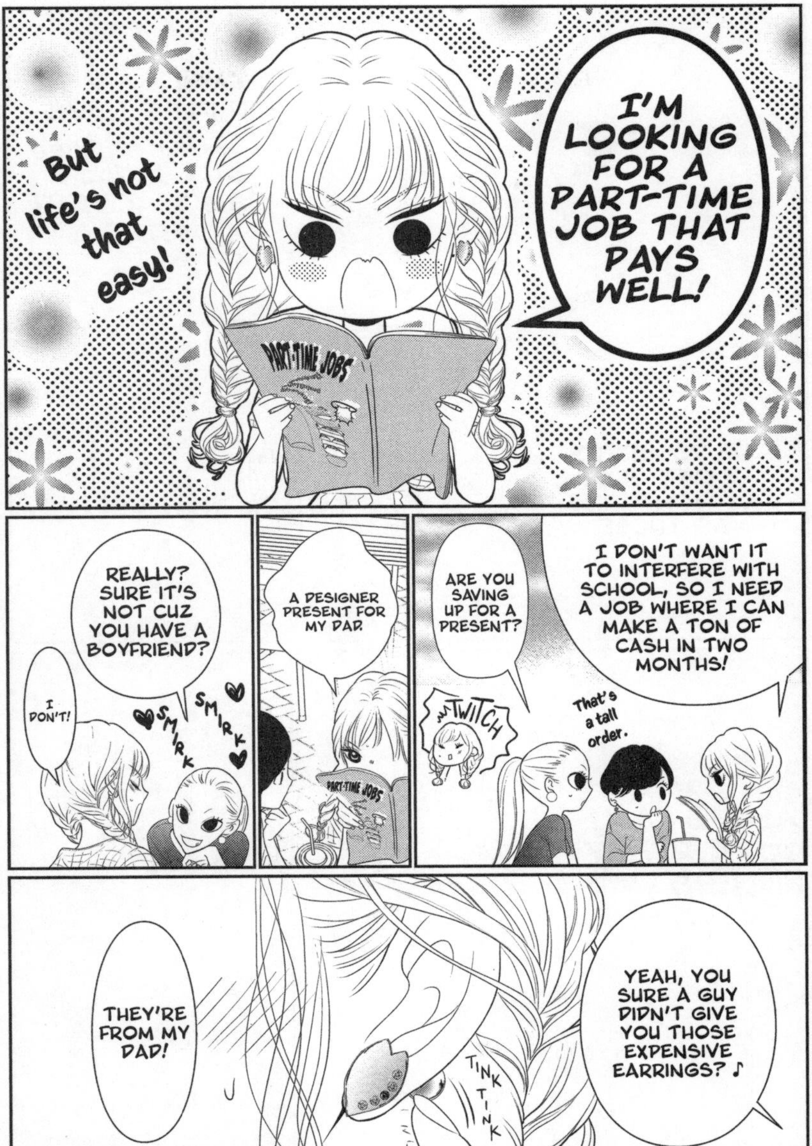
I'M LOOKING FOR A PART-TIME JOB THAT PAYS WELL!
But life's not that easy!
PART-TIME JOBS
I DON'T WANT IT TO INTERFERE WITH SCHOOL, SO I NEED A JOB WHERE I CAN MAKE A TON OF CASH IN TWO MONTHS!
That's a tall order.
ARE YOU SAVING UP FOR A PRESENT?
TWITCH
A DESIGNER PRESENT FOR MY DAD.
PART-TIME JOBS
REALLY? SURE IT'S NOT CUZ YOU HAVE A BOYFRIEND?
SMIRK
SMIRK
I DON'T!
YEAH, YOU SURE A GUY DIDN'T GIVE YOU THOSE EXPENSIVE EARRINGS? ♪
TINK
TINK
THEY'RE FROM MY DAD!

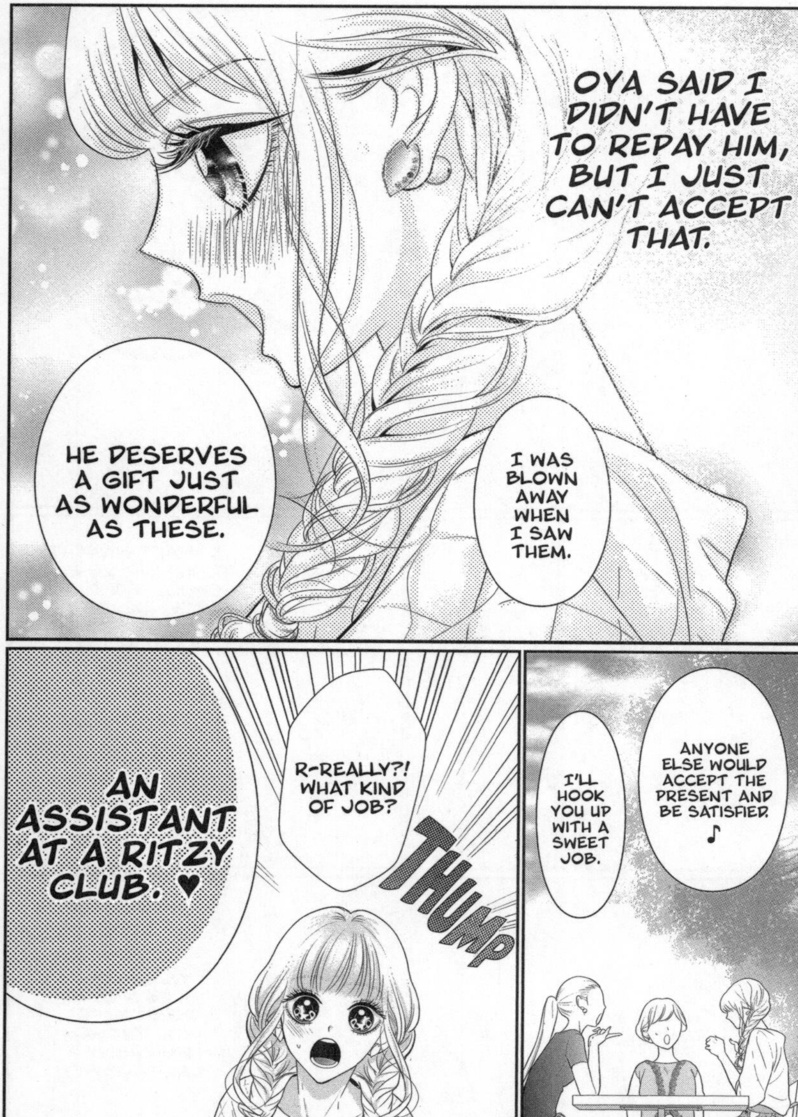
OYA SAID I DIDN'T HAVE TO REPAY HIM, BUT I JUST CAN'T ACCEPT THAT.
I WAS BLOWN AWAY WHEN I SAW THEM.
HE DESERVES A GIFT JUST AS WONDERFUL AS THESE.
ANYONE ELSE WOULD ACCEPT THE PRESENT AND BE SATISFIED. ♪
I'LL HOOK YOU UP WITH A SWEET JOB.
R-REALLY?! WHAT KIND OF JOB?
THUMP
AN ASSISTANT AT A RITZY CLUB. ♥

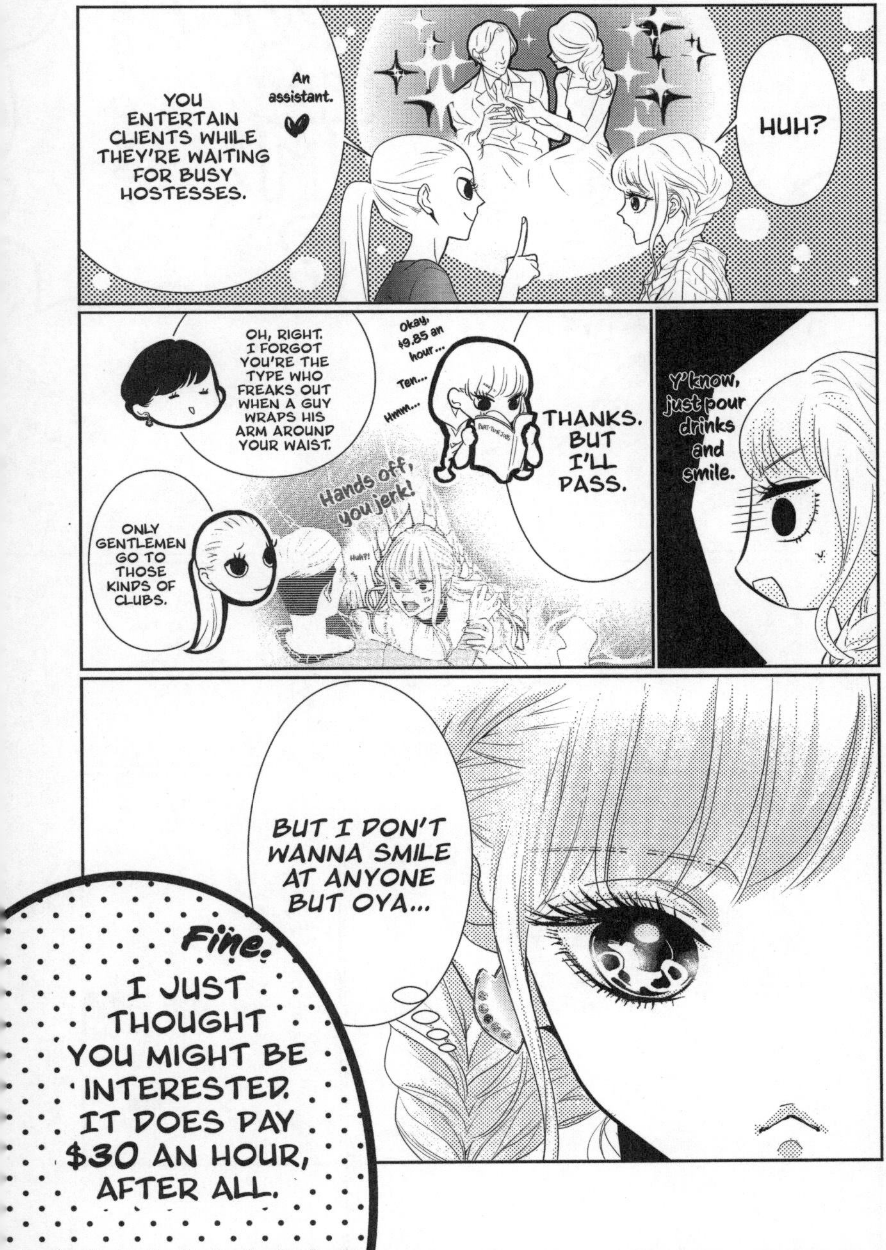
An assistant.
YOU ENTERTAIN CLIENTS WHILE THEY'RE WAITING FOR BUSY HOSTESSES.
HUH?
Y'know, just pour drinks and smile.
THANKS. BUT I'LL PASS.
Okay, $9.85 an hour...
Ten...
Hmm...
PART-TIME JOBS
OH, RIGHT. I FORGOT YOU'RE THE TYPE WHO FREAKS OUT WHEN A GUY WRAPS HIS ARM AROUND YOUR WAIST.
Hands off, you jerk!
Huh?!
ONLY GENTLEMEN GO TO THOSE KINDS OF CLUBS.
BUT I DON'T WANNA SMILE AT ANYONE BUT OYA...
Fine. I JUST THOUGHT YOU MIGHT BE INTERESTED. IT DOES PAY $30 AN HOUR, AFTER ALL.

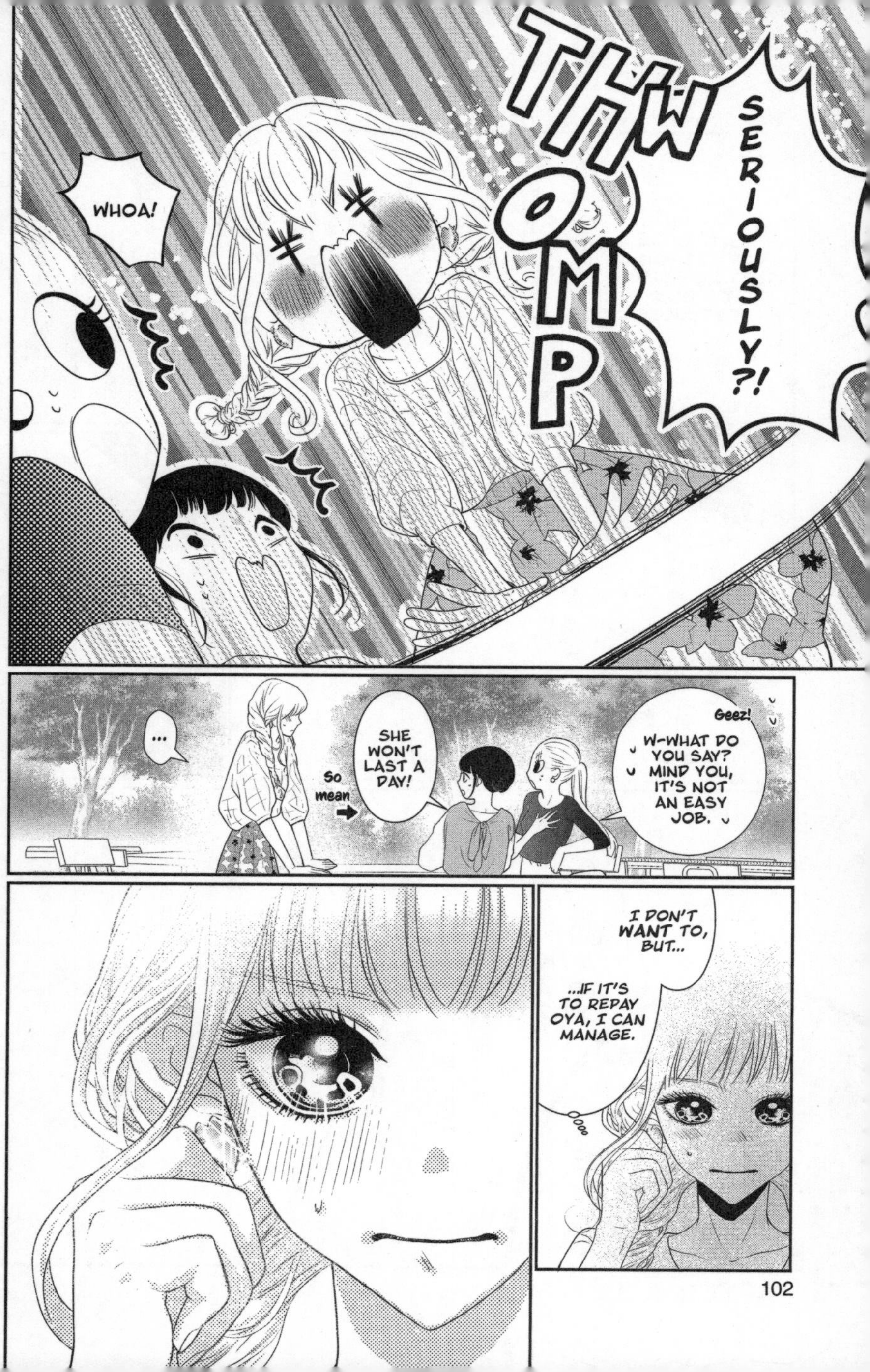
THWOMP
SERIOUSLY?!
WHOA!
Geez!
W-WHAT DO YOU SAY? MIND YOU, IT'S NOT AN EASY JOB.
SHE WON'T LAST A DAY!
So mean
...
I DON'T WANT TO, BUT...
...IF IT'S TO REPAY OYA, I CAN MANAGE.

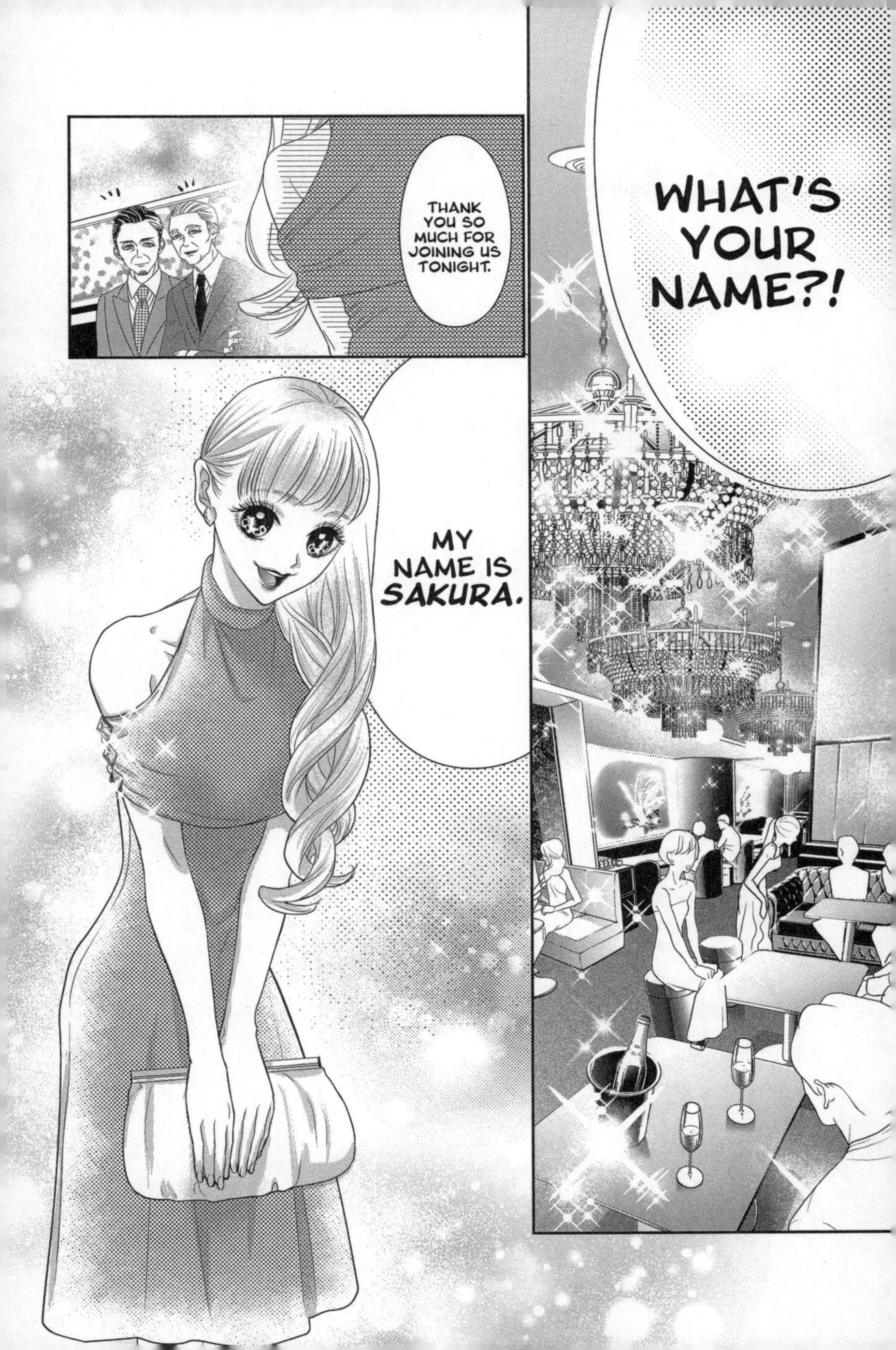
WHAT'S YOUR NAME?!
THANK YOU SO MUCH FOR JOINING US TONIGHT.
MY NAME IS SAKURA.

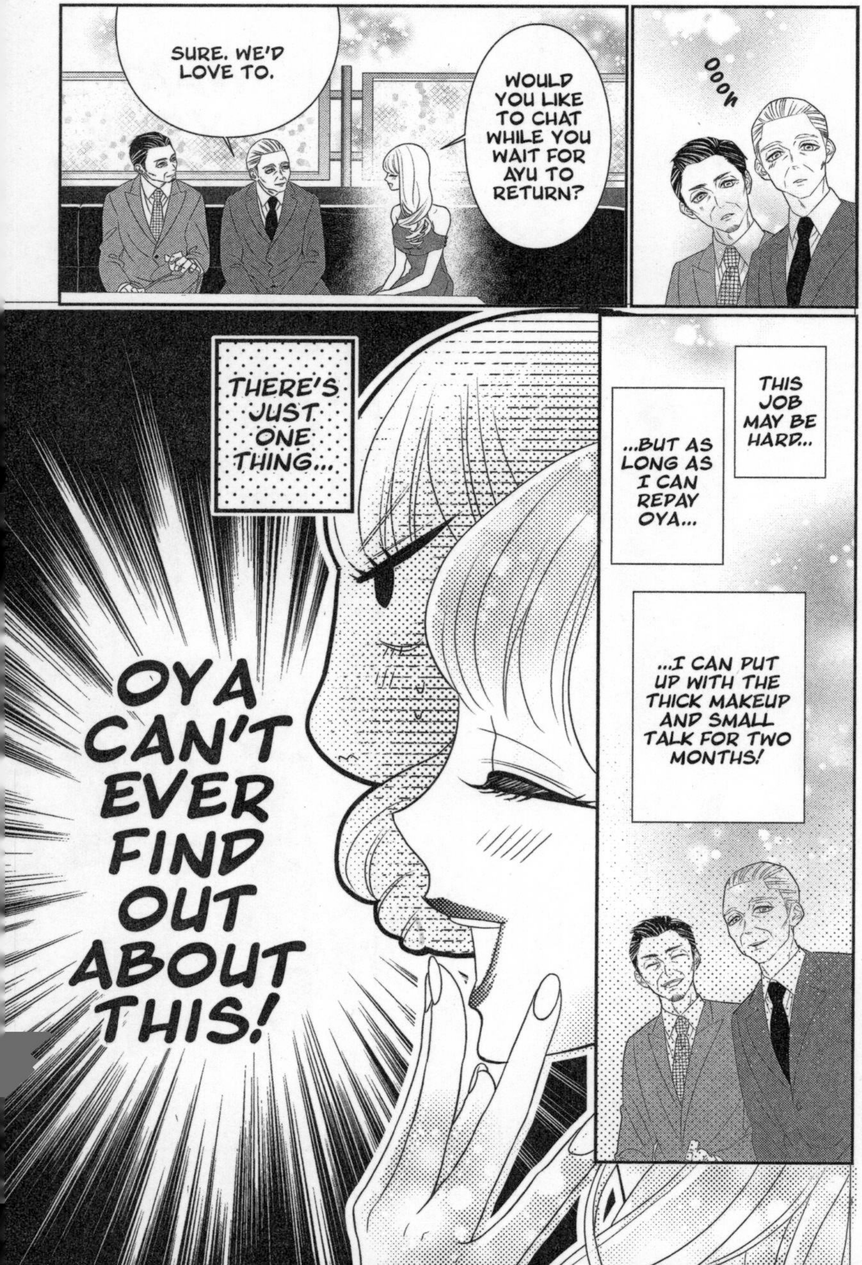

OOOH
WOULD YOU LIKE TO CHAT WHILE YOU WAIT FOR AYU TO RETURN?
SURE. WE'D LOVE TO.
THIS JOB MAY BE HARD...
...BUT AS LONG AS I CAN REPAY OYA...
...I CAN PUT UP WITH THE THICK MAKEUP AND SMALL TALK FOR TWO MONTHS!
THERE'S JUST ONE THING...
OYA CAN'T EVER FIND OUT ABOUT THIS!

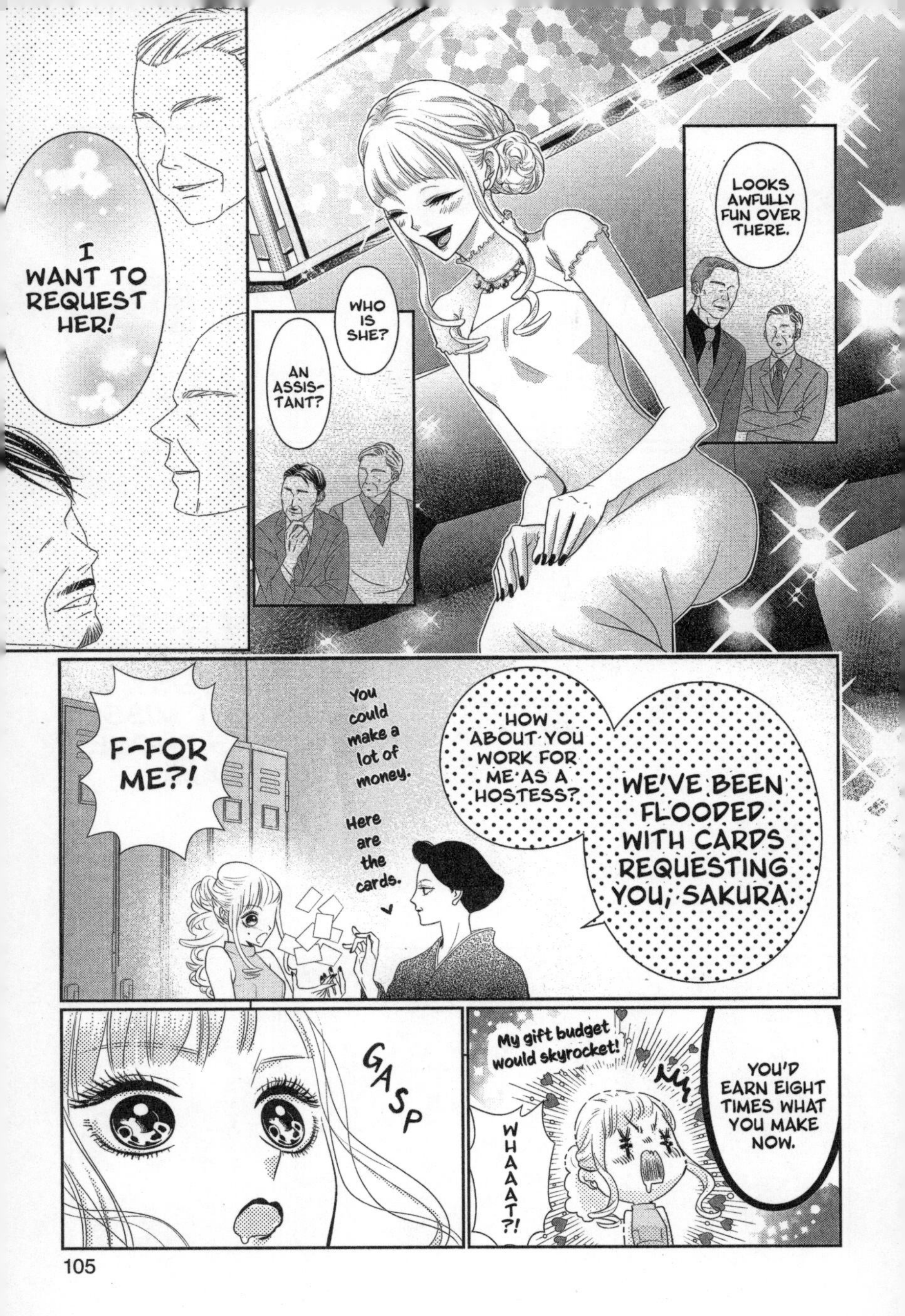
LOOKS AWFULLY FUN OVER THERE.
WHO IS SHE?
AN ASSISTANT?
I WANT TO REQUEST HER!
WE'VE BEEN FLOODED WITH CARDS REQUESTING YOU, SAKURA.
HOW ABOUT YOU WORK FOR ME AS A HOSTESS?
You could make a lot of money.
Here are the cards.
F-FOR ME?!
YOU'D EARN EIGHT TIMES WHAT YOU MAKE NOW.
WHAAAAT?!
My gift budget would skyrocket!
GASP

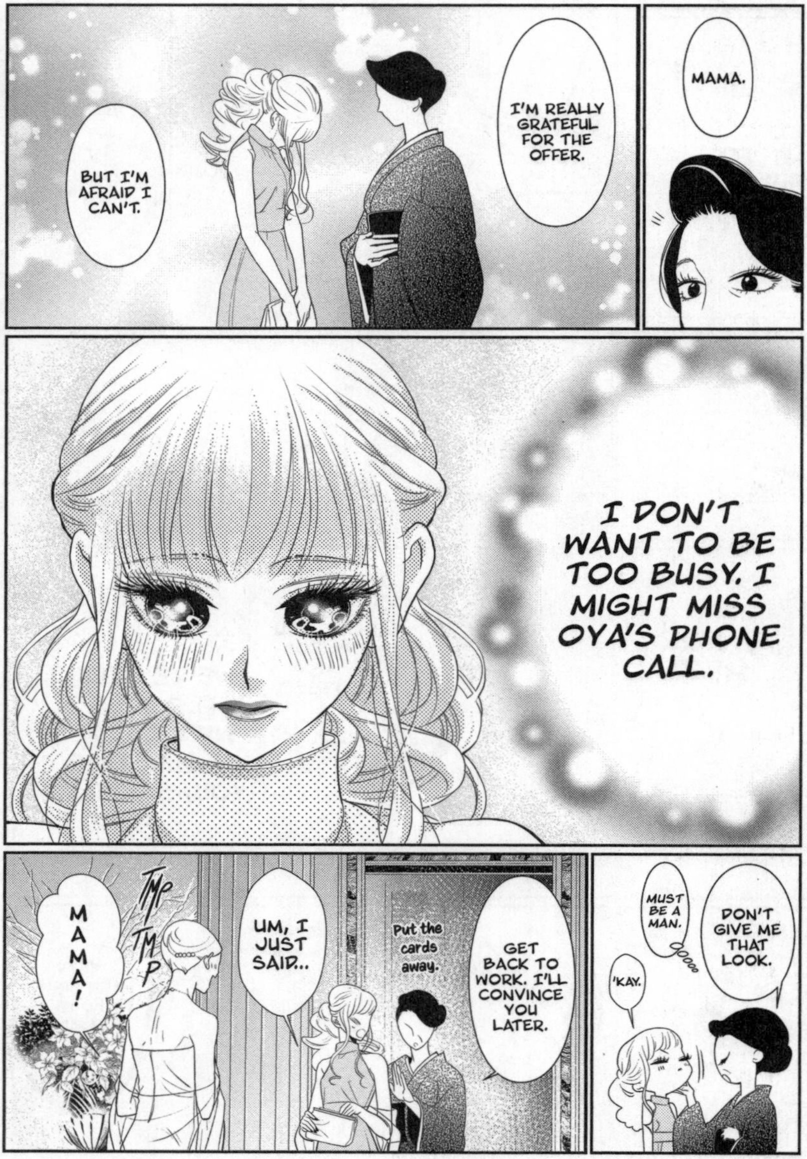
MAMA.
I'M REALLY GRATEFUL FOR THE OFFER.
BUT I'M AFRAID I CAN'T.
I DON'T WANT TO BE TOO BUSY. I MIGHT MISS OYA'S PHONE CALL.
DON'T GIVE ME THAT LOOK.
MUST BE A MAN.
'KAY.
GET BACK TO WORK. I'LL CONVINCE YOU LATER.
Put the cards away.
UM, I JUST SAID...
TMP TMP
MAMA!

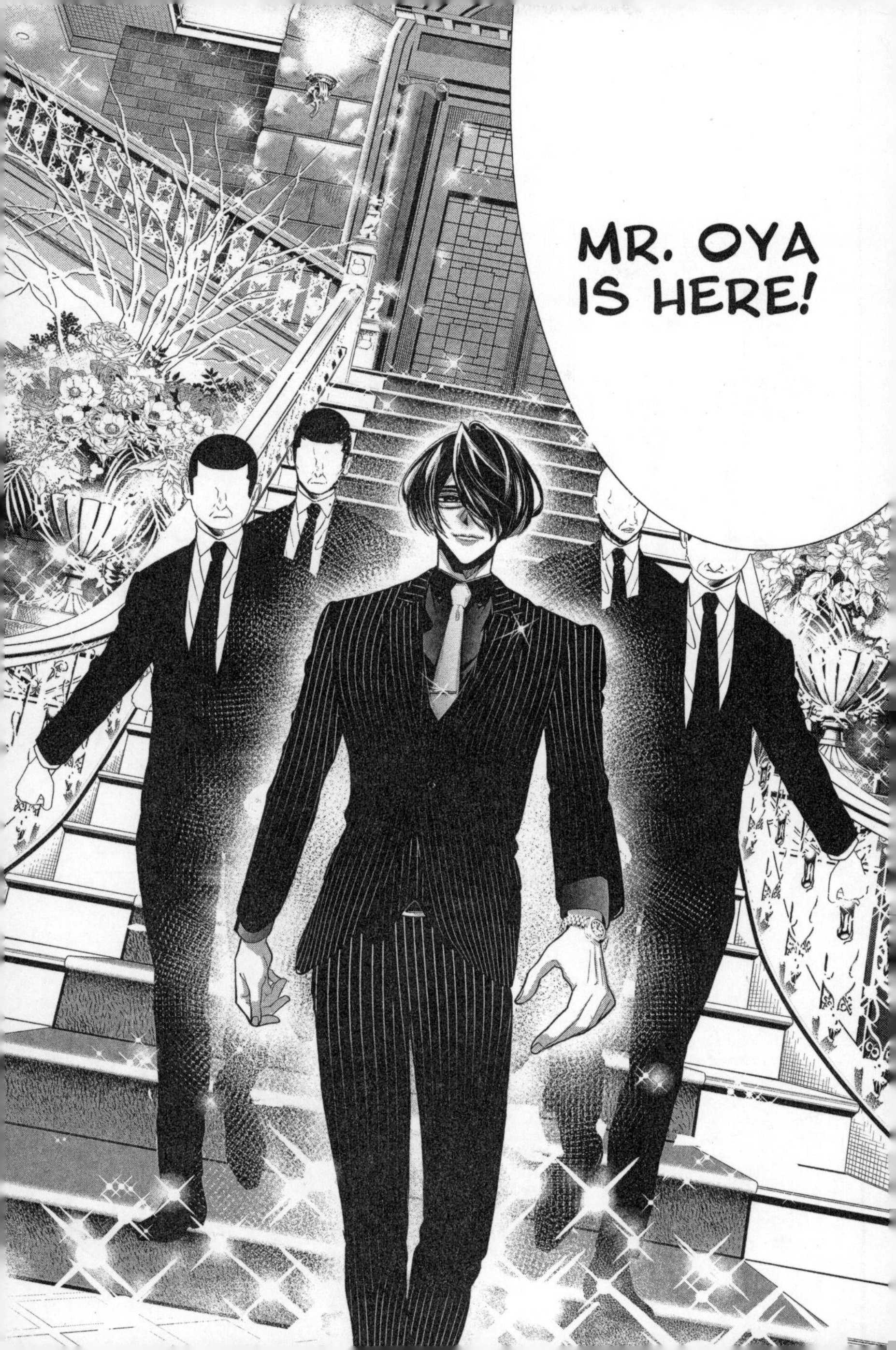
MR. OYA IS HERE!

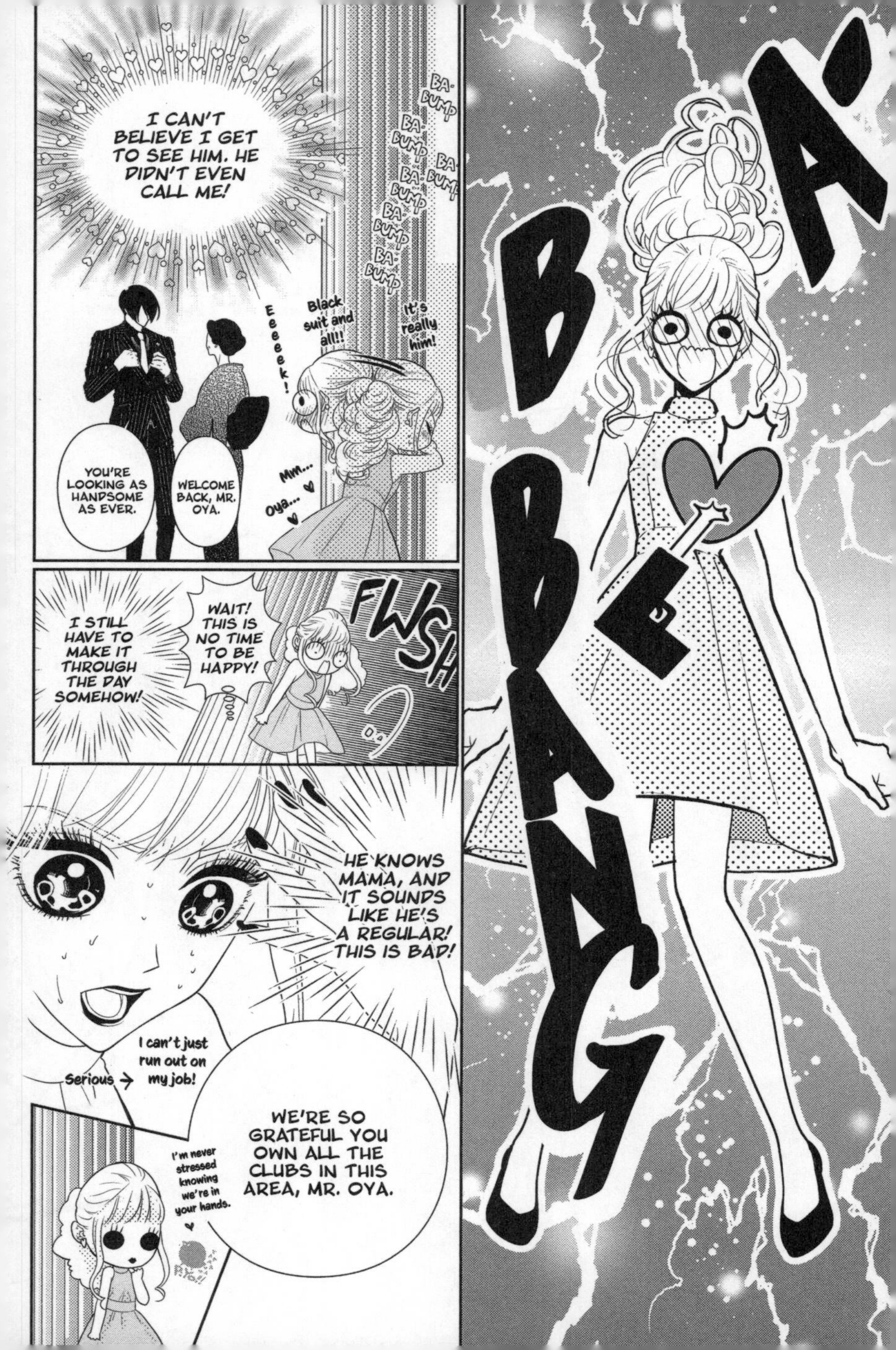
BA
BANG
BA-BUMP BA-BUMP BA-BUMP BA-BUMP BA-BUMP BA-BUMP
I CAN'T BELIEVE I GET TO SEE HIM. HE DIDN'T EVEN CALL ME!
It's really him!
Black suit and all!!
Eeeeeek!
Mm... Oya...
WELCOME BACK, MR. OYA.
YOU'RE LOOKING AS HANDSOME AS EVER.
FWSH
WAIT! THIS IS NO TIME TO BE HAPPY!
I STILL HAVE TO MAKE IT THROUGH THE DAY SOMEHOW!
HE KNOWS MAMA, AND IT SOUNDS LIKE HE'S A REGULAR! THIS IS BAD!
I can't just run out on my job!
Serious →
WE'RE SO GRATEFUL YOU OWN ALL THE CLUBS IN THIS AREA, MR. OYA.
I'm never stressed knowing we're in your hands.

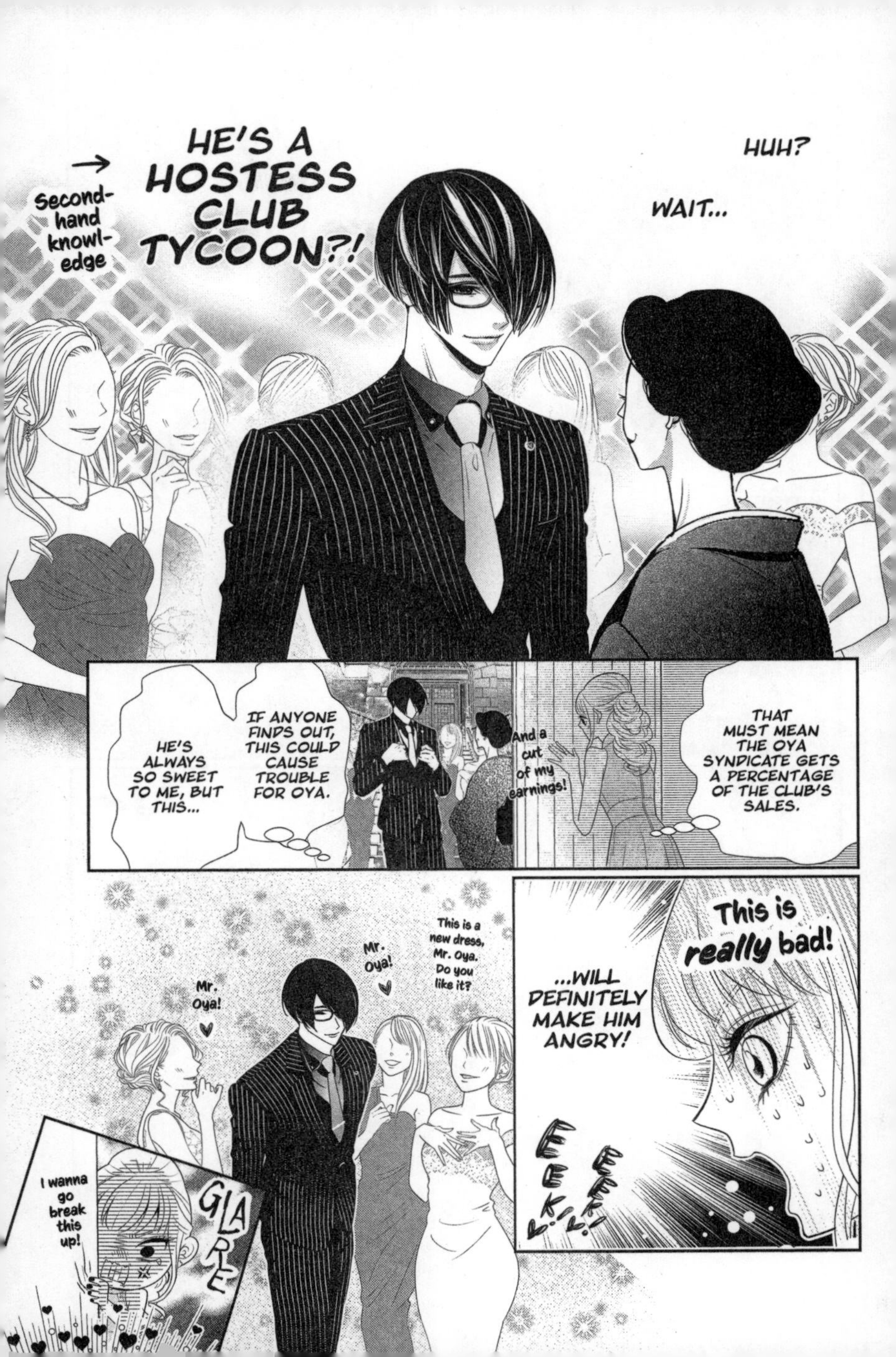
HUH?
WAIT...
HE'S A HOSTESS CLUB TYCOON?!
Second-hand knowl-edge
THAT MUST MEAN THE OYA SYNDICATE GETS A PERCENTAGE OF THE CLUB'S SALES.
And a cut of my earnings!
IF ANYONE FINDS OUT, THIS COULD CAUSE TROUBLE FOR OYA.
HE'S ALWAYS SO SWEET TO ME, BUT THIS...
This is really bad!
...WILL DEFINITELY MAKE HIM ANGRY!
EEK! EEK!
This is a new dress, Mr. Oya. Do you like it?
Mr. Oya!
Mr. Oya!
GLARE
I wanna go break this up!

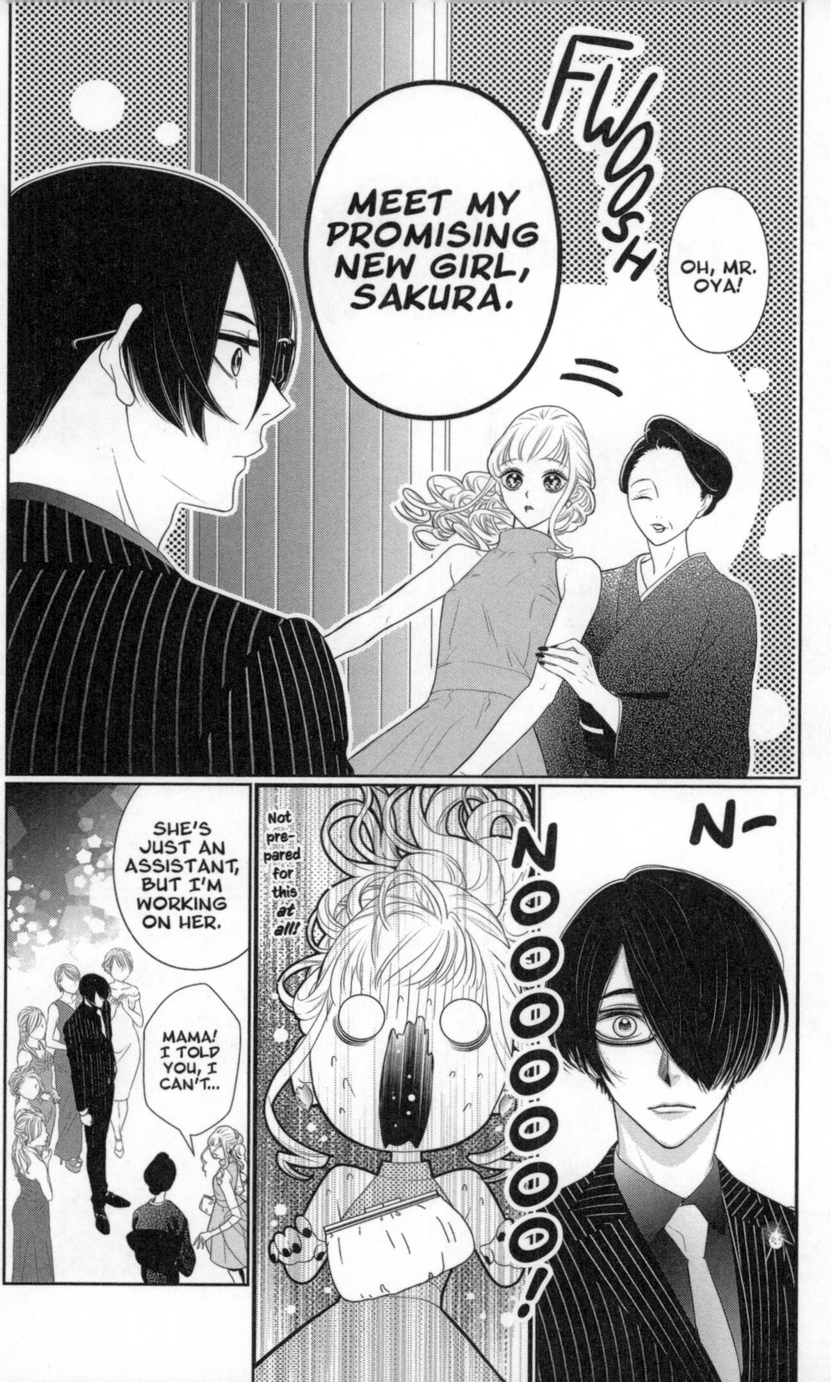
FWOOSH
OH, MR. OYA!
MEET MY PROMISING NEW GIRL, SAKURA.
N-
NOOOOOOOOOOO!
Not prepared for this at all!
SHE'S JUST AN ASSISTANT, BUT I'M WORKING ON HER.
MAMA! I TOLD YOU, I CAN'T...

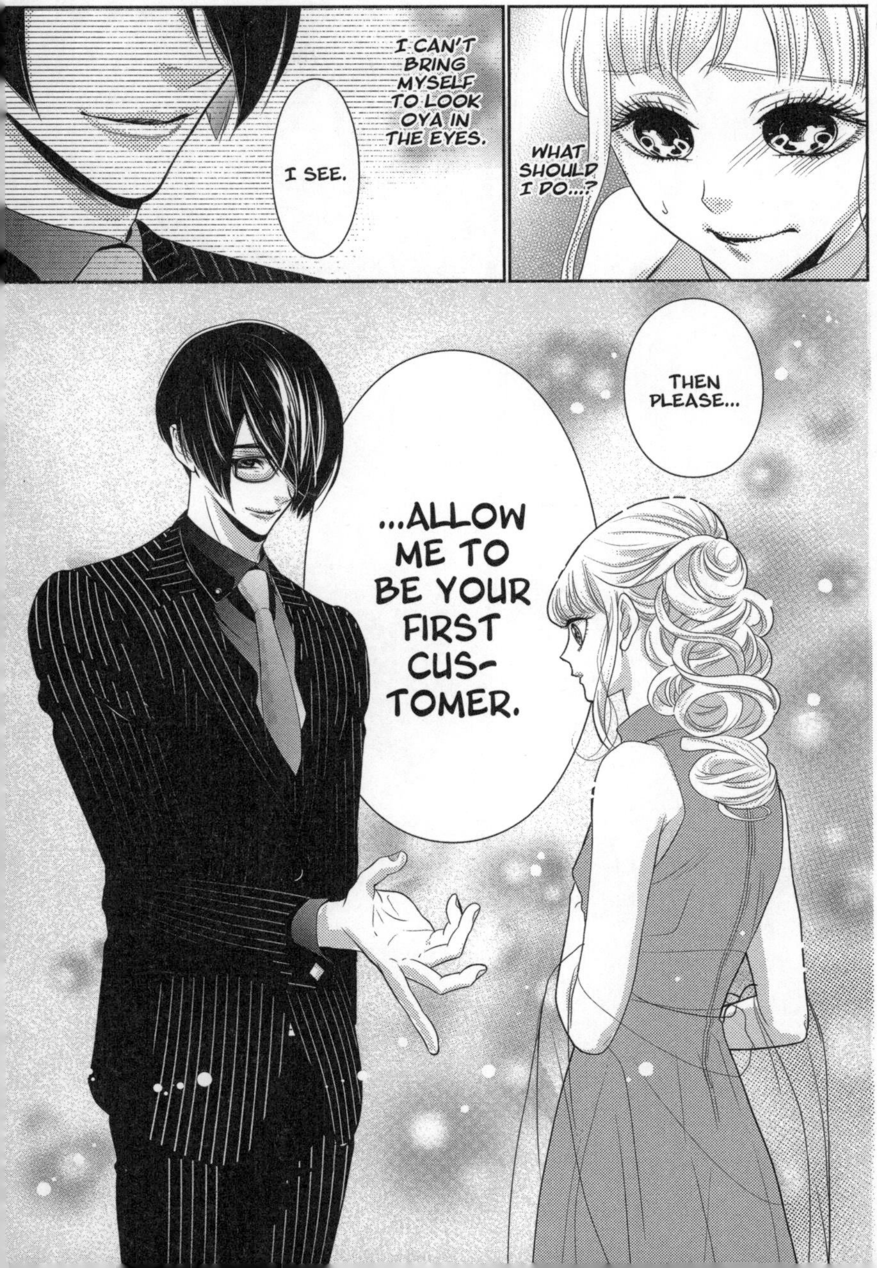
WHAT SHOULD I DO...?
I CAN'T BRING MYSELF TO LOOK OYA IN THE EYES.
I SEE.
THEN PLEASE...
...ALLOW ME TO BE YOUR FIRST CUS-TOMER.

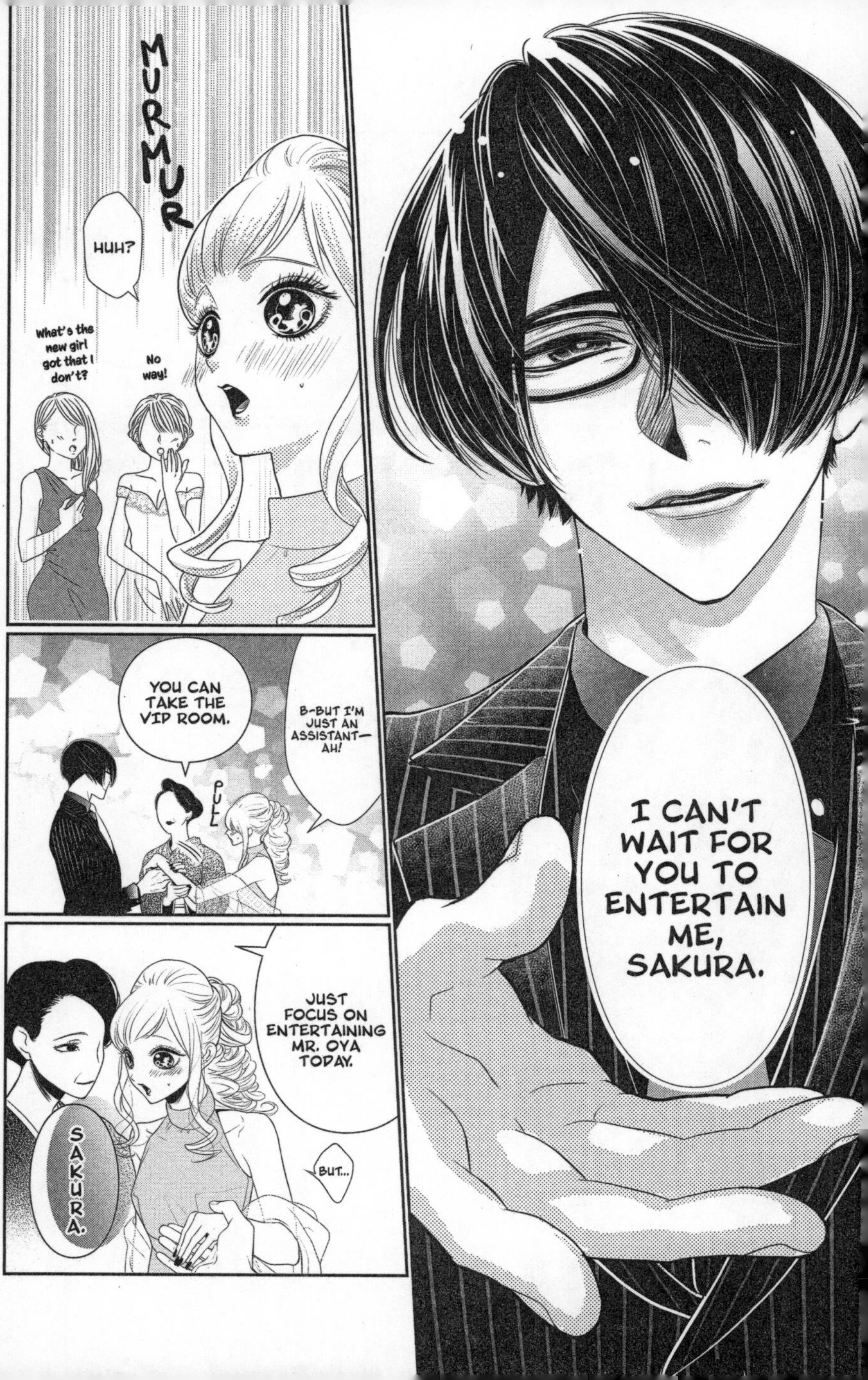
I CAN'T WAIT FOR YOU TO ENTERTAIN ME, SAKURA.
MURMUR
HUH?
No way!
What's the new girl got that I don't?
B-BUT I'M JUST AN ASSISTANT—AH!
PULL
YOU CAN TAKE THE VIP ROOM.
JUST FOCUS ON ENTERTAINING MR. OYA TODAY.
BUT...
SAKURA.

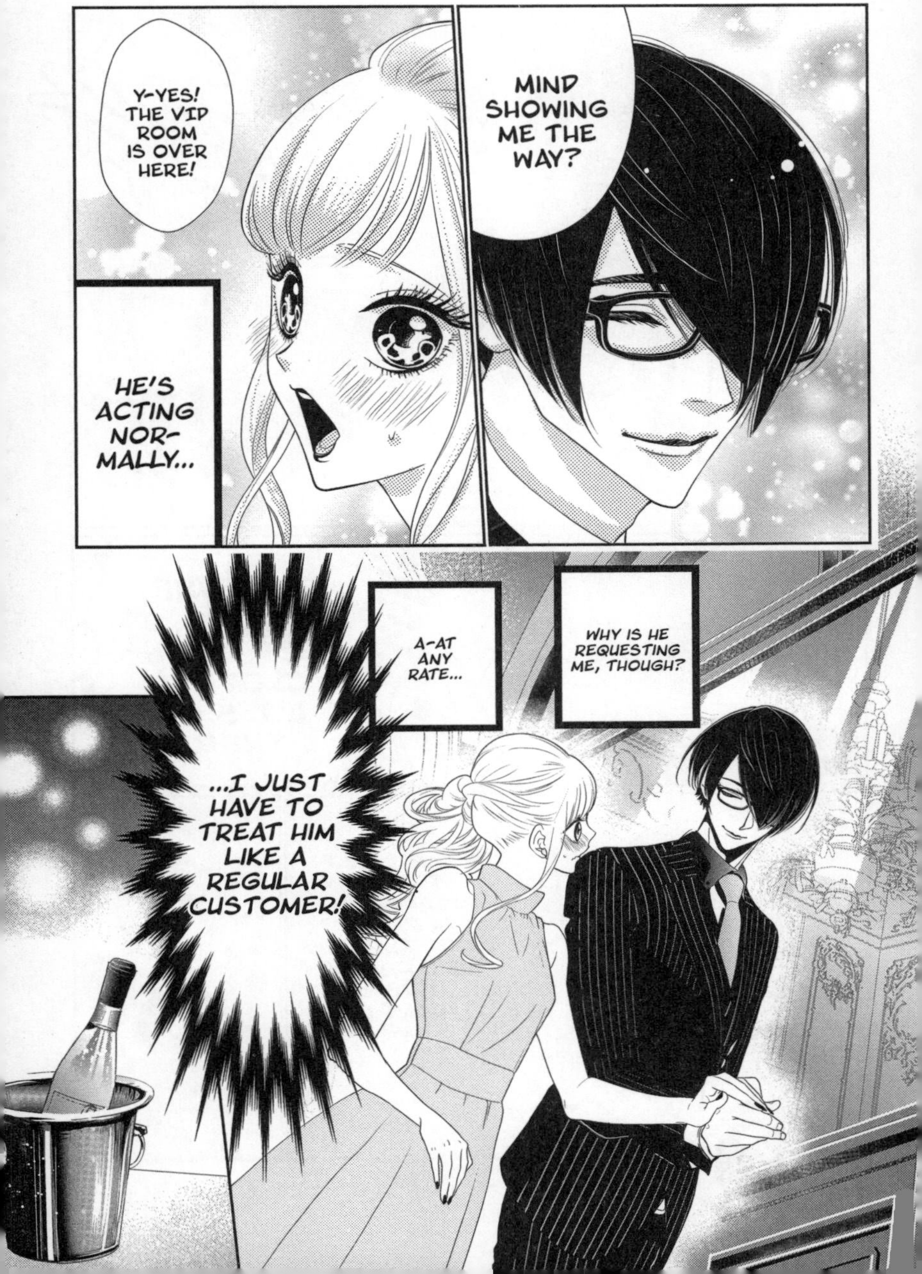
MIND SHOWING ME THE WAY?
Y-YES! THE VIP ROOM IS OVER HERE!
HE'S ACTING NOR-MALLY...
WHY IS HE REQUESTING ME, THOUGH?
A-AT ANY RATE...
...I JUST HAVE TO TREAT HIM LIKE A REGULAR CUSTOMER!

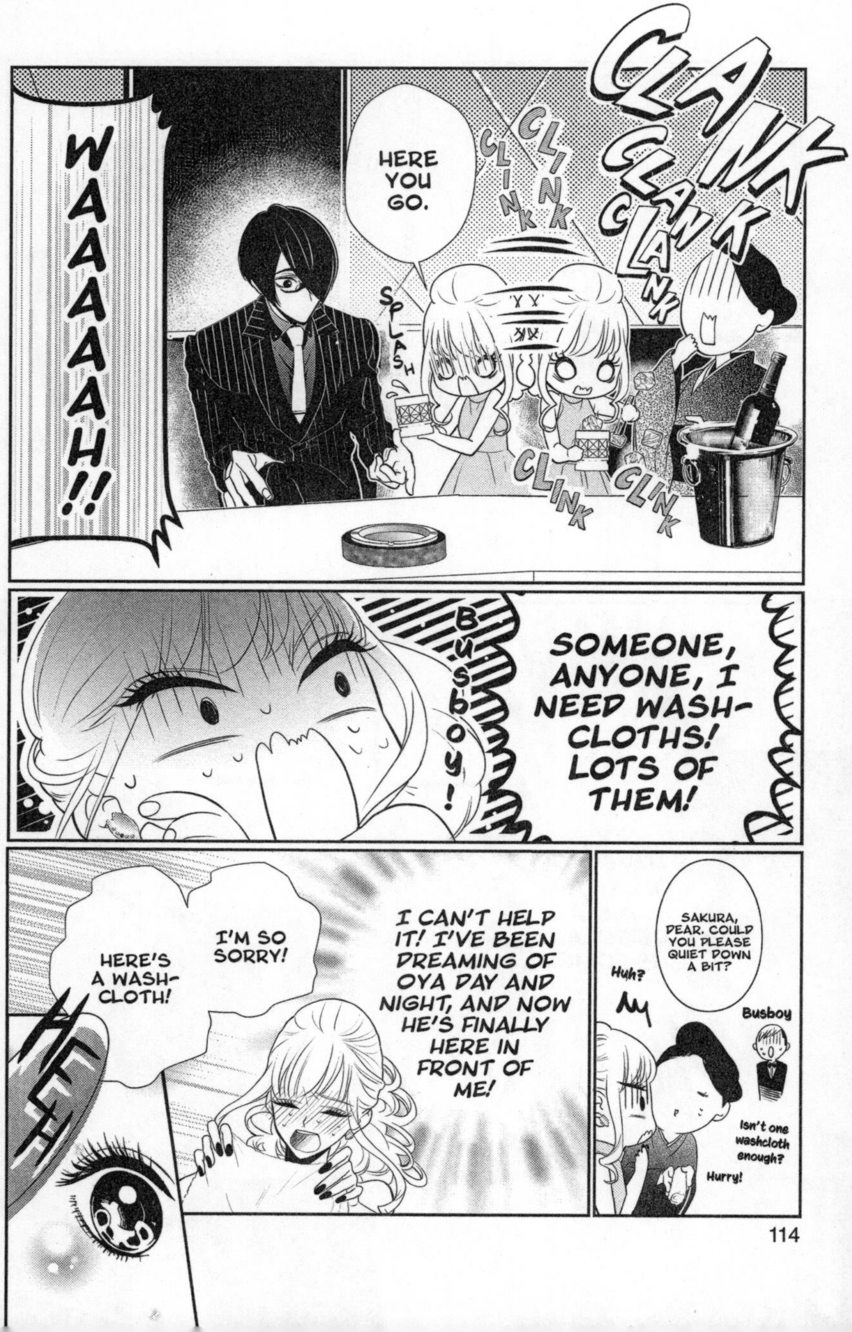
CLANK
CLANK
CLANK
CLANK
CLINK
CLINK
HERE YOU GO.
SPLASH
CLINK
CLINK
WAAAAAAAH!!
SOMEONE, ANYONE, I NEED WASH-CLOTHS! LOTS OF THEM!
Busboy!
SAKURA, DEAR. COULD YOU PLEASE QUIET DOWN A BIT?
Huh?
Busboy
Isn't one washcloth enough?
Hurry!
I CAN'T HELP IT! I'VE BEEN DREAMING OF OYA DAY AND NIGHT, AND NOW HE'S FINALLY HERE IN FRONT OF ME!
I'M SO SORRY!
HERE'S A WASH-CLOTH!
HEFT

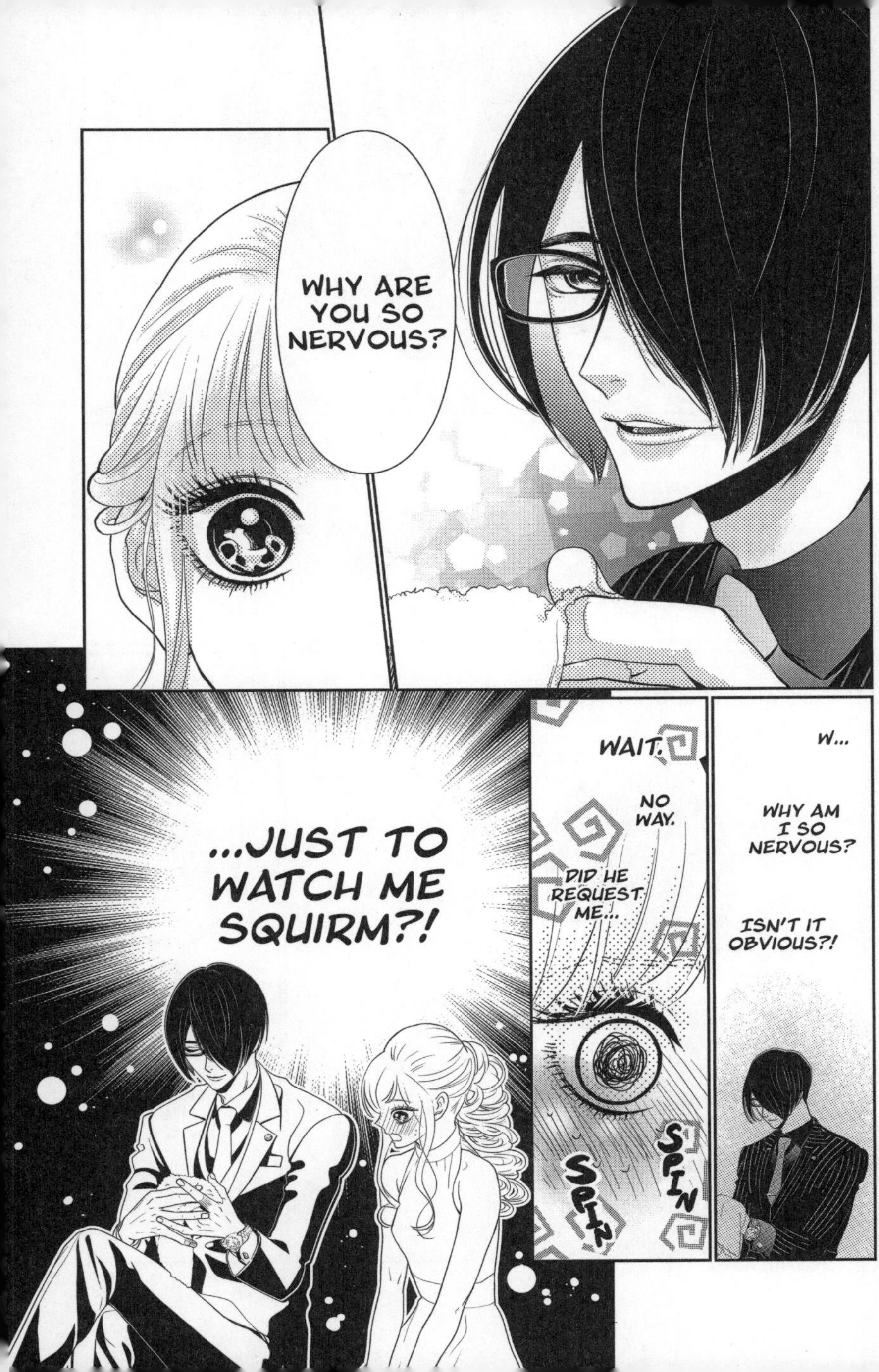
WHY ARE YOU SO NERVOUS?
W...
WHY AM I SO NERVOUS?
ISN'T IT OBVIOUS?!
WAIT.
NO WAY.
DID HE REQUEST ME...
SPIN
SPIN
SPIN
...JUST TO WATCH ME SQUIRM?!

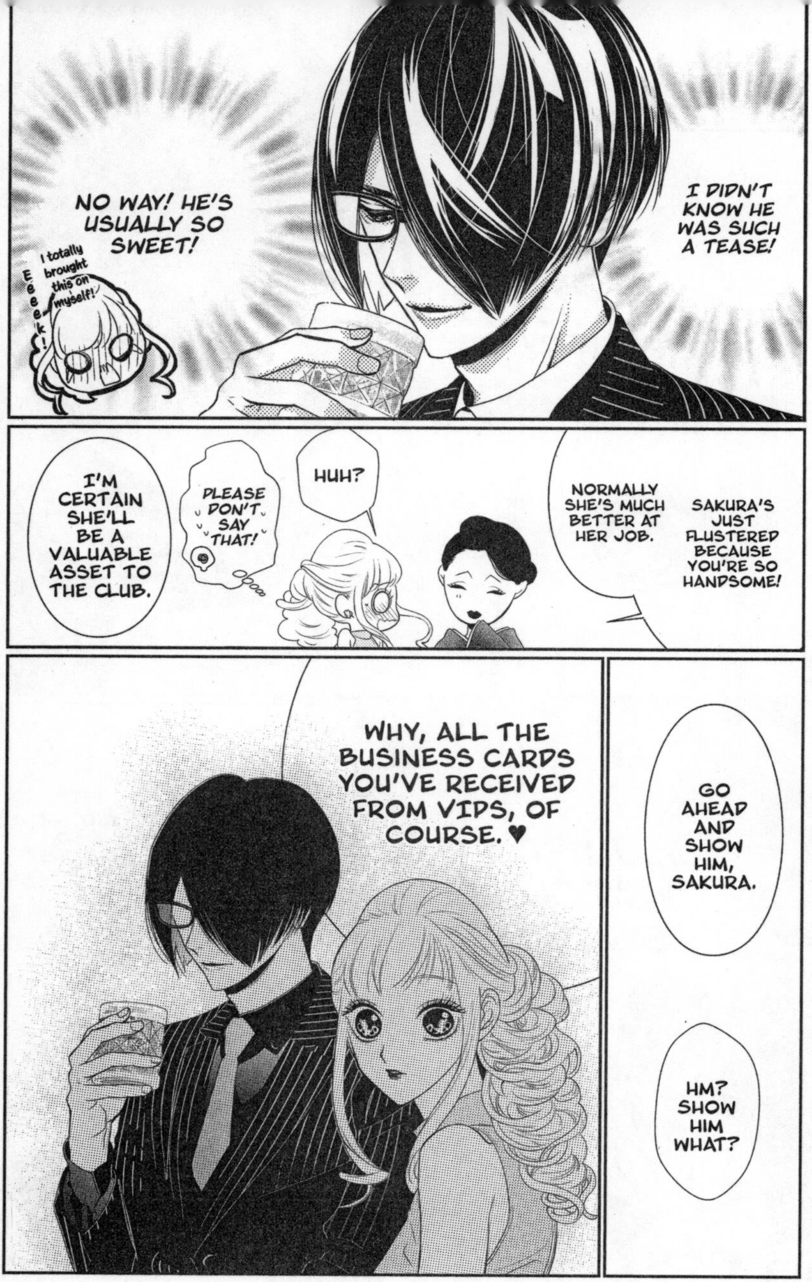
I DIDN'T KNOW HE WAS SUCH A TEASE!
NO WAY! HE'S USUALLY SO SWEET!
I totally brought this on myself!
Eeeek!
SAKURA'S JUST FLUSTERED BECAUSE YOU'RE SO HANDSOME!
NORMALLY SHE'S MUCH BETTER AT HER JOB.
HUH?
PLEASE DON'T SAY THAT!
I'M CERTAIN SHE'LL BE A VALUABLE ASSET TO THE CLUB.
GO AHEAD AND SHOW HIM, SAKURA.
HM? SHOW HIM WHAT?
WHY, ALL THE BUSINESS CARDS YOU'VE RECEIVED FROM VIPS, OF COURSE. ♥

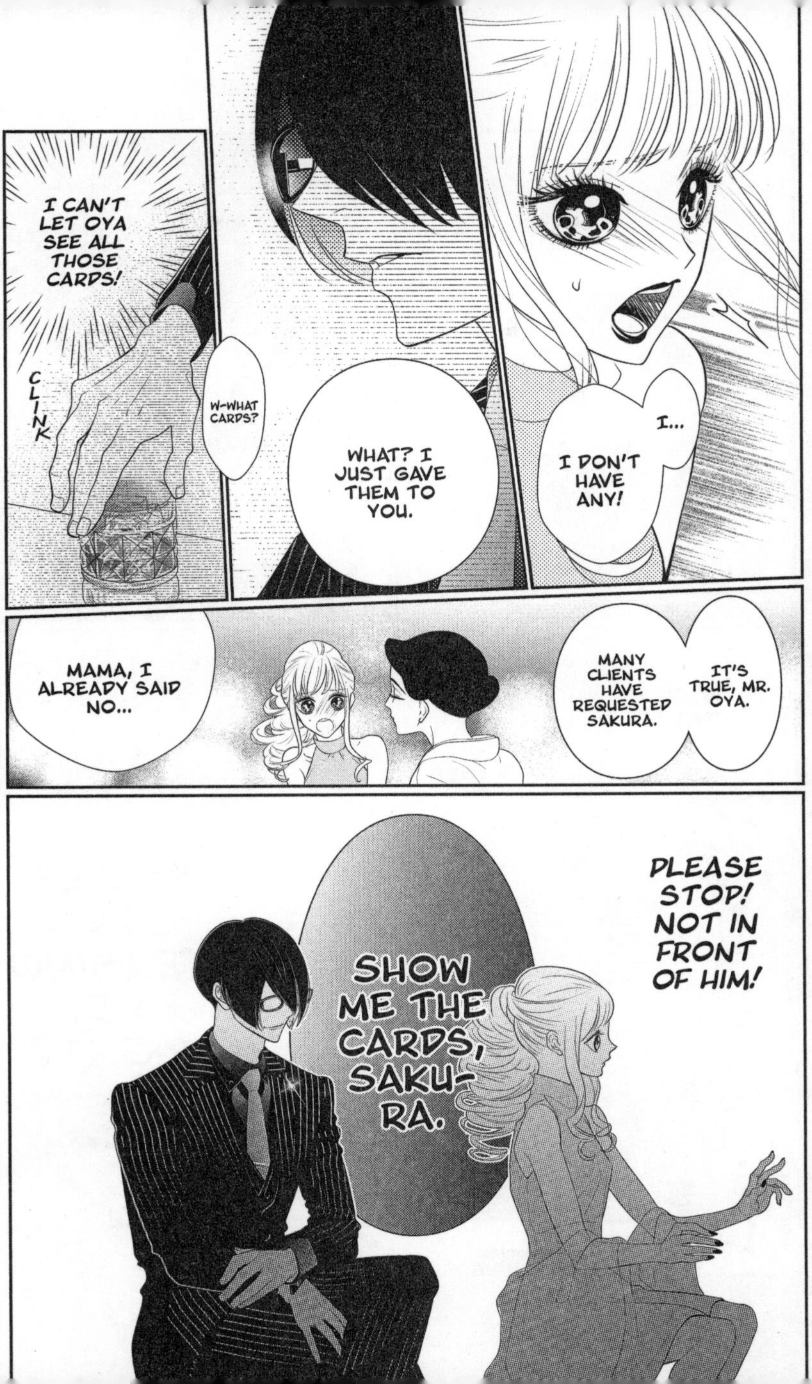
I...
I DON'T HAVE ANY!
WHAT? I JUST GAVE THEM TO YOU.
W-WHAT CARDS?
I CAN'T LET OYA SEE ALL THOSE CARDS!
CLINK
IT'S TRUE, MR. OYA.
MANY CLIENTS HAVE REQUESTED SAKURA.
MAMA, I ALREADY SAID NO...
PLEASE STOP! NOT IN FRONT OF HIM!
SHOW ME THE CARDS, SAKU-RA.

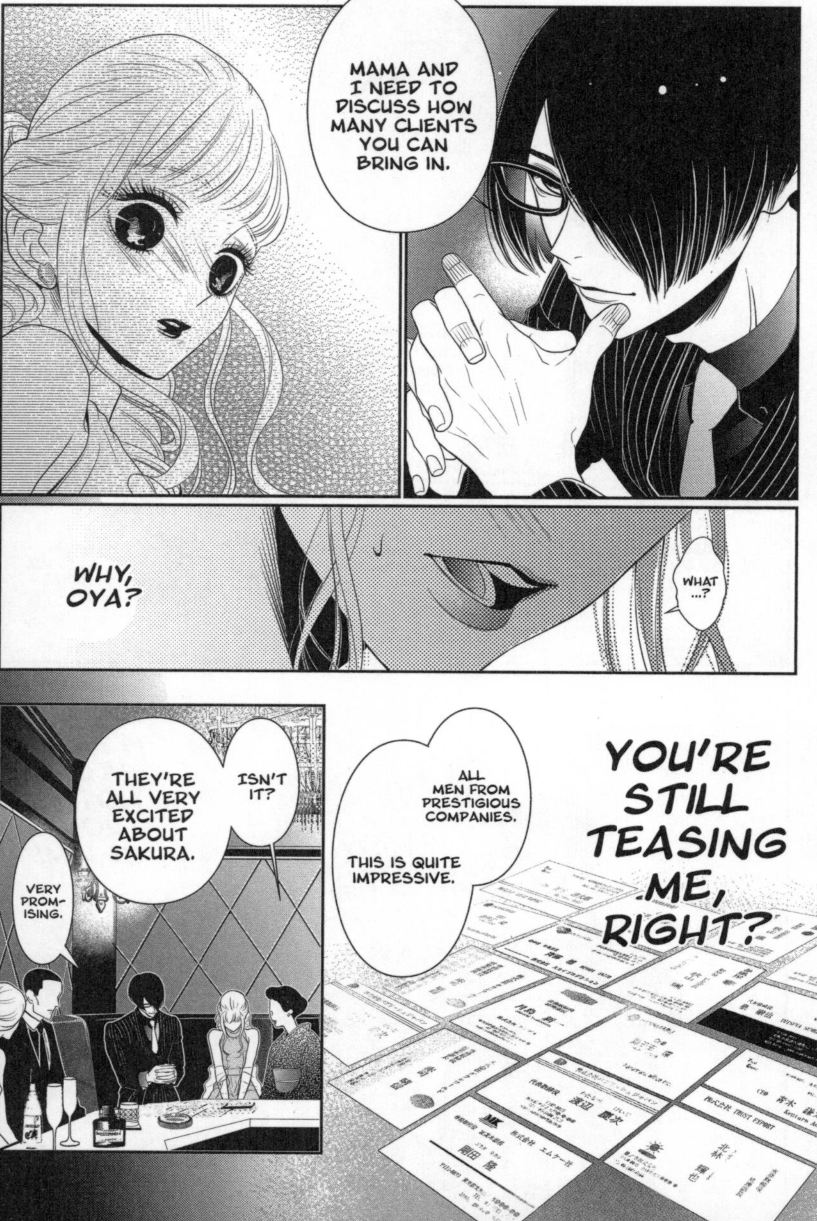
MAMA AND I NEED TO DISCUSS HOW MANY CLIENTS YOU CAN BRING IN.
WHAT ...?
WHY, OYA?
YOU'RE STILL TEASING ME, RIGHT?
ALL MEN FROM PRESTIGIOUS COMPANIES.
THIS IS QUITE IMPRESSIVE.
ISN'T IT?
THEY'RE ALL VERY EXCITED ABOUT SAKURA.
VERY PROM-ISING.

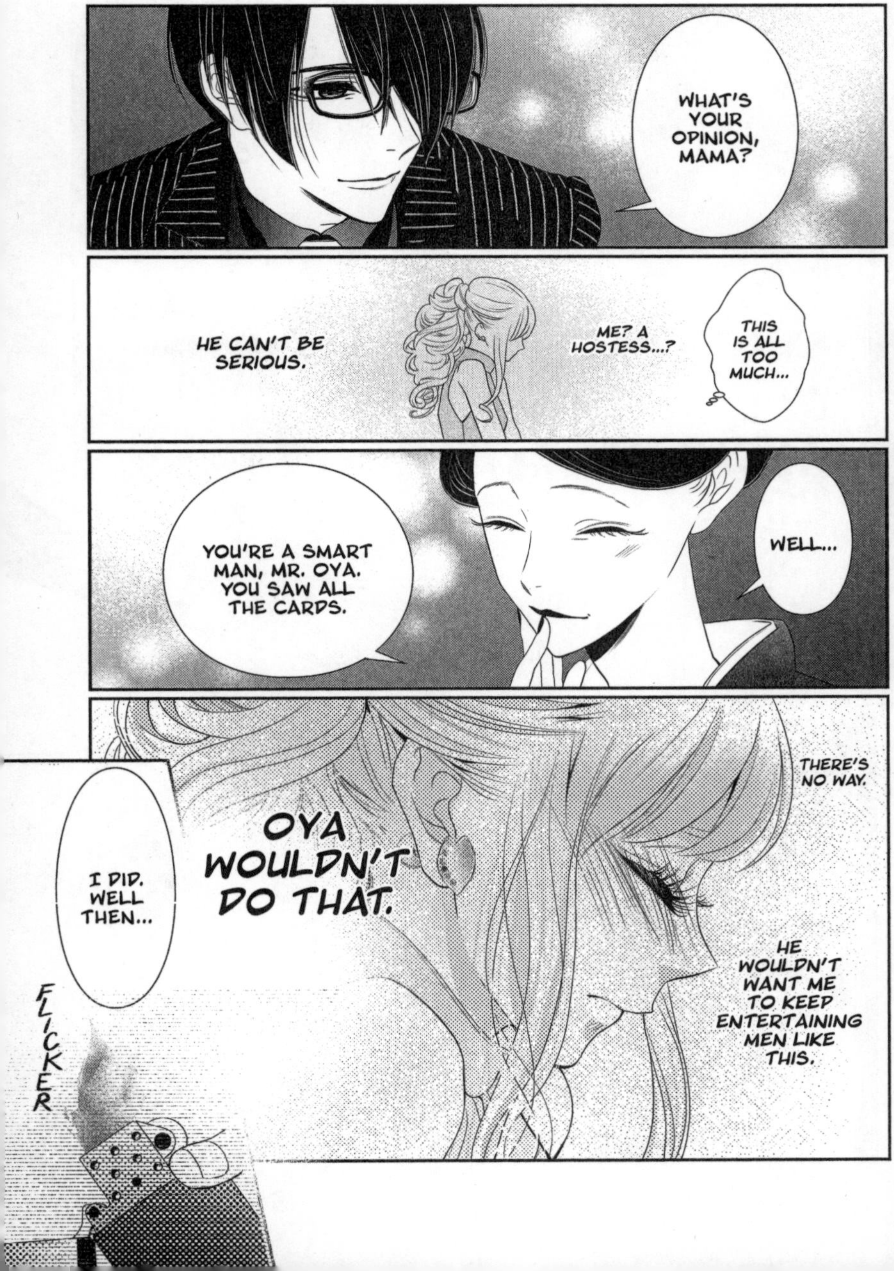
WHAT'S YOUR OPINION, MAMA?
THIS IS ALL TOO MUCH...
ME? A HOSTESS...?
HE CAN'T BE SERIOUS.
WELL...
YOU'RE A SMART MAN, MR. OYA. YOU SAW ALL THE CARDS.
THERE'S NO WAY.
HE WOULDN'T WANT ME TO KEEP ENTERTAINING MEN LIKE THIS.
OYA WOULDN'T DO THAT.
I DID. WELL THEN...
FLICKER

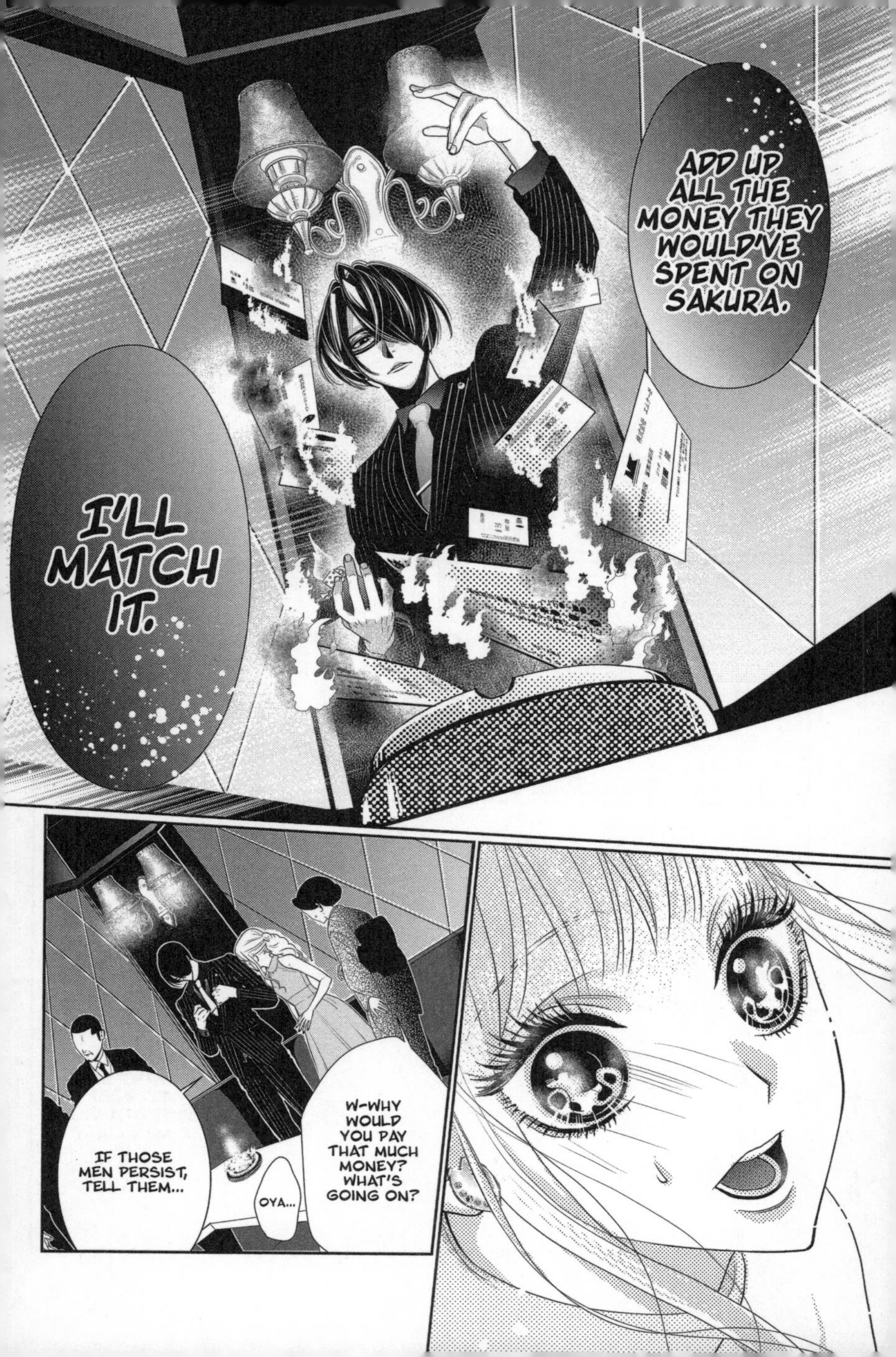
ADD UP ALL THE MONEY THEY WOULD'VE SPENT ON SAKURA.
I'LL MATCH IT.
W-WHY WOULD YOU PAY THAT MUCH MONEY? WHAT'S GOING ON?
OYA...
IF THOSE MEN PERSIST, TELL THEM...

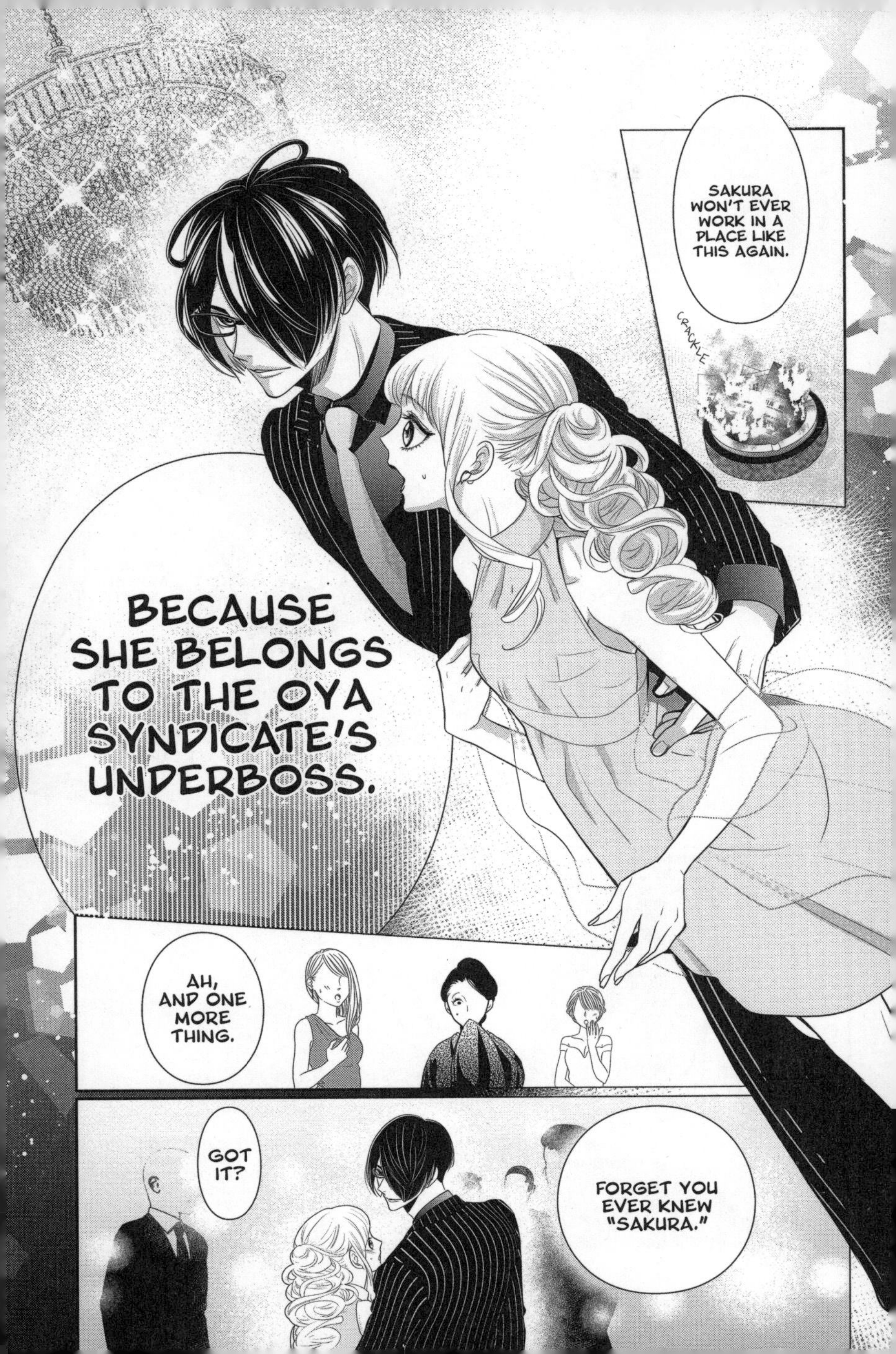
SAKURA WON'T EVER WORK IN A PLACE LIKE THIS AGAIN.
CRACKLE
BECAUSE SHE BELONGS TO THE OYA SYNDICATE'S UNDERBOSS.
AH, AND ONE MORE THING.
FORGET YOU EVER KNEW "SAKURA."
GOT IT?

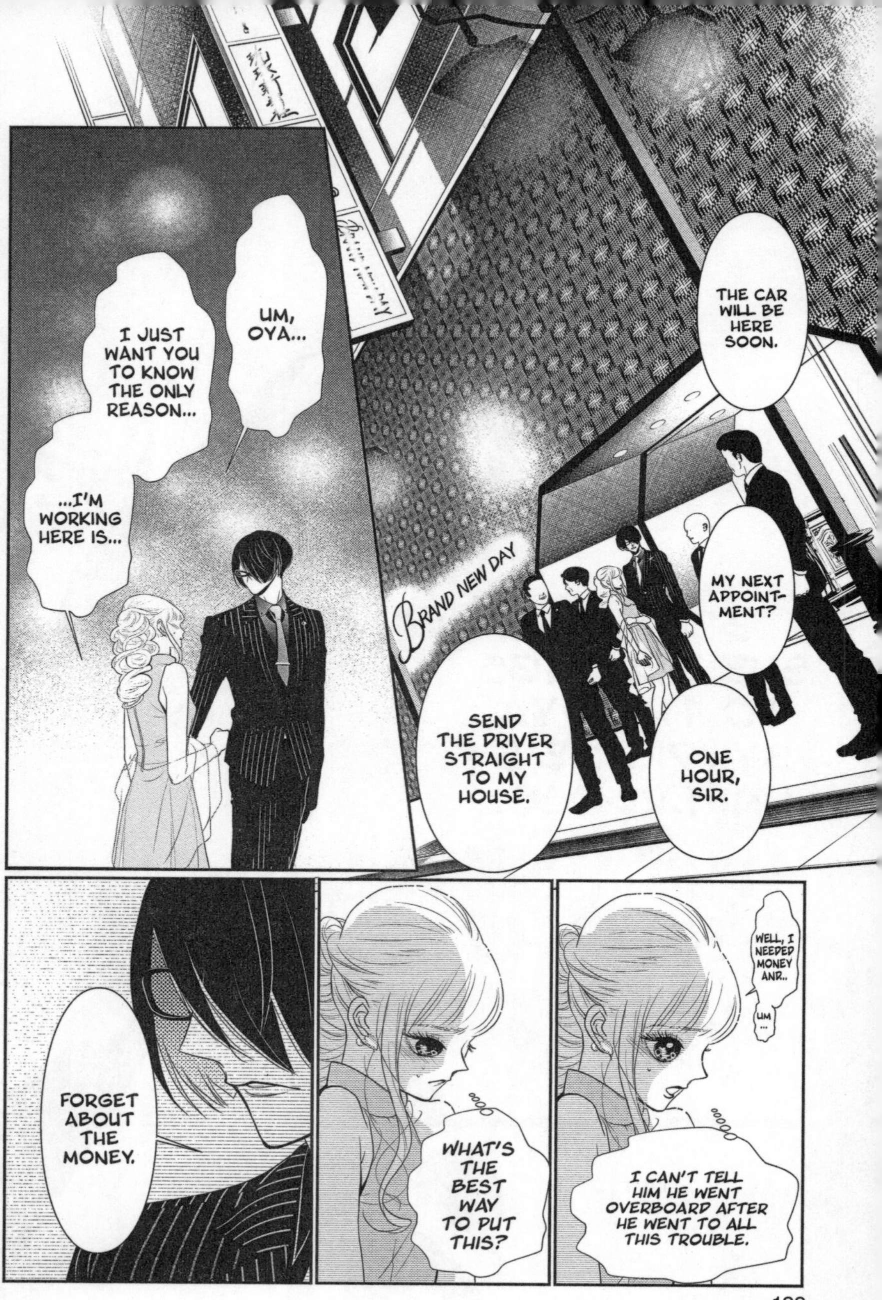
THE CAR WILL BE HERE SOON.
MY NEXT APPOINTMENT?
ONE HOUR, SIR.
SEND THE DRIVER STRAIGHT TO MY HOUSE.
BRAND NEW DAY
UM, OYA...
I JUST WANT YOU TO KNOW THE ONLY REASON...
...I'M WORKING HERE IS...
WELL, I NEEDED MONEY AND...
UM ...
I CAN'T TELL HIM HE WENT OVERBOARD AFTER HE WENT TO ALL THIS TROUBLE.
WHAT'S THE BEST WAY TO PUT THIS?
FORGET ABOUT THE MONEY.

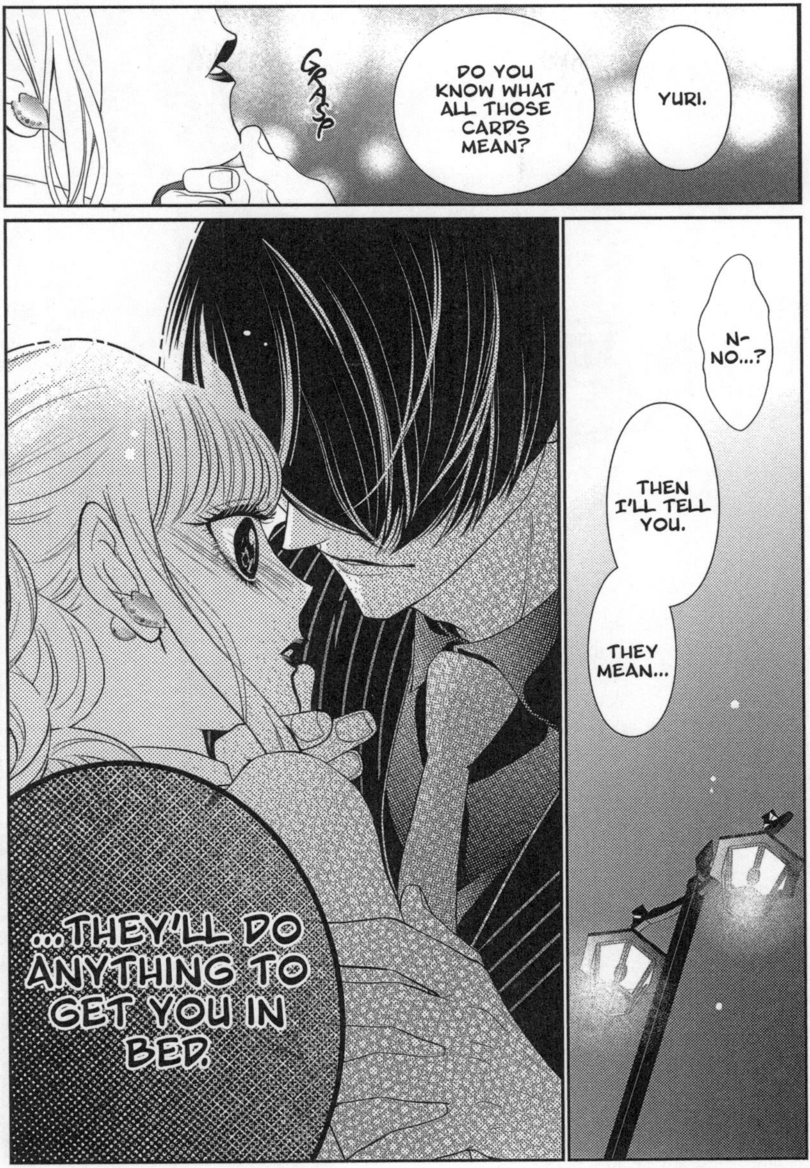
YURI.
DO YOU KNOW WHAT ALL THOSE CARDS MEAN?
GRASP
N-NO...?
THEN I'LL TELL YOU.
THEY MEAN...
...THEY'LL DO ANYTHING TO GET YOU IN BED.

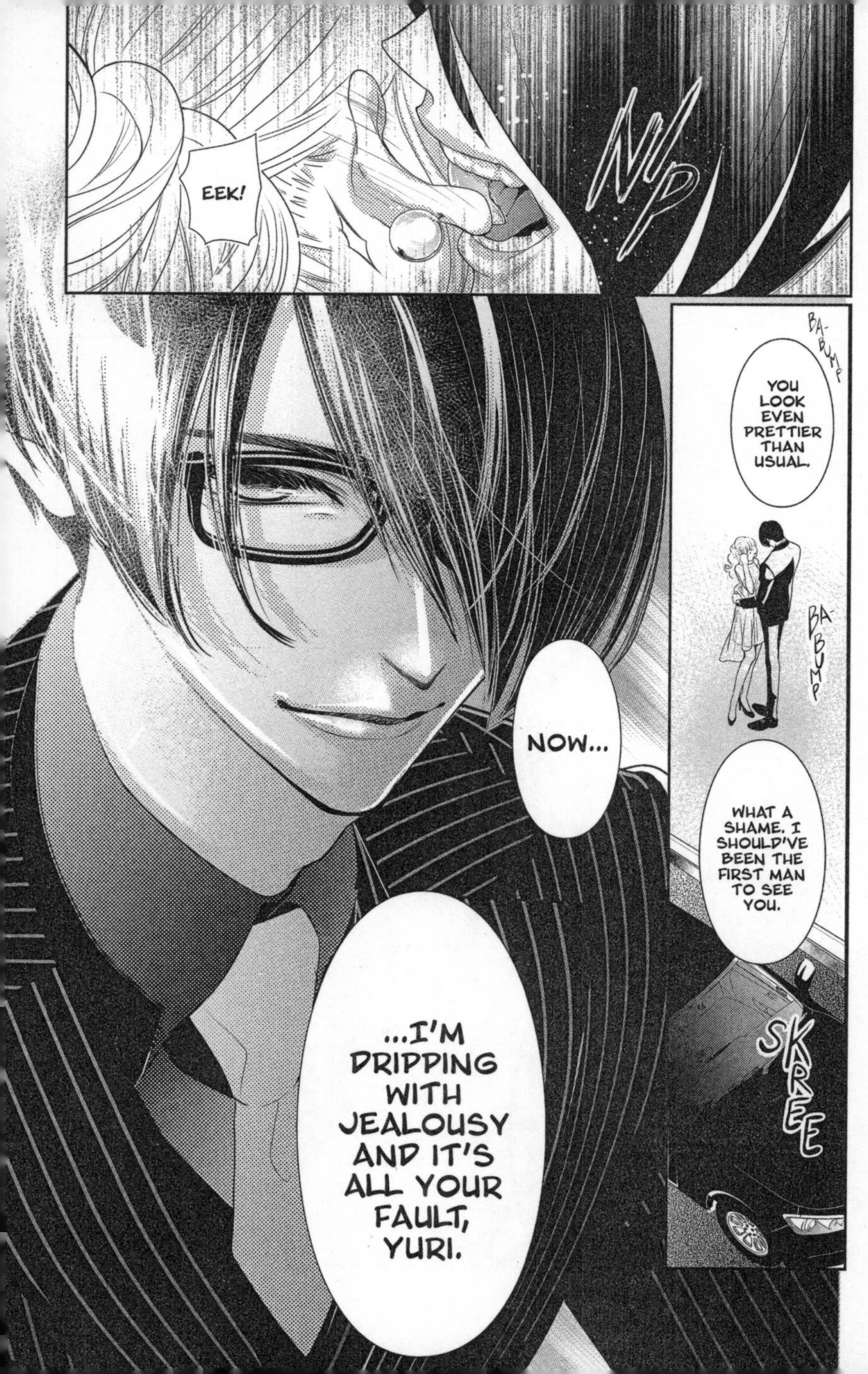
NIP
EEK!
BA-BUMP
YOU LOOK EVEN PRETTIER THAN USUAL.
BA-BUMP
WHAT A SHAME. I SHOULD'VE BEEN THE FIRST MAN TO SEE YOU.
SKREEE
NOW...
...I'M DRIPPING WITH JEALOUSY AND IT'S ALL YOUR FAULT, YURI.

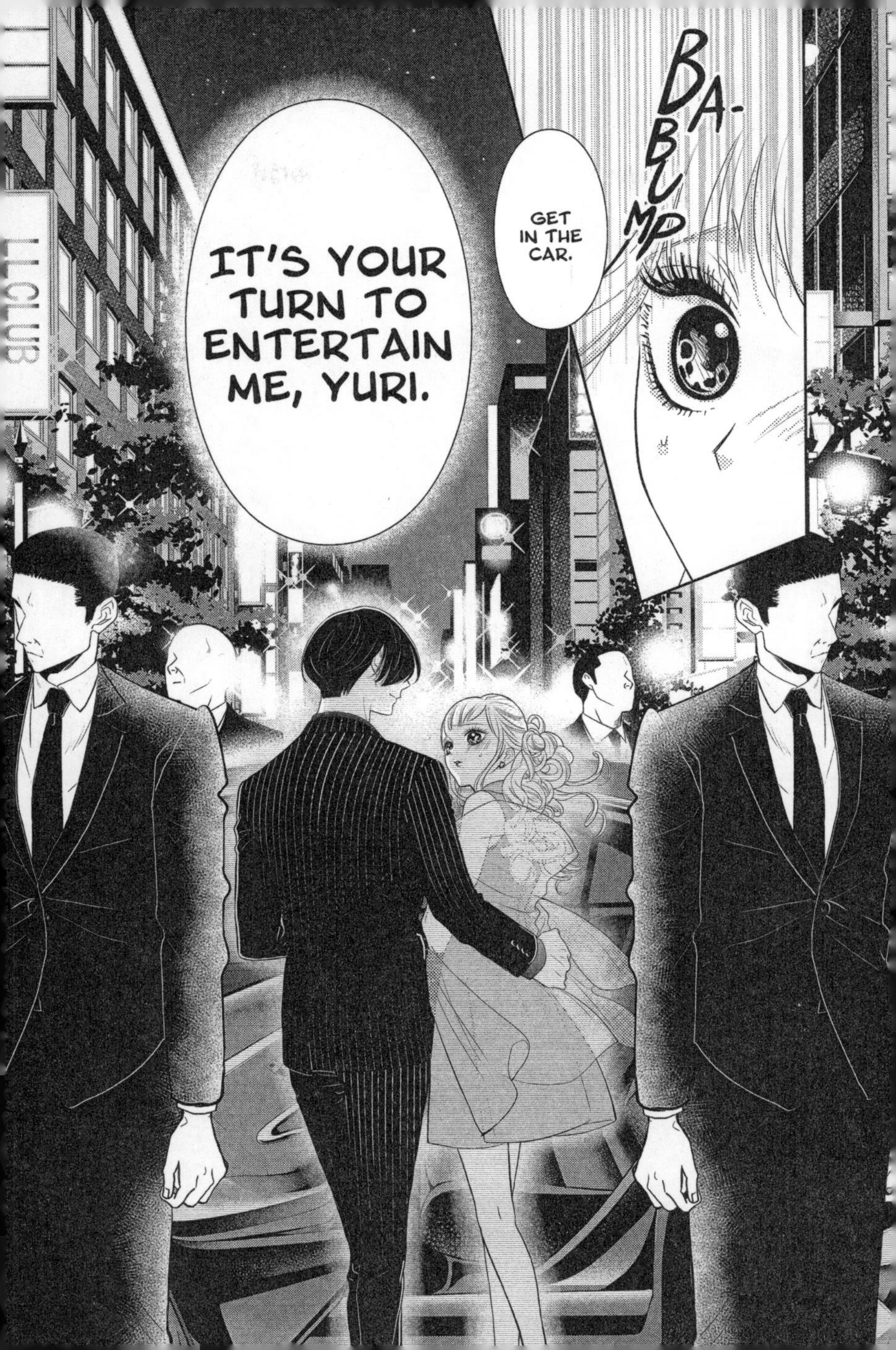
BA-BUMP
GET IN THE CAR.
IT'S YOUR TURN TO ENTERTAIN ME, YURI.
LL CLUB

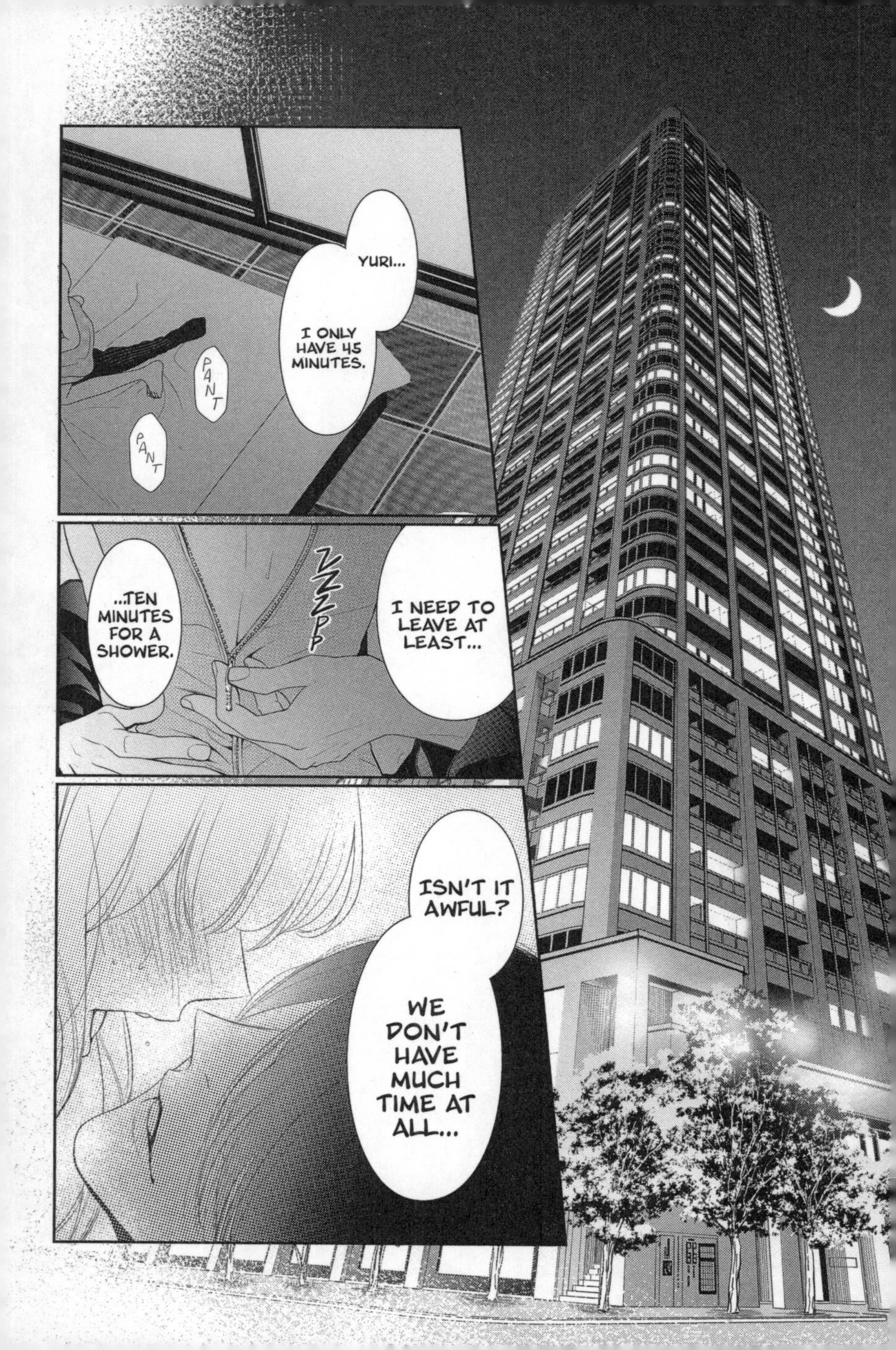
YURI...
I ONLY HAVE 45 MINUTES.
PANT
PANT
I NEED TO LEAVE AT LEAST...
ZZZPP
...TEN MINUTES FOR A SHOWER.
ISN'T IT AWFUL?
WE DON'T HAVE MUCH TIME AT ALL...

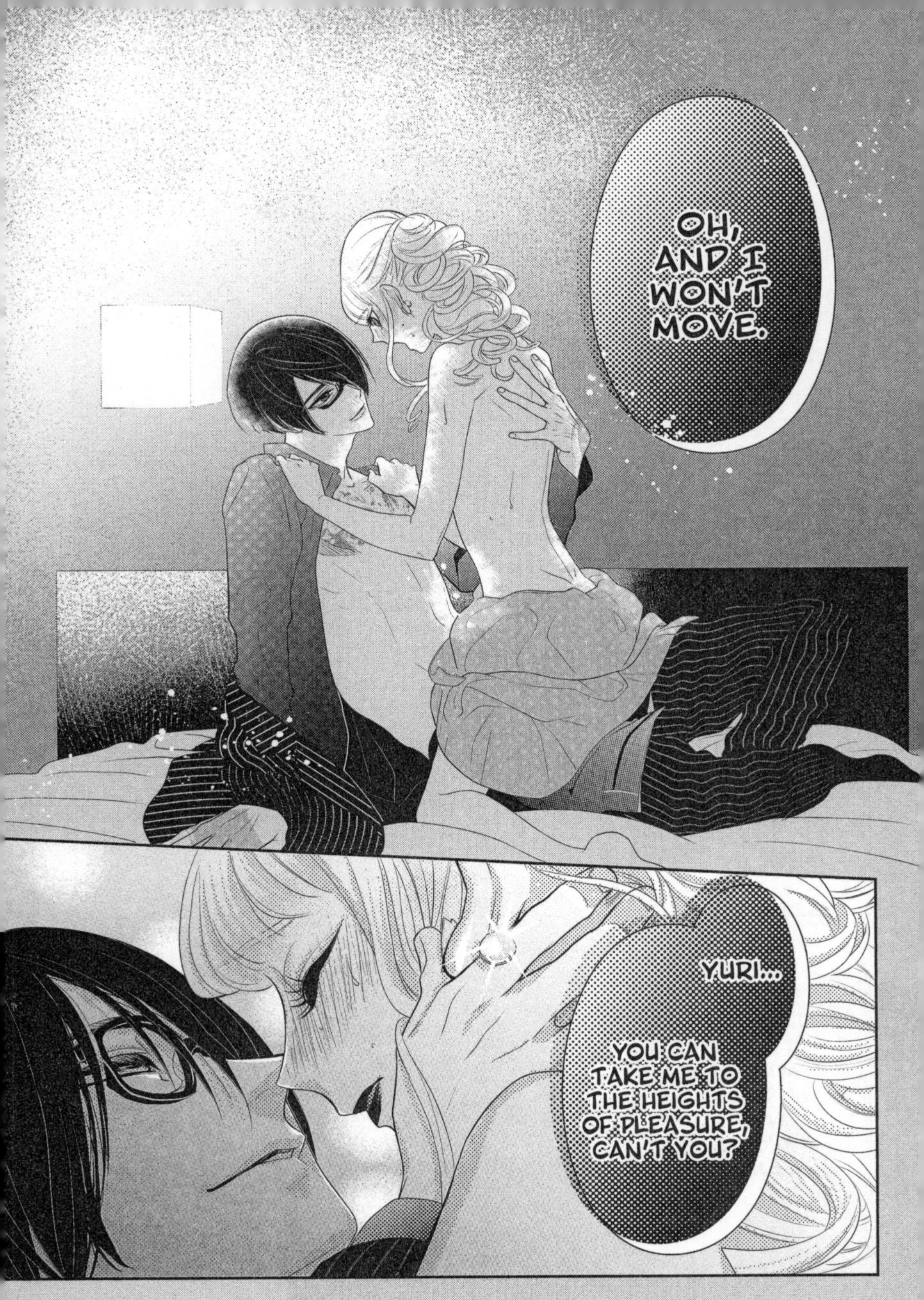
OH, AND I WON'T MOVE.
YURI...
YOU CAN TAKE ME TO THE HEIGHTS OF PLEASURE, CAN'T YOU?

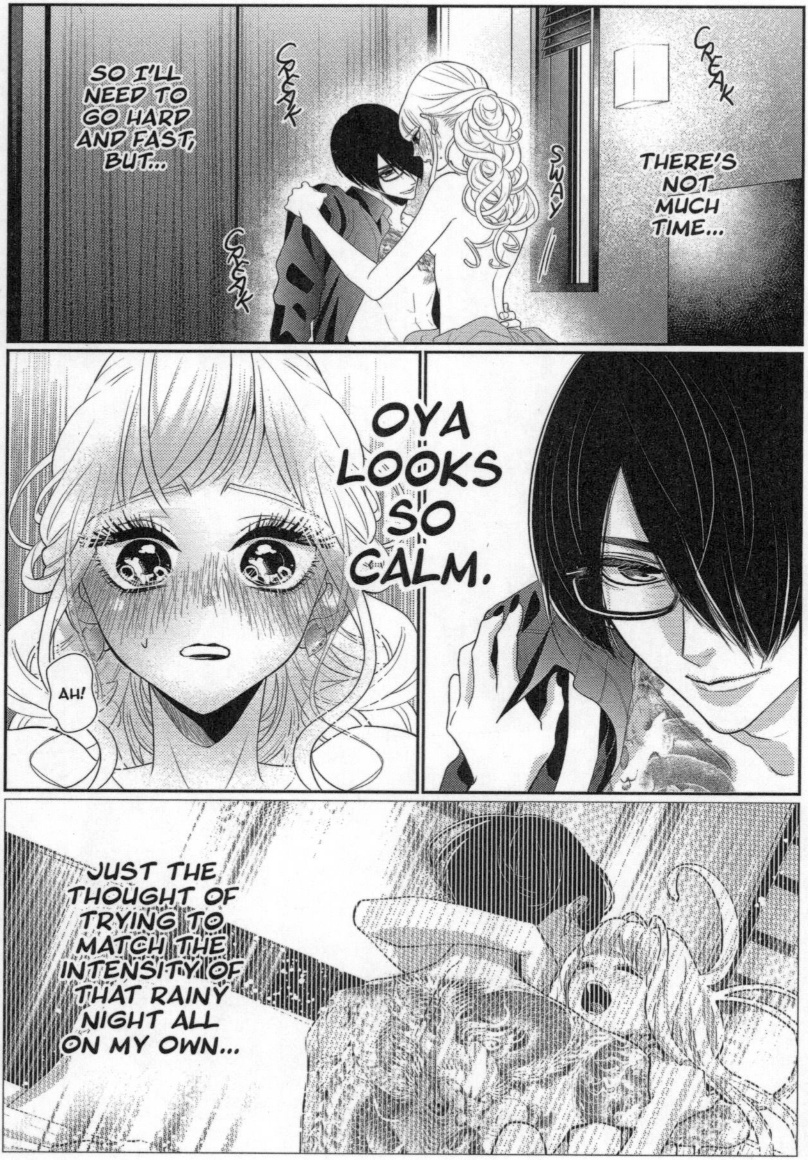
CREAK
THERE'S NOT MUCH TIME...
SWAY
CREAK
SO I'LL NEED TO GO HARD AND FAST, BUT...
CREAK
OYA LOOKS SO CALM.
AH!
JUST THE THOUGHT OF TRYING TO MATCH THE INTENSITY OF THAT RAINY NIGHT ALL ON MY OWN...

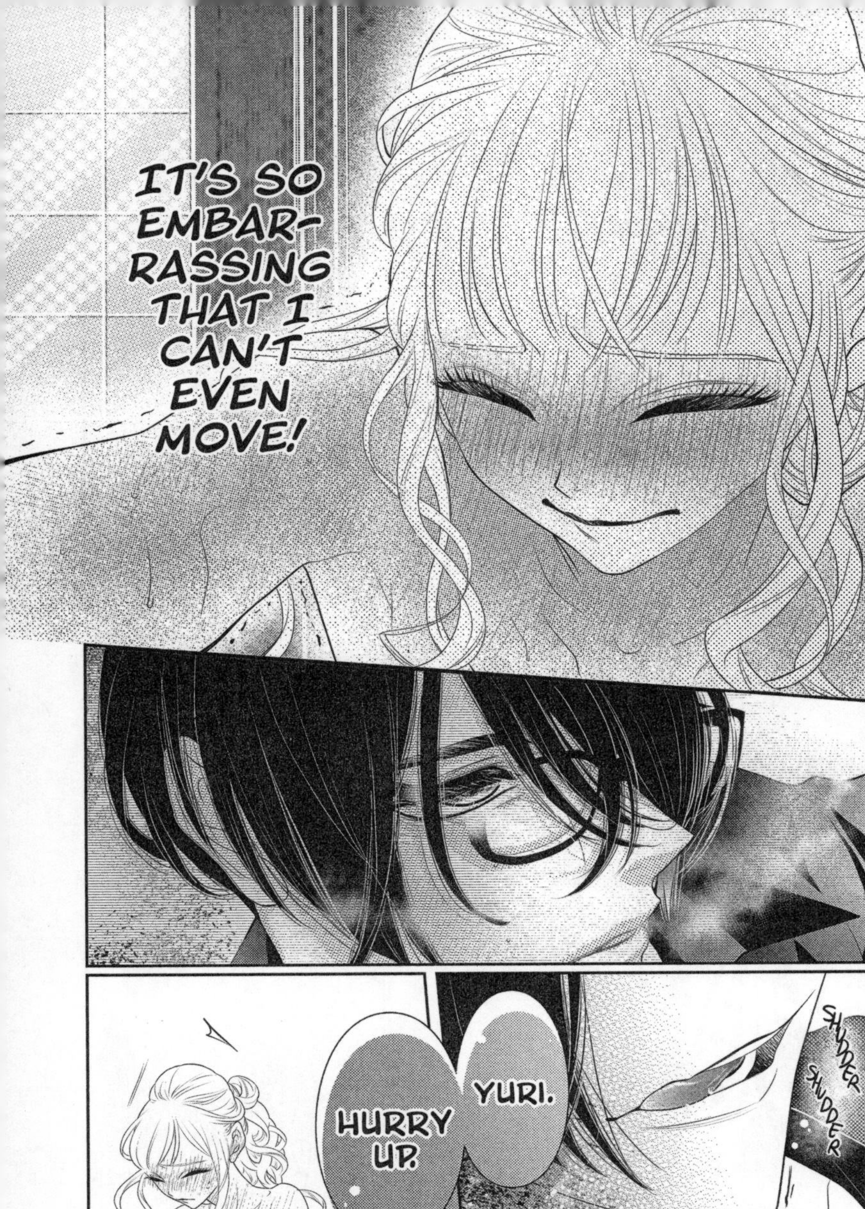
IT'S SO EMBARRASSING THAT I CAN'T EVEN MOVE!
SHUDDER SHUDDER
YURI.
HURRY UP.

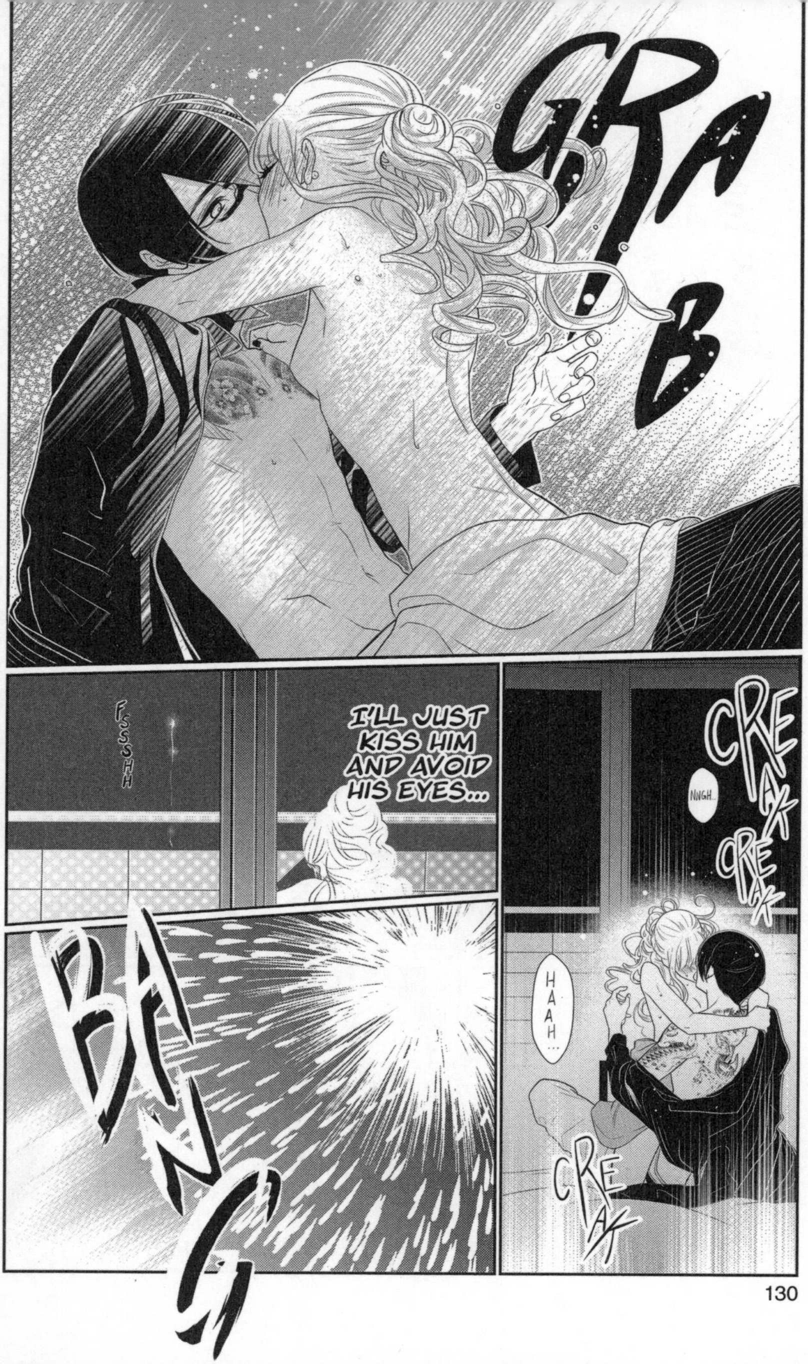
GRAB
CREAK
NNGH...
CREAK
HAAH...
CREAK
FSSSHH
I'LL JUST KISS HIM AND AVOID HIS EYES...
BANG

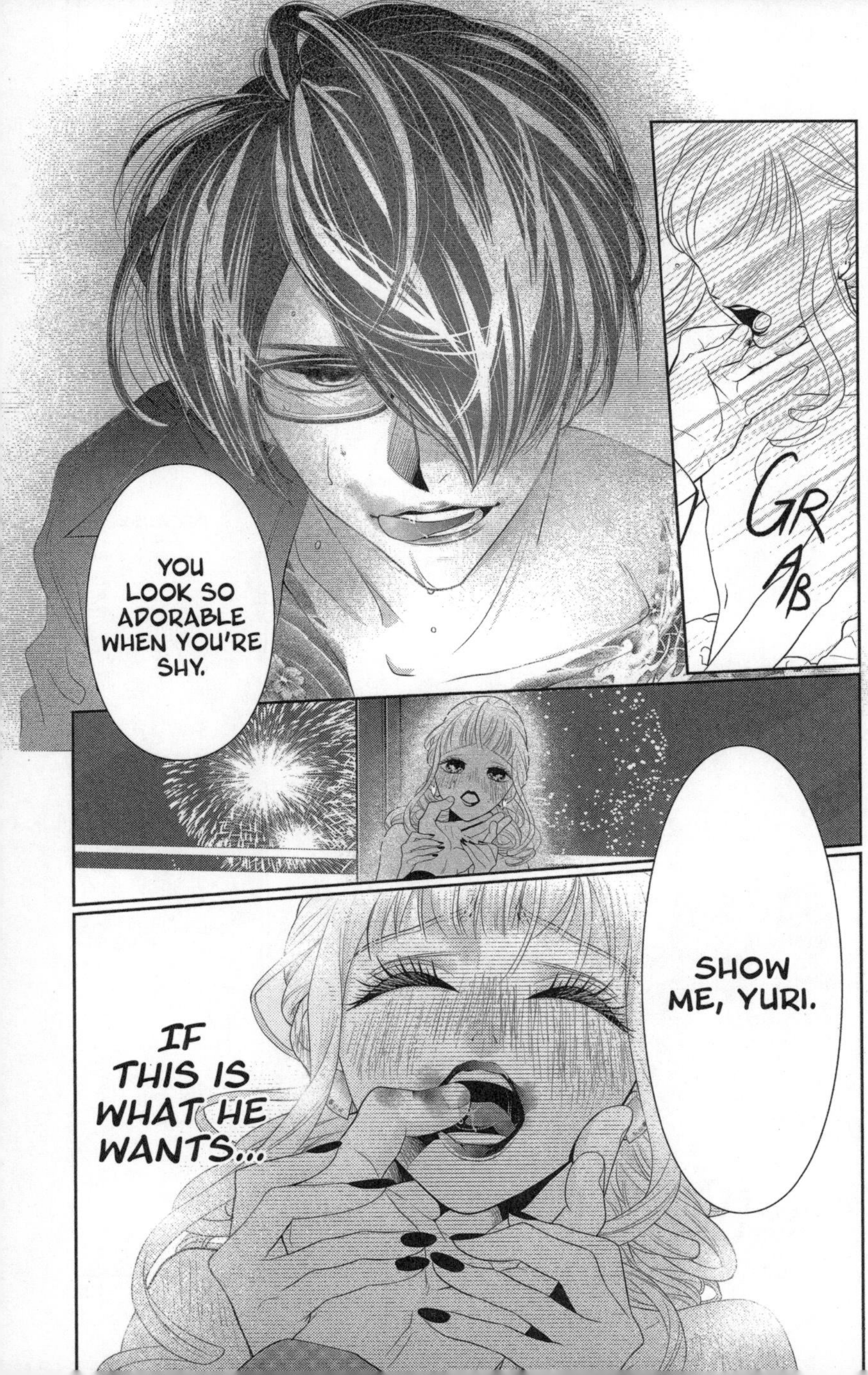
GRAB
YOU LOOK SO ADORABLE WHEN YOU'RE SHY.
SHOW ME, YURI.
IF THIS IS WHAT HE WANTS...

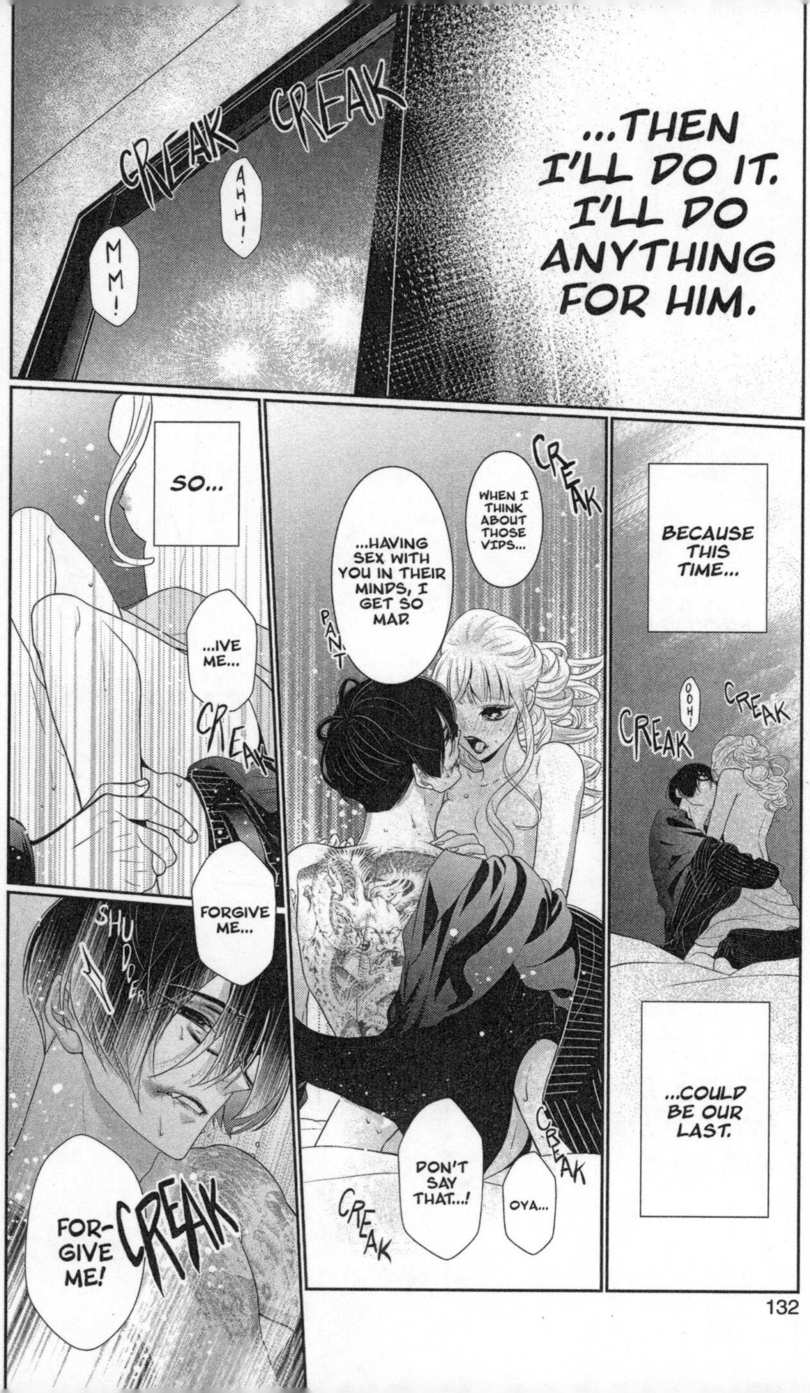
...THEN I'LL DO IT. I'LL DO ANYTHING FOR HIM.
CREAK
CREAK
AHH!
MM!
BECAUSE THIS TIME...
OOH!
CREAK
CREAK
...COULD BE OUR LAST.
CREAK
WHEN I THINK ABOUT THOSE VIPS...
...HAVING SEX WITH YOU IN THEIR MINDS, I GET SO MAD.
PANT
CREAK
OYA...
DON'T SAY THAT...!
CREAK
SO...
...IVE ME...
CREAK
FORGIVE ME...
SHUDDER
FOR-GIVE ME!
CREAK

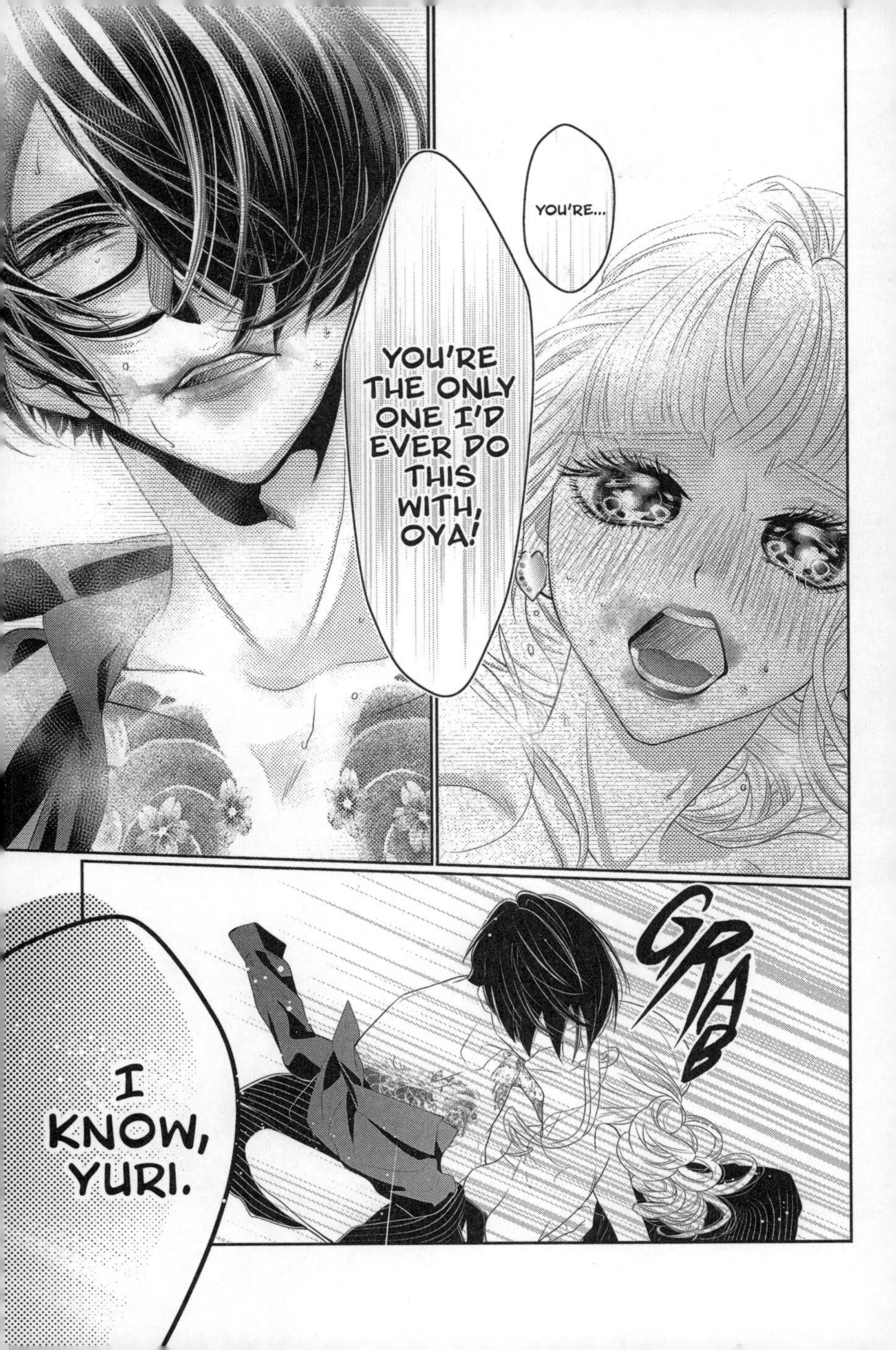
YOU'RE...
YOU'RE THE ONLY ONE I'D EVER DO THIS WITH, OYA!
GRAB
I KNOW, YURI.

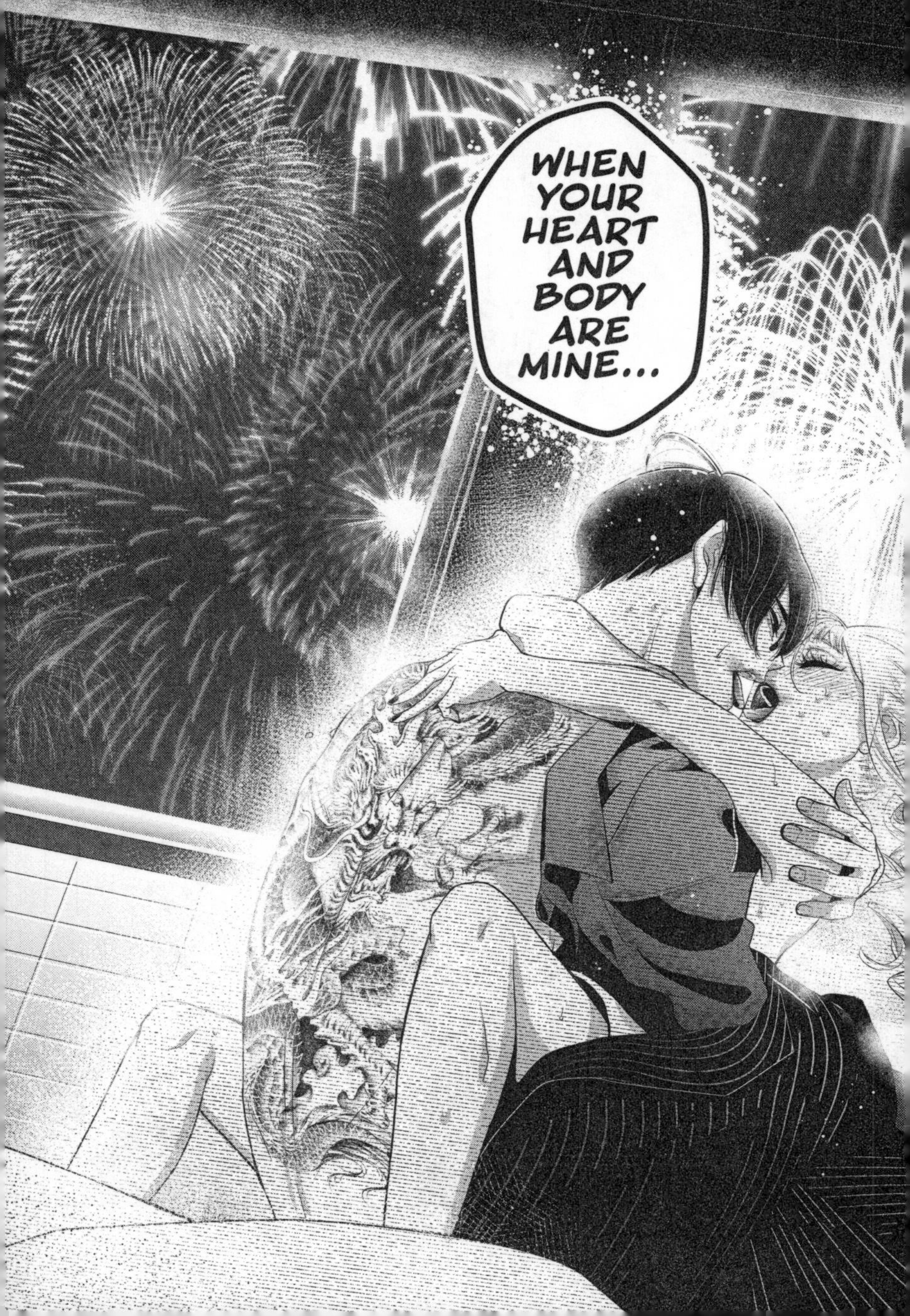
WHEN YOUR HEART AND BODY ARE MINE...

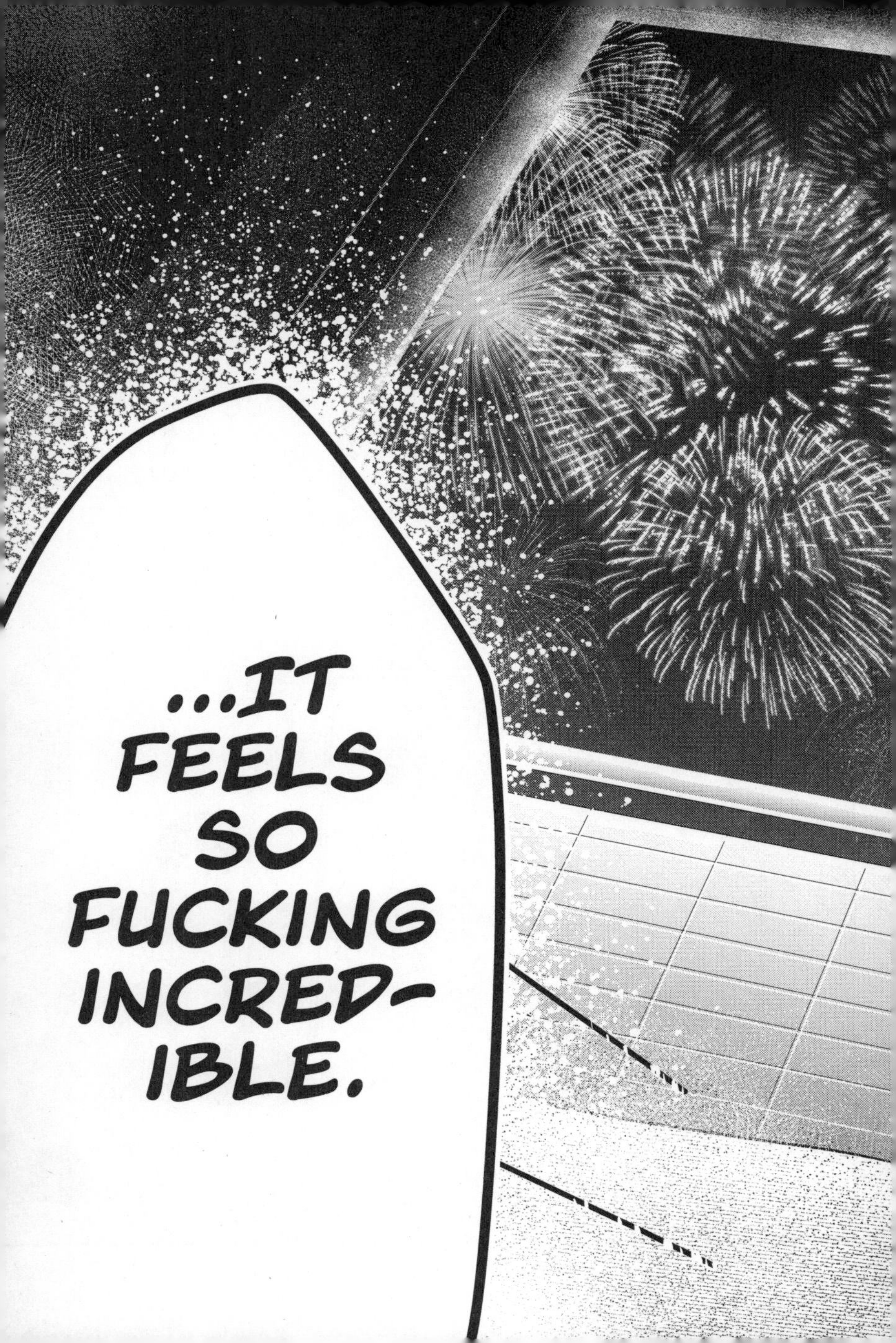
...IT FEELS SO FUCKING INCRED-IBLE.

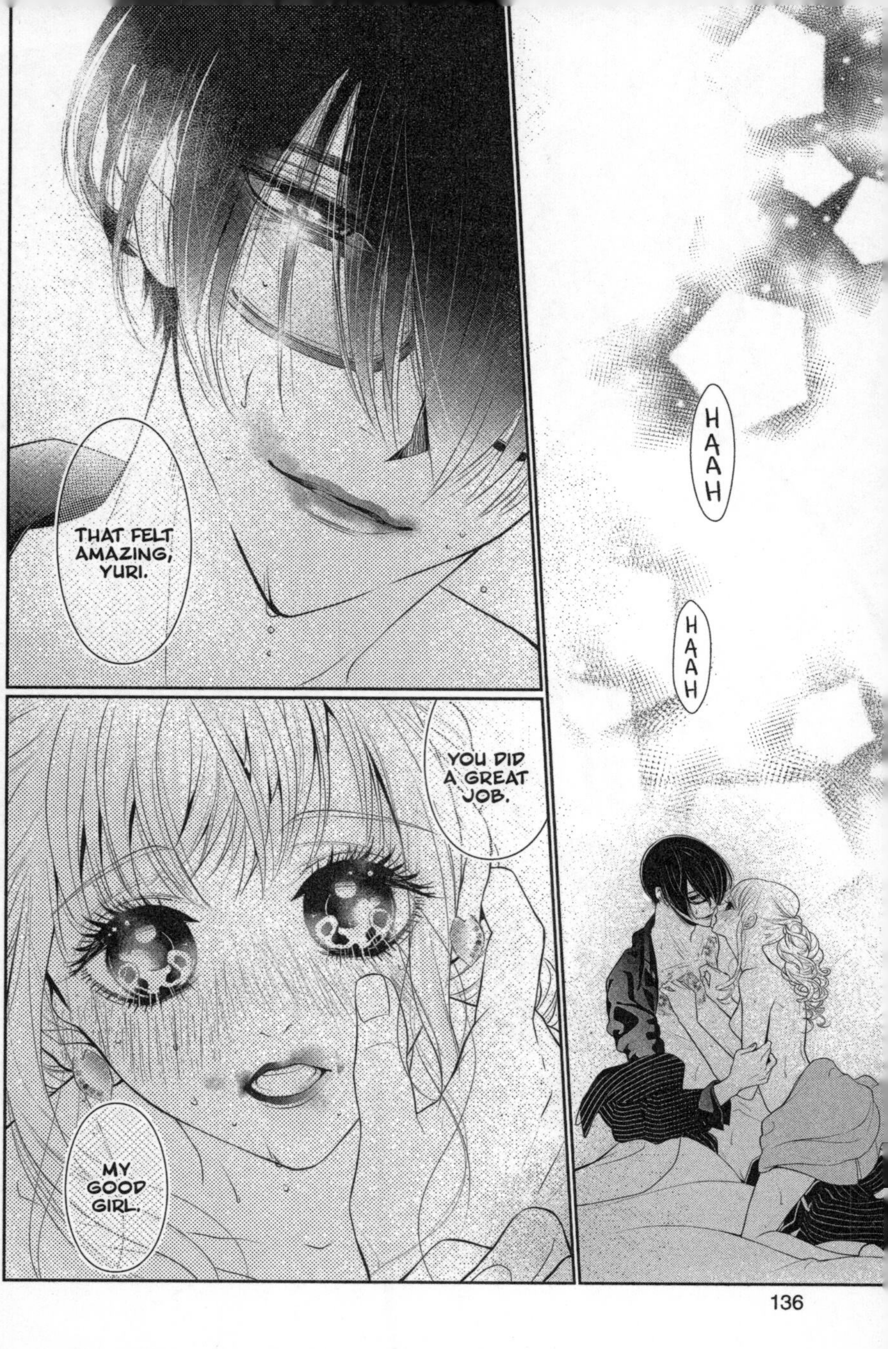
HAAH
HAAH
THAT FELT AMAZING, YURI.
YOU DID A GREAT JOB.
MY GOOD GIRL.

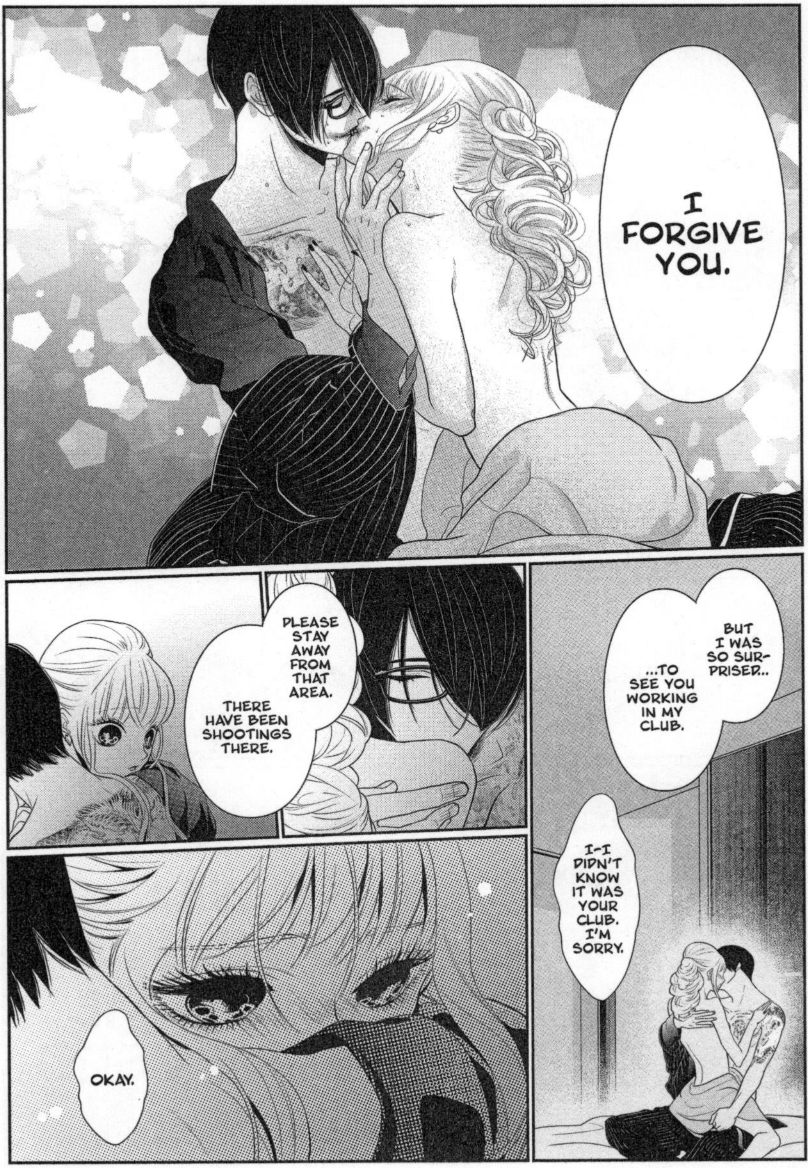
I FORGIVE YOU.
BUT I WAS SO SUR-PRISED...
...TO SEE YOU WORKING IN MY CLUB.
I-I DIDN'T KNOW IT WAS YOUR CLUB. I'M SORRY.
PLEASE STAY AWAY FROM THAT AREA.
THERE HAVE BEEN SHOOTINGS THERE.
OKAY.

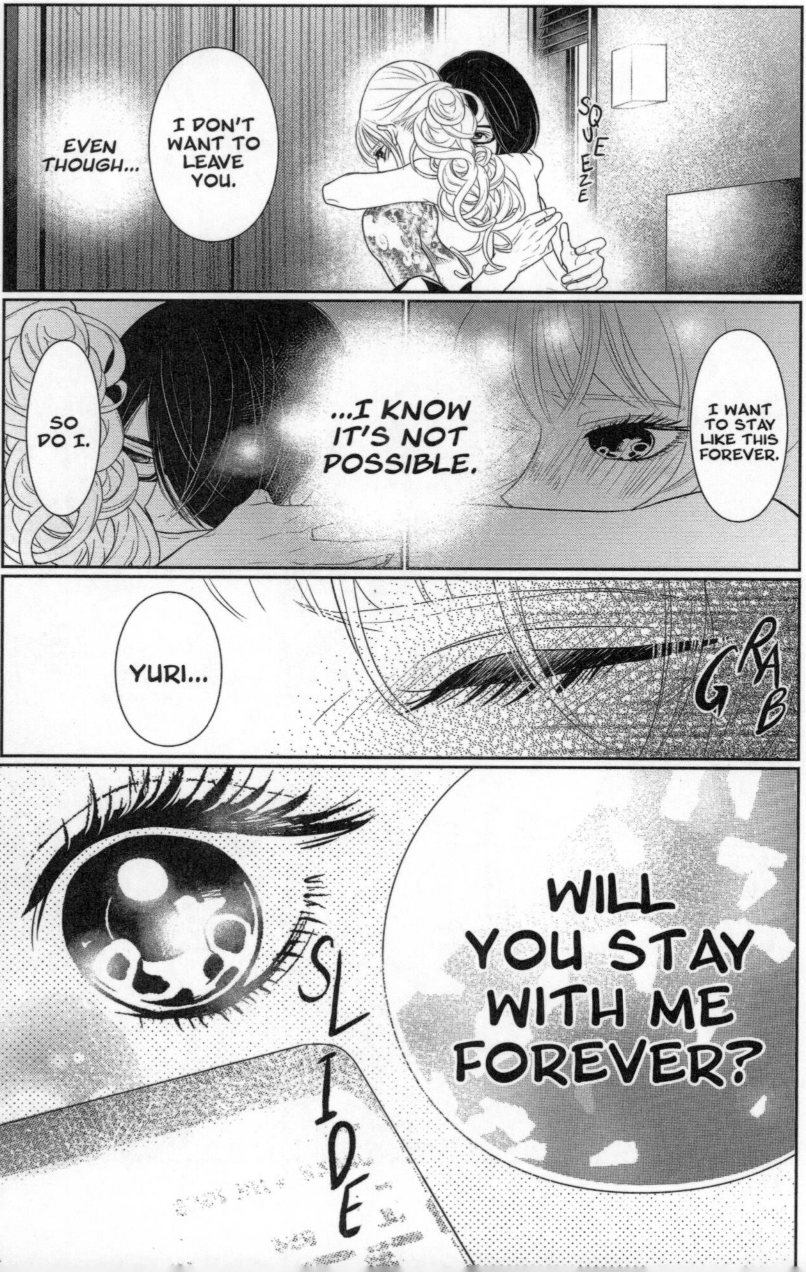
SQUEEZE
I DON'T WANT TO LEAVE YOU.
EVEN THOUGH...
I WANT TO STAY LIKE THIS FOREVER.
...I KNOW IT'S NOT POSSIBLE.
SO DO I.
GRAB
YURI...
WILL YOU STAY WITH ME FOREVER?
SLIDE

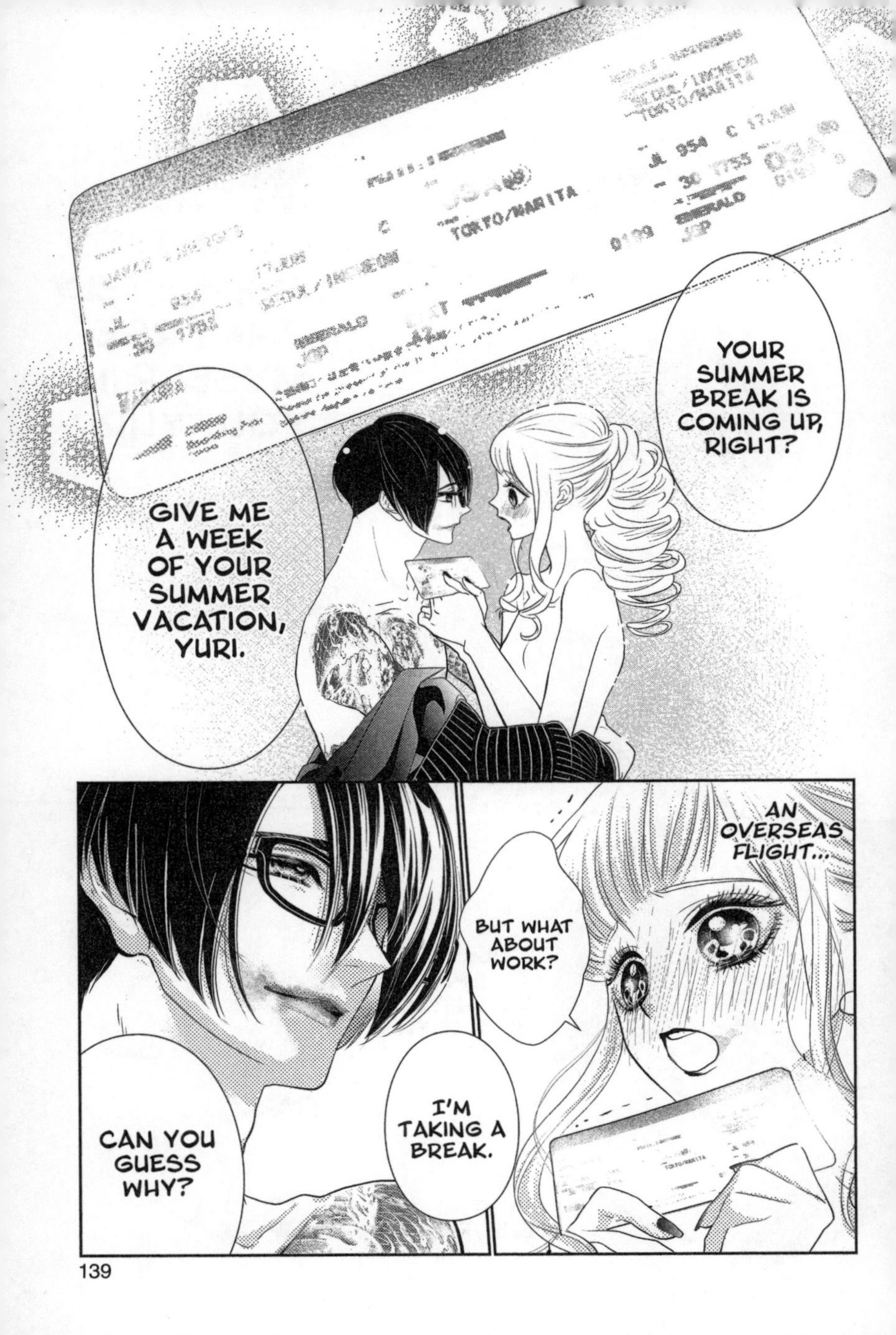
YOUR SUMMER BREAK IS COMING UP, RIGHT?
GIVE ME A WEEK OF YOUR SUMMER VACATION, YURI.
AN OVERSEAS FLIGHT...
BUT WHAT ABOUT WORK?
I'M TAKING A BREAK.
CAN YOU GUESS WHY?

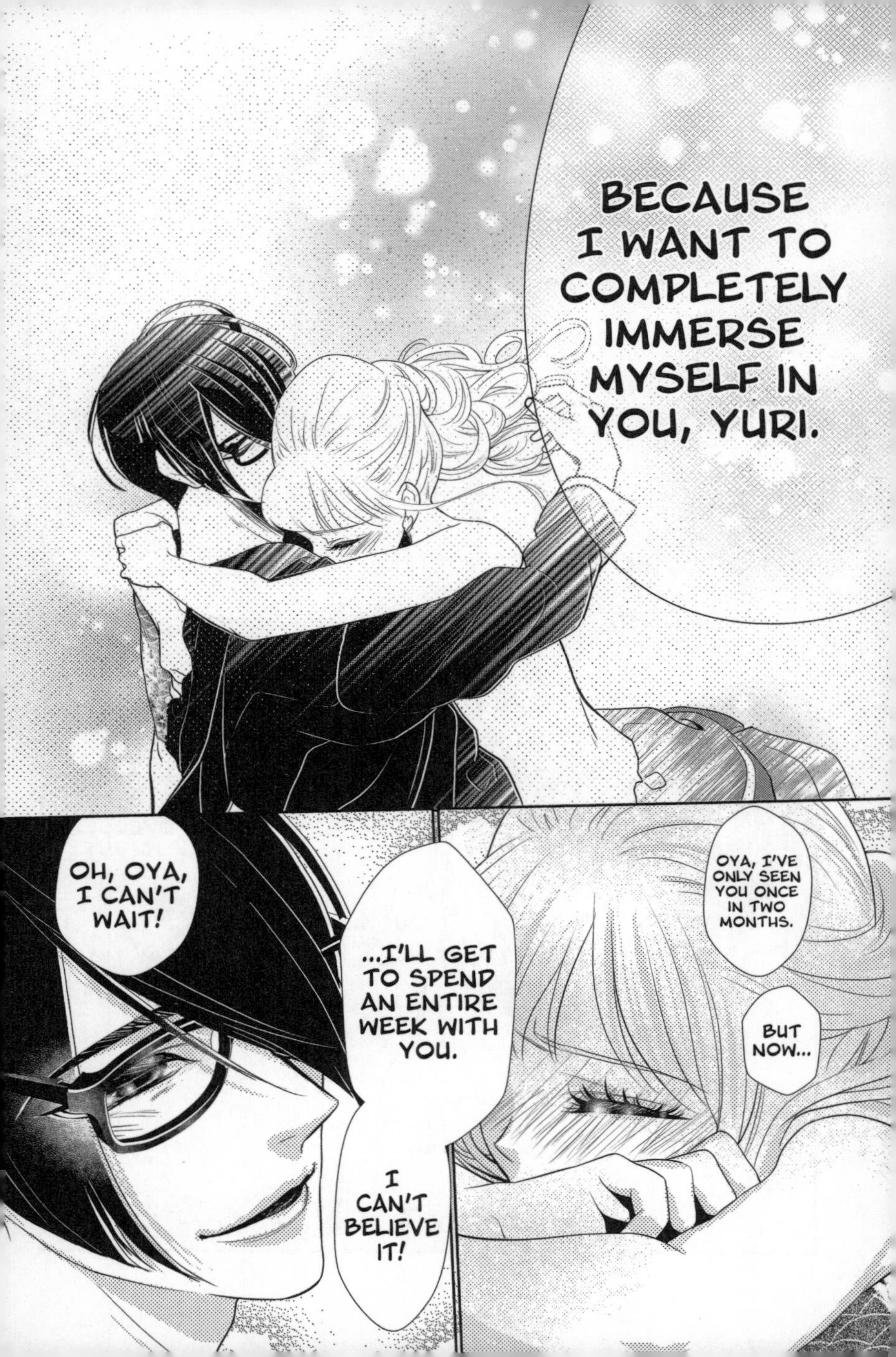
BECAUSE I WANT TO COMPLETELY IMMERSE MYSELF IN YOU, YURI.
OYA, I'VE ONLY SEEN YOU ONCE IN TWO MONTHS.
BUT NOW...
...I'LL GET TO SPEND AN ENTIRE WEEK WITH YOU.
I CAN'T BELIEVE IT!
OH, OYA, I CAN'T WAIT!

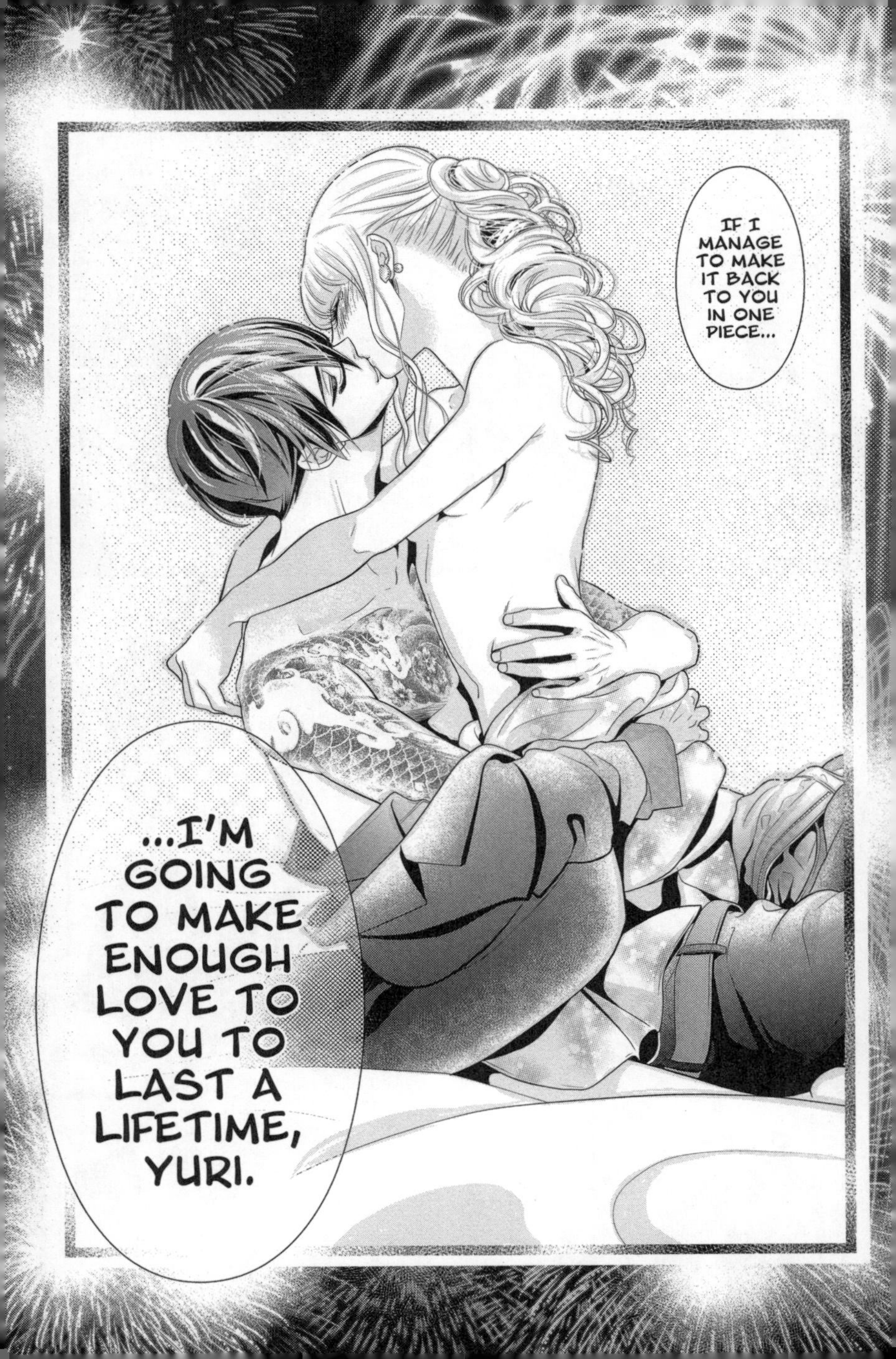
IF I MANAGE TO MAKE IT BACK TO YOU IN ONE PIECE...
...I'M GOING TO MAKE ENOUGH LOVE TO YOU TO LAST A LIFETIME, YURI.

bonus
bullet 03 secret scene

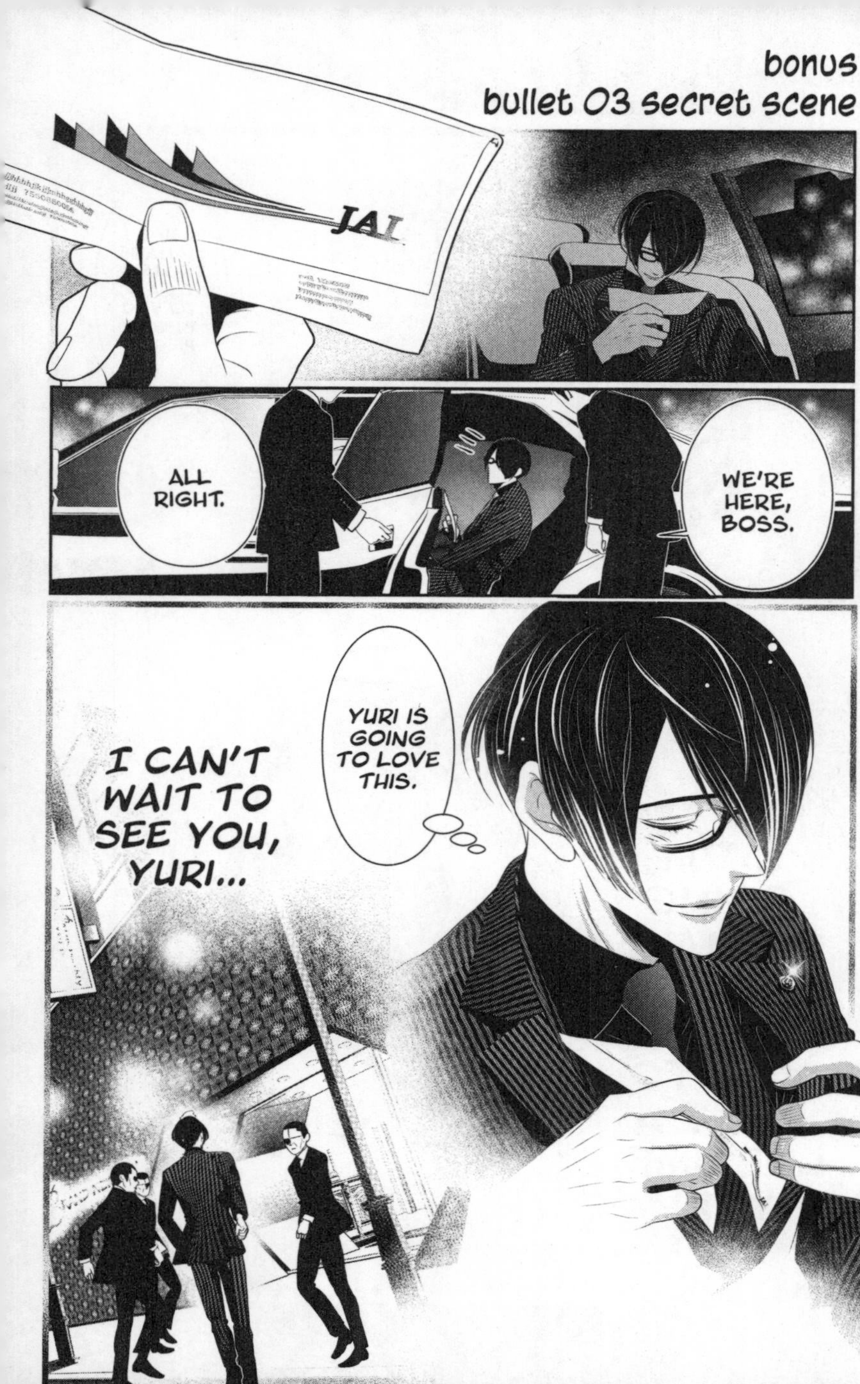
JAL
WE'RE HERE, BOSS.
ALL RIGHT.
YURI IS GOING TO LOVE THIS.
I CAN'T WAIT TO SEE YOU, YURI...

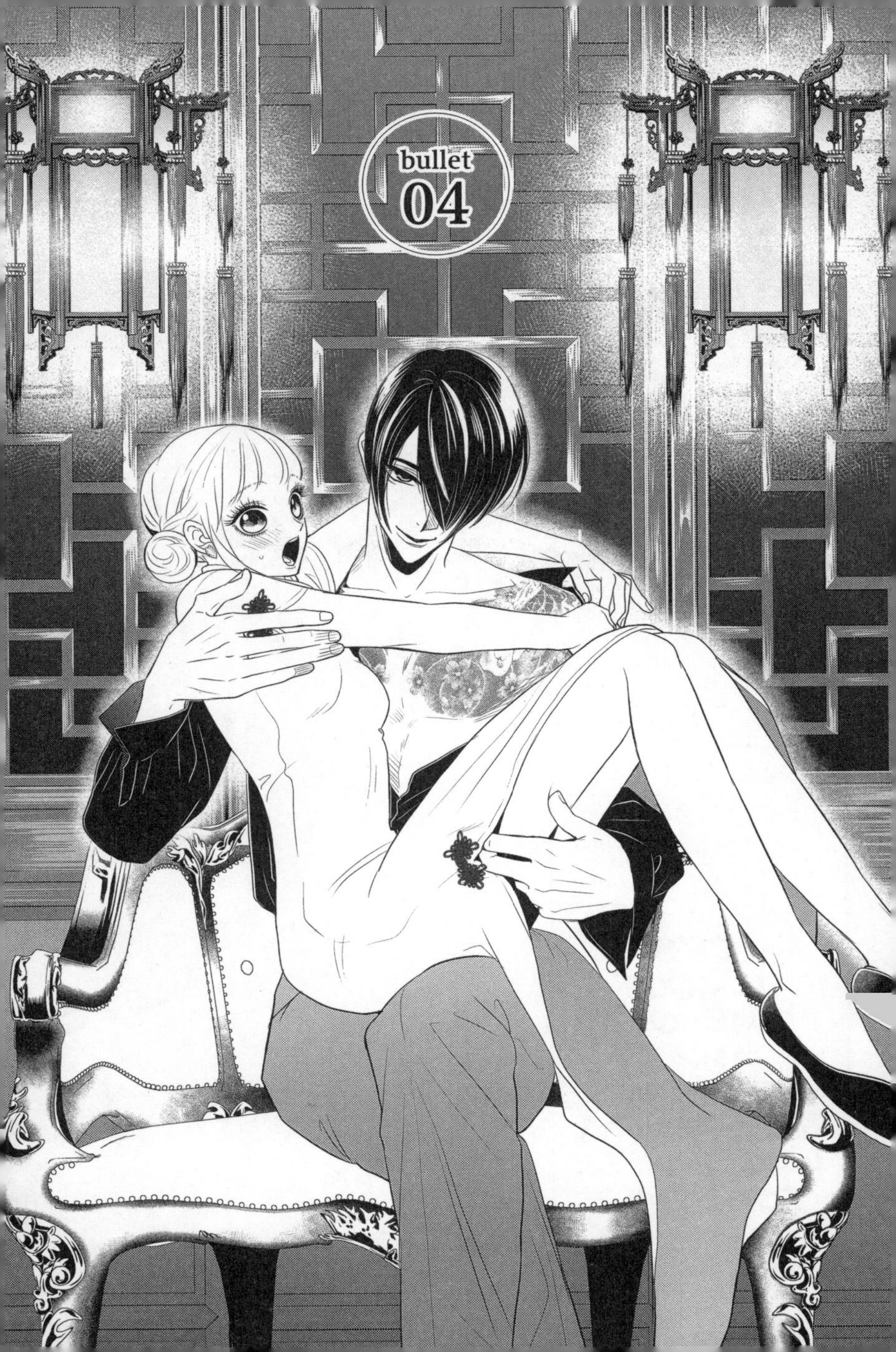
bullet
04

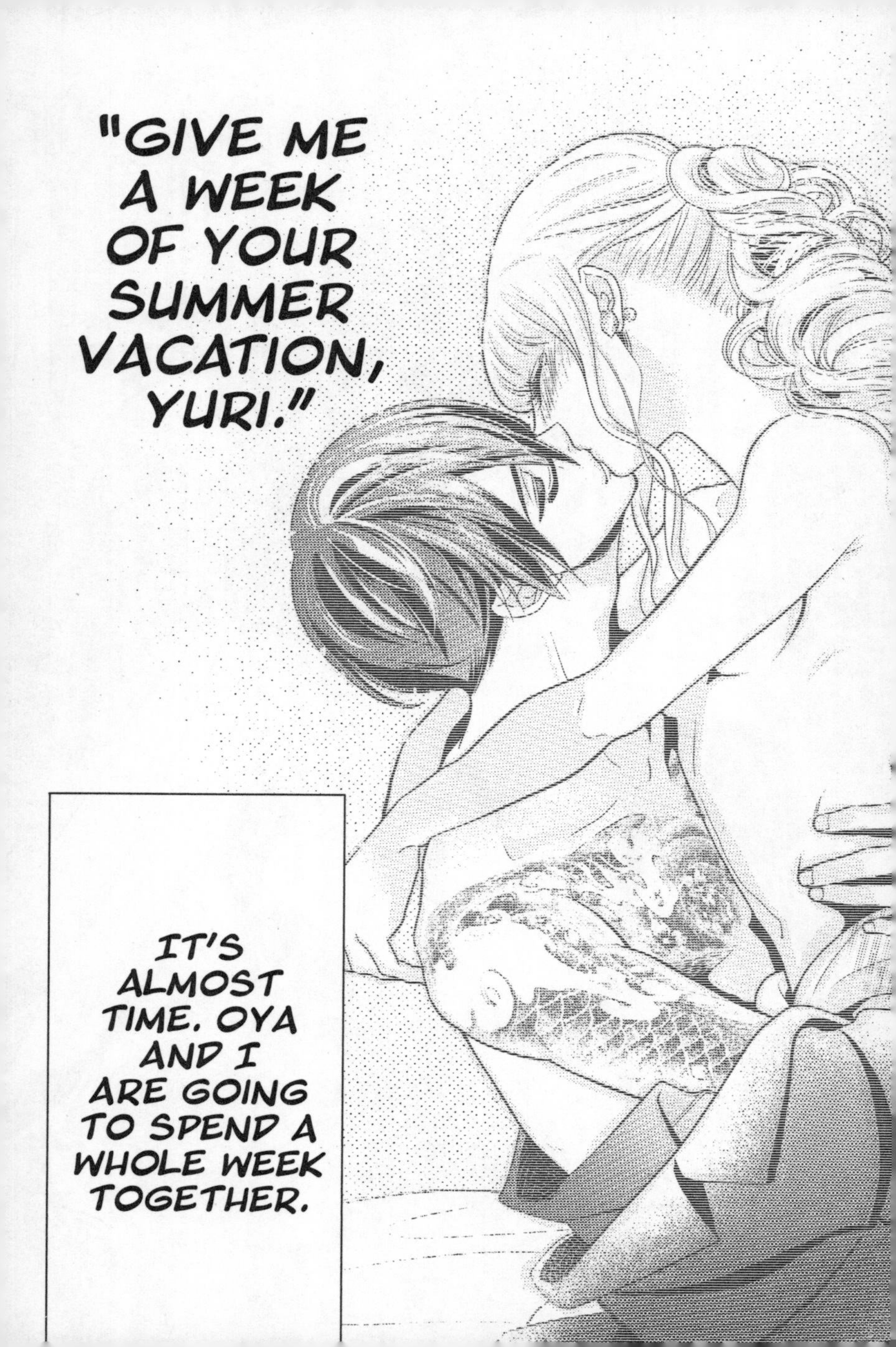
"GIVE ME A WEEK OF YOUR SUMMER VACATION, YURI."
IT'S ALMOST TIME. OYA AND I ARE GOING TO SPEND A WHOLE WEEK TOGETHER.

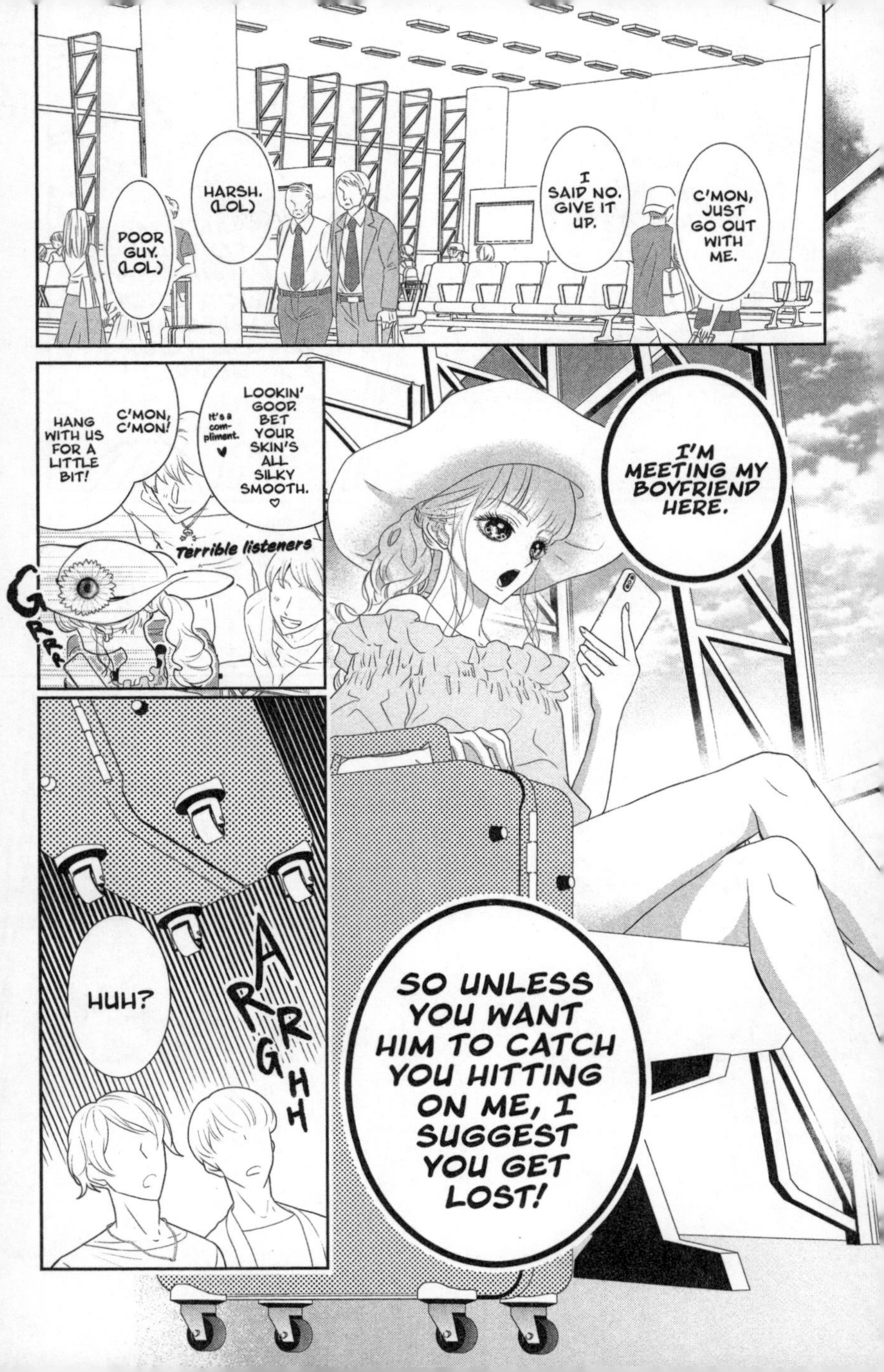
C'MON, JUST GO OUT WITH ME.
I SAID NO. GIVE IT UP.
HARSH. (LOL)
POOR GUY. (LOL)
I'M MEETING MY BOYFRIEND HERE.
SO UNLESS YOU WANT HIM TO CATCH YOU HITTING ON ME, I SUGGEST YOU GET LOST!
LOOKIN' GOOD. BET YOUR SKIN'S ALL SILKY SMOOTH. ♡
It's a compliment. ♥
C'MON, C'MON!
HANG WITH US FOR A LITTLE BIT!
Terrible listeners
GRRRR
ARRGHH
HUH?

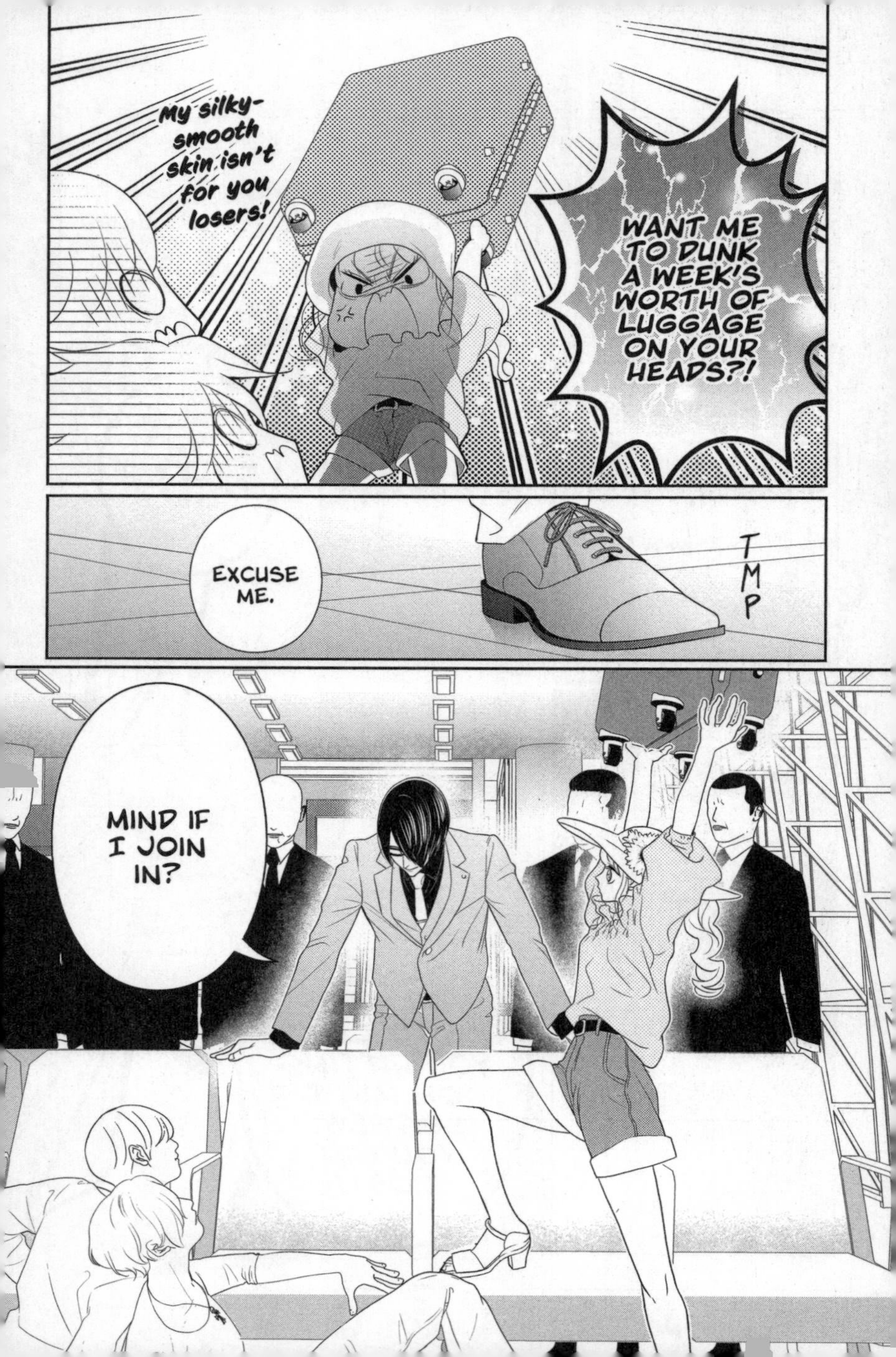
WANT ME TO DUNK A WEEK'S WORTH OF LUGGAGE ON YOUR HEADS?!
My silky-smooth skin isn't for you losers!
TMP
EXCUSE ME.
MIND IF I JOIN IN?

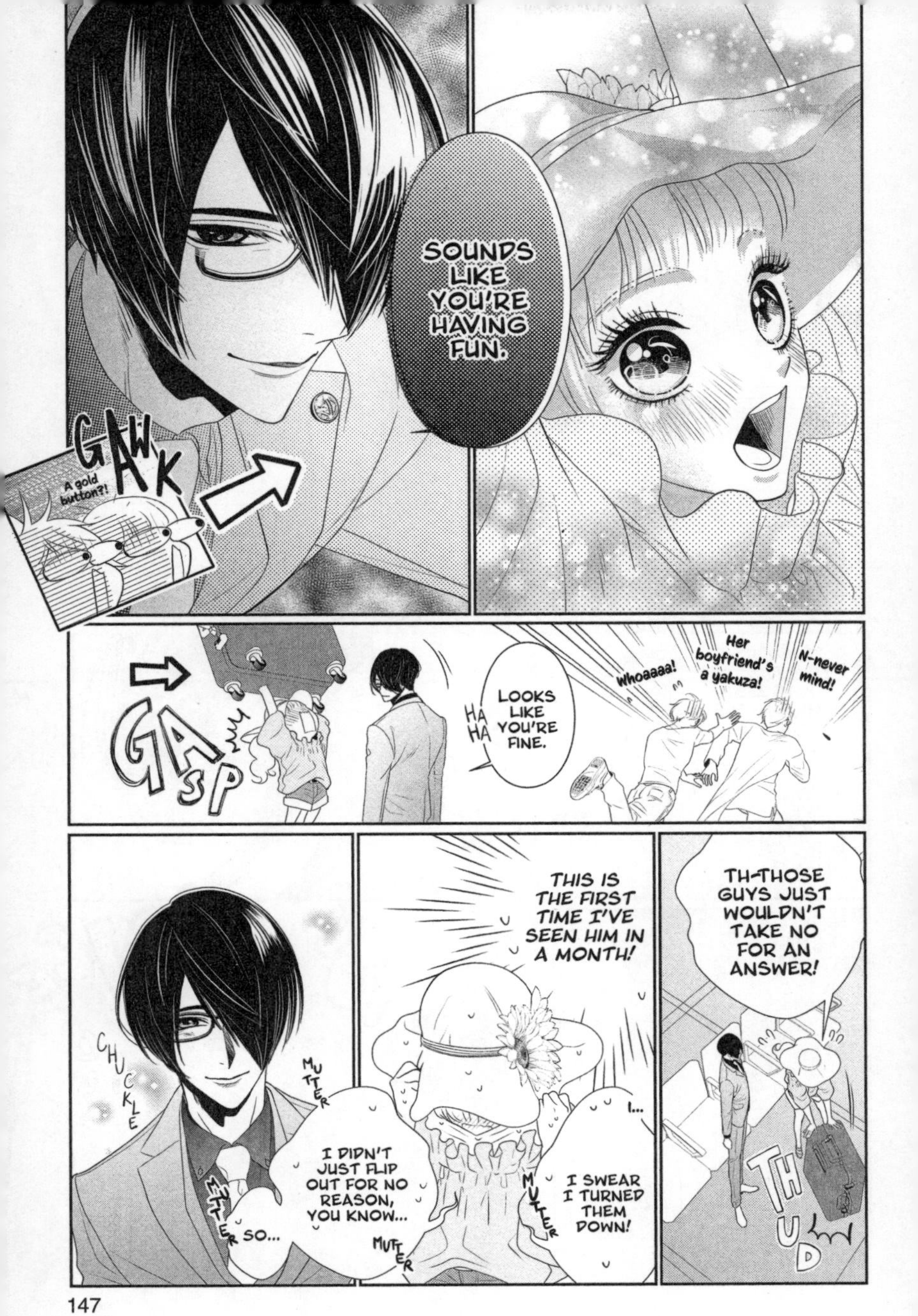
SOUNDS LIKE YOU'RE HAVING FUN.
GAWK
A gold button?!
N-never mind!
Her boyfriend's a yakuza!
Whoaaaa!
HA HA
LOOKS LIKE YOU'RE FINE.
GASP
TH-THOSE GUYS JUST WOULDN'T TAKE NO FOR AN ANSWER!
THUD
THIS IS THE FIRST TIME I'VE SEEN HIM IN A MONTH!
I...
I SWEAR I TURNED THEM DOWN!
MUTTER
I DIDN'T JUST FLIP OUT FOR NO REASON, YOU KNOW...
MUTTER
MUTTER
SO...
MUTTER
CHUCKLE

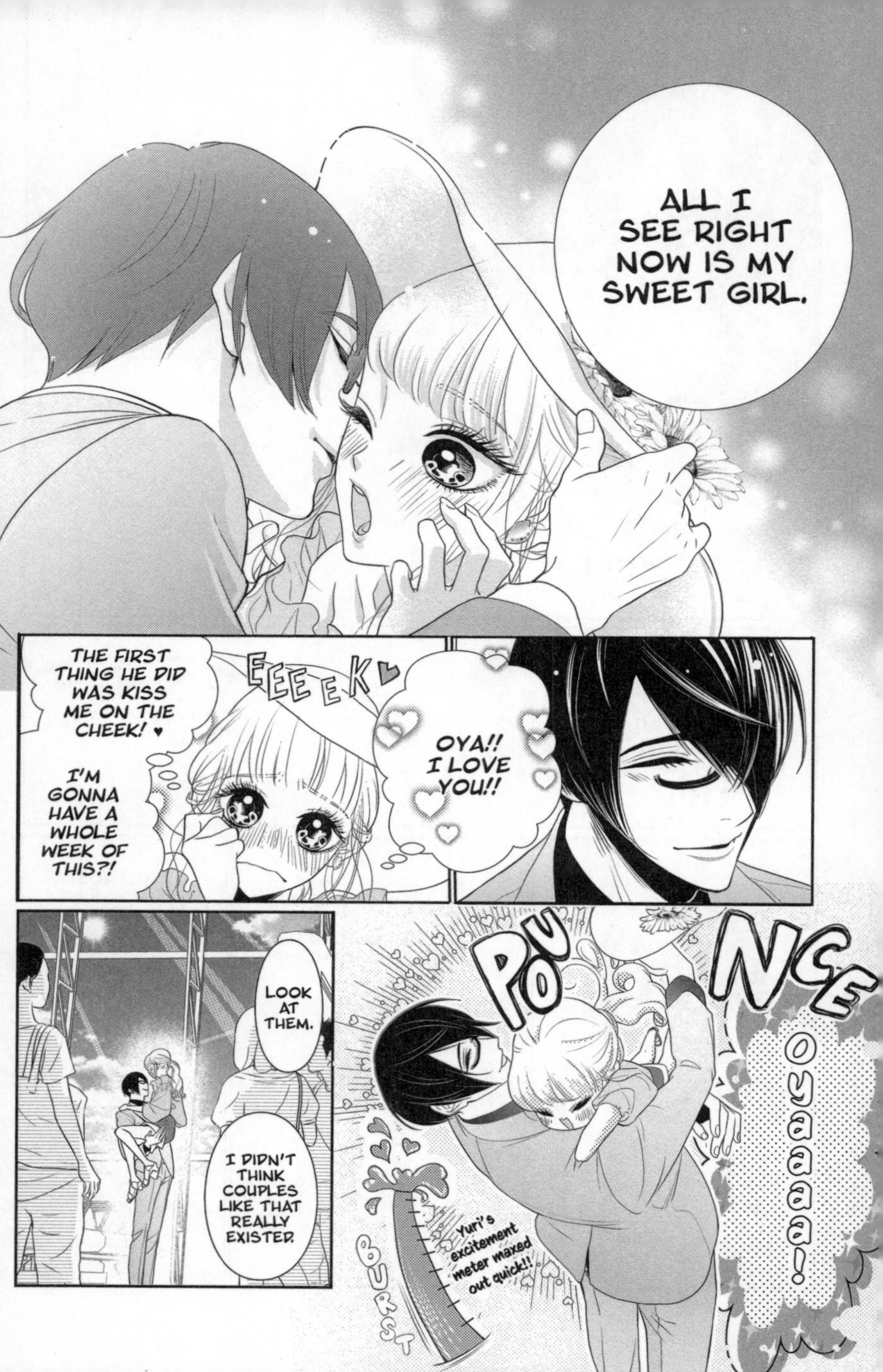
ALL I SEE RIGHT NOW IS MY SWEET GIRL.
OYA!! I LOVE YOU!!
EEEEK ♥
THE FIRST THING HE DID WAS KISS ME ON THE CHEEK! ♥
I'M GONNA HAVE A WHOLE WEEK OF THIS?!
POUNCE
Oyaaaaaa!
Yuri's excitement meter maxed out quick!!
BURST
LOOK AT THEM.
I DIDN'T THINK COUPLES LIKE THAT REALLY EXISTED.

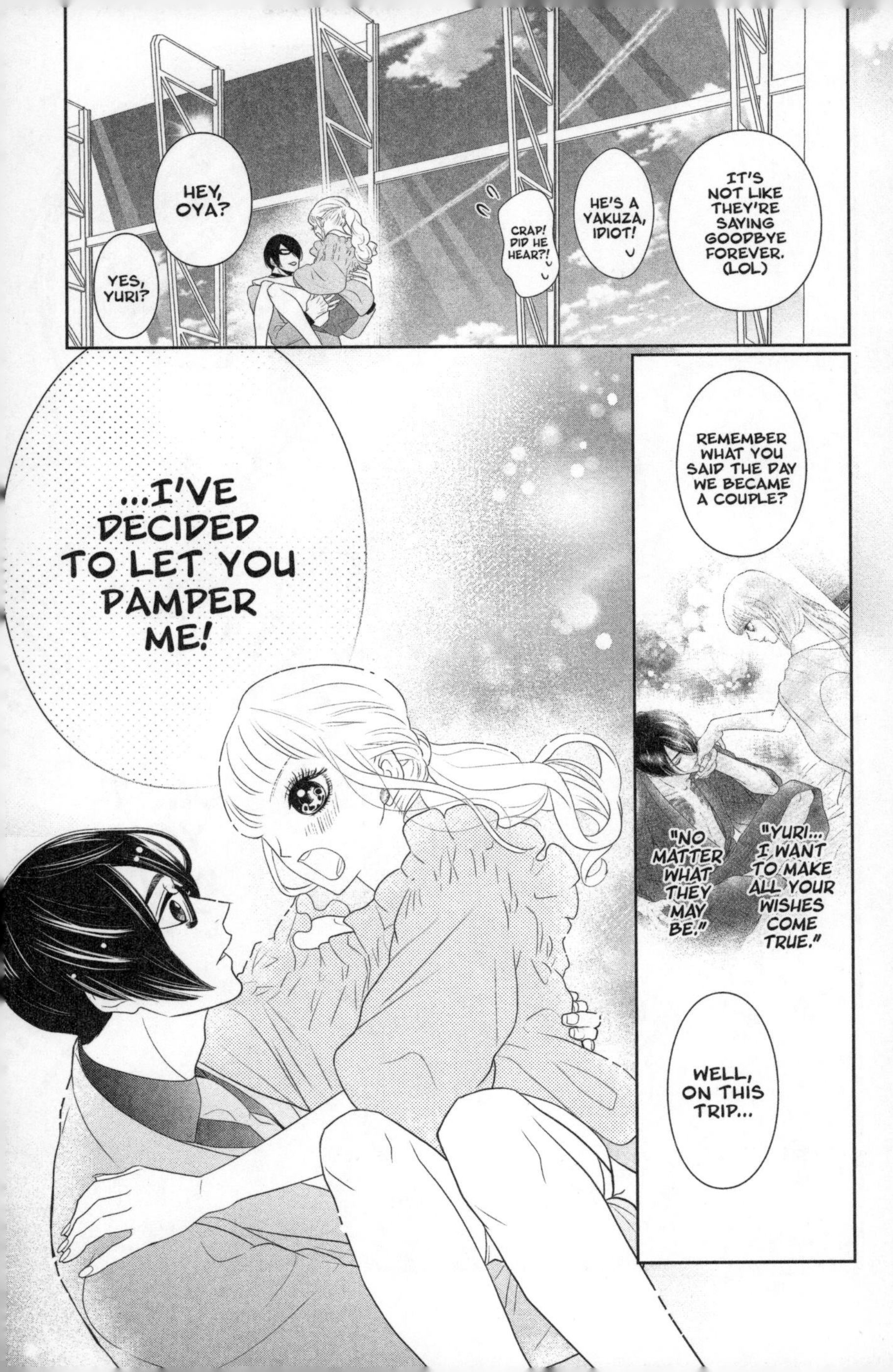
IT'S NOT LIKE THEY'RE SAYING GOODBYE FOREVER. (LOL)
HE'S A YAKUZA, IDIOT!
CRAP! DID HE HEAR?!
HEY, OYA?
YES, YURI?
REMEMBER WHAT YOU SAID THE DAY WE BECAME A COUPLE?
"YURI... I WANT TO MAKE ALL YOUR WISHES COME TRUE."
"NO MATTER WHAT THEY MAY BE."
WELL, ON THIS TRIP...
...I'VE DECIDED TO LET YOU PAMPER ME!

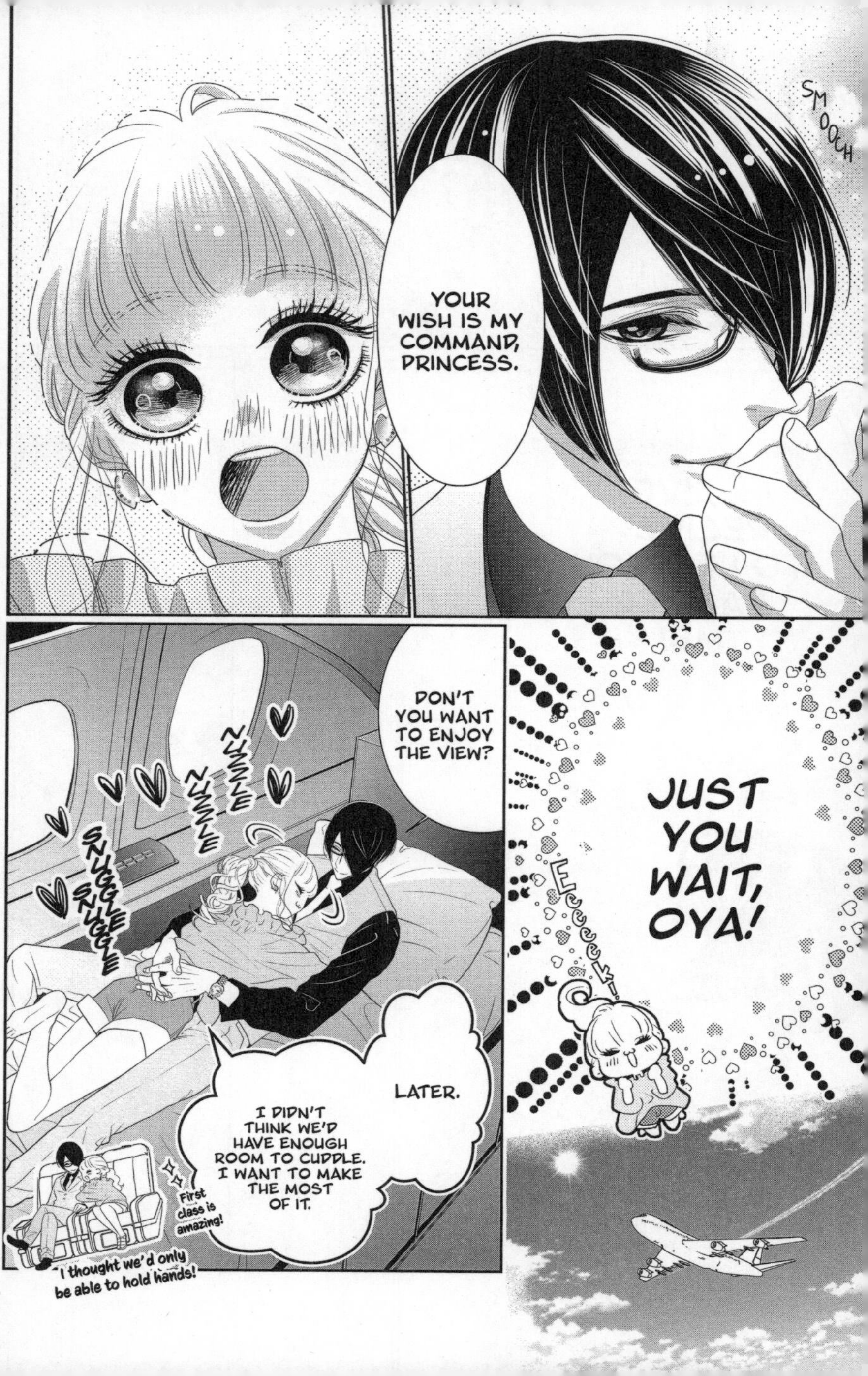
SMOOCH
YOUR WISH IS MY COMMAND, PRINCESS.
JUST YOU WAIT, OYA!
Eeeeek!
DON'T YOU WANT TO ENJOY THE VIEW?
NUZZLE NUZZLE
SNUGGLE SNUGGLE
LATER.
I DIDN'T THINK WE'D HAVE ENOUGH ROOM TO CUDDLE. I WANT TO MAKE THE MOST OF IT.
First class is amazing!
I thought we'd only be able to hold hands!

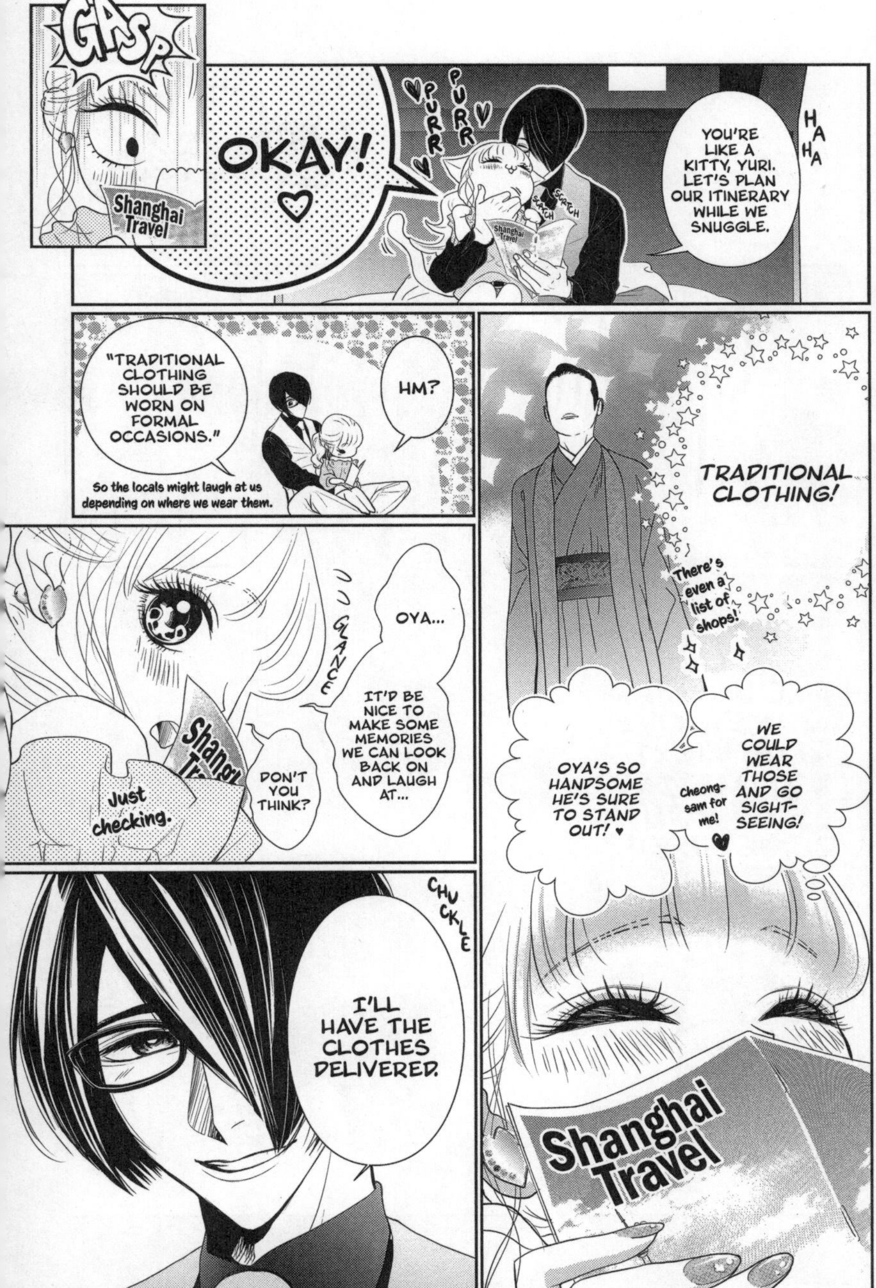
HA HA
YOU'RE LIKE A KITTY, YURI. LET'S PLAN OUR ITINERARY WHILE WE SNUGGLE.
PURR PURR
SCRATCH SCRATCH
Shanghai Travel
OKAY! ♥
GASP
Shanghai Travel
TRADITIONAL CLOTHING!
There's even a list of shops!
WE COULD WEAR THOSE AND GO SIGHT-SEEING!
Cheong-sam for me!
OYA'S SO HANDSOME HE'S SURE TO STAND OUT! ♥
Shanghai Travel
HM?
"TRADITIONAL CLOTHING SHOULD BE WORN ON FORMAL OCCASIONS."
So the locals might laugh at us depending on where we wear them.
OYA...
GLANCE
IT'D BE NICE TO MAKE SOME MEMORIES WE CAN LOOK BACK ON AND LAUGH AT...
DON'T YOU THINK?
Shanghai Travel
Just checking.
CHUCKLE
I'LL HAVE THE CLOTHES DELIVERED.

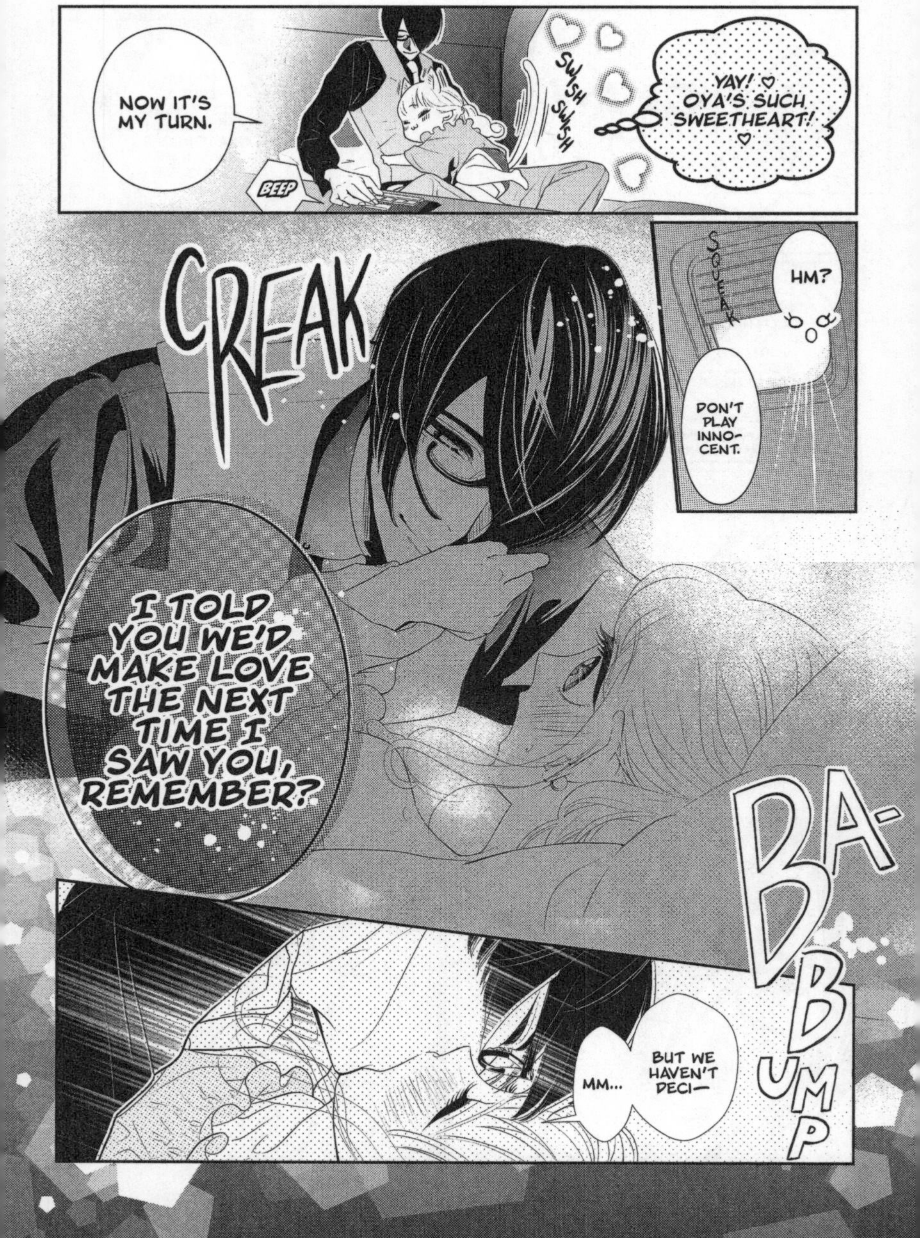
YAY! ♡ OYA'S SUCH SWEETHEART! ♡
SWISH SWISH
NOW IT'S MY TURN.
BEEP
SQUEAK
HM?
DON'T PLAY INNO-CENT.
CREAK
I TOLD YOU WE'D MAKE LOVE THE NEXT TIME I SAW YOU, REMEMBER?
BA-BUMP
BUT WE HAVEN'T DECI—
MM...

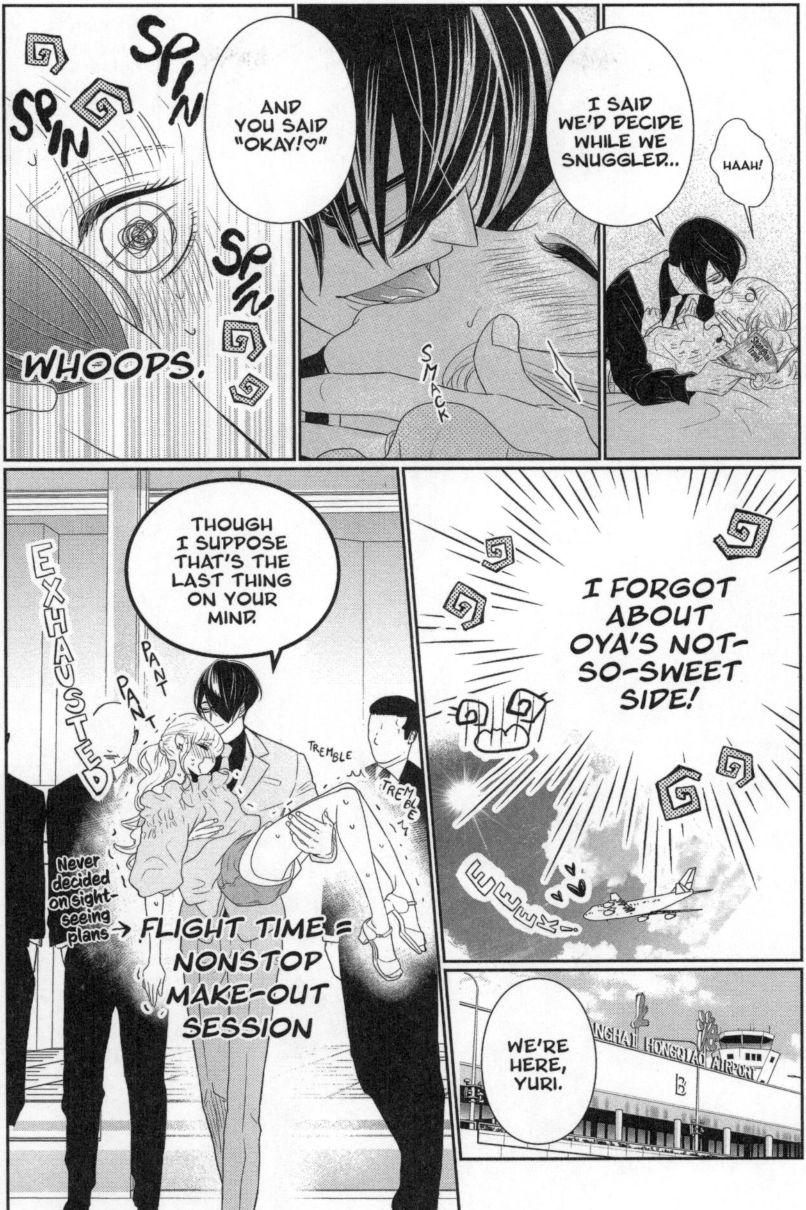
I SAID WE'D DECIDE WHILE WE SNUGGLED...
HAAH!
AND YOU SAID "OKAY!♡"
SMACK
SPIN
SPIN
SPIN
WHOOPS.
I FORGOT ABOUT OYA'S NOT-SO-SWEET SIDE!
EEEEK-!
WE'RE HERE, YURI.
NGHAI HONGQIAO AIRPORT
THOUGH I SUPPOSE THAT'S THE LAST THING ON YOUR MIND.
EXHAUSTED
PANT
PANT
TREMBLE
TREMBLE
Never decided on sight-seeing plans → FLIGHT TIME = NONSTOP MAKE-OUT SESSION

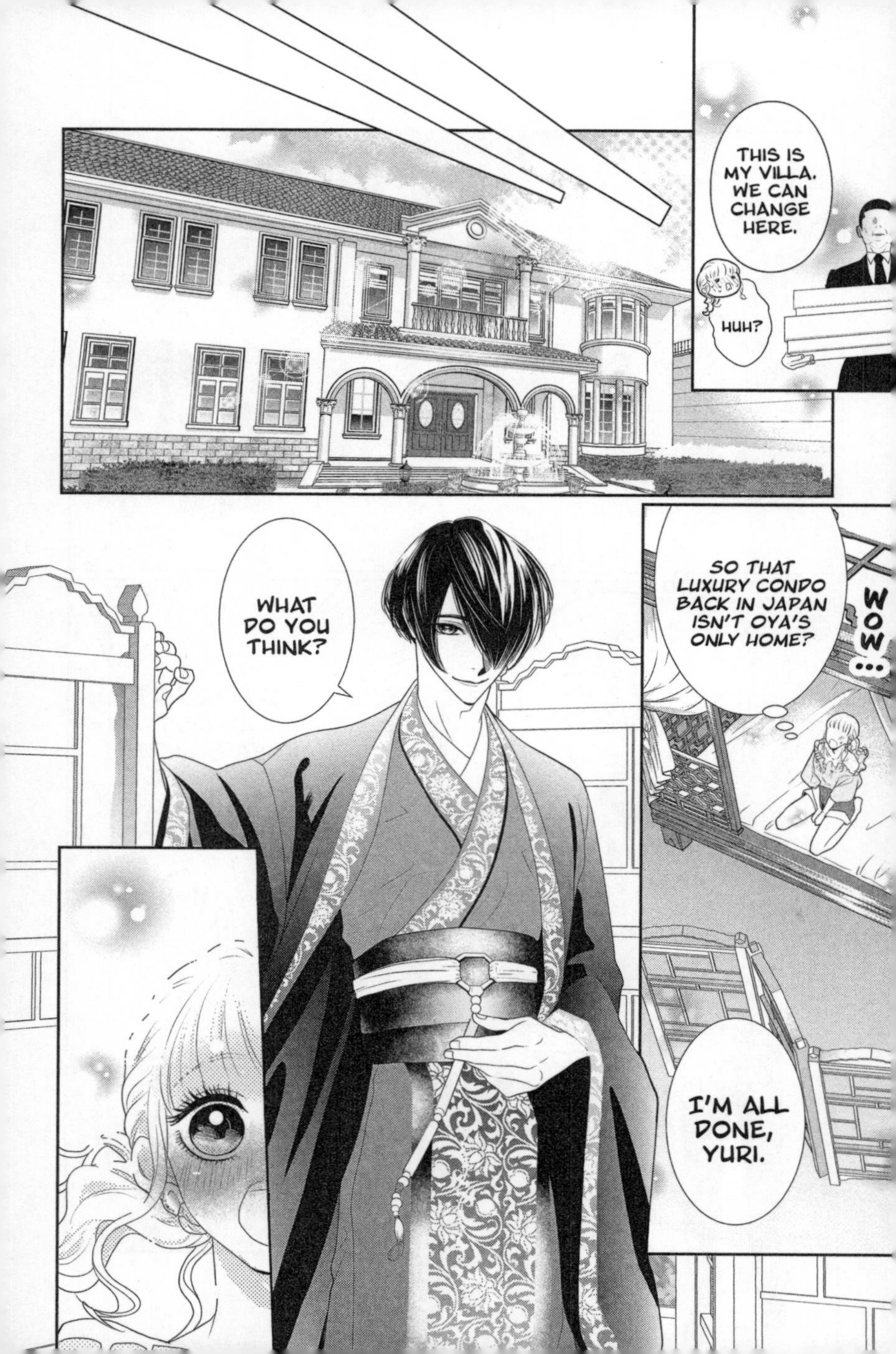

THIS IS MY VILLA. WE CAN CHANGE HERE.
HUH?
SO THAT LUXURY CONDO BACK IN JAPAN ISN'T OYA'S ONLY HOME?
WOW...
I'M ALL DONE, YURI.
WHAT DO YOU THINK?

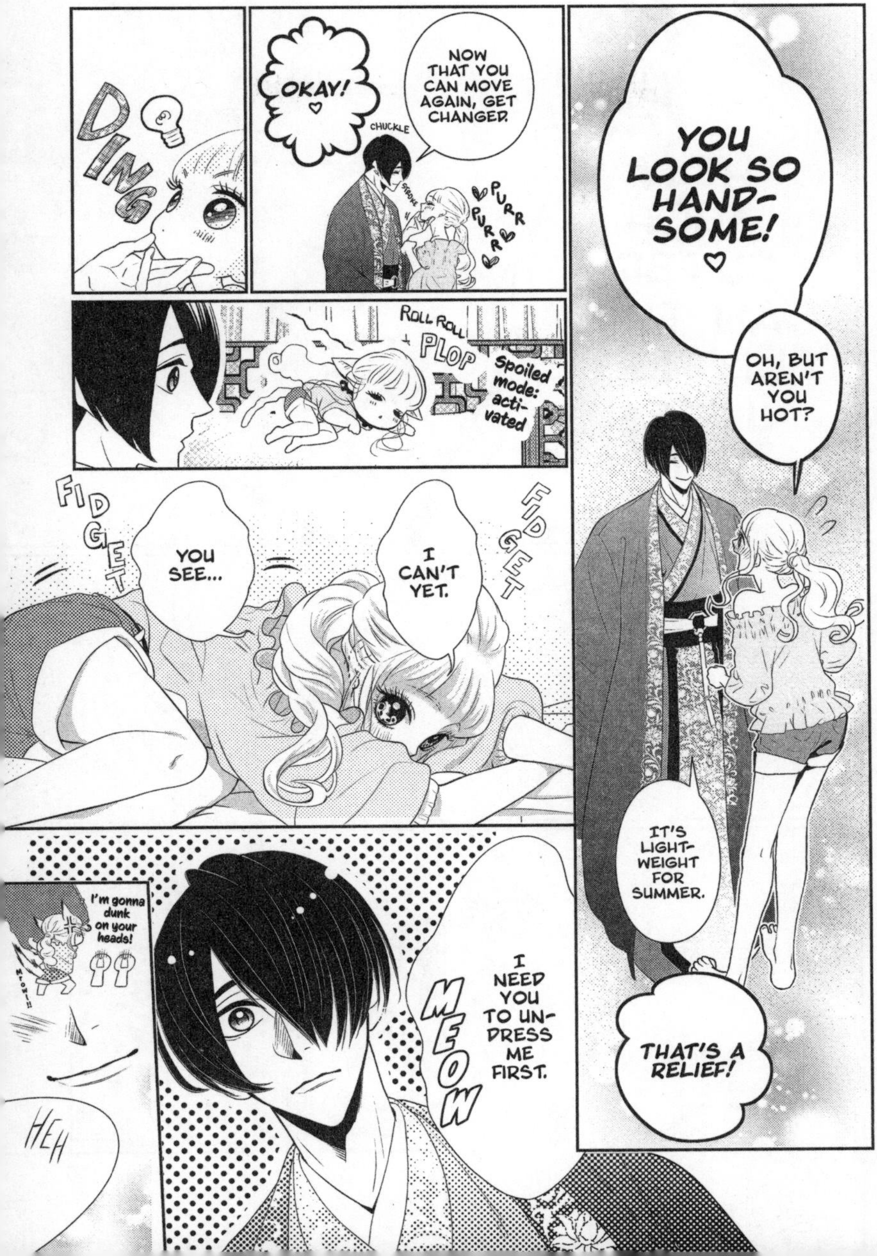
YOU LOOK SO HAND-SOME! ♡
OH, BUT AREN'T YOU HOT?
IT'S LIGHT-WEIGHT FOR SUMMER.
THAT'S A RELIEF!
NOW THAT YOU CAN MOVE AGAIN, GET CHANGED.
OKAY! ♡
CHUCKLE
STROKE
PURR PURR
DING
ROLL ROLL
PLOP
Spoiled mode: activated
FIDGET
I CAN'T YET.
YOU SEE...
FIDGET
I NEED YOU TO UN-DRESS ME FIRST.
MEOW
I'm gonna dunk on your heads!
HEH

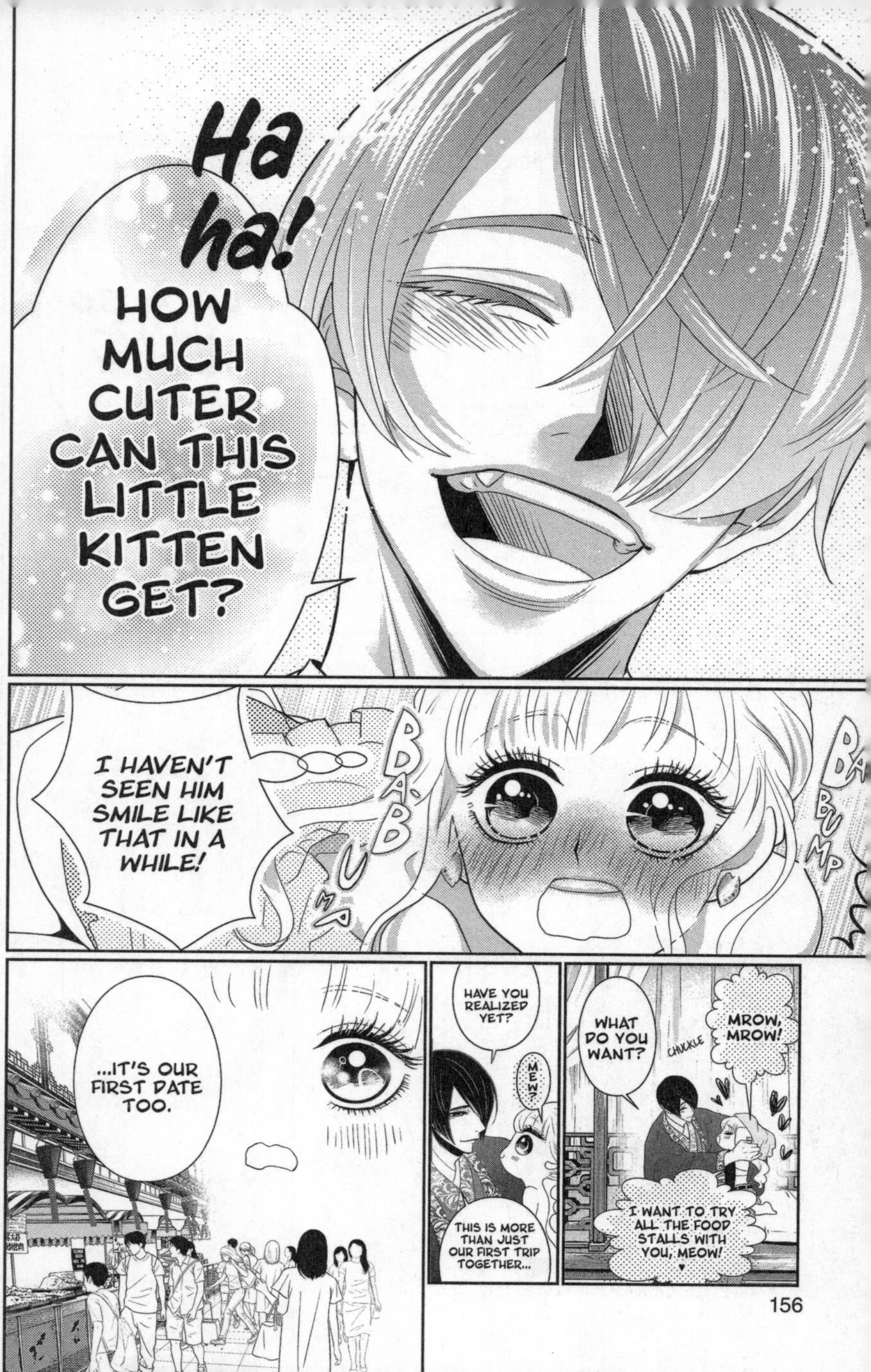
Ha ha!
HOW MUCH CUTER CAN THIS LITTLE KITTEN GET?
BA-BUMP
I HAVEN'T SEEN HIM SMILE LIKE THAT IN A WHILE!
BA-BUMP
MROW, MROW!
WHAT DO YOU WANT?
CHUCKLE
I WANT TO TRY ALL THE FOOD STALLS WITH YOU, MEOW!
HAVE YOU REALIZED YET?
MEW?
THIS IS MORE THAN JUST OUR FIRST TRIP TOGETHER...
...IT'S OUR FIRST DATE TOO.

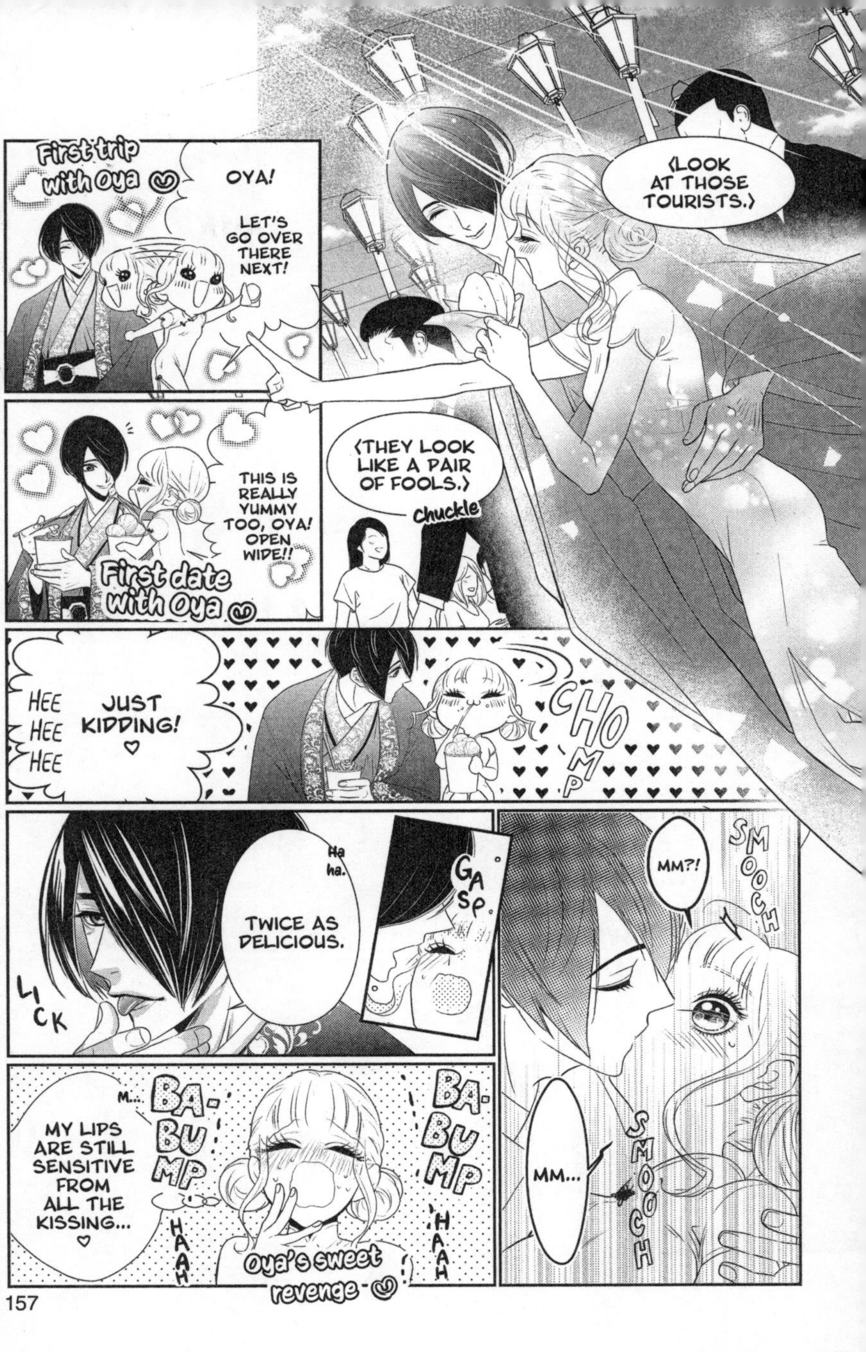

⟨LOOK AT THOSE TOURISTS.⟩
⟨THEY LOOK LIKE A PAIR OF FOOLS.⟩
Chuckle
First trip with Oya
OYA!
LET'S GO OVER THERE NEXT!
THIS IS REALLY YUMMY TOO, OYA! OPEN WIDE!!
First date with Oya
CHOMP
HEE HEE HEE
JUST KIDDING!
MM?!
SMOOCH
MM...
SMOOCH
GASP
Ha ha.
TWICE AS DELICIOUS.
LICK
BA-BUMP
BA-BUMP
M...
MY LIPS ARE STILL SENSITIVE FROM ALL THE KISSING...
HAAH
HAAH
Oya's sweet revenge

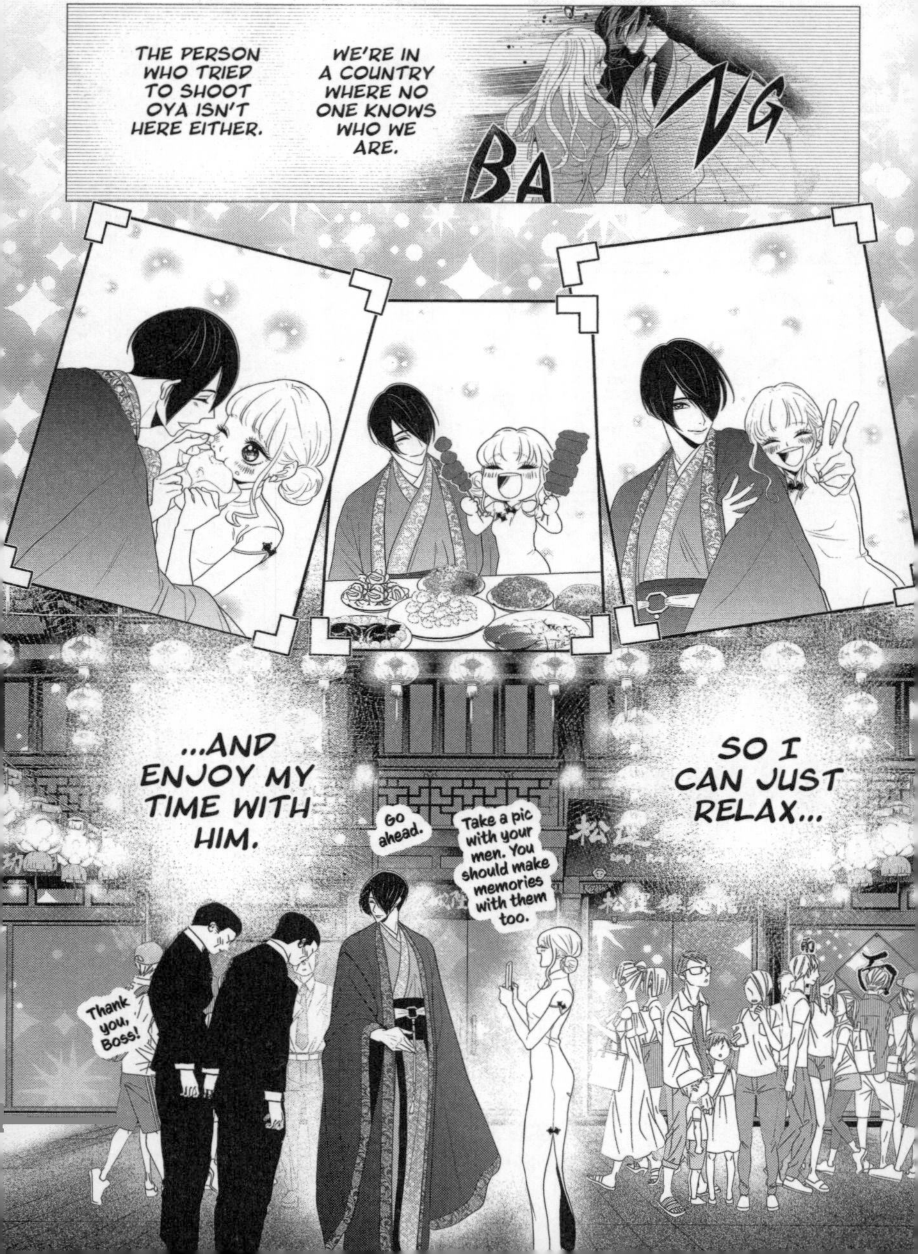
BANG
WE'RE IN A COUNTRY WHERE NO ONE KNOWS WHO WE ARE.
THE PERSON WHO TRIED TO SHOOT OYA ISN'T HERE EITHER.
SO I CAN JUST RELAX...
Take a pic with your men. You should make memories with them too.
Go ahead.
...AND ENJOY MY TIME WITH HIM.
Thank you, Boss!

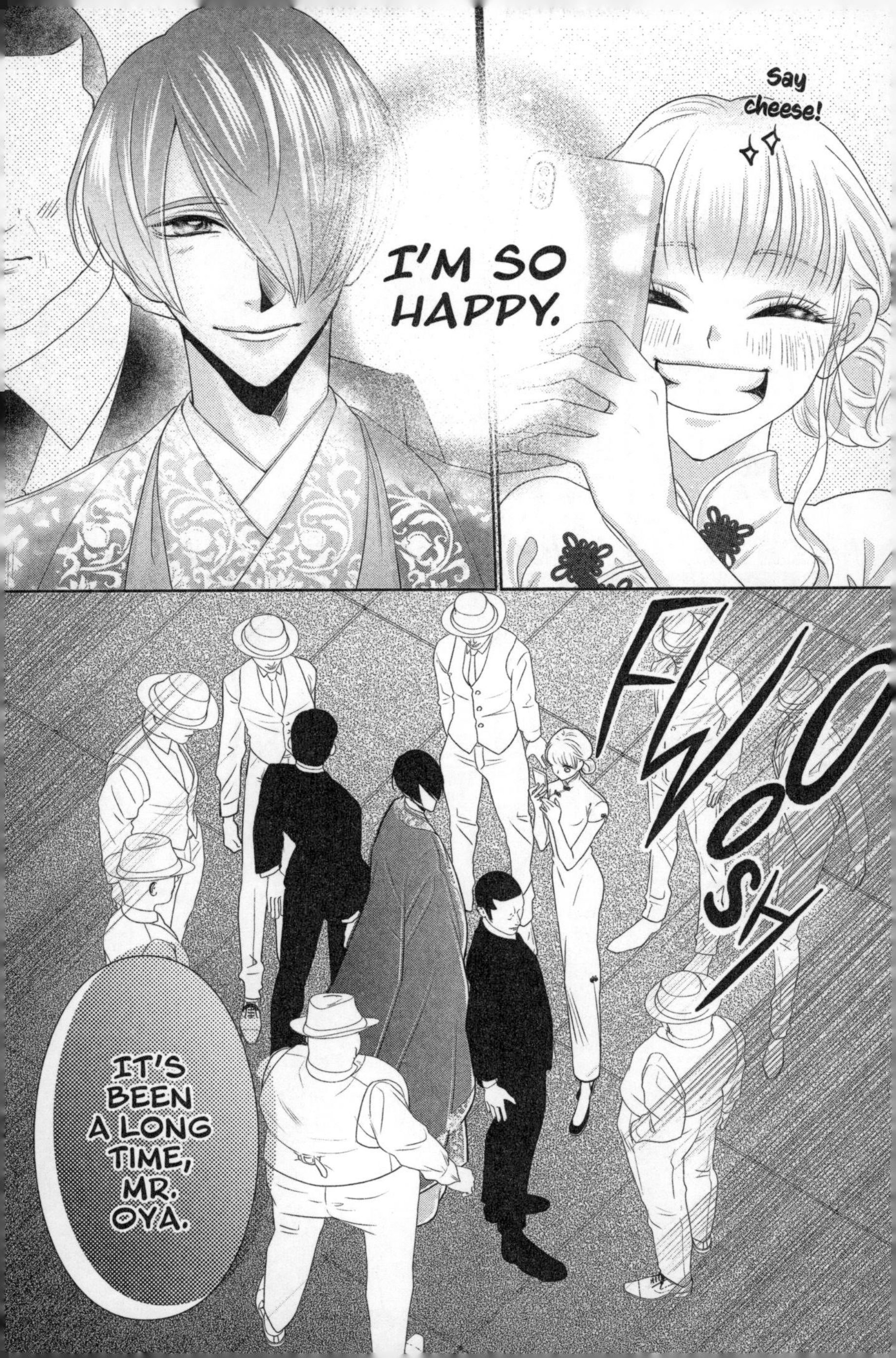
Say cheese!
I'M SO HAPPY.
FWOOSH
IT'S BEEN A LONG TIME, MR. OYA.

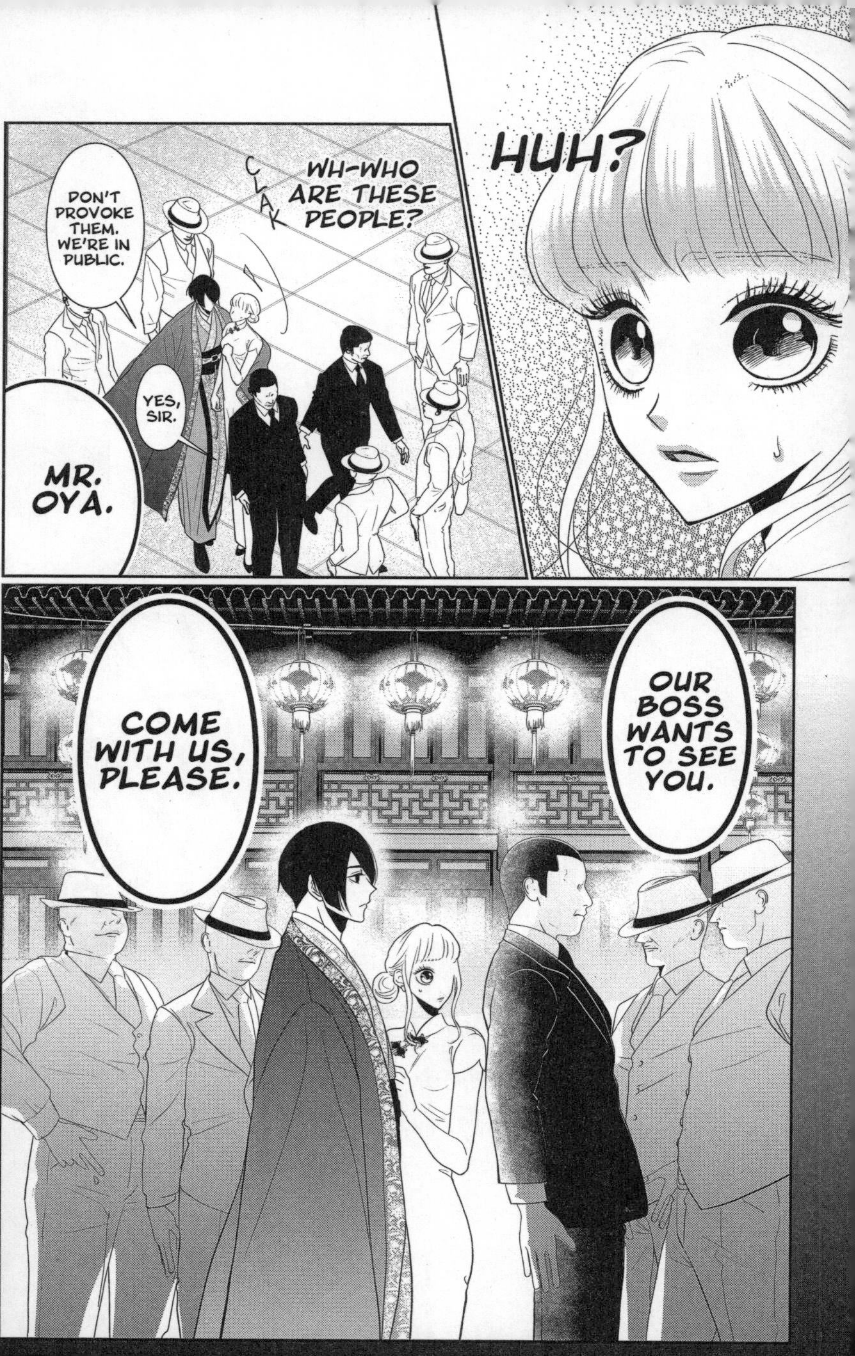
HUH?
WH-WHO ARE THESE PEOPLE?
CLAK
DON'T PROVOKE THEM. WE'RE IN PUBLIC.
YES, SIR.
MR. OYA.
OUR BOSS WANTS TO SEE YOU.
COME WITH US, PLEASE.

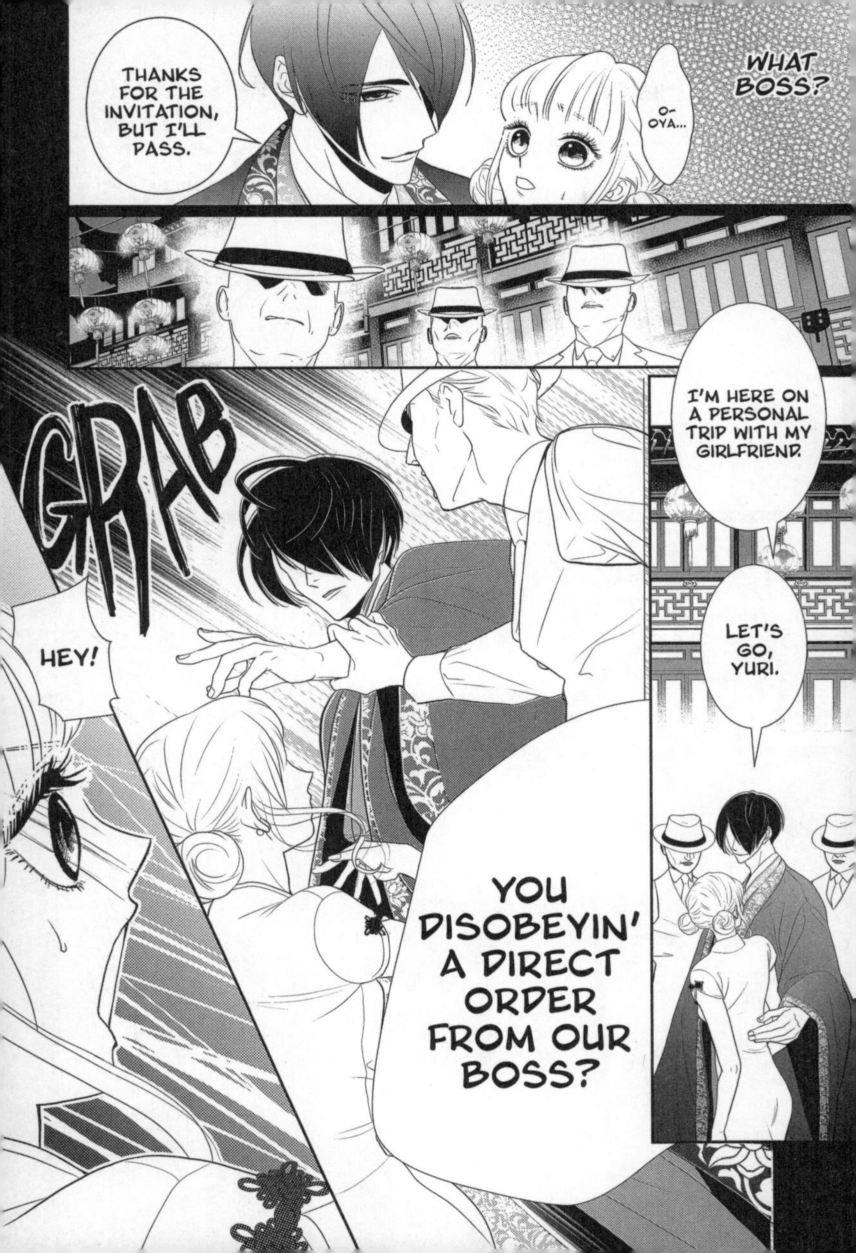
WHAT BOSS?
O-OYA...
THANKS FOR THE INVITATION, BUT I'LL PASS.
I'M HERE ON A PERSONAL TRIP WITH MY GIRLFRIEND.
LET'S GO, YURI.
GRAB
HEY!
YOU DISOBEYIN' A DIRECT ORDER FROM OUR BOSS?

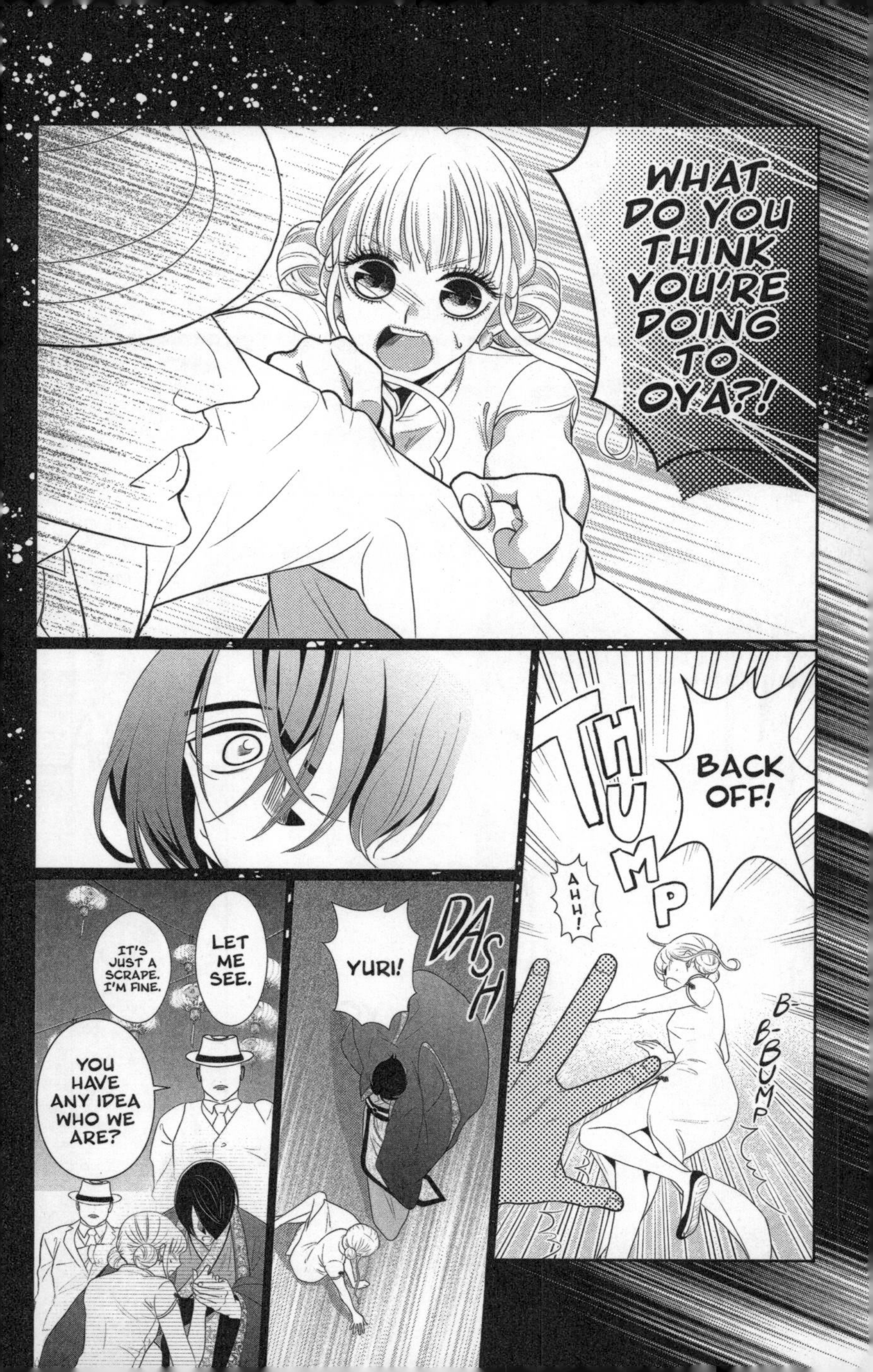
WHAT DO YOU THINK YOU'RE DOING TO OYA?!
BACK OFF!
THUMP
AHH!
B-B-BUMP
DASH
YURI!
LET ME SEE.
IT'S JUST A SCRAPE. I'M FINE.
YOU HAVE ANY IDEA WHO WE ARE?

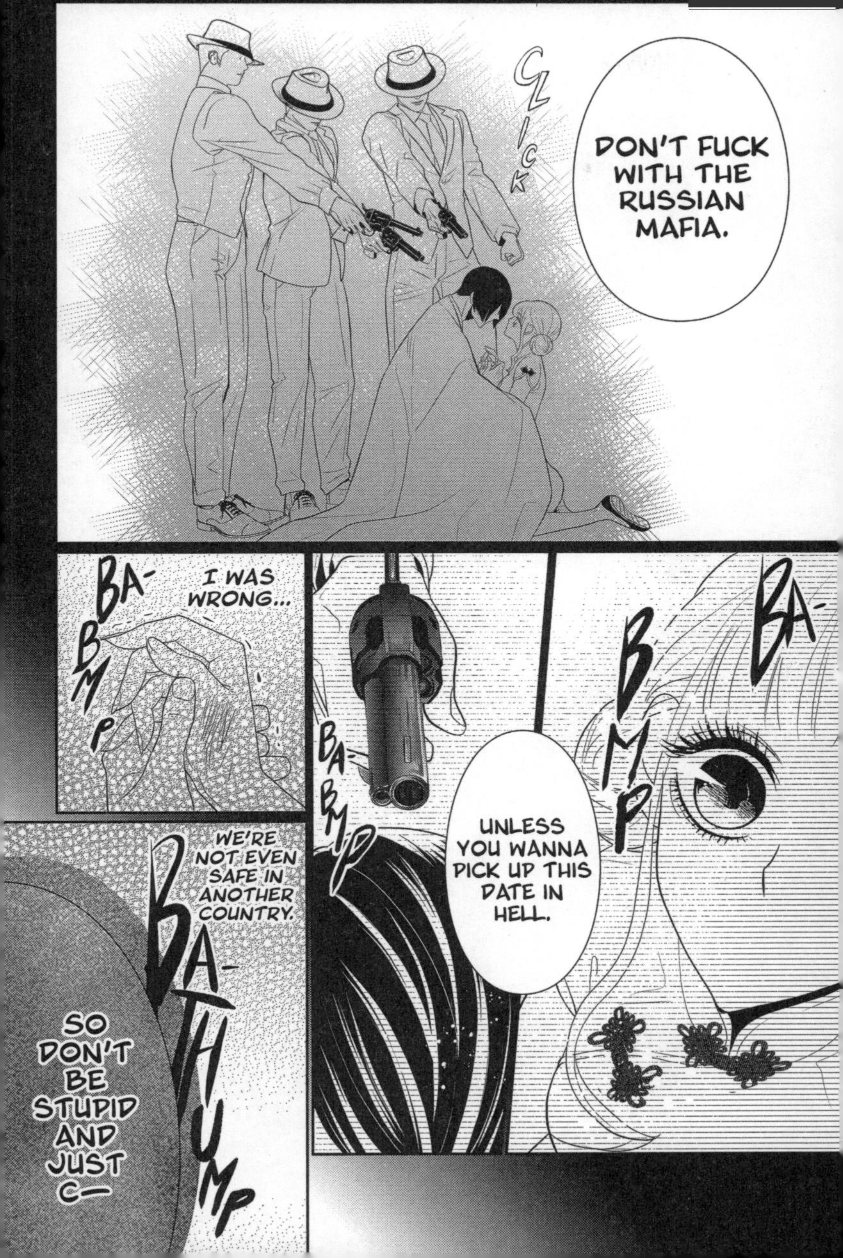
CLICK
DON'T FUCK WITH THE RUSSIAN MAFIA.
BA-BUMP
UNLESS YOU WANNA PICK UP THIS DATE IN HELL.
BA-BUMP
BA-BUMP
I WAS WRONG...
WE'RE NOT EVEN SAFE IN ANOTHER COUNTRY.
BA-THUMP
SO DON'T BE STUPID AND JUST C—

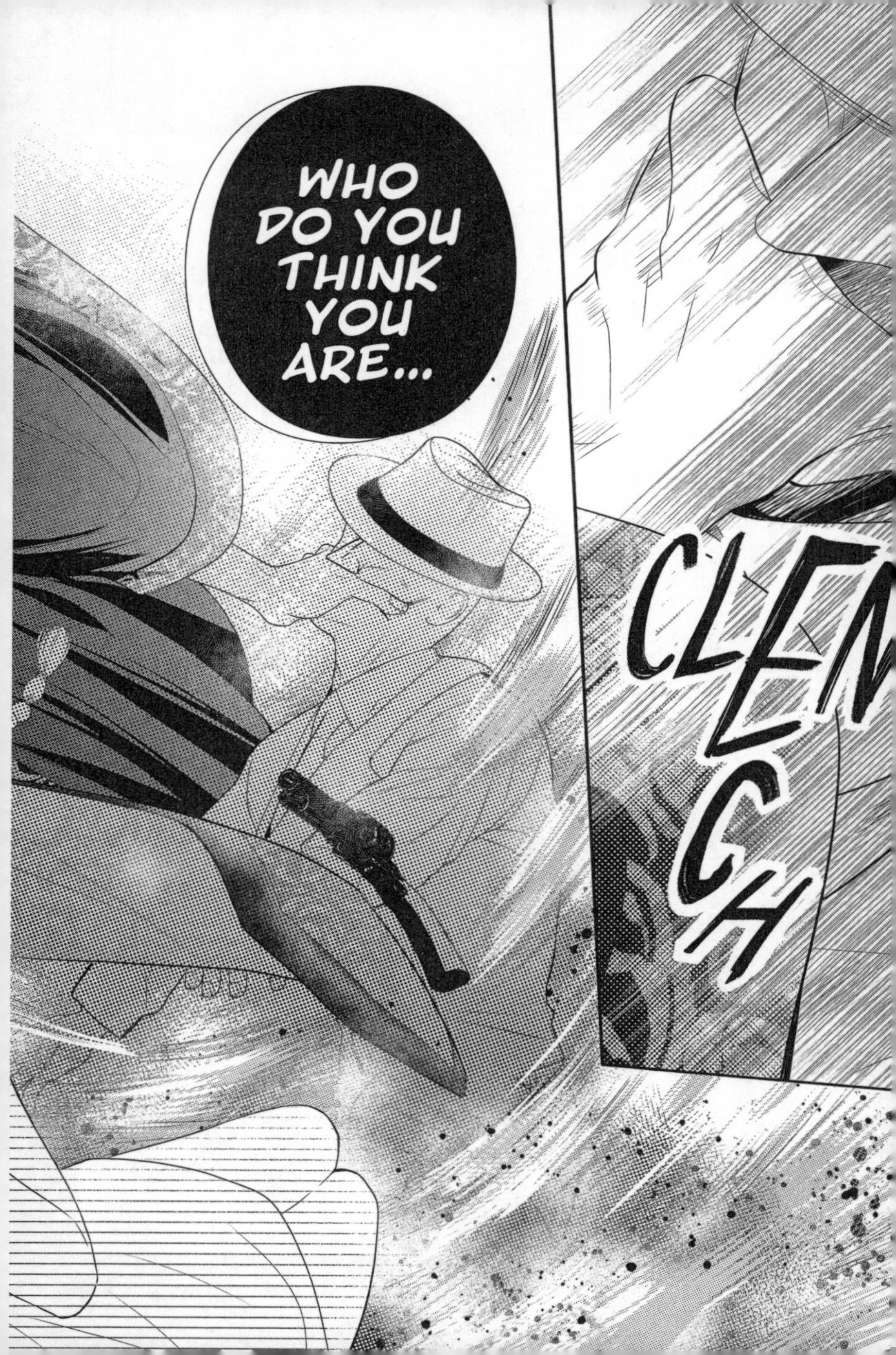
CLENCH
WHO DO YOU THINK YOU ARE...

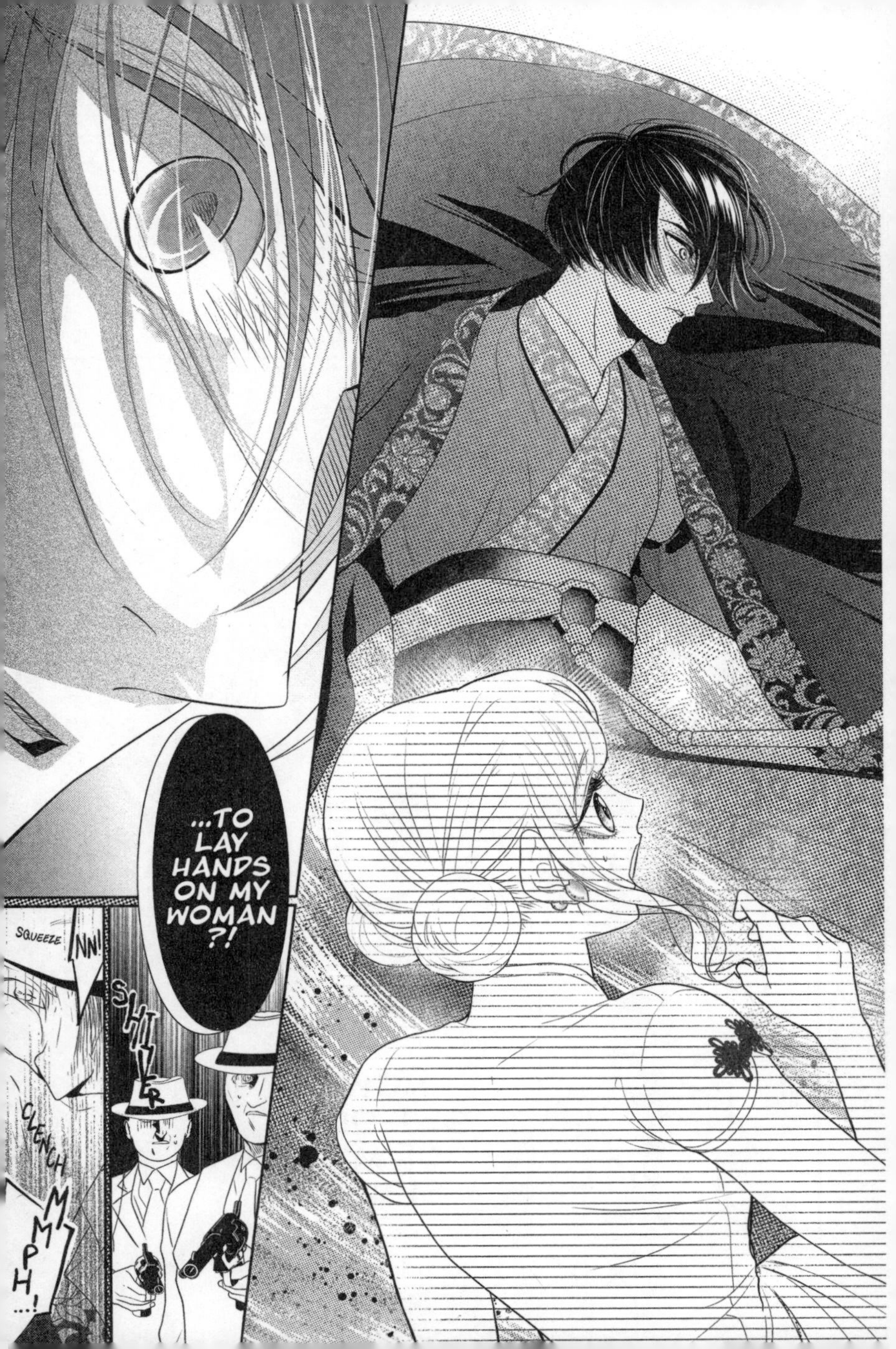
...TO LAY HANDS ON MY WOMAN?!
SQUEEZE
NN!
SHIVER
CLENCH
MMPH...!

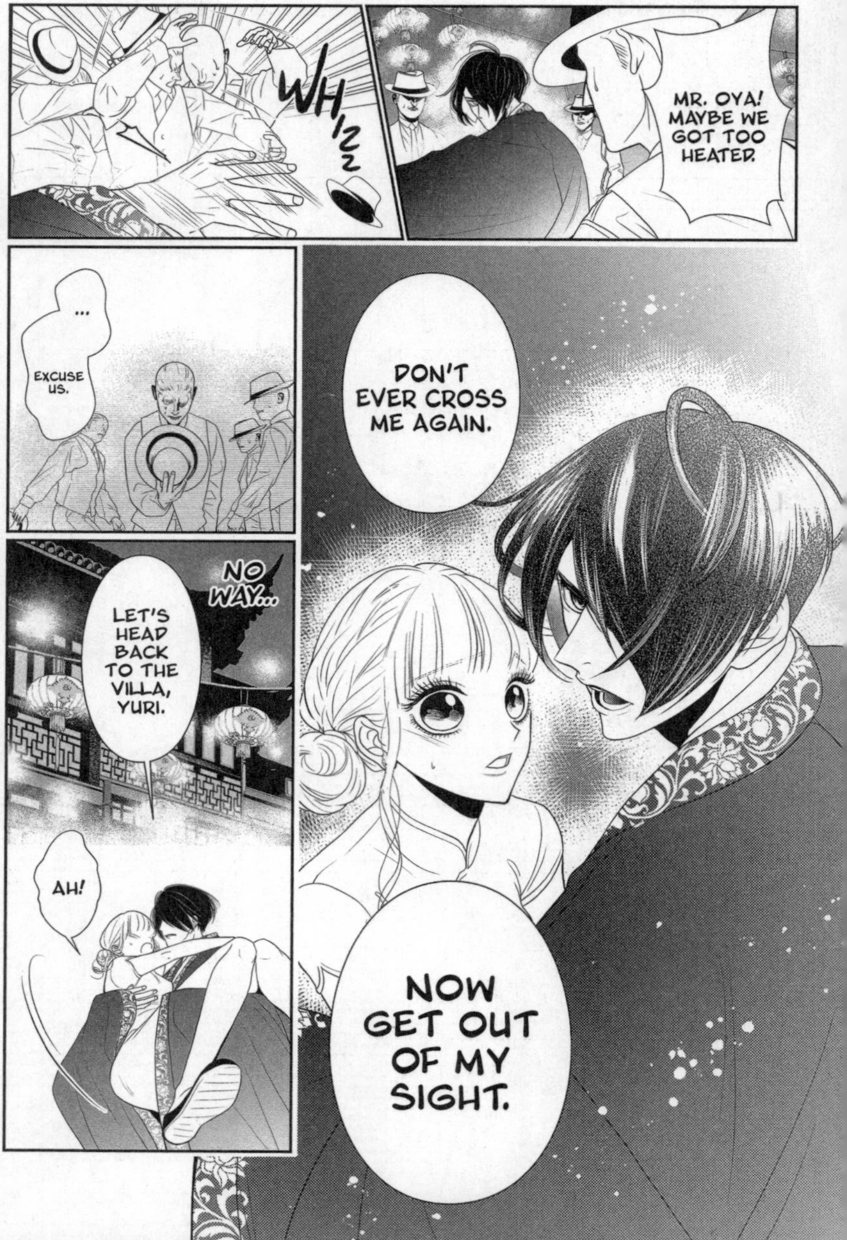
MR. OYA! MAYBE WE GOT TOO HEATED.
WHIZZ
DON'T EVER CROSS ME AGAIN.
NOW GET OUT OF MY SIGHT.
...
EXCUSE US.
NO WAY...
LET'S HEAD BACK TO THE VILLA, YURI.
AH!

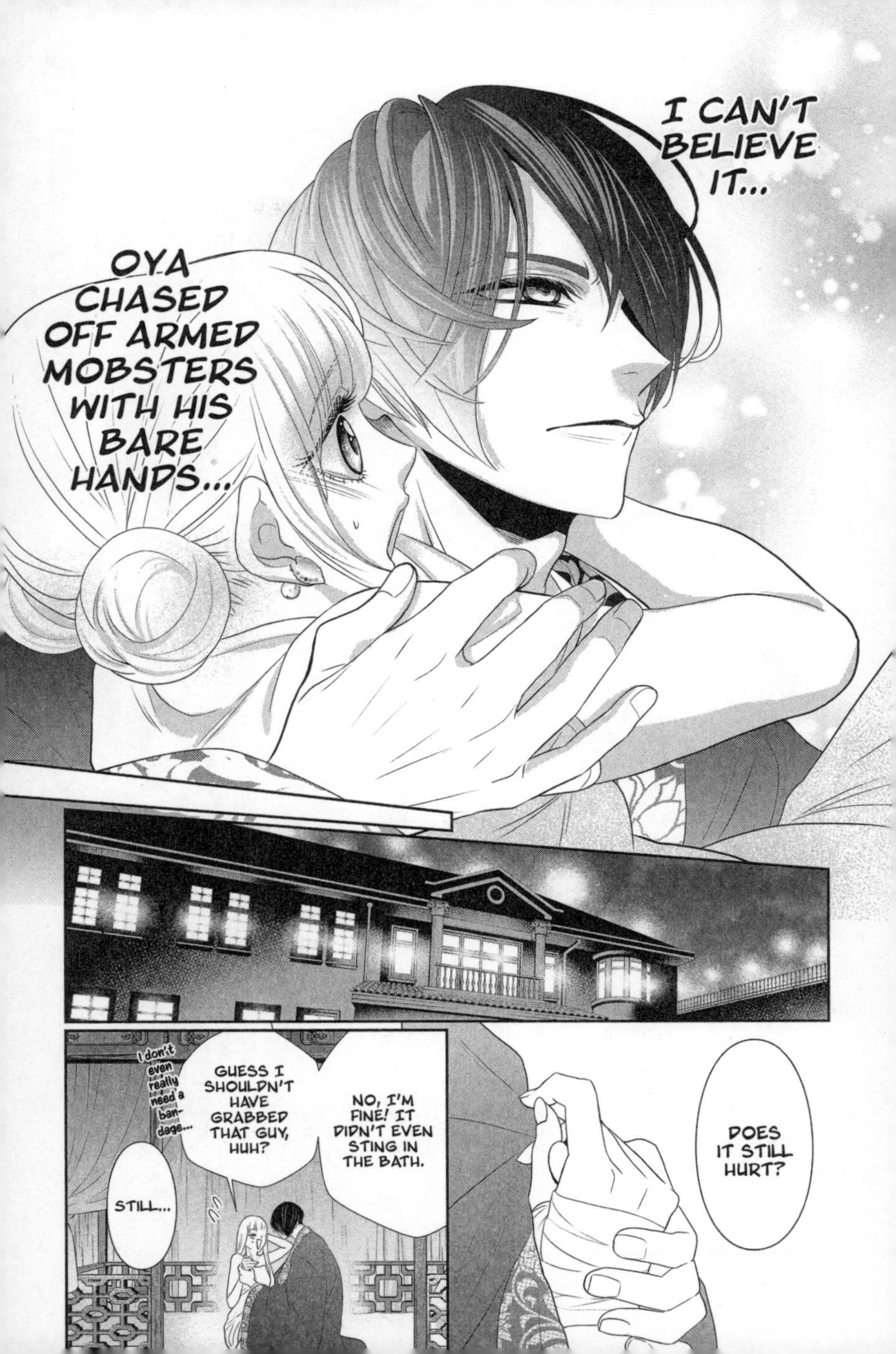
I CAN'T BELIEVE IT...
OYA CHASED OFF ARMED MOBSTERS WITH HIS BARE HANDS...
DOES IT STILL HURT?
NO, I'M FINE! IT DIDN'T EVEN STING IN THE BATH.
GUESS I SHOULDN'T HAVE GRABBED THAT GUY, HUH?
I don't even really need a ban-dage...
STILL...

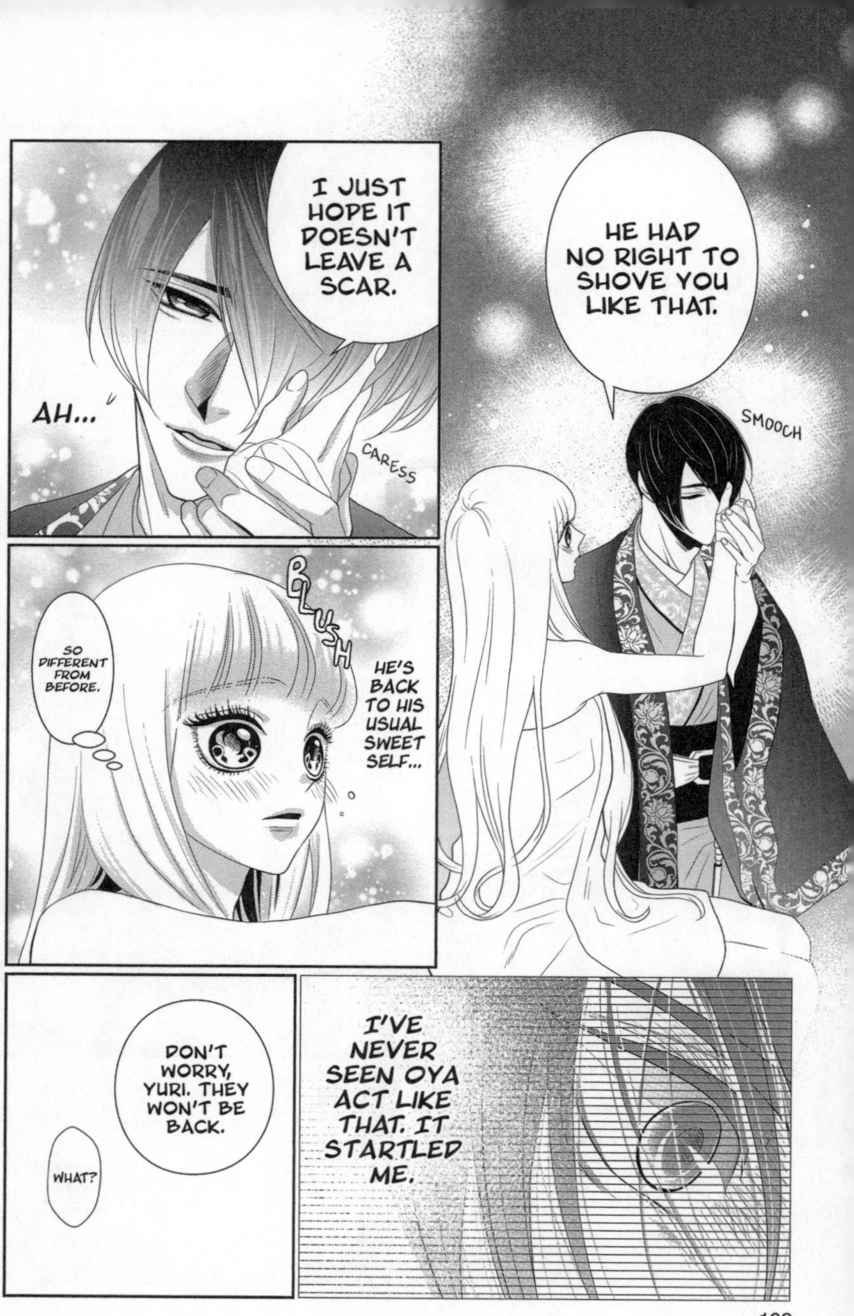
HE HAD NO RIGHT TO SHOVE YOU LIKE THAT.
SMOOCH
I JUST HOPE IT DOESN'T LEAVE A SCAR.
AH...
CARESS
BLUSH
HE'S BACK TO HIS USUAL SWEET SELF...
SO DIFFERENT FROM BEFORE.
I'VE NEVER SEEN OYA ACT LIKE THAT. IT STARTLED ME.
DON'T WORRY, YURI. THEY WON'T BE BACK.
WHAT?

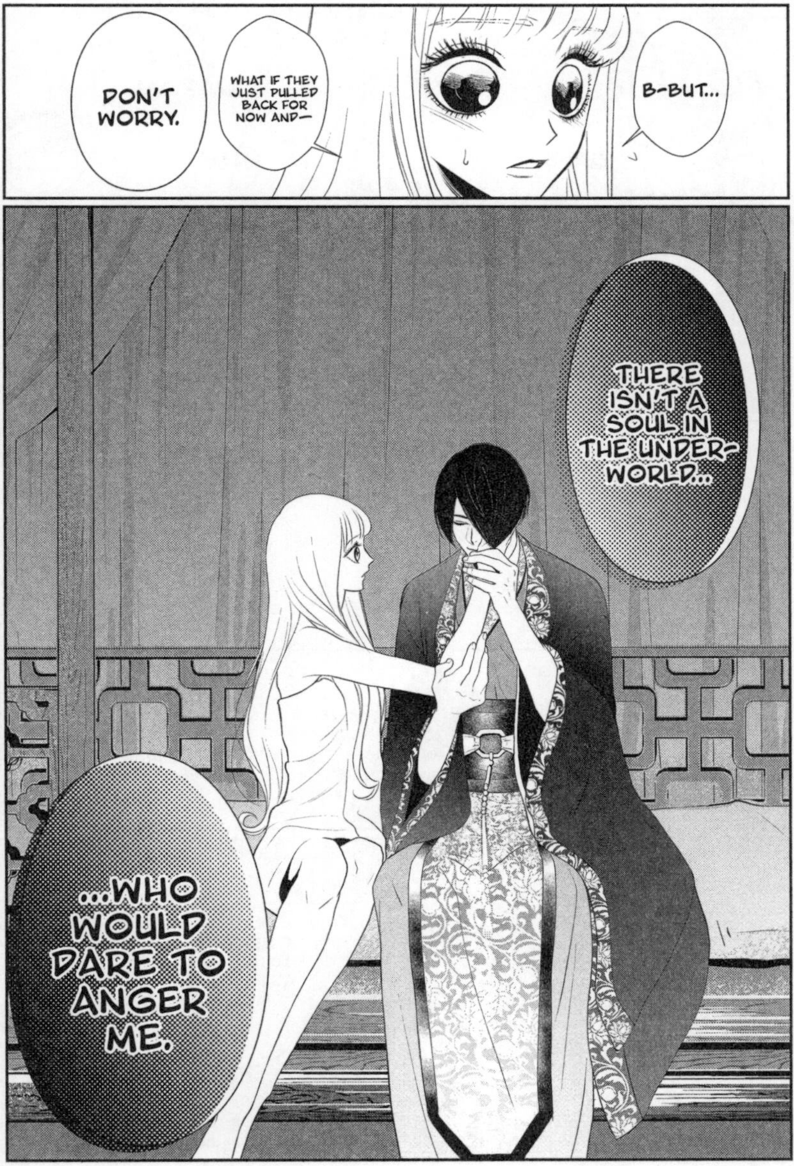
B-BUT...
WHAT IF THEY JUST PULLED BACK FOR NOW AND—
DON'T WORRY.
THERE ISN'T A SOUL IN THE UNDER-WORLD...
...WHO WOULD DARE TO ANGER ME.

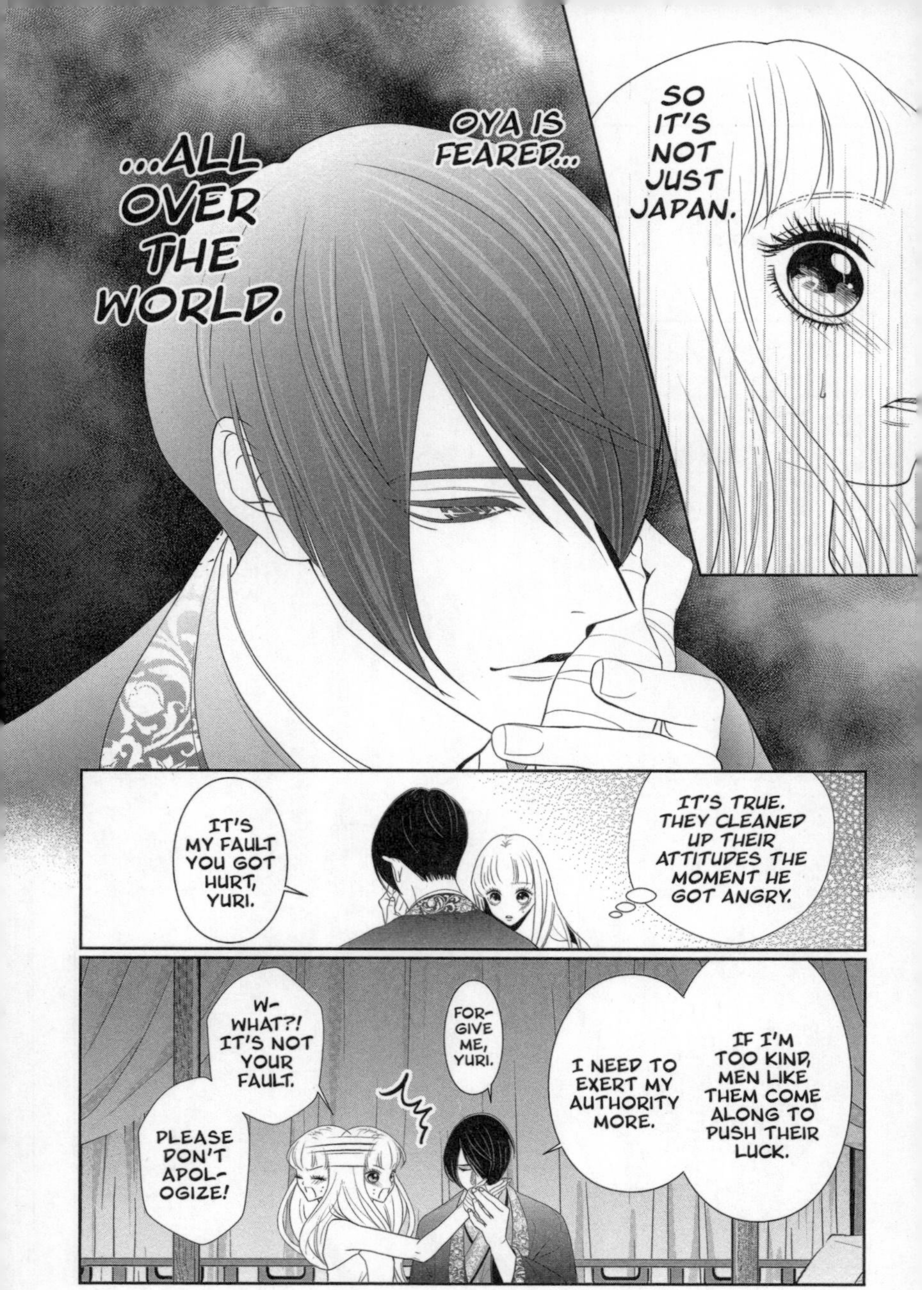
SO IT'S NOT JUST JAPAN.
OYA IS FEARED...
...ALL OVER THE WORLD.
IT'S TRUE. THEY CLEANED UP THEIR ATTITUDES THE MOMENT HE GOT ANGRY.
IT'S MY FAULT YOU GOT HURT, YURI.
IF I'M TOO KIND, MEN LIKE THEM COME ALONG TO PUSH THEIR LUCK.
I NEED TO EXERT MY AUTHORITY MORE.
FOR-GIVE ME, YURI.
W-WHAT?! IT'S NOT YOUR FAULT.
PLEASE DON'T APOLO-GIZE!

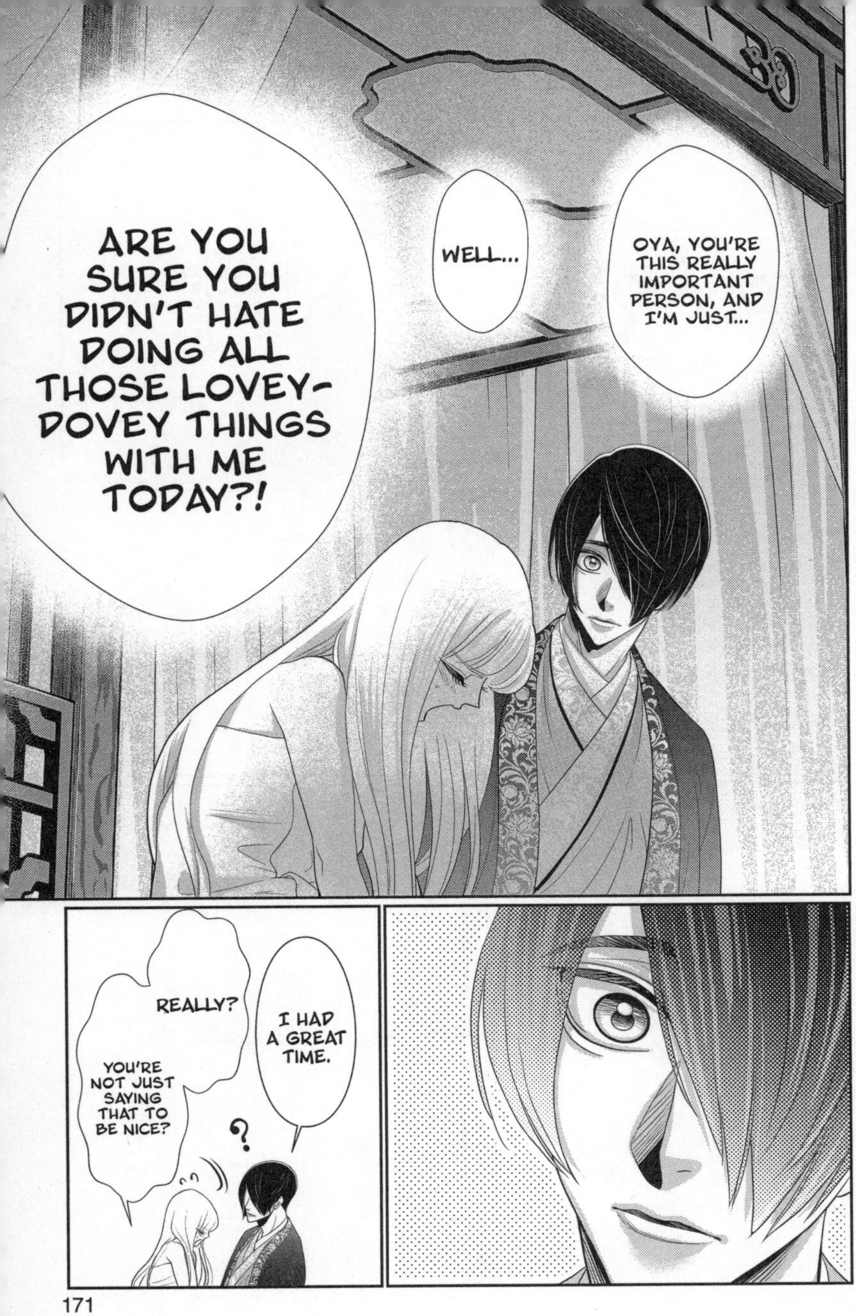
OYA, YOU'RE THIS REALLY IMPORTANT PERSON, AND I'M JUST...
WELL...
ARE YOU SURE YOU DIDN'T HATE DOING ALL THOSE LOVEY-DOVEY THINGS WITH ME TODAY?!
I HAD A GREAT TIME.
?
REALLY?
YOU'RE NOT JUST SAYING THAT TO BE NICE?

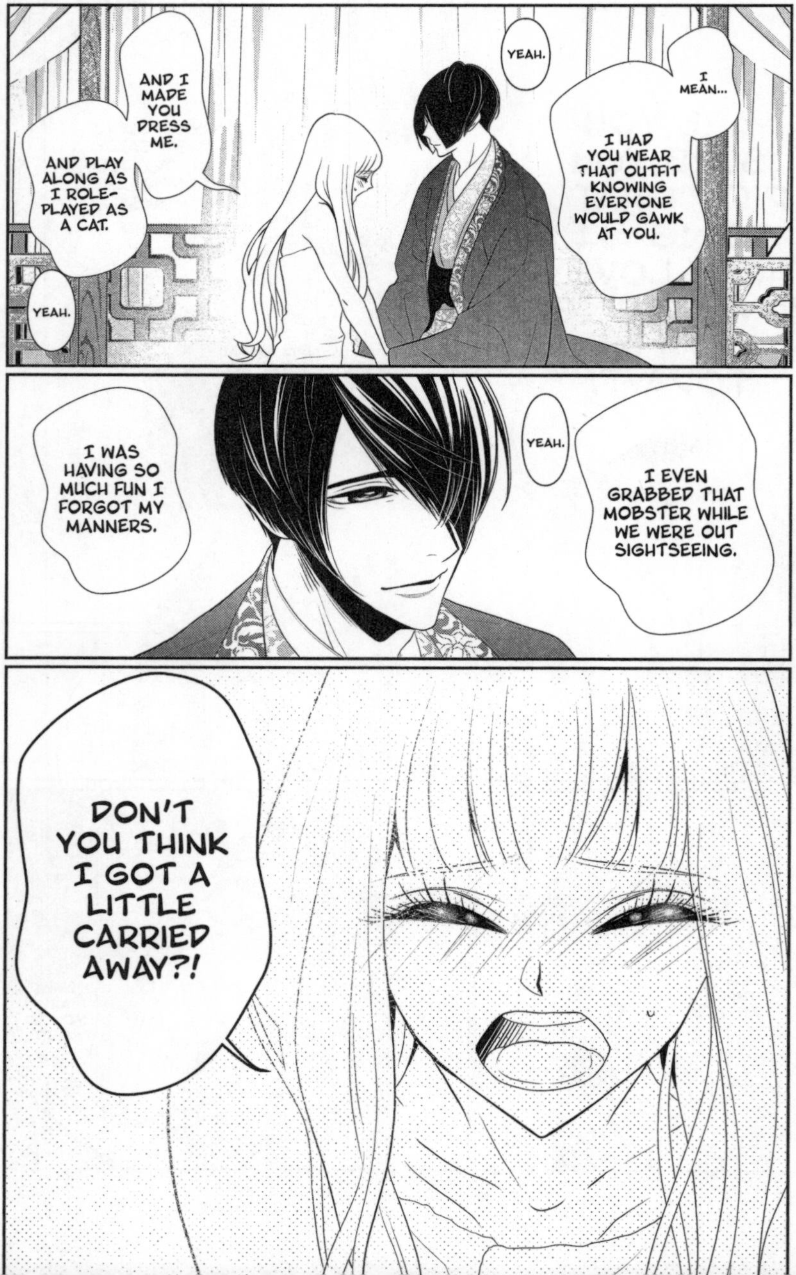
I MEAN...
I HAD YOU WEAR THAT OUTFIT KNOWING EVERYONE WOULD GAWK AT YOU.
YEAH.
AND I MADE YOU DRESS ME.
AND PLAY ALONG AS I ROLE-PLAYED AS A CAT.
YEAH.
I EVEN GRABBED THAT MOBSTER WHILE WE WERE OUT SIGHTSEEING.
YEAH.
I WAS HAVING SO MUCH FUN I FORGOT MY MANNERS.
DON'T YOU THINK I GOT A LITTLE CARRIED AWAY?!

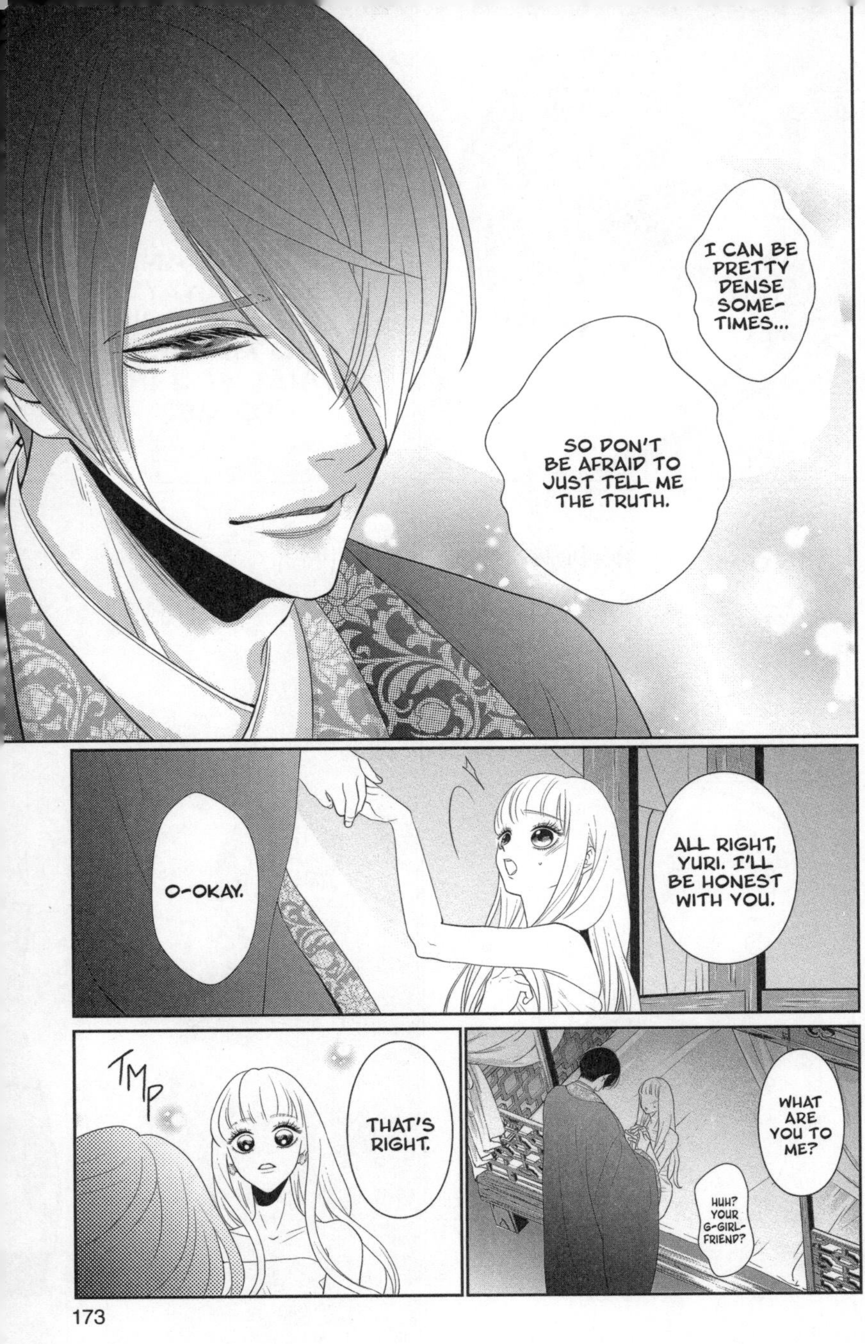
I CAN BE PRETTY DENSE SOME-TIMES...
SO DON'T BE AFRAID TO JUST TELL ME THE TRUTH.
ALL RIGHT, YURI. I'LL BE HONEST WITH YOU.
O-OKAY.
WHAT ARE YOU TO ME?
HUH? YOUR G-GIRL-FRIEND?
THAT'S RIGHT.
TMP

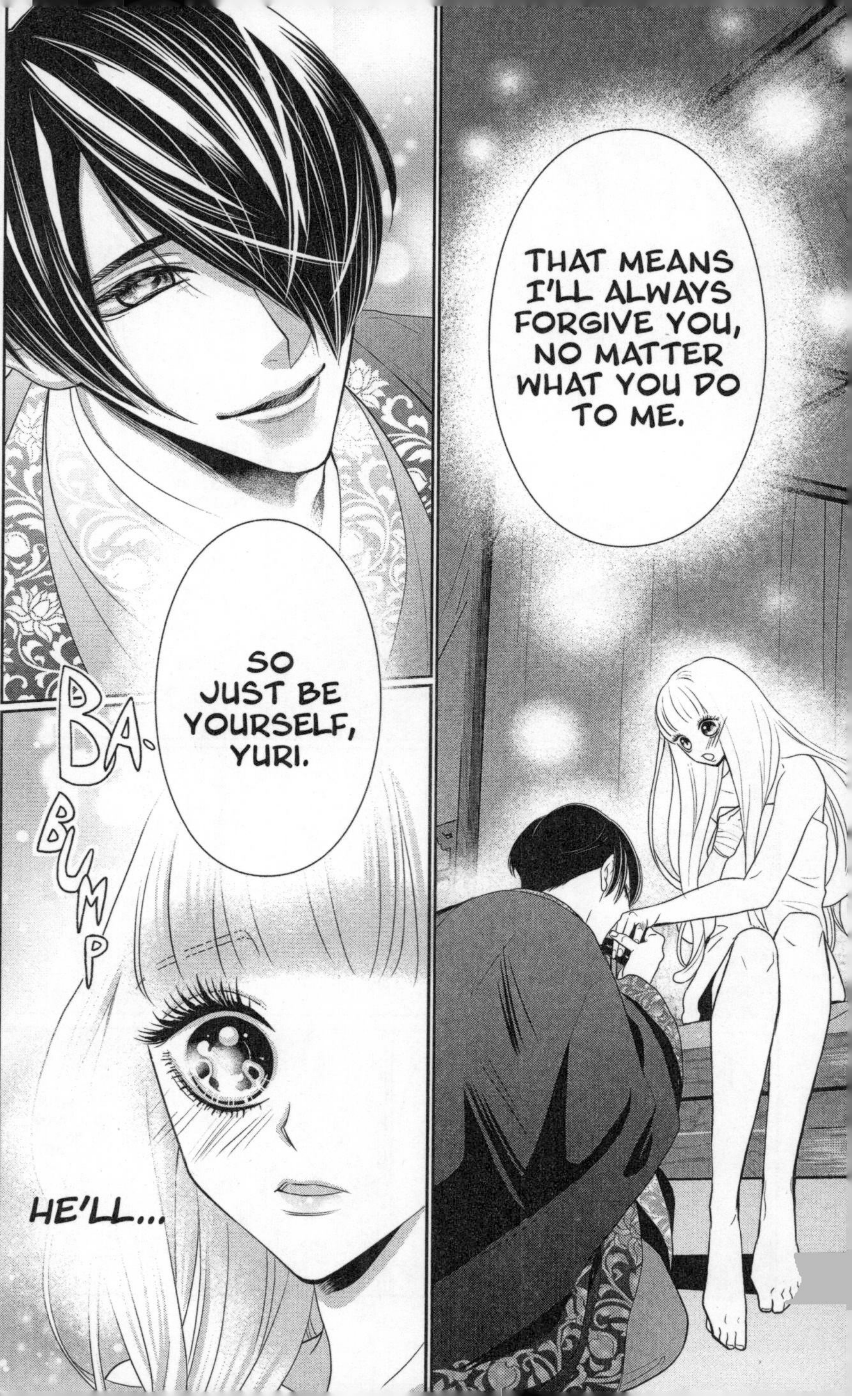
THAT MEANS I'LL ALWAYS FORGIVE YOU, NO MATTER WHAT YOU DO TO ME.
SO JUST BE YOURSELF, YURI.
BA-BUMP
HE'LL...

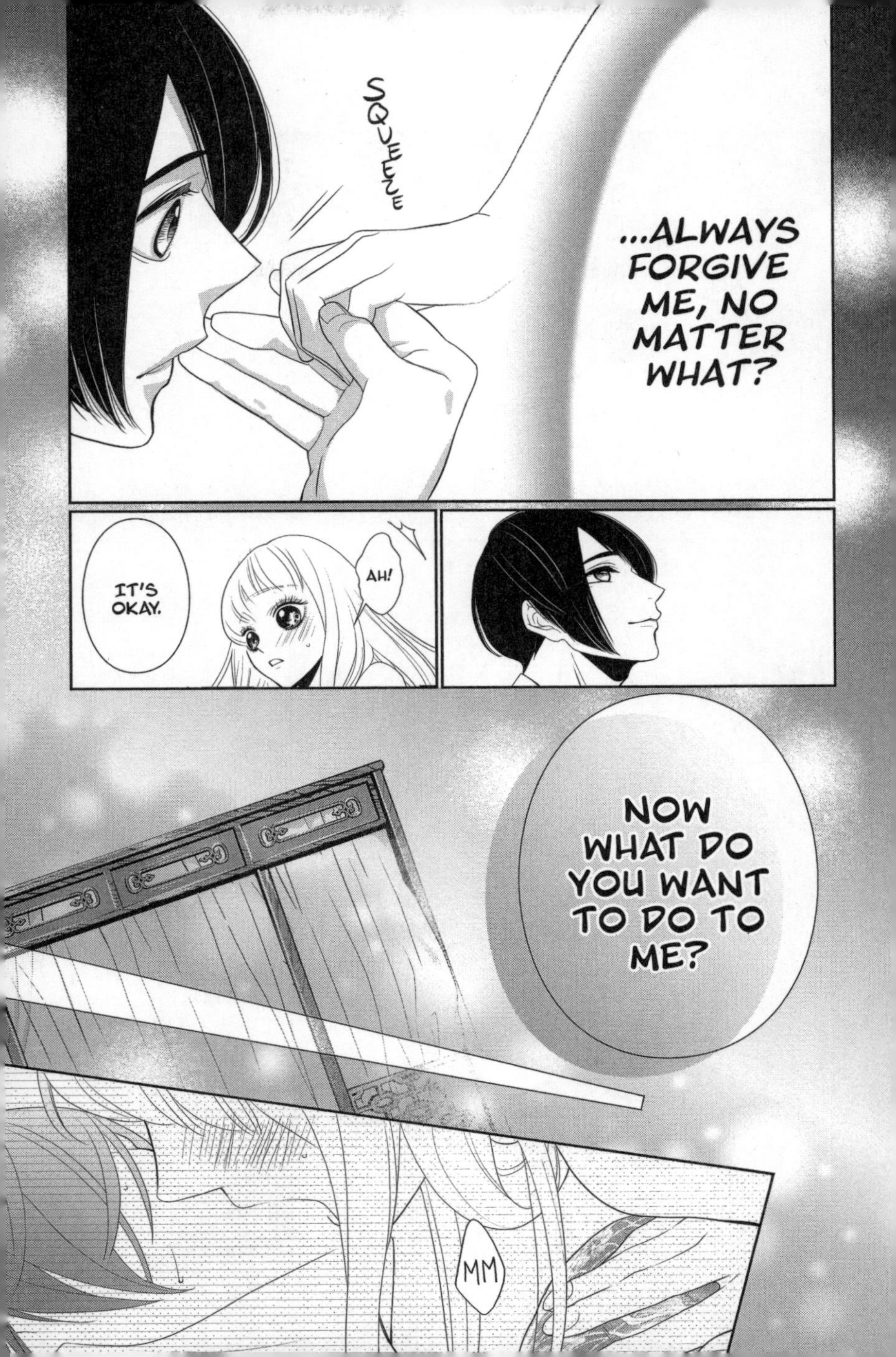
...ALWAYS FORGIVE ME, NO MATTER WHAT?
SQUEEZE
AH!
IT'S OKAY.
NOW WHAT DO YOU WANT TO DO TO ME?
MM

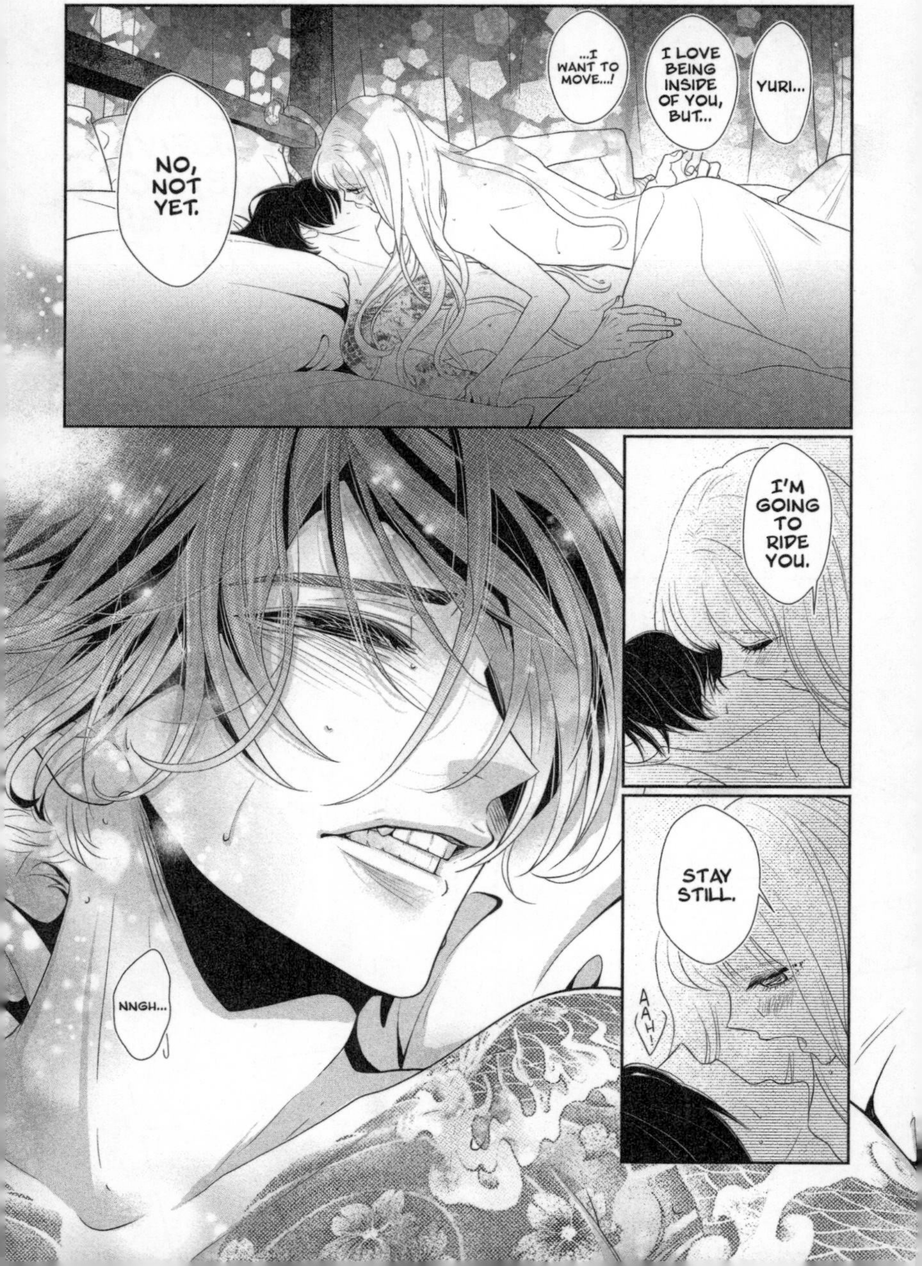
YURI...
I LOVE BEING INSIDE OF YOU, BUT...
...I WANT TO MOVE...!
NO, NOT YET.
I'M GOING TO RIDE YOU.
STAY STILL.
AAH!
NNGH...

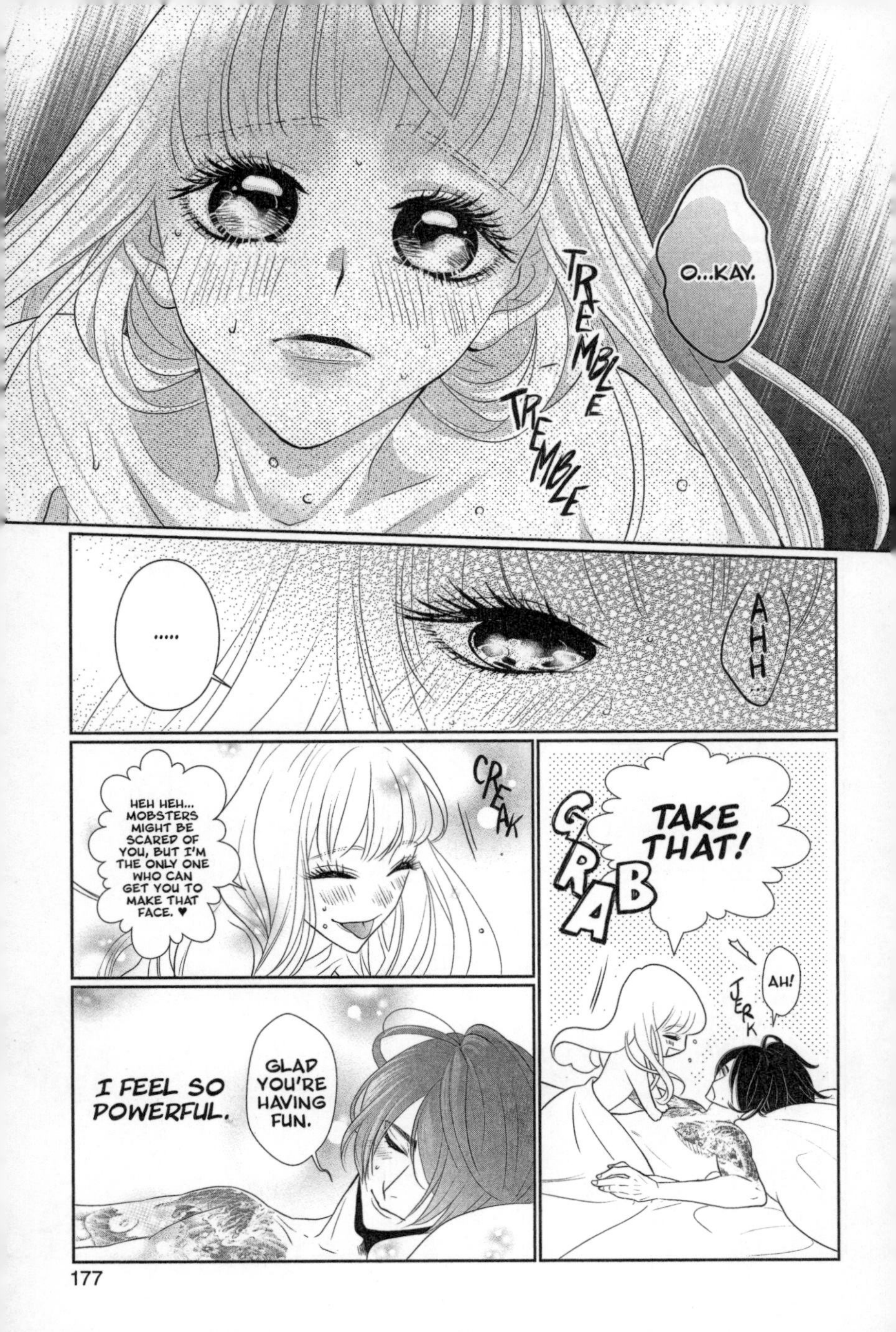
O...KAY.
TREMBLE
TREMBLE
AHH...
.....
TAKE THAT!
GRAB
AH!
JERK
CREAK
HEH HEH... MOBSTERS MIGHT BE SCARED OF YOU, BUT I'M THE ONLY ONE WHO CAN GET YOU TO MAKE THAT FACE. ♥
GLAD YOU'RE HAVING FUN.
I FEEL SO POWERFUL.

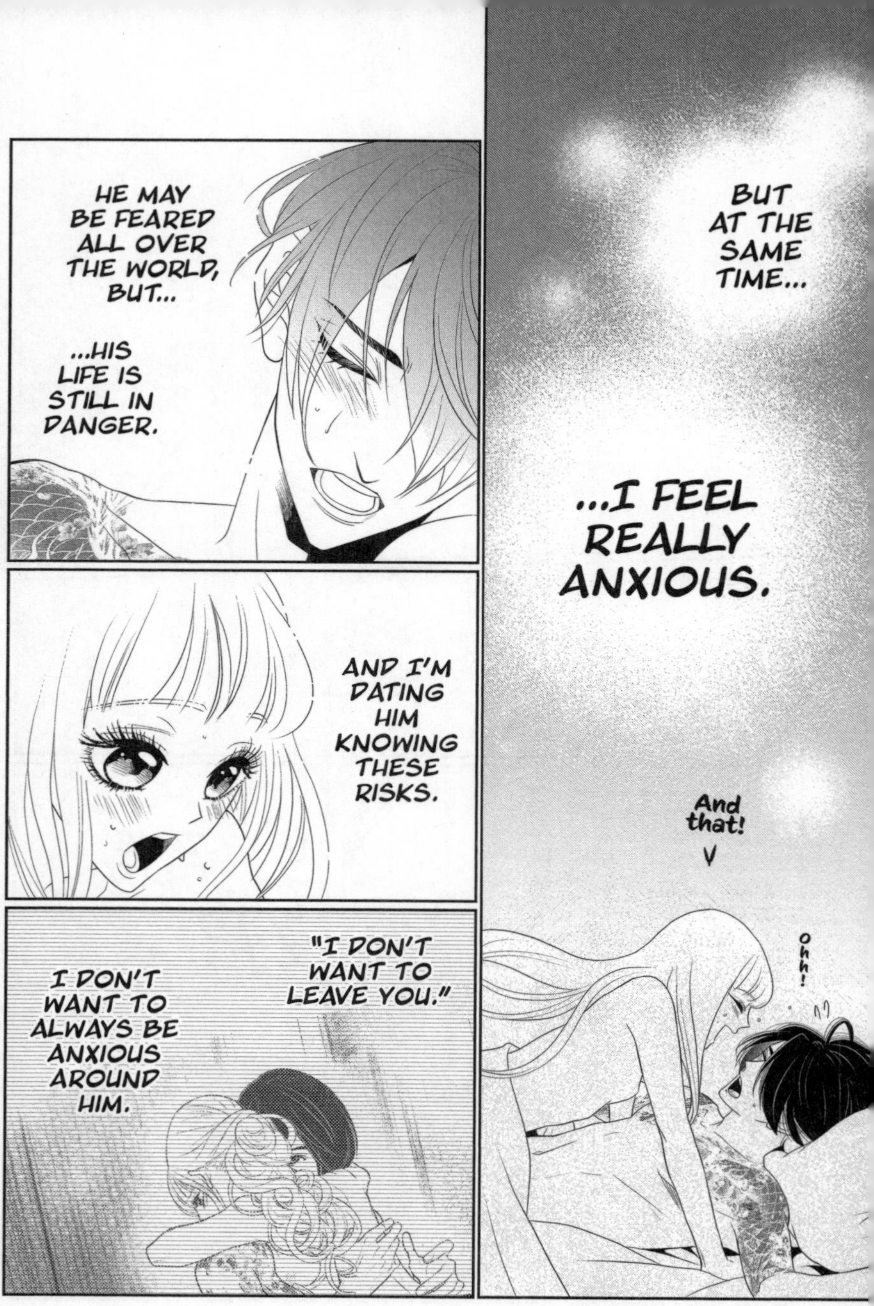
BUT AT THE SAME TIME...
...I FEEL REALLY ANXIOUS.
And that!
Ohh!
HE MAY BE FEARED ALL OVER THE WORLD, BUT...
...HIS LIFE IS STILL IN DANGER.
AND I'M DATING HIM KNOWING THESE RISKS.
"I DON'T WANT TO LEAVE YOU."
I DON'T WANT TO ALWAYS BE ANXIOUS AROUND HIM.

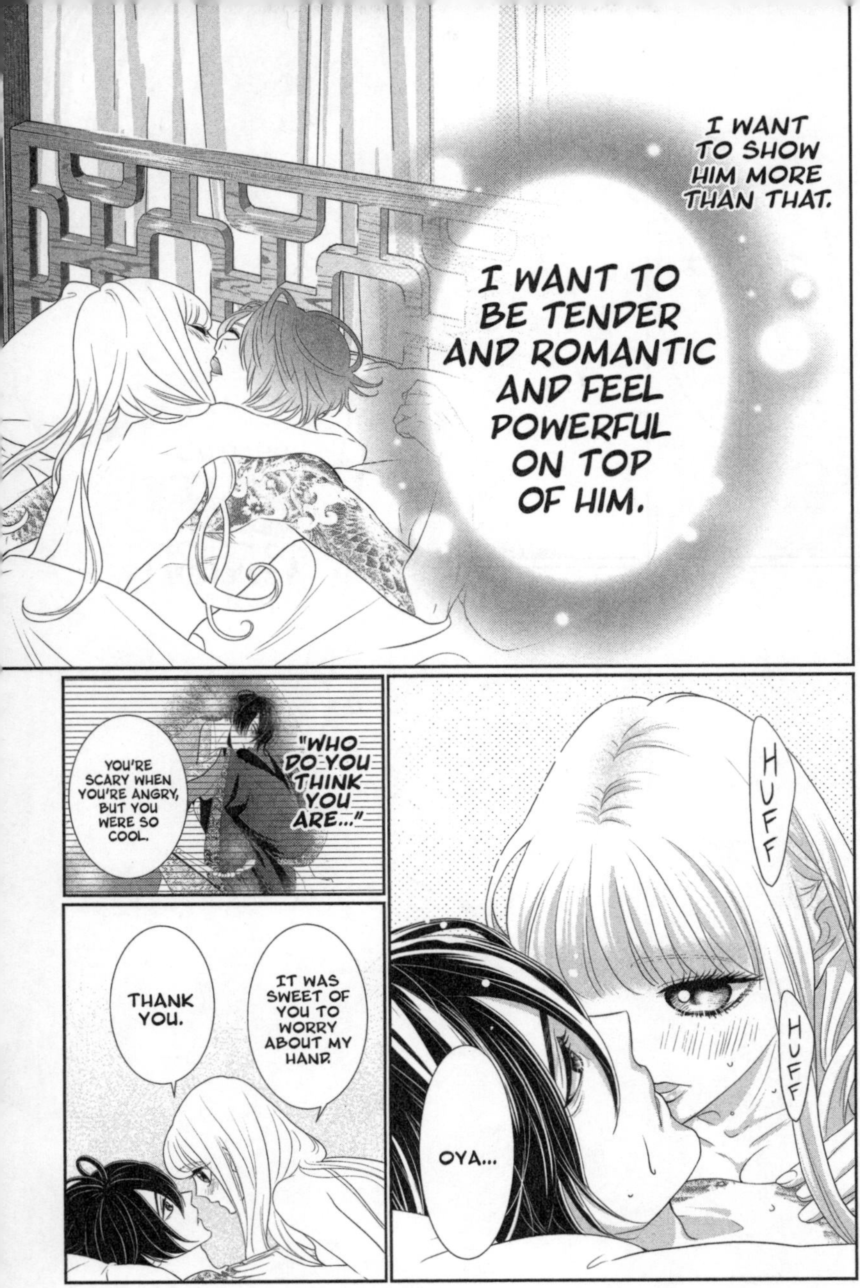
I WANT TO SHOW HIM MORE THAN THAT.
I WANT TO BE TENDER AND ROMANTIC AND FEEL POWERFUL ON TOP OF HIM.
HUFF
HUFF
OYA...
"WHO DO YOU THINK YOU ARE..."
YOU'RE SCARY WHEN YOU'RE ANGRY, BUT YOU WERE SO COOL.
IT WAS SWEET OF YOU TO WORRY ABOUT MY HAND.
THANK YOU.

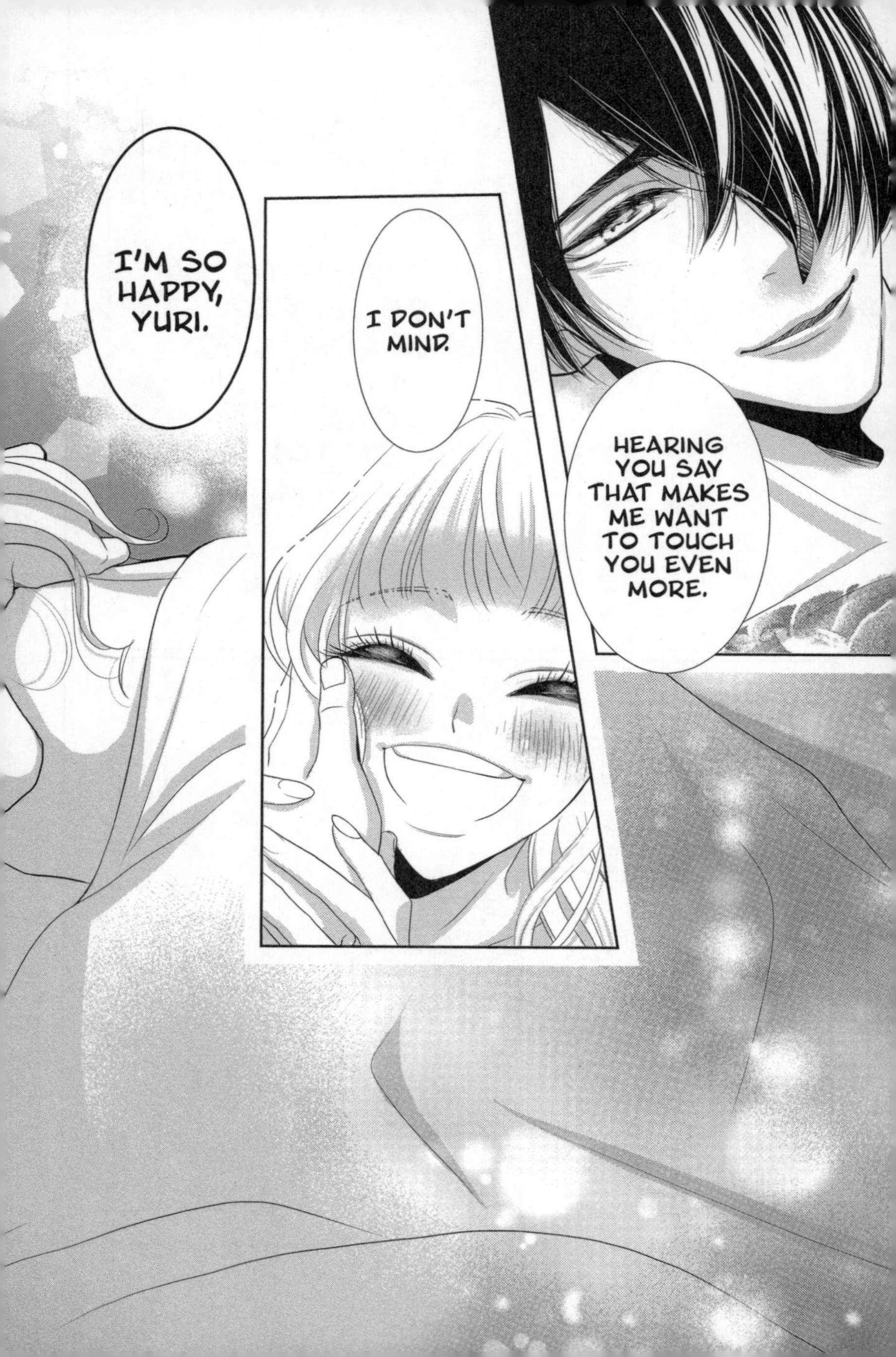
I DON'T MIND.
HEARING YOU SAY THAT MAKES ME WANT TO TOUCH YOU EVEN MORE.
I'M SO HAPPY, YURI.

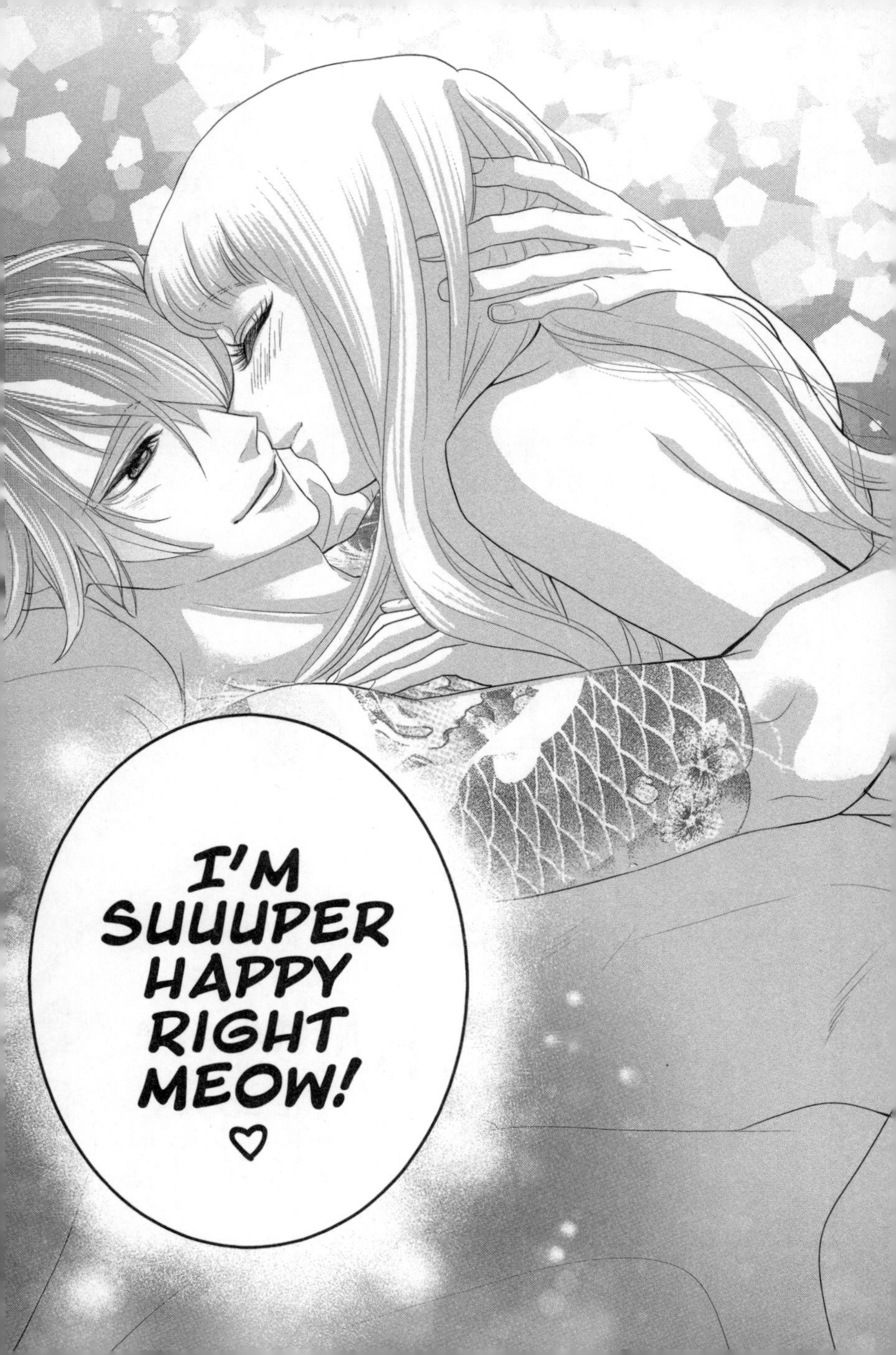
I'M SUUUPER HAPPY RIGHT MEOW! ♡

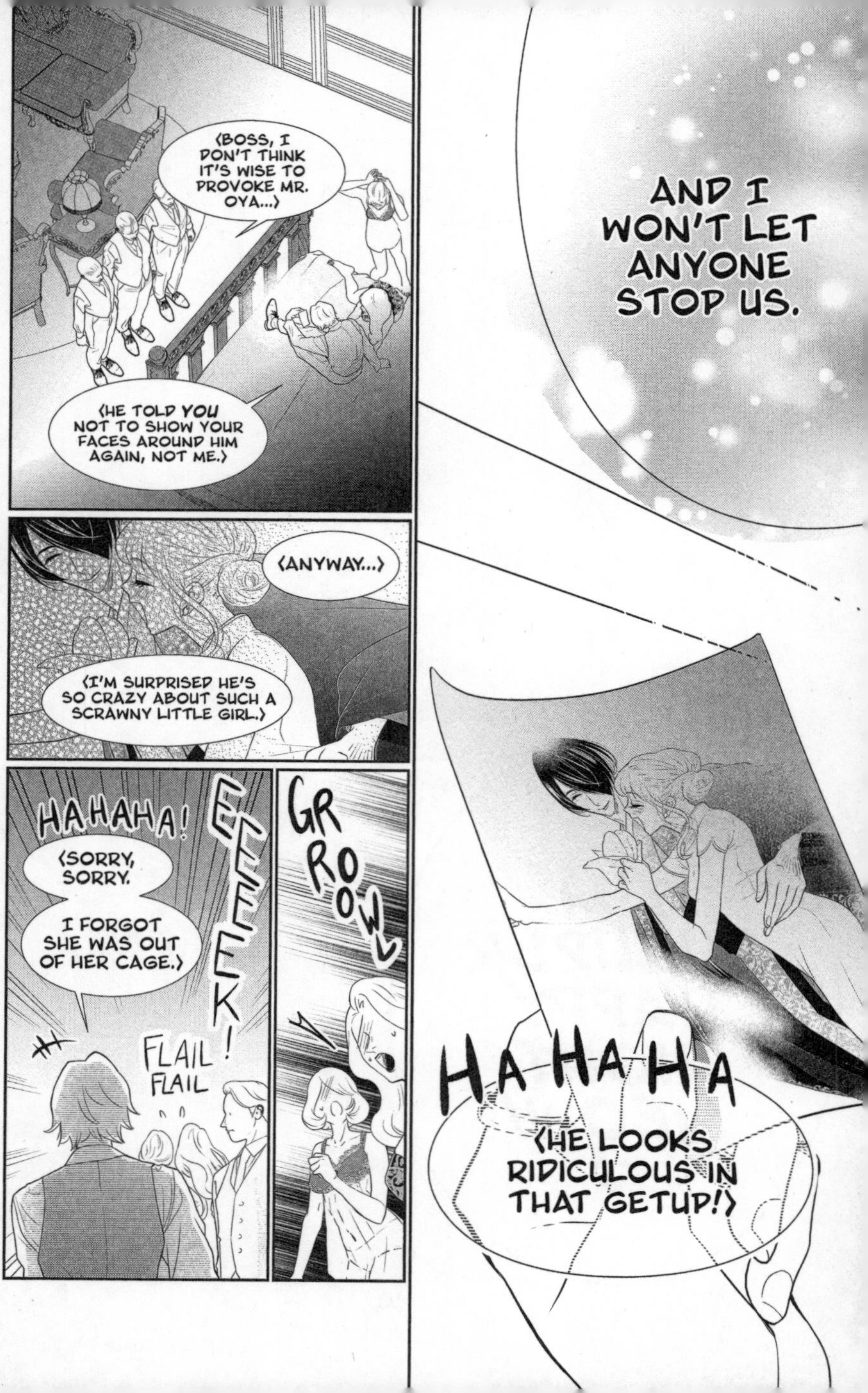
AND I WON'T LET ANYONE STOP US.
HA HA HA HA
〈HE LOOKS RIDICULOUS IN THAT GETUP!〉
〈BOSS, I DON'T THINK IT'S WISE TO PROVOKE MR. OYA...〉
〈HE TOLD *YOU* NOT TO SHOW YOUR FACES AROUND HIM AGAIN, NOT ME.〉
〈ANYWAY...〉
〈I'M SURPRISED HE'S SO CRAZY ABOUT SUCH A SCRAWNY LITTLE GIRL.〉
GRROWL
EEEEEK!
HAHAHA!
〈SORRY, SORRY.
I FORGOT SHE WAS OUT OF HER CAGE.〉
FLAIL FLAIL

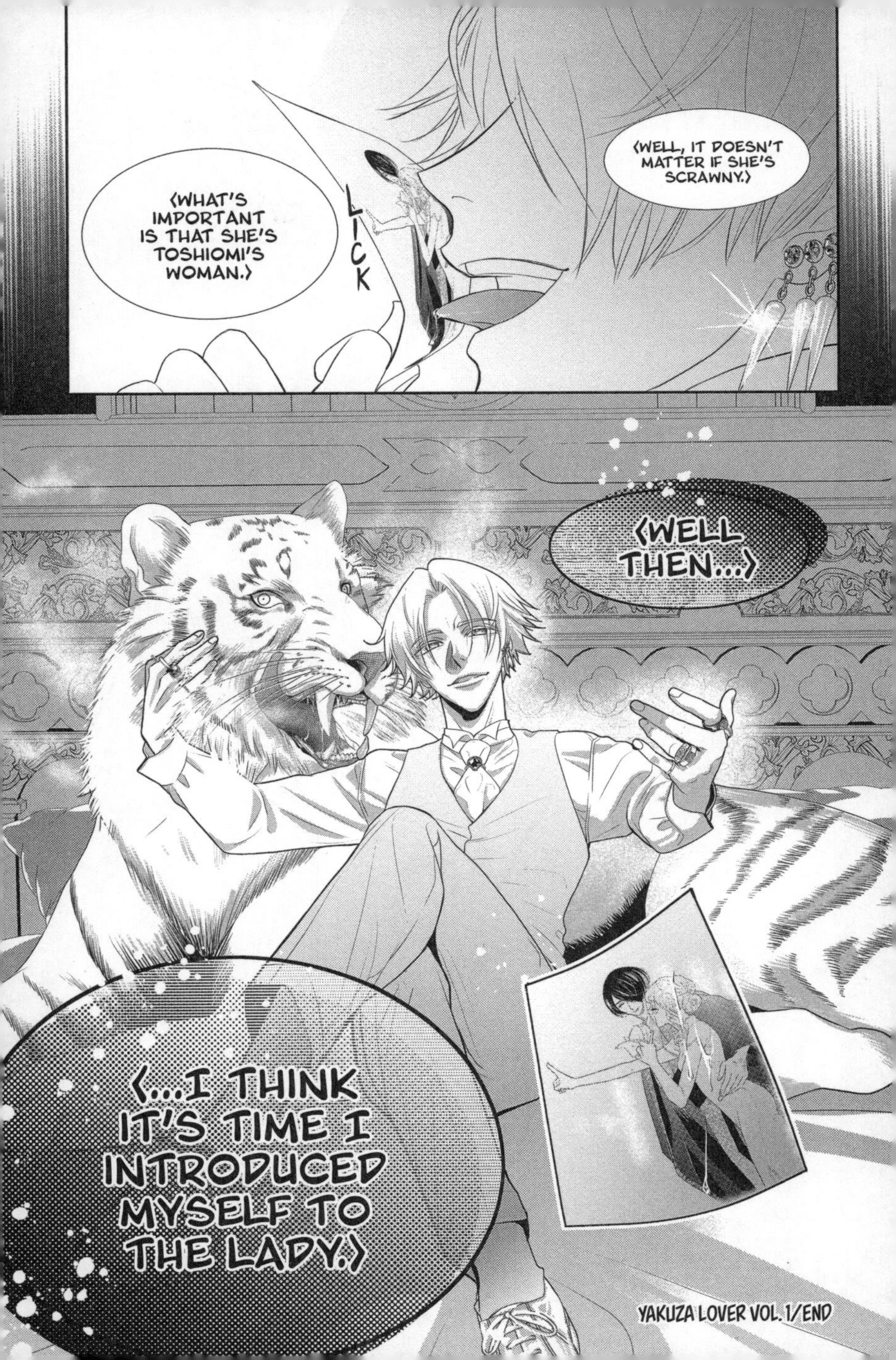
‹WELL, IT DOESN'T MATTER IF SHE'S SCRAWNY.›
LICK
‹WHAT'S IMPORTANT IS THAT SHE'S TOSHIOMI'S WOMAN.›
‹WELL THEN...›
‹...I THINK IT'S TIME I INTRODUCED MYSELF TO THE LADY.›
YAKUZA LOVER VOL. 1/END

bonus secret scene: Toshiomi Oya Takes a Break

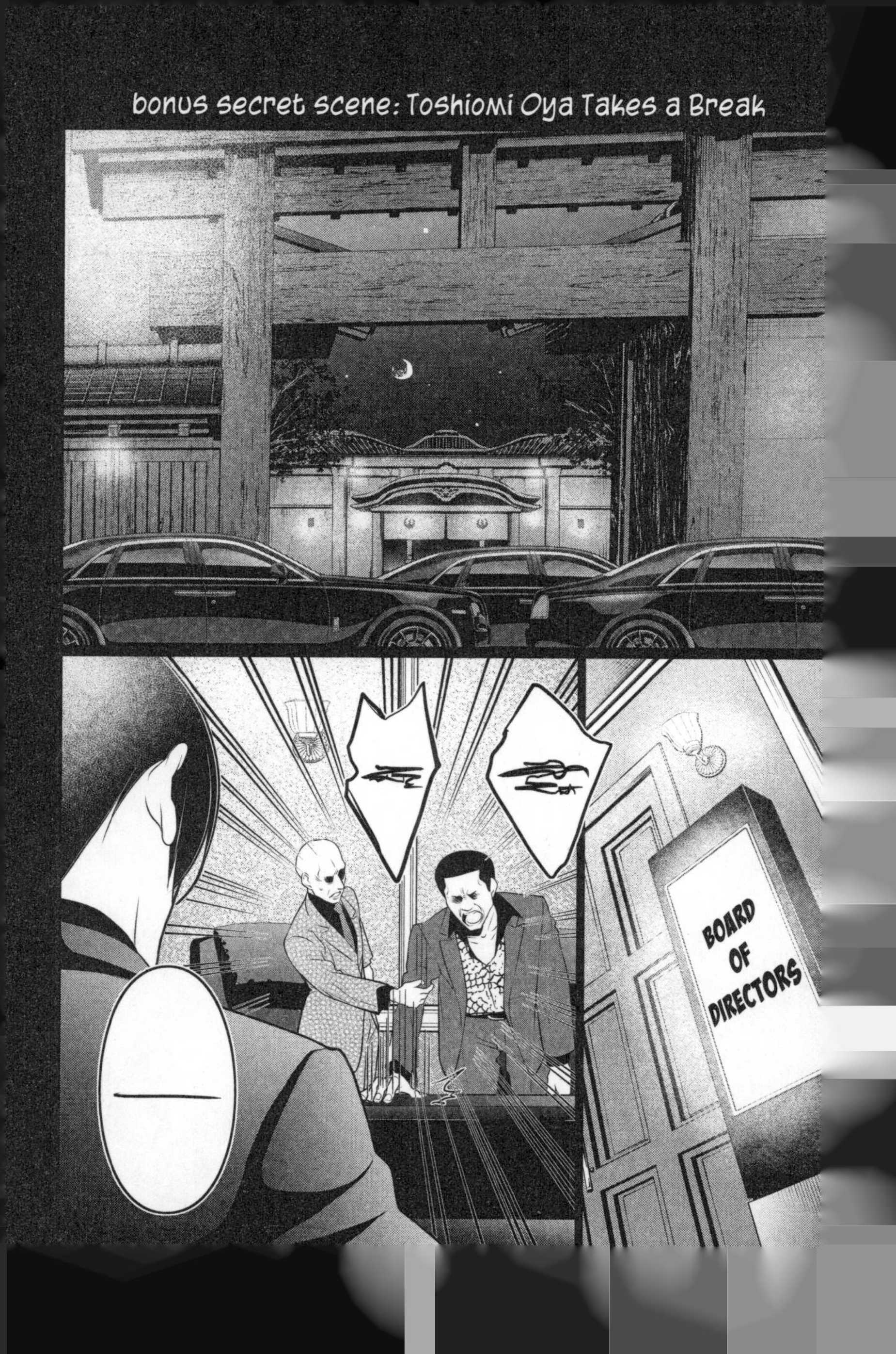
BOARD OF DIRECTORS
—

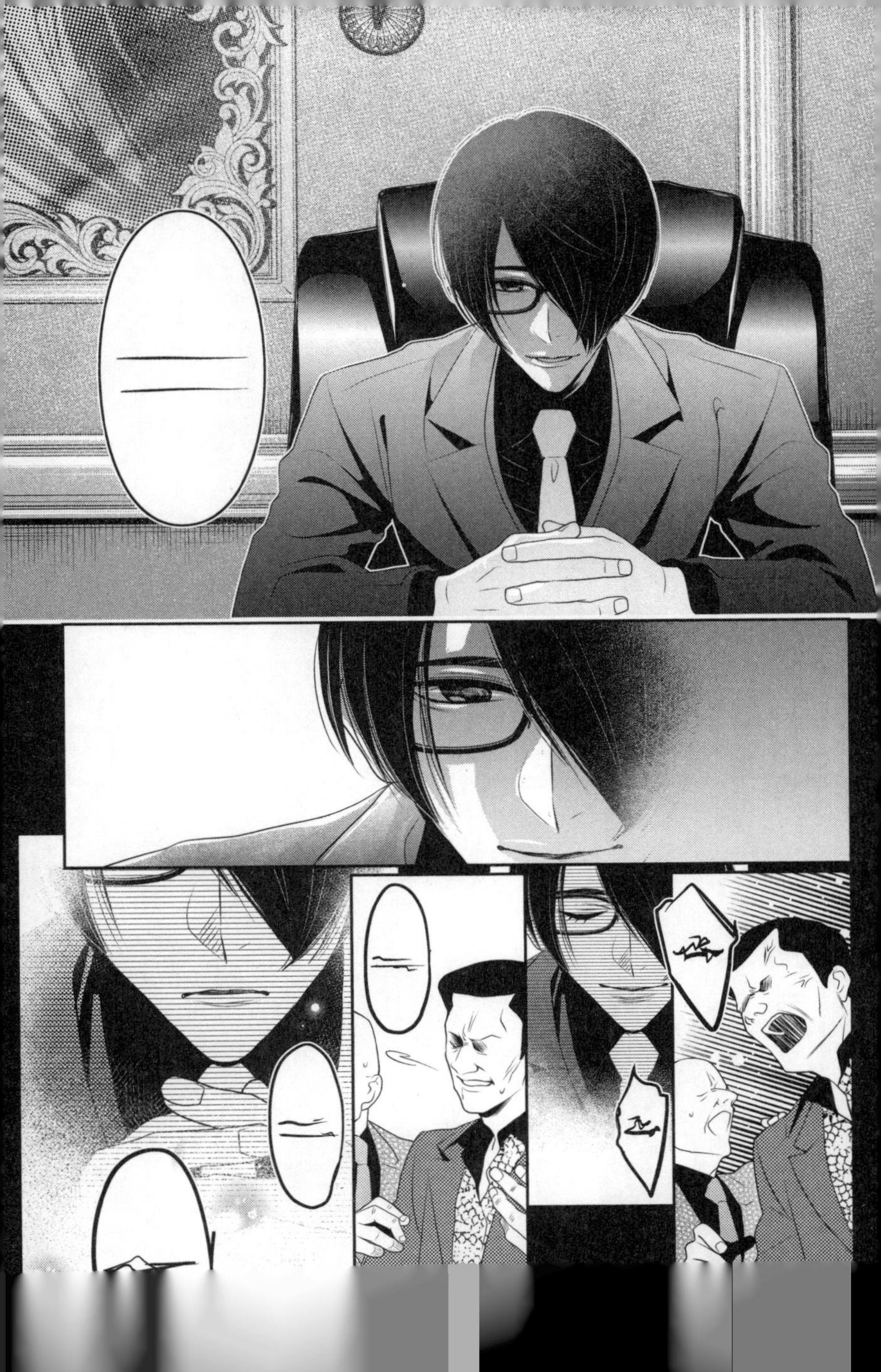
——

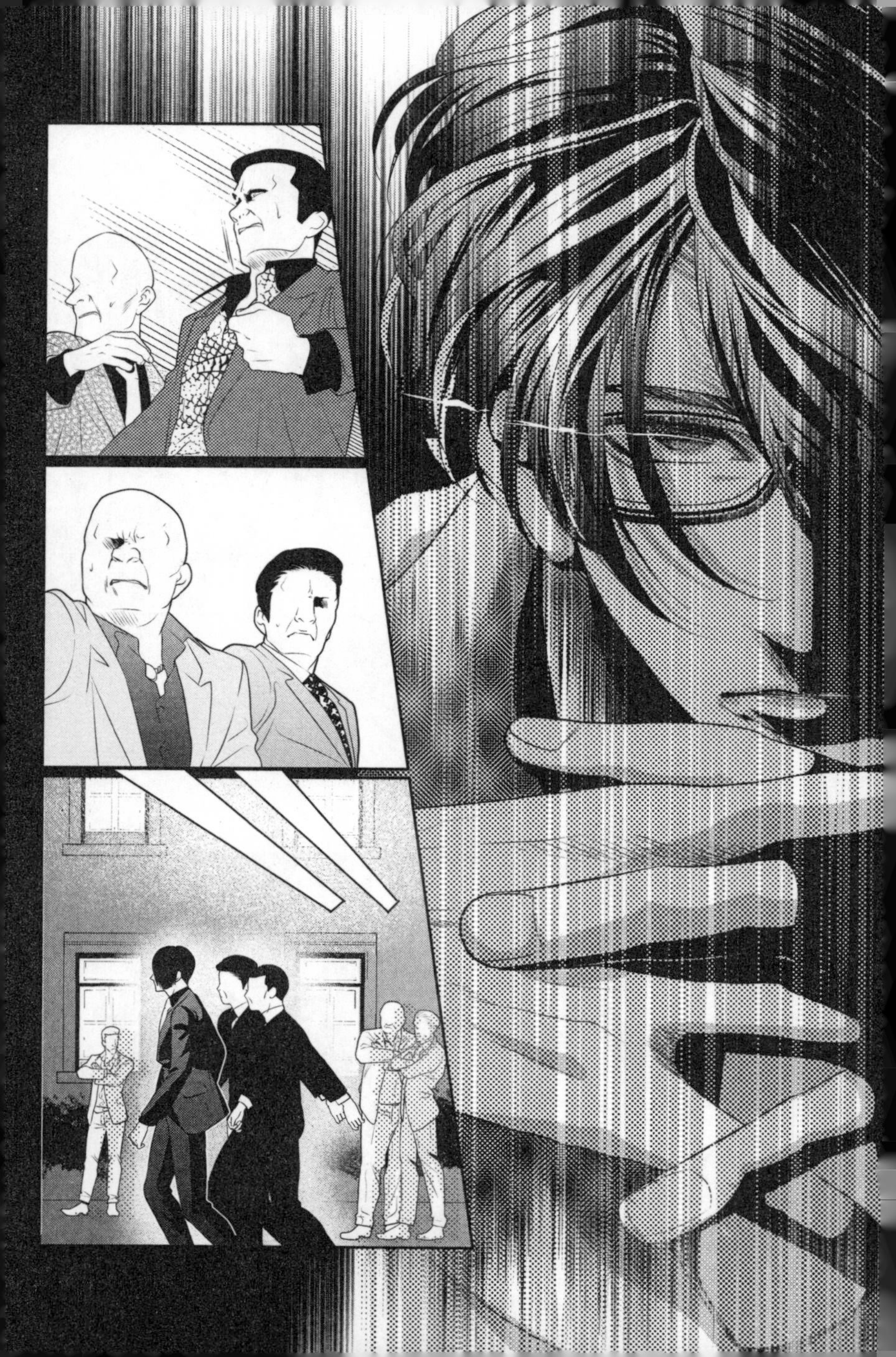

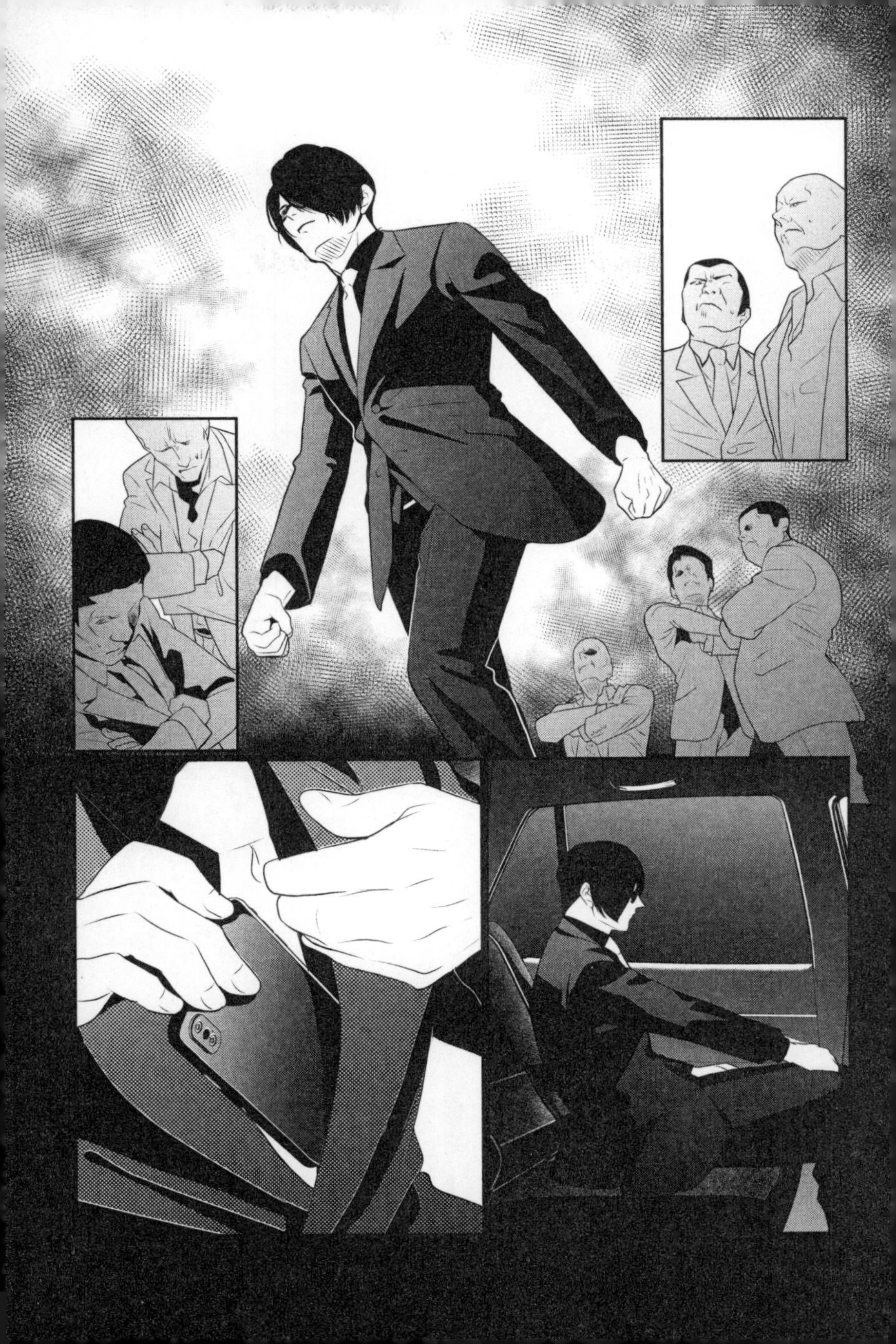

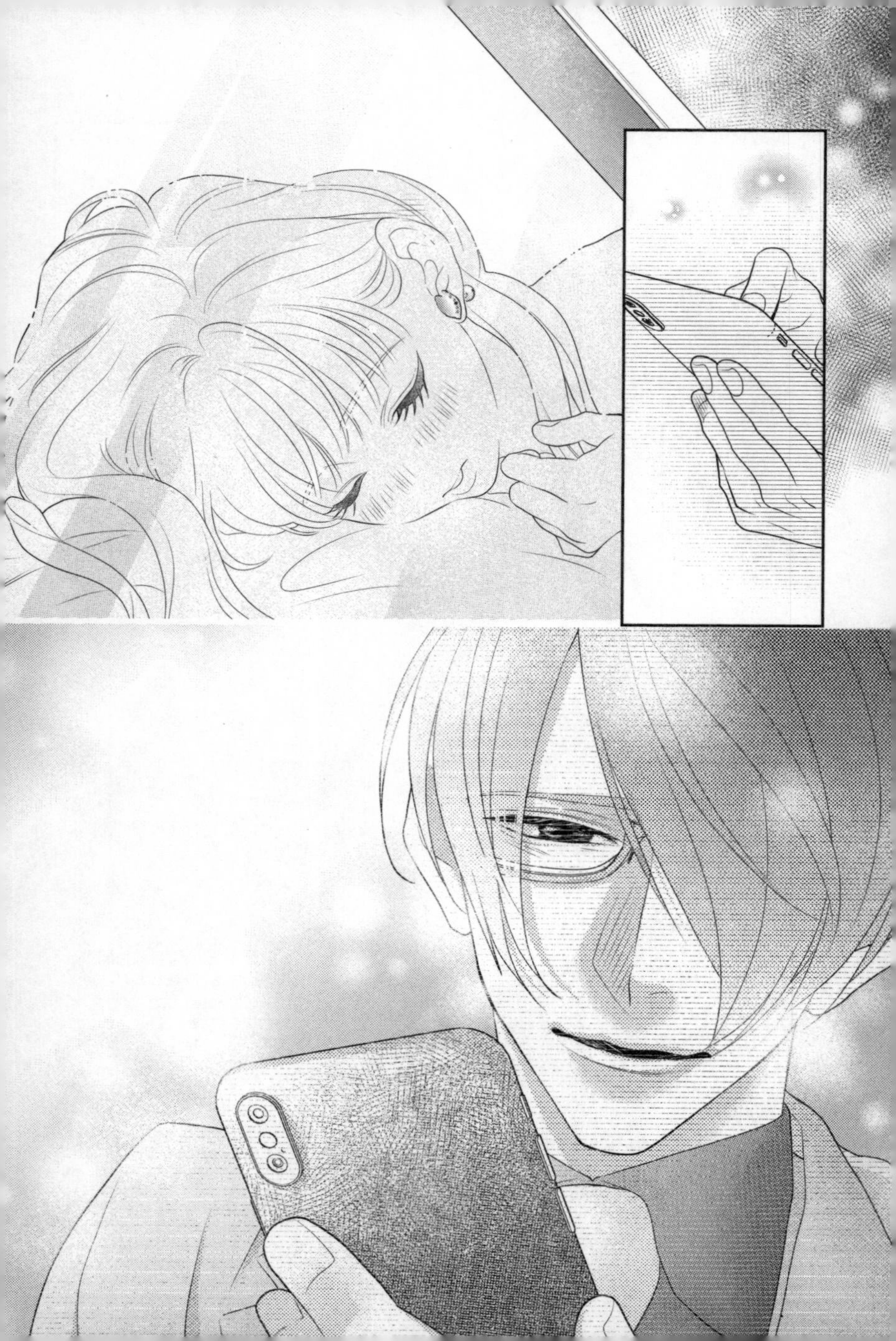

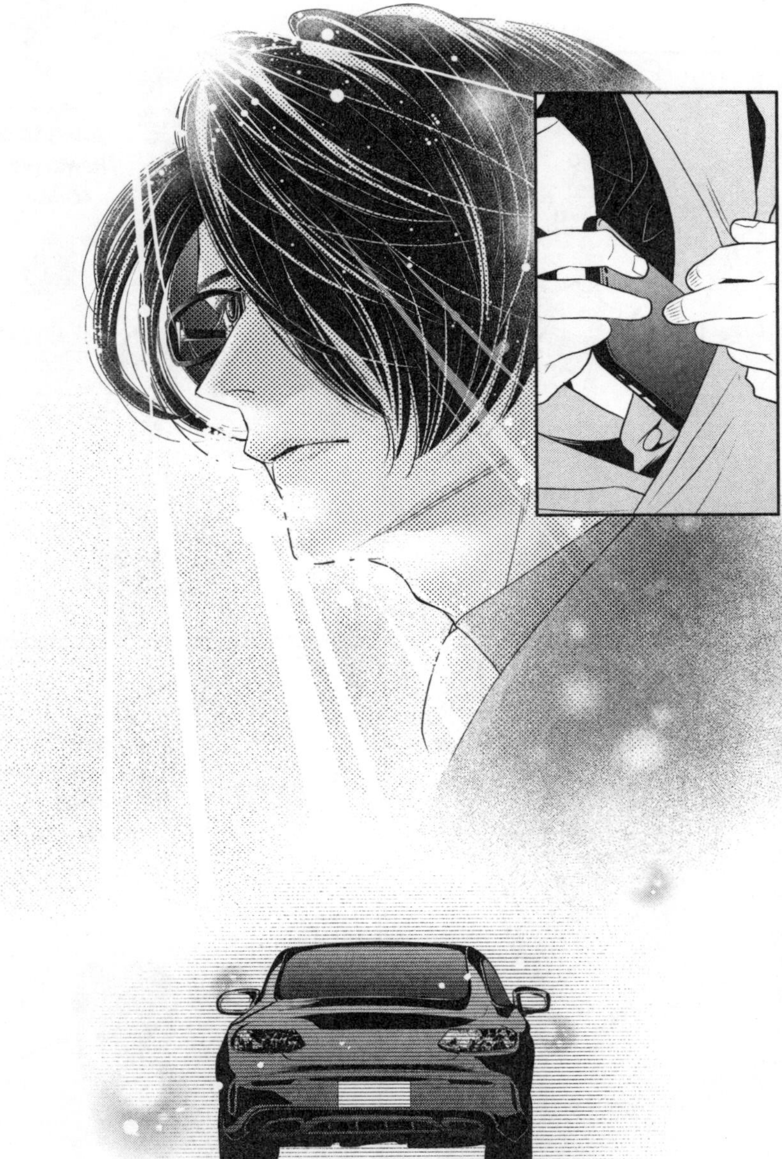

bonus secret scene: Toshiomi Oya Takes a Break/end

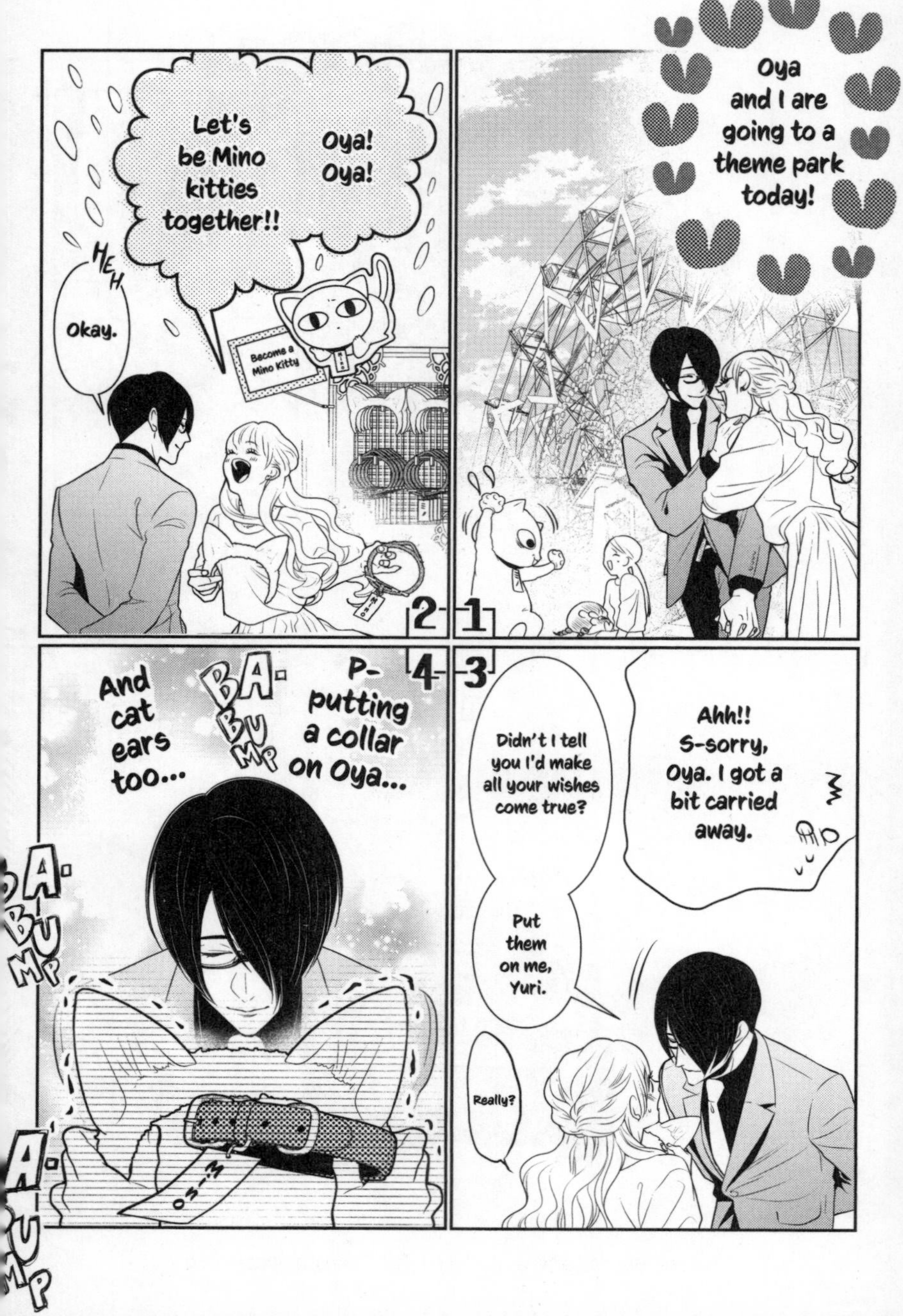
Oya and I are going to a theme park today!
Oya! Oya!
Let's be Mino kitties together!!
Become a Mino Kitty
HEH
Okay.
Ahh!! S-sorry, Oya. I got a bit carried away.
Didn't I tell you I'd make all your wishes come true?
Put them on me, Yuri.
Really?
P-putting a collar on Oya...
BA-BUMP
And cat ears too...
BA-BUMP
BA-BUMP

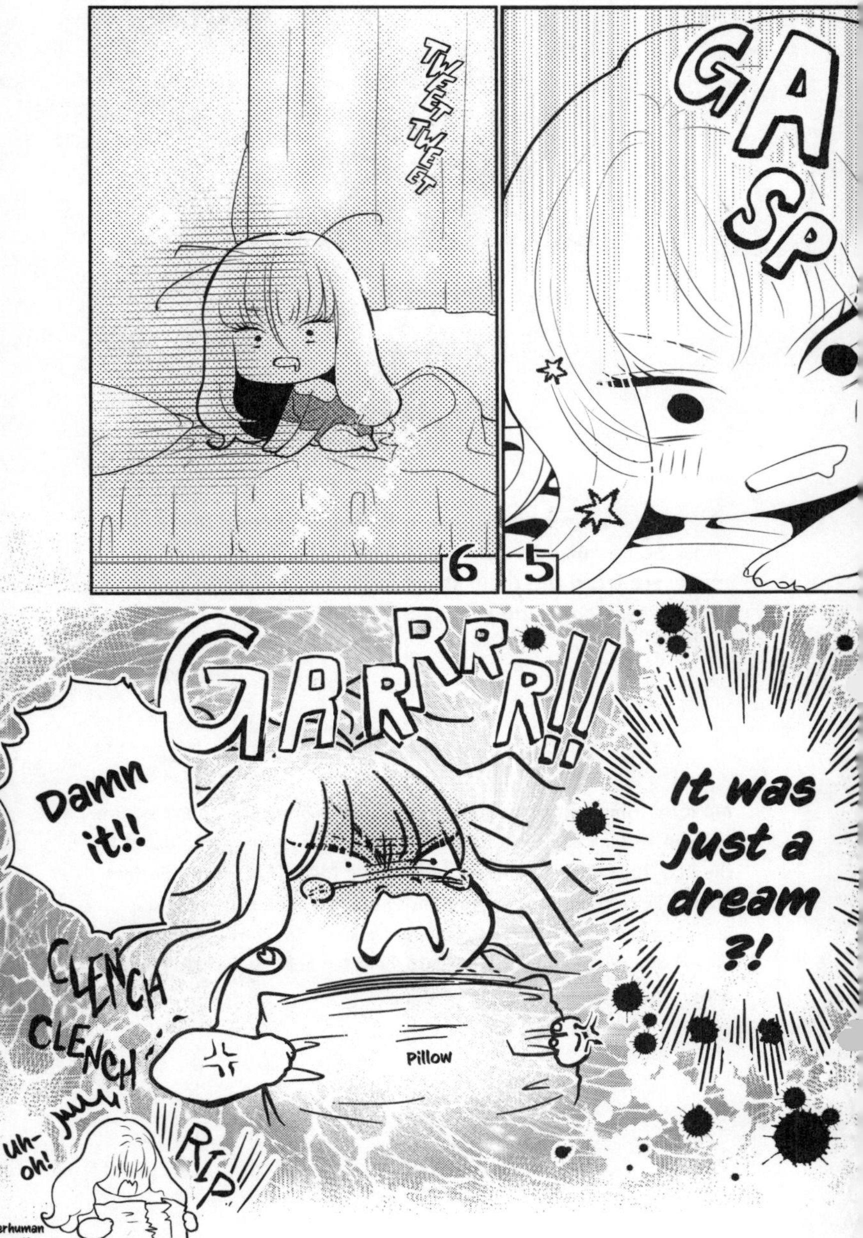
GASP
5
TWEET TWEET
6
GRRRR!!
It was just a dream?!
Damn it!!
CLENCH CLENCH
Pillow
RIP
uh-oh!
Superhuman strength

MEOW

It's me.

Hello.

FLIP

(I'm bad at smiling.)

Yakuza Lover ran bimonthly in *Premium Cheese!* but will now be serialized in *Cheese!* I'll be including shorts separate from the main story in *Premium Cheese!* too. I hope you'll continue reading.

—Nozomi Mino

. . . .

Nozomi Mino was born on February 12 in Himeji, Hyogo Prefecture, in Japan, making her an Aquarius. She made her shojo manga debut in the May 2006 issue of *Cheese!* with "LOVE MANTEN" (Love Perfect Score). Since then, she has gone on to publish numerous works, including *Sweet Marriage*, *Wagamama Otoko wa Ichizu ni Koisuru* (Selfish Guys Love Hard) and *LOVE x PLACE.fam*. Her hobbies include going on drives and visiting cafes.